History on the Run

KNOWLTON NASH

History on the Run

The Trenchcoat Memoirs of a Foreign Correspondent

McClelland and Stewart

McClelland and Stewart Limited
The Canadian Publishers
25 Hollinger Road
Toronto, Ontario
M4B 3G2

Canadian Cataloguing in Publication Data

Nash, Knowlton
   History on the run

Includes index.
ISBN 0-7710-6701-1

1. Nash, Knowlton.   2. Foreign correspondents –
Canada – Biography.   I. Title.

PN4913.N38A3 1984   070.4′33′0924   C84-099085-5

Printed and bound in Canada

CONTENTS

To Lorraine
who taught me how to share

PREFACE

The English poet Matthew Arnold once said that journalism is "literature in a hurry." I'm not so sure about it being literature, but, to paraphrase Arnold, I am sure that journalism is history on the run.

This book is by no means a definitive history of the period covered. It is simply my own recollections of what I saw and reported, mostly from Washington, especially during the chaotic 1960s, and, with the advantage of hindsight, more sober reflections on the people and events I've covered. These pages are also a salute to those trenchcoated commandos, the correspondents, who risk life, limb, and personal well-being in pursuit of the news. And finally, this is the story of how I paid my journalistic dues. This book reflects all of these things, and, in a very personal sense, it has been a way of sharing my journalistic life with my wife Lorraine.

My major theme is what it was like to be in Washington between 1951 and 1969. As such, it may provide some insight into the kinds of demands and pressures a foreign correspondent faces day after day, as well as a glimpse into some of the private moments of reporters and the world leaders – and would-be leaders – they keep an eye on.

I've been lucky in having worked in just about every aspect of the news business, from selling papers on a Toronto streetcorner to reporting, editing, managing, and anchoring the news for CBC Television and Radio. In addition to my work in broadcast journalism, I've worked for news agencies, weekly and daily newspapers, newsletters, and magazines. My career has taken me around the world many times on assignments to Africa, South and Central America, the Far East, Europe, and all over Canada and the United States on the trail of wars, revolutions, political crises, scandals, and scams. But in retrospect what is particularly important to me is the small part I've been able to play in the development and expansion of the television news

News was something of an afterthought in the early days of television. And the foreign correspondents were among the first honest-to-God news-gathering reporters the CBC had. In the early 1950s, when television first arrived in Canada, people like Tom Earle did some reporting out of Ottawa, but there was little elsewhere except for the correspondents' work. Prior to that, except during the war years, CBC Radio largely regurgitated news from the agencies like British United

Press and Canadian Press. For years, if Canadian Press didn't carry it, we didn't report it – we lost a lot of scoops that way.

I recall an Ottawa meeting in the mid-1960s, between the correspondents and the CBC brass, where the Executive Vice-President, Captain Ted Briggs, was startled at the fact that we were actually covering the news. "You mean to say," he asked us, "that you are actually gathering the news as well as reporting it?"

Things certainly have changed.

Over the years, CBC dramatically increased the number of reporters across Canada so that we could reflect the nation as well as the world. We have substantially increased our production values to tell a story more effectively, added to the length of *The National*, put *The National* into the prime time of 10:00 p.m., introduced satellite collection and distribution of the news, and, most important of all, achieved a much greater respect for the News Service in the corporate upper echelons. This, in turn, has led to more money being spent on providing better journalism.

In the end, however, it always comes down to the individual reporter and the quality of his or her reporting. As a reporter, you need an insatiable curiosity, an implacable demand for accuracy, persistence, patience, stamina, and an ability to communicate. To some degree, I acquired those qualities over the years. But two other essential qualities I inherited from my parents: a spirit of adventure from my mother, who, among other things, was the first woman to fly in a plane over her home town of Hamilton; and a spirit of fun from my father, who always said that if you're not having fun in what you do, do something else.

Being a correspondent was more fun than any other job I can imagine in journalism. But it's a life that takes its toll. My mind reels at the pace we used to set and most still do.

There are scores of people and organizations I should thank, but I'm particularly grateful to the editors of what used to be called British United Press, who gave me my real start; to my bosses at the International Federation of Agricultural Producers (IFAP), who took me to Washington in the first place; to the editors of the *Windsor Star* and *Vancouver Sun*, for whom I worked in Washington; and most especially to the people at Maclean Hunter, primarily the *Financial Post* and its editor Ron McEachern, who gave me a chance to do some of what I found was my most satisfying reporting and writing. Above all, my thanks go to the editors and managers of CBC News, both radio and television, whose encouragement and guidance have given me the greatest joy of my professional life.

Insofar as this book is concerned, I owe a large debt of gratitude to my editor, Rick Archbold, whose constant prodding for threads and texture helped me to anchor anecdotes and recollections within a cohesive framework. I'm also grateful to my colleague, Jean Bruce, who helped in typing the original manuscript as she has helped me for so many years. And I owe more than I could ever repay in a dozen lifetimes to my wife Lorraine, for her encouragement, patience, understanding, and sensitivity.

My reportorial reminiscing in these pages is based on my notes, articles, scripts, old film clips, programs, and memories as a front-line journalist. Others may view people and events differently, but I call them as I see them and this is how I saw them.

PROLOGUE

Washington, D.C., November 24, 1963 ...

I was standing on the driveway just below the north portico of the White House, waiting. In a few minutes, the big African mahogany box containing the body of John Fitzgerald Kennedy would be taken to the rotunda of the U.S. Capitol where it would lie in state. For the moment, it rested just inside the front door of the White House.

It had been foggy and raining all weekend, but now the sun broke through the clouds. And, as we waited, the incredible word came from the White House Press Office, whispered from reporter to reporter, that the assassin Lee Harvey Oswald had himself just been shot in Dallas. It felt like some unclean intrusion.

Like all my colleagues, I'd been working twenty hours a day doing radio, television, and newspaper reports on the assassination and the succession. If I wasn't writing or broadcasting, I was on the phone or on the move gathering every scrap of information I could – doing my job, as a professional reporter. Now, for the first time in two days, I had nothing to do except wait, and reflect.

Good reporters are supposed to be objective. They are supposed to distance themselves emotionally from the events they're covering; they strive to be as objective as humanly possible. To do otherwise is to colour factual reporting with personal feelings. On this noon hour, I failed to meet that criterion. There's an old Irish saying that the world will break your heart sometime. But this was too soon. Just a thousand days before I'd seen John Kennedy go into the White House as President for the first time, and now he was coming out for the last time.

My reflections were broken as Jackie Kennedy came out the White House door, each hand clinging fiercely to a child. Robert Kennedy was just behind her, tense and vacant. They stood, momentarily transfixed and translucent, at the top of the front steps under a big hanging lamp. Perhaps to escape the agony of the moment, I wondered whether that lamp would come crashing down on top of them.

"Hail To The Chief" blared from the trumpets as the Kennedys and the new President, Lyndon Johnson, watched while a military casket team carried the coffin of the dead President down the steps and pushed it onto the gun carriage. Then the Kennedy family, the Johnsons, and other mourners slumped into their black limousines and the death march to Capitol Hill – forty minutes and twenty blocks away – began.

A general led the march, followed by soldiers in dress blues with white gloves, sailors carrying fixed bayonets that flashed in the sun, clergymen, the Joint Chiefs of Staff, and then the horse-drawn gun carriage carrying the coffin. The carriage was flanked by six matched grey horses and followed by a riderless horse – a bad-tempered seventeen-year-old called Black Jack – with reversed boots in the stirrups, traditional for a warrior killed in battle. The procession passed before silent, blurred eyes as we reporters standing on the White House driveway surrendered to the tragedy. At the end came the limousines with the Kennedy and Johnson families. At our request, the President's office allowed White House reporters to join the march as the last contingent.

And so perhaps fifty or a hundred of us walked with John Kennedy for the last time. For me, it remains a blur: tens of thousands of mourners, many of them young people, most in tears, lined the street. Many were holding flags, as were the soldiers stationed along the route; the flags dipped as the coffin passed by; the boots of the soldiers and sailors ahead of us thumped on the pavement in counterpoint to the clatter of horses' hooves. Looking up, I noted the trees were leafless and lifeless.

But however misty the scene before me may have been, the one searing sensation overwhelming all others was the relentless beating of the drums. To this day, I am haunted by them pounding, pounding, pounding. One hundred beats to the minute by two bass and sixteen snare drums cloaked in black. Those terrible drums still echo in my head, capturing more than anything else the awful reality of a dream destroyed.

1 WRITING FOR THE KANSAS CITY MILKMAN

Toronto, June 24, 1940 ...

"Star, Tely, paper here! Read all about it! France surrenders! Read all about it! France surrenders!"

I was twelve years old, my voice was hoarse from yelling, and my short pants were nearly falling off under the weight of hundreds of pennies as I stood at the corner of Bathurst and Eglinton announcing the German victory. I sold more *Toronto Stars* and *Toronto Telegrams* that Monday after the French surrender than ever before. Throughout that year, as World War II unfolded across the ocean, I sold papers each day after school – the price was three cents a paper and on a good day I sold as many as 100 papers.

It was thrilling to watch the trucks dump off the *Star* and *Telegram* at my corner, knowing I'd be the first to open the bundles and see the news. I revelled in my fledgling connection to the process of getting out the news. I suppose it was an embryonic form of what I would do decades later as a foreign correspondent and then as anchor of *The National* on CBC Television. It was my small entrance into the exciting world of journalism. (Actually, my entrance had begun four years earlier when I pecked out on the family typewriter eight pages of neighbourhood and school news, and sold ads to local stores – one quarter page for five licorice whips.)

Being a reporter was a future I dreamed of. One career I knew even then that I'd never pursue was acting. In Grade Four I played the role of Friar Tuck in a school play about Robin Hood. My opening line, uttered in response to Robin Hood's query, "Who goes there?", was "It is I, Fire Truck." My future clearly lay elsewhere.

I soon went from selling papers on the street corner to writing letters to the editors of the Toronto daily papers on everything from Canadian politics to world affairs. I reported high school football games for the Toronto *Globe and Mail* and, at seventeen, I dropped out of school to become editor of *Canadian High News* at $15 a week. It was a weekly tabloid paper distributed to most high schools in southern Ontario and I loved every minute of our twelve-hour days and six-day weeks, writing, editing, organizing, laying out, and proofreading. I was intoxicated by the smell of newsprint and ink as I watched the paper roll off the Maclean Hunter presses, a smell familiar from selling my papers on that Toronto street corner.

At *Canadian High News* we worked out of the back end of the second floor of an old rattletrap building in downtown Toronto on Adelaide Street. My colleagues included Patrick Scott as jazz columnist, Keith Davey as sports columnist, Bob McMichael as photographer, and Bill Torgis as publisher. Patrick went on to become a distinguished newspaper columnist and editor. Keith is now known to everyone as the Liberal Party "Rainmaker." Bob has his name on a distinguished collection of Canadian paintings at Kleinberg, Ontario. And Bill is a successful Toronto businessman.

But in less than a year I left the editorship over a matter of principle now long forgotten and bounced from job to job between bouts of unemployment and lunches of ketchup sandwiches and lemon cokes. In one moment of pecuniary desperation, I even took a job in a bank. I quit at the end of the first day, convinced more than ever that journalism was the career for me. It took a while to get there, though.

For a few months, I worked as an editor at the Dutchess Publishing Company, helping put out a couple of magazines called *Candid Crime* and *Candid Confessions*. Most of our authors were in prison and, for some strange reason, most were at the Oklahoma State Penitentiary in Ada, Oklahoma. Half the time we'd be answering letters from the warden asking if a prisoner-author could make a living "outside" as a writer. That was a bit doubtful because, once out of prison, their sources of information, namely their cell mates, would dry up.

A couple of hard-drinking, old-time journalistic vagabonds right out of *The Front Page* also worked at The Dutchess, as we called the company. One had been run out of the Canadian Army after it was discovered he was involved in a big black market operation in Italy during the war. The other had misbehaved badly by drinking too much and being too boisterous while working at a paper in Philadelphia.

Mentors or Walter Lippmanns they were not, but they had an inexhaustible knowledge of the colourful, seamy side of journalism. I was an avid listener to their tales of outrageous derring-do, of stealing diaries and pictures, hiding court witnesses, bribing cops, and conspiring with shyster lawyers.

One of them had two especially impressive talents: he could smell a bottle of gin being opened a block away and he also claimed to be the best dog tail-biter in Toronto. He claimed to double his salary by biting off dogs' tails for people who felt this was a particularly effective way of having their pets ''detailed'' – or bobbed. When he got a call in the office, he'd drop everything, exercise his jaws for a few minutes, and then dash out the door.

A fall in the circulation of *Candid Crime* and *Candid Confessions* led to my being fired, and I was on the street again looking for a job. This time I wound up as a reporter for a Toronto neighbourhood newspaper called *The St. Clair Leader*, but that lasted only a few months. Then, former editorial colleagues from my *Canadian High News* days and I bought a couple of Toronto neighbourhood weekly papers and launched, full of hope, into the publishing world. It wasn't our money since none of us had any. We'd somehow persuaded Patrick Scott's stockbroker brother to finance us instead of paying for Patrick to go to university. It turned out to be a dubious decision because we never did get out of the red ink.

Our advertising staff was forever talking about the big contracts we were going to get in a few months, but meanwhile, little advertising was coming in for the next issue. We all went out selling ads, and I found this wasn't a particularly fruitful field for me. Once I went into a funeral home near Eglinton and Dufferin and started my advertising pitch to a chap sitting in a chair in the front room. He seemed to listen intently and I thought I was clearly making an impression. I waxed eloquently over the virtues of advertising in our papers but he neither spoke nor even nodded, and it slowly dawned on me that he was dead. The funeral home director came out after five minutes or so, picked up the body, and shouted ''No!'' over his shoulder as he carted away my would-be client.

After a few months of determined but unsuccessful efforts, we mournfully gave up our tiny publishing empire.

Toronto, January, 1947 ...

Here I was, nineteen years old, broke, unemployed, and determined to pursue my ambition to become a journalist. After knocking on the doors of every newspaper, radio station, and magazine in town and trying freelance writing, I finally got my first real professional job. I was hired as Toronto night editor with British United Press.

BUP's main competition in Canada was Canadian Press (CP), which was affiliated with Associated Press (AP) and Reuters. In those days before television, when the newspaper was still king of the news media, international news was almost all gathered and disseminated by a few large wire services. Newspapers and radio networks, with rare exceptions, could afford few, if any, of their own correspondents.

With a head office in Montreal and BUP bureaus across the country, we supplied foreign and domestic news to newspapers on one wire and to radio stations on another wire. Most of our work in the Toronto bureau was for radio stations and we would send out fifty to sixty Ontario stories every day. News from the rest of Canada and around the world was fed onto the radio wire from Montreal. Our editors in Montreal and sometimes at UP headquarters in New York would occasionally ask us to write stories for the newspaper wire.

In salary terms, I hadn't come very far in two years – my starting pay at BUP was $16 a week. But the job had all the romance and excitement a nineteen-year-old journalistic dreamer could imagine.

When I walked into that BUP office, I crossed the threshold into the romantic, exciting world of international journalism that I'd fantasized about after seeing a trenchcoated Joel McRae try to stop World War II from happening in *Foreign Correspondent*. It was all here in this paper-strewn, noisy, cramped little office. We were on the second floor of a creaky old building across the street from the King Edward Hotel in downtown Toronto, but it seemed like the centre of the world to me with reports coming in from across the country and from UP correspondents in Tokyo, Berlin, London, Cairo, and Moscow (where the UP correspondent was a young fellow named Walter Cronkite). Twenty-four hours a day the teletype clattered and rang with "URGENTS," which were given three bells, "BULLETINS," which got five bells, and the very rare "FLASHES" at ten bells. This was truly the big time – my dream come true.

Brian Tobin, the BUP bureau manager who hired me, was a handsome, tall, thin, worried, and weary man in his early thirties. Tobin was tight with a nickel, to put it mildly. I was quickly told that when on assignment I was always to walk or take a streetcar, never a cab. My stories were to be typed on both sides of the paper, pencils were to be saved and not taken home, and I was constantly admonished to "downhold" expenses.

Two of my three co-workers in the bureau were World War II veterans and the other was fresh off the boat from Fleet Street, while I was the baby still living at home in northern Toronto with my parents. I was awed by my new colleagues who'd seen so much of the world.

In those days at BUP, we primarily "scalped" news from the newspapers. Scalping was when you simply rewrote a story that had appeared elsewhere. This was distinct from "researching," which meant you rewrote a story that had appeared in two or more papers, blending the information.

We worked different shifts, rewriting, editing, reporting, and "punching" the wire (that is, typing the teletype) ourselves. I was grateful that I'd learned the touch system of typing in high school while my more seasoned workmates had to use the painfully slow two-finger "hunt-and-peck" system. Every hour or so, we filed what we called a "split," which consisted of at least half a dozen stories. I always tried to file as many stories as possible on my shift. Montreal filed the main radio wire and every bureau would insert its own regional stories each time Montreal "split" the wire.

My shift was 4:00 p.m. to 1:00 a.m. but usually I'd get in early to read what had gone on so far that day. The biggest pressure was between 4:00 and 6:00, when we filed a heavy run of stories during our split for the evening newscasts on our client radio stations. At dinnertime, I'd munch a sandwich while reading the wires and papers. The pressure picked up again about 9:00 when I got the *Globe and Mail* and scalped everything in sight.

By midnight, my writing was finished and the radio wire primarily carried feature stories for the next day. Once or twice a week, I'd work till about 2:00 a.m. on a feature story; other nights I'd settle down to read through the out-of-town newspapers we received and gradually work my way through every scrap of correspondence the bureau had written or received over the previous half-dozen years. I was young and ambitious, and hungry for every snippet of journalistic knowledge I could glean.

The most important lesson I learned in those first few months with BUP was always to write clearly, simply, and colourfully. "Write it so the Kansas City milkman can understand" was the UP motto. We hardly wrote anything without thinking of that milkman in Kansas City. As a result, UP and BUP stories were usually better written than our opposition Canadian Press and Associated Press, but CP had a better reputation for accuracy.

After I'd been at BUP for a few months, I began to get the chance to cover stories assigned by our Montreal and New York offices. I got the assignments because I volunteered to do the reporting in addition to my full normal shift. In those days, we never dreamed of overtime; I simply did it for the experience. Soon I was regularly covering the major sports in Toronto: NHL hockey, Big Four football (forerunner of the Canadian Football League), and professional basketball (the short-lived Toronto Huskies).

When I was a youngster growing up in Toronto, my father used to take me to see the Leafs play. We'd sit high up in the greys – the cheapest seats available – and watch players like Syl Apps, Gordie Drillon, Red Horner, and Turk Broda. Now, here I was sitting in the exotic precincts of the press box, surrounded by veteran sports writers such as Jim Vipond of the *Globe*, Joe Perlove of the *Star*, Baz O'Meara of the *Montreal Star*, and sharply dressed, wisecracking writers from New York, Detroit, and Boston.

Working for a wire service, I had to write a running account and file it as the game progressed – and I had to be quick if I was to beat the opposition. So I'd bang away at my typewriter continually and shout for the CN or CP telegraph operator to take my copy for filing to New York. In my exuberant prose, players such as Apps, Howie Meeker, Rocket Richard, and Ted Kennedy never simply scored a goal. They "dented the cords," "potted a shot," "sent the rubber home," "rifled," "swatted," and "batted" the puck.

I was a natural to cover major horse races since my father was a racetrack betting manager and I'd worked for him from time to time at tracks in Hamilton and Niagara Falls, usually in the ticket room preparing tickets to be sold each day and running money to the paddock or the infield cashiers. The racing world was part of my growing up. When a husky brown gelding named Last Mark won the King's Plate in 1948, my story was the lead in the *New York Times* sports section. There was no byline, but there it was at the top of the page with a UP slug and a Toronto dateline. Heady stuff for someone who was just starting out in the profession.

But the most exciting news stories I covered were in the Ontario legislature. Since my daily shift at BUP didn't start until four, I could spend part of the morning and early afternoon in the press gallery at Queen's Park watching Premier George Drew and his Conservative colleagues run roughshod over the opposition. The only members Drew had trouble with were the two Communist MPPs of the Labour Progressive Party, Joe Salsberg and A.A. MacLeod. Drew never could beat them in debate and he grew especially red-faced in frustration when MacLeod would mischievously quote the Bible to support his position.

Politics was and remains my journalistic passion. In 1942, as a young teen-ager, I once rode an elevator with John Bracken, the then newly elected leader of the Progressive Conservative Party. He had been a long-time Premier of Manitoba, a leader in the Progressive Party, and had insisted on liberalizing the image of the Conservatives by putting the word "Progressive" in front of the party name before he would accept its leadership. When Bracken got off the elevator in the Royal Connaught Hotel in Hamilton, I got off, too, and like a kid sneaking under the flap of a circus tent, I followed him into the political meeting where he was speaking. I don't remember what he said, but I was captivated by the noise, the smoke, the smell, and the feel of the place and the sense of important things happening. As a BUP reporter I had that same feeling of excitement as I looked down from the press gallery at the Ontario legislative chamber at George Drew and his fellow politicians.

Drew was a hard person to get to know. He was aloof, austere, and shy. He was also probably the world's worst storyteller, as was clearly evident at one off-the-record dinner with Queen's Park press gallery members. He tried to tell a risqué joke, but stammered his way through, got utterly mixed up, and forgot the punch line. His audience laughed politely anyway.

Covering a provincial legislature in those days could be a profitable sideline. In Ontario, we received what was called a "stationery allowance" from the government in power. As I remember it, this was about $50 a year, equal at that time to about three weeks' pay for me. But in fact, in the press gallery we got all our stationery free, so this little bonus was presumably a way of trying to make us less hostile to the government of the day. In Quebec the stationery allowance was substantially more – several hundred dollars. One of our BUP reporters collected the bonus several times over since he represented several small Quebec daily papers as well as BUP.

One action of the Drew government I covered at the time was passage of a law allowing bars. At the time you couldn't buy a glass of whisky in the province except at a bootlegger's or a private club. But Drew changed that and I was on hand reporting the opening of the first bar in Toronto – the Silver Rail. When I got there the line-up was three blocks long. I waited an hour in line, was given fifteen minutes to drink, and then had to go back to the end of the line again. It was a good story, but personally I confined my drinking to the smoky, raucous Toronto Men's Press Club on Yonge Street a couple of blocks from the BUP bureau. There I could watch in fascination as Toronto's hard-boiled, loud-talking veteran reporters and editors gathered to drink, sing, and argue. At my impressionable age, to see the likes of columnists Ted "The Moaner" Reeve, Jim Coleman, and Frank Tumpane, photographers Nat and Lou Turofsky, and a dozen others singing at an out-of-tune piano and slopping booze on the piano keys was close to heaven.

In March of 1947 I covered the trial of the sensational "Torso Murder Case" involving a glamorous Hamilton lady of shady reputation, Evelyn Dick, her boy friend, and her streetcar-conductor husband whose body was found in the trunk of a car on Hamilton Mountain. A year earlier, when I was freelancing, I had talked to the detective in charge; he was careful not to call it murder just yet.

"But the body was cut up into pieces," I said.

"Yes, I know," he replied, "and we suspect foul play."

Eventually, Evelyn was found not guilty of killing her husband but was convicted of manslaughter in the death of her infant son, an event which occurred about the same time.

Later that year I undertook my first real effort at investigative journalism – a term not then current. There had been rumours of Jewish terrorist groups recruiting members in Canada for their revolt against the British in an attempt to establish a separate Jewish state in Palestine. One such group was the Irgun Zvai Leumi, led by Menachem Begin. I spent days in the Jewish area around Spadina Avenue going in and out of scores of stores and offices and stopping people on the street to ask if they knew how I could join up. Finally, I got a lead from a boastful, unemployed young man who sent me up two floors into a dingy office over a rundown store on Spadina. There, I met a smiling but roughly dressed representative of the Irgun who was just finishing a lunchtime sandwich. When he curtly asked me what I wanted I promptly replied, "To join." He was sceptical.

I told him of being in school with many Jewish friends, of my admiration for Zionism and my desire for adventure. I did not tell him I was a reporter. He either believed me or humoured me, but in any event he had me sign some papers swearing allegiance to the Irgun and told me to keep quiet and come back in a week. Exhilarated with my scoop, I said "Sure" and ran down the stairs as an official terrorist, at least on paper. I went straight to BUP to write the story and got congratulations from my bureau chief and from Montreal. But while my exposé was carried across the country, to my chagrin the Toronto papers ignored it.

Nevertheless, for this and for my general zealousness, I was given a raise, something rare at BUP in those days. A three-page letter of praise from BUP head man Bob Keyserlingk announced my increase from $16 to $18 a week, effective immediately.

Halifax, June, 1948 ...

A few months after my raise, in the late spring of 1948, things began to look up even more. I was sent to Halifax as British United Press bureau manager. The promotion meant I was in charge of our coverage of Newfoundland, Labrador, Nova Scotia, New Brunswick, and Prince Edward Island. It was a grand-sounding job description, but I would be in charge of only a two-man bureau: me and an assistant. However, I would be earning $27.50 a week.

In many ways, Halifax seemed like the end of the earth. I'd been living at home until then and this was a complete break with family and friends. As an only child, my family ties were strong. And yet, with our White Anglo-Saxon Protestant heritage, we prided ourselves on not showing deep emotions. We bottled up our love for each other so much that we never really knew how close a family we were until it was too late. Both my mother and father were happy-go-lucky souls who lived relatively well from paycheque to paycheque, enjoying parties, dinners out, and winter trips to Miami.

At the time I heard about my promotion to Halifax, my father was working in Hamilton, preparing for the summer meeting of the Hamilton Jockey Club. The next morning, I took the train over to say good-bye to him and to my mother, who was with him.

My mother bit back tears as we kissed good-bye in her hotel room and told me to "be good." My father, a sensitive, sweet man, didn't know what to say, or more likely couldn't say what his heart told him, and the only way he could express his love was to press a $20 bill into my hand. His lined, soft face crinkled into a smile, but a tear trickled down his cheek. I knew what he was feeling because I, too, was deeply moved. But we said nothing and silently shared our leave-taking. A few hours later I was on the train to Montreal and Halifax.

Stepping off the CNR Ocean Limited into a Halifax summer dusk, I lugged my suitcase a few blocks to a rooming house right across the street from where I'd be working. The rent was $6 a week for a front room with a bathroom just down the hall. I unpacked and walked across the street to the BUP office located on the second floor of radio station CHNS. (CHNS is still there.) My one-room office was complete with a battered old desk, two typewriters vintage 1920, a cot, and a hot plate.

It may have been a small operation, but I was the boss in charge of covering a huge territory and selling to it all the products of BUP and UP, from the radio and news wires to feature columnists and comic strips. At age twenty, I was British United Press in the Atlantic region.

As in Toronto, my main competition was Canadian Press, but I think

21

my CP colleagues with their vaster resources looked upon me more with pity than with competitive apprehension. CP bureau chief Jack Brayley and his staff were newsmen of long experience with contacts everywhere and they usually beat us with scoops and exclusives. Still, we were able to pull off the occasional coup and get the banner line in the *Halifax Herald* and papers in Moncton and Sydney.

We did it sometimes by better writing and sometimes by just working harder, getting up earlier, and staying later than our opposition. I established a lengthy phone check list of police, fire, Air Force Search and Rescue, and other contacts that we phoned every three or four hours, and I set up a network of part-time stringers in communities throughout the region who sometimes gave us exclusives and beats. So we not infrequently beat CP on disasters at sea and fires. And because of friendships I developed with some union officials, we often got the jump on labour stories. Our stringer in Newfoundland often kept us ahead of CP on the negotiations leading to the then British-run Commission Government joining Canada.

One of the first stories I wrote after arriving in Halifax was on this question, and we were well ahead of CP with it:

St. John's, Nfld., Aug. 6—(BUP)—The five man delegation that will go to Ottawa to open Confederation talks, has been appointed. Included in the talks are ... Confederation leader Joseph R. Smallwood ...''

We did stories, too, on those opposed to Newfoundland joining Canada, such as St. John's broadcaster Don Jamieson, who wanted Newfoundland to become part of the United States. He later changed his mind, and, much later, became Trudeau's Minister for External Affairs.

My colleague in the Halifax bureau was a hard-working, nervous, quiet, and gentle youth (he was nineteen and I was all of twenty) named Stan McCabe. Together, we each put in fourteen- to eighteen-hour days, feeding news reports onto the BUP radio and news wires, making our phone checks, rewriting, and doing much original reporting instead of just scalping the pages of the *Halifax Herald* and *Halifax Chronicle* (later merged into a single daily). In addition, I called on customers for the BUP and UP services among radio stations and newspapers of the Atlantic region and flew up a couple of times to do stories on the big American air base at Goose Bay, Labrador.

We certainly didn't have much spare time. I usually took the early shift starting at 5:30 a.m., jarred awake by a pre-arranged telephone call from the CN telegraph office. To this day, I leap up in fright whenever the phone rings when I'm in bed. I would generally work through to 8:00 or 9:00 p.m. Stan would start a couple of hours later than I did and stay until 10:00 or 11:00 p.m. Whenever I was out of the office, I always had to leave a phone number where I could be reached by Stan or by our head office in Montreal in case a news story was breaking. We lived with the constant fear of missing a story, a fear that haunted me throughout my reportorial career.

Late at night, we'd occasionally repair to the bootlegger's house just across the street from the police station to sit and sip rum in a quiet front room. Once in a while I'd go to a Saturday night party with friends from CHNS or to a Navy bash. It was in Halifax where I learned the delights of dark rum, the impact of which seemed far more immediate and comforting than the rye and coke I had previously favoured. With our strenuous working pace we needed as fast a relaxer as we could get.

Drinking seemed to be much more of a major pastime among my Maritime colleagues than in Toronto, and even, or especially, on melancholy occasions. An Irish neighbour of mine died one day, and that night a wake was held. I watched transfixed from my next-door rooming-house window until well past midnight as the party got rowdier and rowdier. I could see my former neighbour propped up in a casket in the kitchen beside an impromptu bar. At one point, five guys gathered around the corpse, bellowing out an off-key version of "My Wild Irish Rose." Although the scene amazed and shocked me at the time, I came to feel that such post-mortem merriment was a simply marvellous way to celebrate the life of a deceased friend rather than mourning his death. Ever since, I've believed in the bittersweet celebration of an old-fashioned wake as the best possible salute to the dead.

If rum was a relaxer for us, food was merely something to keep us working. We ate irregularly and imprudently. For breakfast, I'd cook bacon and eggs on the hot plate in our office, distressing the radio station employees on the first floor below as the smell of eggs and bacon cooking wafted down the stairs and into their offices. Generally I'd skip lunch, and dinner was almost invariably a tuna steak at a nearby drug store soda fountain. Sometimes, instead of the drug store, I'd go to a restaurant called the Green Lantern or, as we called it, the Green Latrine. Sundays, though, were special. I'd get dressed up and treat myself to a seafood dinner in the formal dining room of the fancy Nova Scotian Hotel.

Halifax in 1948 was a medium-sized city with little night life and less glitter, still a bit dingy from its wartime role as the staging point of the Atlantic convoys. Perhaps because of my work schedule, I never really had time to feel a part of the city. I had no time at all to sail or fish as most others did. I liked the people and the picturesque nearby towns of Peggy's Cove and Chester, but I yearned for the vibrancy of the big city, as I thought Toronto to be. Coming home to my room at midnight after a drink at the bootlegger's or straight from a long siege at the office, I'd lie abed, moodily listening to the torch songs of Phyllis Marshall wafting over the airwaves from the CBC in Toronto, evoking in me a sense of melancholy loneliness.

Halifax then was a Navy town as it still is today. Most of our stories were about the sea: the Navy, merchant shipping, RCAF Search and Rescue, ships lost at sea. Not all Maritime stories were tragic, of course. One day not long after I arrived, the Royal Canadian Navy aircraft carrier *Magnificent* took a wrong turn and wound up on a golf course – and the captain wound up in a court-martial.

One night in the fall of 1948 the Navy took me and half a dozen other news people out to sea on submarine-chasing training man-oeuvres. As luck would have it, we were caught in the tail end of a hurricane in the North Atlantic and our little minesweeper crashed up and down relentlessly in the great waves as it was battered by wind and rain. Everyone except the captain was seasick, crew included. The skipper was a hale and hearty soul who revelled in the angry seas. At one point he called all the correspondents into his cramped quarters to show us exactly what the minesweeper's mission was. After unrolling a chart on his table, he said, "Now here we are."

All of us leaned over the map to see where he pointed. Suddenly the ship rolled, dipped, and pitched and two of the newsmen threw up all over the map. Unfazed, the captain laughed heartily, swept away the mess, and carried on with his briefing.

Twenty-four hours later we were back in Halifax, the crew smartly dressed and the captain full of exuberance at a challenge well met, while a struggling, wobbling group of pale reporters made their precarious way down the gangplank.

A few weeks later that fall of 1948, Canadians, along with most everybody else in the British Commonwealth, were waiting for the birth of Princess Elizabeth's first baby. We in BUP and UP were determined to be first with the big news. And we were, as a ten-bell FLASH clanged across our wire late Sunday afternoon, November 14, announcing, "It's a girl." This was quickly followed by general copy describing Princess Elizabeth's first-born child as a bouncing baby girl. The trouble was, the baby was a boy – Prince Charles.

Our subscriber radio stations around the world, including CHNS in

Halifax, broke into scheduled programs to breathlessly announce the birth of the baby princess. At BUP Halifax, we stayed with the story for seven or eight minutes. Then, suddenly, more bells clanged and KILL came on the teletype, followed by a story saying, "It's a boy."

There was mortification in every UP bureau and none more than in Halifax, but London was to blame. In an attempt to beat AP and Reuters by a few seconds, UP London had punched two tapes ahead of time – one for a boy and one for a girl. The London teletype operator picked up the wrong tape and sent it through.

It was professionally inexcusable and especially mortifying because every newsman I met reminded me of an earlier occasion on which UP had been first but wrong. In November, 1918, Roy Howard, the president of UP, had been visiting France and saw a telegram to an admiral in Brest that he thought announced the end of World War I. He immediately reported the news to UP New York, which fired it out around the world, causing great celebrations. The report, however, was four days too soon and UP had never lived down that false armistice.

In Halifax there was the occasional international story that UP New York wanted covered, and whenever New York called we jumped. One such story was the annual International Tuna Fishing Tournament held at the time off Wedgeport, Nova Scotia, near Yarmouth. At dawn every morning, I'd be out on "Soldier's Rip" watching the fishing and occasionally seeing a thousand-pound tuna hit someone's line. It was a totally enjoyable few days spent fishing all day, drinking rum all night, and in between writing copy for the New York office.

A running story New York wanted us to cover was the arrival in Nova Scotia of thousands of Estonian and Latvian refugees. Somewhat like the refugee "boat people" fleeing Vietnam in the late-1970s, the Estonians and Latvians made their harrowing Atlantic crossing in small boats piloted by greedy Swedish captains who charged their passengers inflated prices and landed them illegally on Canadian shores. But the refugees were willing to take any means to escape communism in their homeland. They came in every kind of vessel: some ships carried as few as thirty and some as many as 400. Many were sick during the passage; others died. When I interviewed some who'd made it, I found them desperate to stay in Canada. Eventually most of them were admitted to the country.

On a tip from our Annapolis Valley stringer one day, I unearthed another story for New York. The story was about a man named Otto Strasser. He may be largely forgotten today, but then he was an important historical figure with still-influential friends in Germany. Strasser was an ex-Nazi official who broke with Hitler in a policy dispute in 1930 and eventually fled to Canada. I met him at the farm of a friend of his where he was staying. He was a chunky, balding man in his fifties. He told me he had tried to force Hitler toward socialism, but Hitler accused him of "democracy and liberalism" and threw him out of the Nazi Party. He then formed his own National Socialist Party, known as "The Black Front," but failed to win enough support. When the Nazis gained power, he was forced to flee for his life. His brother Gregor, also an original organizer of the Nazi Party, and one-time number-two man to Hitler, was one of hundreds murdered by Hitler in the Roehm Purge of 1934. Strasser was trying to get back to Germany to renew his political career, but the Canadian government had five times refused to let him leave the country. He finally did get back, but he was never again a political force.

Vancouver, August, 1949 ...

In the summer of 1949 I had three major personal changes: I got a raise to $50 a week; I married an old Toronto girl friend from *Canadian High News* days with whom I'd been carrying on a long-distance, letter-writing courtship; and I got a promotion to run the BUP West Coast bureau out of Vancouver. BUP Vancouver was a three-man bureau, not just two, and we worked closely with the Seattle UP bureau. I'd been in Halifax just over a year and felt I had learned as much as I could, so I was enthusiastic about my new personal and professional challenges.

As befitted my newly married status, on arrival in Vancouver, my wife and I moved into two rooms and a kitchen, with a shared bathroom right outside our hall door.

We needed all this space because a few months later a baby was on the way. When I called my parents to tell them the news, my father was so excited he could only exclaim, "Caesar's Ghost!", his strongest expletive, as he quickly handed the phone to my mother. "Caesar's Ghost!" were the last words I ever heard from my father; he died a few weeks later from a heart attack.

I was filing a story on the BUP Vancouver radio wire when our Toronto bureau cut in with a message for me: "Knowlton ... your father has died." The world was knocked out from under me; I lost my breath and felt dizzy. Yet I said not a word, finished the story I was sending, and only then sat down at my desk to reflect on the news. I didn't cry until one evening two weeks later, coming out of the movie

Gone with the Wind, I suddenly burst into uncontrollable tears, sobbing that "there's too much dying in that movie."

Getting to my father's funeral was a financial problem as well as an emotional one because I didn't have the air fare and my friends had no savings to lend me. I raided the office petty cash and came up with $25, not enough for a plane ticket. By luck, though, Jawaharlal Nehru, the Prime Minister of India, was visiting Vancouver and flying out the next day to Madison, Wisconsin. I'd been covering his visit and so asked his news secretary if I could hitchhike with them to Wisconsin. From there I could get a train to Chicago and Toronto. Nehru agreed, and thanks to him, I was able to get to my father's funeral. Although I am not a religious man in any formal sense, when our daughter Anne was born seven months later, it seemed to me almost as if God were giving a new life after taking an old one. It gave me a sense of continuity and comfort knowing my father's blood ran in her veins.

During my year and a half in Vancouver, the big ongoing story was the Doukhobors, particularly the radical "Sons of Freedom" sect. The Doukhobors were founded by a Prussian sergeant in the mid-eighteenth century at Kharkov and came to the Canadian West from Russia at the start of the twentieth century, seeking religious freedom. They had rebelled against persecution in Czarist Russia and they rebelled in Canada, too, refusing to send their children to school or obey other laws. The "Sons of Freedom" sect claimed God wanted them to burn and strip as a protest against the laws of Canada and so for two generations they set fire to their homes and marched nude in protest. Their outbreaks ran in cycles and in 1950 a new burst of Doukhobor defiance of the law exploded in a series of bombings, burnings, and stripping, and it became a story in which UP New York was especially interested.

The "Sons of Freedom" leaders would tell their members to "don the red hats," which meant they should set their homes afire and stand naked watching the flames. Usually it was the older men and women who burned and bared, but I vividly remember one march of naked teen-age Doukhobors held at Krestova (meaning City of Christ) in the southeast corner of British Columbia. I was in nearby Nelson, B.C., at the time, covering the various Doukhobor outbreaks. I first got word of the march from a local RCMP sergeant, Larry Smith. "Half the town is running around naked over there," he told me. That was enough to get me and my competitors driving the twenty miles to Krestova as quickly as we could.

Sure enough, there were forty naked teen-agers shouting and marching along the highway just outside town, led by a pretty nineteen-year-old girl named Vera Kanigan. There were several farm horses travelling alongside the marchers.

The event provided an object lesson for me in the way the pressure of competition and the demand to be colourful sometimes overwhelm the quest for truth. It doesn't happen nearly so much nowadays because we journalists have become a bit more honest and because television can show you exactly what is happening. But in those days, we occasionally took a bit of liberty with reality.

My first lead on the story read: "Krestova, B.C.—(UP)—Led by a pretty young girl, 40 naked teen-age Doukhobors marched in protest here today." The Canadian Press improved on that. "Krestova, B.C.—(CP)—Led by a blonde beauty, 40 teen-age Doukhobors stripped in a protest march today here." Not to be outdone, our rewrite desk in Seattle noted that several paragraphs down in my story I'd mentioned horses. The desk simply put the girl leader atop one of the horses, changed the colour of her hair, and the new lead read: "Krestova, B.C.—(UP)—Led by a bare-breasted, raven-haired beauty straddling a frisky horse, 40 naked teen-age Doukhobors marched in protest here today." Putting her on that horse did it. UP scored front pages all across the U.S. with AP left out in the cold. The Kansas City milkman must have loved it.

The teen-agers wound up burning a 1920 model car, which the owner, also a Doukhobor, had surrendered to them. The owner told me later that a car was a "seduction to young people." His son John was among the naked youngsters and he said, "As I watched John and the girls and boys standing there undressed and burning it, I felt a little sad because I had to work hard for the $200 which I paid for it, but the car is a luxury and we don't need luxuries."

After the burning, Vera and her friends put their clothes back on and, as she put on her print dress and flowered slip, she told a group of us reporters, "We will undress and burn again and again as we must." Nobody was arrested on this occasion, but later there were many arrests as the Doukhobors blew up bridges and burned houses.

Some years after I'd left British Columbia, John Diefenbaker ran into a similar protest during an election campaign while he was Prime Minister. When a group of Doukhobors stood up and stripped stark naked in the middle of Diefenbaker's speech, his eyes nearly popped out of his head, his eyebrows wiggled, and then he smiled a little nervously and said, "Ah but boys, I've seen that before."

Vancouver was a busy bureau. Apart from the Doukhobors, there were floods, plane crashes, the occasional murder, and the never-ending fascination of B.C. politics – as wild then as it is today. At one point, I interviewed Canada's official hangman, a mild-mannered little fellow named John Ellis who seemed more like a clerk in a bookstore. He was visiting Vancouver in the course of his duty.

"It's an easy business to get into," he told me, "but hard to get out of." I told him I'd watched one hanging and found it cruel and grotesque. "Oh, it's not so bad," he replied. "It's all in the knot."

In the news business, death is always a story and especially if it's dramatic. Christmas of 1950 saw a Canadian Pacific plane crash into a mountain near Penticton, B.C., killing the pilot and co-pilot while the fifteen passengers and stewardesses miraculously survived. I was on the phone eighteen hours a day getting details and sending out reports on the story that turned out to be the biggest one anywhere in North America that Christmas. As a result, UP New York was hot on my tail for more detail and more colour. Because of my efforts, we were miles ahead of CP and everybody else, and it was my story with a BUP slug on it that splashed across the top of the *Vancouver Sun*. That was a rare achievement since the *Sun* demanded its own reporters write any banner story that occurred in British Columbia.

As I was going home on the bus at the end of that long day, I stood looking proudly at people reading my *Sun* lead story. I think I must have achieved journalistic nirvana when I heard someone point to the front page and say, "Look at that, will you!" I was about to proudly announce that I was the author when I heard him add, "Yeah, look at that. It's going to rain again tomorrow." The incident taught me a lesson I'll never forget: my own preoccupation with news scoops and beats was not shared by everybody.

I got my first taste of Hollywood celebrities with BUP in Vancouver. It was a bit sour. Bing Crosby often came up to fish off the B.C. coast and would come into town after a week or so, unshaven and still wearing his fishing clothes. Once he was refused a room at the Hotel Vancouver because the room clerk didn't recognize him and thought he was a bum. In an interview, I found Crosby charming at first, but less so later as he leered at and flirted with waitresses, maids, and anyone in a skirt.

Rudy Vallee had a different problem. He was cheap. I spent a couple of hours with him in his dressing room at a Vancouver nightclub, and all he talked about was ways to save money. At one point, his assistant went to the hotel to get something for him. When he returned, Vallee exploded in anger when he discovered the assistant had taken a cab to the hotel. "What the hell for?" he shouted. "You could have taken a streetcar. The cab'll come out of your pay as a lesson."

Toronto, January, 1951 ...

When the time came I was sad to leave Vancouver but eager to tackle new responsibilities as BUP's Toronto bureau manager at $60 a week. Toronto was our biggest bureau outside of the Montreal head office and I was proud and excited about running it. As much as I enjoyed Vancouver and its people, I missed the immediacy and sense of involvement in national affairs I'd had in Toronto. The West Coast seemed to me to be cut off by the Rocky Mountains in those pre-television days. My Vancouver friends, of course, couldn't understand why I was leaving – to them it seemed like a demotion. Nevertheless, I said farewell to the mountains and the ocean and returned home. In two-and-a-half years I had come full circle.

When I'd left Toronto I was the lowly night editor of BUP and now I was coming back as the top man. The Toronto bureau had expanded to five people and had one-man bureaus in Hamilton and Windsor reporting to it. It all gave me a heady sense of power. The bureau had also moved into a bigger office beside Track 7 at the Toronto Union Station, which meant we could get out-of-town on stories more quickly. It also meant the gambling mad Union Station redcaps came into our office all the time to read the race results off the UP sports wire. Every Saturday I'd find a bottle of Seagram's VO left for me in a wastebasket by the grateful station porters.

Another thing that had changed was the degree of Canadian autonomy. UP New York had taken more control of BUP, sending in two new bosses to Montreal: Phil Curran, a rotund, friendly, smooth-talking salesman who was named head man, and Denny Landry, a small, vinegary old news workhorse who ran the editorial side. One of the first memos I got when I arrived in Toronto was from Landry, complaining about one of my staff and warning me, "If he can't straighten up and cut the mustard, it'll be curtains for him."

It was, in time.

One thing that hadn't changed in my years with BUP was the general stinginess of the operation. I had chafed at my first boss Brian Tobin's tightness with a penny and now here I was sitting in his chair and demanding much the same financial vigilance from my staff. While we travelled a lot in BUP we travelled cheap, with free passes from the railroads and by foot and streetcar. Our entertaining of clients was modest, as one B.C. expense account of mine showed for a trip to Victoria: "lunch, $2.10 with station owner; coffee, 40 cents with editor, *Victoria Times*."

The Toronto staff were sometimes a handful and I had to fire more than one employee. My best staffer was Ray Timson, now managing editor of the *Toronto Star*. He was also the most creative person I've ever met when it came to excuses for being late for work. Once he arrived about three hours behind schedule. His neighbour's wife had been coming out of the house, he explained.

"She was crying and told me her husband had just died." In her grief, he said, she had fallen down some stairs and broken her leg, and so he'd had to take her to hospital and then get the body to the undertaker.

"That's why I'm late," he said. None of it was true, of course, but it had a nice ring to it.

As bureau manager, I did less reporting than before, but one story I covered was watching a man called "Red" Hill try to go over Niagara Falls in a "barrel" and live to tell about it. He didn't.

William "Red" Hill had been a Niagara riverman for years, pulling out the occasional body and working around the docks. He thought he could make a lot of money by going over the Horseshoe Falls in a sort of barrel made of thirteen inner tubes strung together with canvas netting. He showed them to me a day before his attempt and I told him he was crazy. "No, no," he said. "I can do it and we'll make a potful of money."

The night before, he went out beer-drinking with his buddies and began to have second thoughts. But having boasted to his buddies and talked to the press, he was grimly determined to do it. "People say it can't be done," he told me. "But I say it can. I think." He was wrong.

The next morning before 7:00 a.m., the thirty-five-year-old Hill squeezed his 155 pounds into what he called "The Thing" and pushed off from the river bank above the Falls where he'd hidden it. The police were trying to stop him but couldn't find his craft. "It's a sure thing, boys," he said.

I was down at the Maid of the Mist landing below the Falls with Hill's mother and brother and other reporters while up on the cliffs were thousands of people who'd come to watch. Some of Hill's friends went through the crowds collecting money. Suddenly, there he was bobbing at the edge of the Falls and he was swept out and over. In mid-air the netting broke, the inner tubes flew apart, and he plummeted 170 feet to the rocks below.

I was beside his mother as she screamed, "Where is he? Where is he? That's my oldest boy, and I want him!" His brother, Corky, zipped off in a small boat. When he came back, he yelled, "There's no one in it!"

As soon as I knew Red was dead, I ran to a telephone in a shed on the dock that I had reserved by bribing a guy in the office with $10. I dictated my story to the rewrite desk at UP New York and then, while one editor was filing the story on the UP wires, I asked another editor to read back to me my story. That way I held on to the only phone available an extra five minutes, keeping it away from my AP competition and giving UP a clear beat on the story. It was one of many times bribery and phone-hogging would be used in my journalistic career to ensure a beat.

When I returned to the scene, another of Red's brothers, Major Hill (Major was his first name, not a title), said to me, "Well, at least he put on a good show." Red Hill's shoes were found in the "barrel," but it was days before his battered body was recovered.

My last assignment for BUP was to cover the royal tour of Princess Elizabeth and the Duke of Edinburgh through southern Ontario in October of 1951. We always had to file lengthy stories on royal tours not only for distribution in Canada, but also for UP New York and for BUP London. It was exciting at first to travel with Elizabeth and Philip, but covering a royal tour very quickly becomes a monumental bore, and I say that even as a committed constitutional monarchist. Day after day, it's the same thing – the same flowers from the same curtsying pretty little girls; the same hospitals and monuments; and the same speech of welcome from every mayor everywhere.

Covering everything from royal tours to murders, a job with a wire service was always considered the best possible introduction to the world of journalism. The pay was bad, the hours endless, and the responsibility heavy. But it was also fun and exciting, and it stretched you to the professional limit. If you survived, you were ready for almost any journalistic challenge, and by the fall of 1951, I felt I'd gone as far as I could with BUP and was considering what to do next. I wanted to be a UP foreign correspondent or to work with UP in New York.

Out of the blue, I heard of a job that dreams are made of. It would mean travelling the world, all expenses paid, living in Washington, and working for double the salary I was then earning. The International Federation of Agricultural Producers (IFAP) was looking for a director of information and I applied. Officials at the Canadian Federation of Agriculture knew of my work with BUP and, as the Canadian member organization of IFAP, asked me to come to Ottawa for a first interview. Actually, I was the second person on their list. The first was an old friend and former colleague from my Halifax days, Keith Morrow of the CBC farm department. But he and his wife felt the Washington climate would be too hot for them, and besides, the CBC had promised him a raise if he would stay. After a successful Ottawa interview I then went to Washington to meet the IFAP secretary-general, who happened to be a Canadian from Saskatchewan named Andy Cairns. At a lunch at the elegant Cosmos Club, we got along fine and I was hired at $7,000 a year plus expenses. After my BUP salary, I felt like a millionaire.

I resigned from BUP, organized my family, said good-bye to my mother, and headed south of the border. Little did I imagine I would not live in Canada again for the next eighteen years.

I'd learned a lot in my nearly five years with BUP: how to write concisely and colourfully; to be relentlessly competitive; to organize news coverage; to hire and fire people; to run a bureau; and to operate on a shoestring budget. Thanks to BUP I had lived at both ends of the country and crossed it more than once. While stationed in Vancouver I made the five-day trip between Toronto and Vancouver nearly a dozen times. I'd experienced not only the grandeur of the north shore of Lake Superior, the Prairies, and the Rockies, but more important, the generosity and genuineness of the people.

I didn't really know it then, but I had developed a strong sense of nationalism, a powerful emotional tie to the country of my birth. Over the next nearly two decades as a globetrotting expatriate, this sense of belonging would be a psychological anchor. Somehow, I always knew that sooner or later I would come home again.

2 *CORRESPONDENT IN WAITING*

Washington, D.C., October, 1951 ...

Washington in late 1951 was still a southern town, at about 600,000 population a little smaller than Toronto, and with one obsession: politics – national and international. It was jokingly known as a city of southern efficiency and northern charm. Clerks, waiters, civil servants, and repairmen dawdled through the day, taking forever to do simple jobs, while brusque officials and politicians rushed about the city in pursuit of power and progress.

For a political junkie and foreign correspondent-in-the-making, the atmosphere was inspirational. Strolling along the grassy mall from Capitol Hill to the White House through a hot, hazy, humid Washington on my first day in town, I was where I'd always wanted to be. As a child, my heroes had been Franklin Roosevelt and Harry Hopkins, not hockey players and movie stars. Looking through the iron fence surrounding the White House at the broad, green, well-manicured presidential lawn, I remembered my parents taking me as a kid of nine to a White House Easter Egg Roll ceremony. We were driving back to Toronto from a Miami winter holiday and had arrived in Washington the night before. In the morning, with hundreds of other youngsters all clutching coloured eggs, we trampled Franklin Roosevelt's lawn rolling eggs on the grass and milling about at what was then an annual American event. Of FDR, I mistily recall a big, laughing man off in the distance who seemed important and nice. In fact, he had recently been inaugurated for his second term as President.

Fourteen years later, here I was again, looking at what was now

34

Harry Truman's lawn and the house where wars were planned, politics plotted, and international crises started and stopped. I'd arrived in Washington in the midst of the Korean War, Truman-era scandals of bribery and pay-offs, McCarthyism, and the beginning of the "Eisenhower for President" boom. What particularly struck me was how noisy and excited everything seemed to be compared to Canada. Day and night the radio blared out everything from accusations and revelations made during live coverage of some congressional hearing to the shouting and screaming of black worshippers at a gospel meeting.

The blacks had reason to cry out. For them, Washington was still very much the South, well below the Mason-Dixon line in mentality as well as geography. Although blacks made up more than half the city's population, the reins of power and influence remained totally in lily-white hands. Blacks still had to ride at the back of the bus, use separate public washrooms, eat in separate restaurants, go to separate movie theatres, get their hair cut in black-only barber shops, and go to segregated schools.

To my innocent and idealistic eyes, this racial discrimination was shocking. Growing up in WASP Toronto in the thirties and forties, I had never seen anything like it, nor had I in Halifax or Vancouver, or on my travels across the country. I was utterly unprepared for such pervasive racism, and especially so in the post-war midst of American idealism about international brotherhood and all the high-minded rhetoric about world peace and future progress. My new job was a product of that post-war idealism, as the International Federation of Agricultural Producers sought to find ways to feed the world's hungry, increase food production, and end the boom-and-bust cycle of international trade in agricultural products.

My IFAP office was on Lafayette Square just across the street from the White House. President Truman would stride by on noon-time walks, a peppy little man, and I would pause in the midst of editing my monthly newsletter, *IFAP News*, to run to the window and watch him pacing along the sidewalk with a couple of Secret Servicemen puffing behind. Then, as now, president-watching was a major Washington pastime and I eagerly joined in.

My IFAP job was valuable training for my later days as a foreign correspondent. For one thing, it meant seeing and rubbing shoulders with some of the famous and powerful and observing them in action. Suddenly, I was a citizen of the world. My work was to write and edit newsletters dealing in agricultural news from around the world, particularly national and international policies and actions on food and fibre, prepare radio programs, organize meetings, and sometimes represent

35

IFAP at conferences at the United Nations, its specialized agencies, and other international organizations.

The International Federation of Agricultural Producers functioned something like the International Chamber of Commerce did for business. It represented 35 million farmers around the world in the international forum, especially at the UN Food and Agriculture Organization (FAO) with its headquarters in Rome.

My work in getting information and representing IFAP meant I was in constant contact with myriad Washington officials – at FAO, the State Department, the Department of Agriculture, the various foreign-aid agencies, the White House, the UN, the World Bank – and with IFAP's own member organizations around the world.

Sometimes I did a reporter's job of getting news for our IFAP publications and sometimes I promoted a particular IFAP policy, arranged a meeting, or simply "schmoozed" with various officials, informally exchanging international gossip and information. It all introduced me to the world of global policy-making and the arcane and immensely complicated interrelationships of national and international bureaucracies.

My IFAP work also introduced me to two journalistic heroes of mine. One was the great CBS newsman, Edward R. Murrow, whom I'd idolized for his dramatic reporting from wartime London and for his more recent thoughtful radio commentaries and early television work. Twice we met in a Washington hotel room to screen and discuss television programs he was preparing on agriculture. He was constantly encircled in cigarette smoke, had a perpetually crinkled forehead, and looked and behaved a bit like my father – tall, thin, long-faced, quiet, and gracious. I wish now I'd sought his guidance on my journalistic ambitions, but I felt that would have been imposing and we talked only about farm problems.

My other hero was James M. Minifie, whom I'd listened to for years on CBC Radio, where he was a regular contributor although his main job was as Washington correspondent for the *New York Herald Tribune*. I first met Don (he was Don to his friends, taking it from his middle name of MacDonald) when he walked into our IFAP office shortly after I arrived. He was looking for background information on the International Wheat Agreement and he had known our secretary-general in Saskatchewan, where he had grown up.

At age fifty-two, Don was a bald, cherub-faced charmer who'd already led a rich professional life. He had reported from Spain during the Spanish Civil War, where he was captured by the Moors and had developed an intense dislike for Ernest Hemingway, whom he consid-

36

ered a boastful liar, both for his reporting from Spain and during World War II. Minifie had been in Rome during the reign of Mussolini (he told me il Duce had haemorrhoids and was in agony whenever he led parades atop his horse – he did it because of the warrior image it projected). He'd also been in London during World War II, where he lost an eye in the blitz. And he had been among the select group of reporters who regularly clustered around the desk of Franklin Roosevelt in his small, informal press conferences. He was a Rhodes Scholar and a man of the world, and I envied and idolized him without imagining at the time that we would become close friends and colleagues. Don Minifie would teach me much about how to report on what was going on in Washington.

One of IFAP's main concerns was trying to harmonize the farm policies of individual nations so that conflicting domestic policies didn't cause havoc in the world marketplace. For instance, we were always battling those who wanted to put heavy subsidies on their farm exports and thereby unfairly undercut the trade of other countries. Another constant concern was to moderate the roller-coaster curves of commodity prices by pushing for more international commodity agreements that would allow prices to fluctuate only within an agreed range. A third preoccupation was urging governments to provide more aid to developing nations.

We took a two-pronged approach to accomplishing our goals: our member organizations in each country (the National Farmers Union in England and Wales, for instance) lobbied their own governments; while on the international scene IFAP lobbied the United Nations and its subsidiary bodies such as the UN Economic and Social Council (ECOSOC), FAO, the World Health Organization (WHO), the International Monetary Fund (IMF), and the World Bank as well as other organizations of global scope. Looking back now, I think IFAP provided a highly effective farmers' voice in world councils, helping to shape government policies for the benefit of the producers of food and the hungry of the world.

We were interested in hundreds of projects, but one WHO project in India stands out in my memory as an example of the difficulty of accomplishing anything at all. It was a very simple population-control scheme. The women in a particular village near Calcutta were each given a string of beads and were instructed to use them to count off the days of the month. When they got to fourteen they were told the next two days were when they were most likely to conceive. They were told not to have sexual intercourse on those days. When officials returned to the village after a couple of years, they found just as many babies being born as before. The women had understood the first half of their instructions, but not the second half. They had been counting the beads all right, but they assumed the counting was all that was necessary to avoid getting pregnant.

In the early 1950s, transatlantic travel was still mostly by ship, and I crossed the Atlantic a dozen times in ships like the *Cristoforo Colombo*, the *Queen Mary*, the *Queen Elizabeth*, the *Liberté*, the *Flandre*, and the *U.S.S. Constitution*. It was an elegant, sophisticated way to travel and I luxuriate in my nostalgia of those leisurely transatlantic crossings of another era.

My IFAP travel took me all over Europe to Belgium, Luxembourg, Germany, Greece, Denmark, the Netherlands, as well as France, the U.K., and Italy. And to Egypt, the Sudan, Kenya, and Mexico. But my most memorable trip was to an IFAP conference in Kenya at the height of the Mau Mau terrorism in the spring of 1954. Native Africans led by Jomo Kenyatta were rebelling against their British colonial rulers. In 1952, they had launched a campaign of terror against the British that eleven years later won them their independence. But in 1954, the British still ruled and wanted to demonstrate to the world they were firmly in control. The Kenya National Farmers Union, an IFAP member, persuaded us to hold our annual conference that year in Nairobi as a part of that effort to demonstrate the British still ran the show.

Upon arrival in Nairobi, the conference delegates were told one horror story after another of Mau Mau atrocities. There were stories of breasts and penises being cut off and eaten in Mau Mau ritual ceremonies where holy men would administer what were called blood oaths. The principal tribe in Kenya, the Kikuyu, had been trained by the British to be the cab drivers, hotel waiters, bartenders, and butlers. It was from the Kikuyus, who were more intelligent and active than members of other tribes, that many of the Mau Mau came, voicing their demands for *uhuru*, which means freedom in Swahili. Hence, you were never entirely sure whether or not your waiter or cab driver was really a terrorist bent on slicing off one of your precious possessions. Almost everyone carried firearms – people checked their guns before going into a movie theatre the way we would check a coat. From the moment of our arrival I could feel the tension in the air.

That first night at Nairobi's New Stanley Hotel, I fell asleep uneasily beneath the mosquito netting, with stories of Mau Mau atrocities dancing in my head. I slept fitfully and was wide awake when, at dawn, I heard my door creak open and heavy feet pad across the floor to my bed. I lay perfectly still with my heart pounding, certain that I was near death.

Suddenly a huge black arm thrust back the bed netting and a deep, gruff voice said cheerfully, "Your morning tea, Bwana!" I collapsed back on the pillow, tipped the waiter outrageously, and nervously sipped my tea, a drink I normally never touch.

While I spent most of my two weeks in Kenya in Nairobi, I was able to travel into the country and meet farm families. I was particularly impressed with the white farm women, many of whom lived alone while their husbands or fathers were away on business or fighting the Mau Mau – the "wogs" and "niggers," as they called them. Even at home men and women carried firearms and sat with their backs to the wall during meals in case of surprise attack. These attacks often came at mealtimes and were frequently made by servants who had worked for a family for years but had become members of the Mau Mau. I talked with several families who had barely escaped murder as they were about to begin their dinner. The servants would come in with the soup and throw it in the faces of their white employers and then attack them with knives and sometimes guns.

One woman told me of a long-time servant about to attack her with a long knife: "I told him, 'Stop it!', and he looked stunned, paused, and then ran away crying. I never saw him again. He was a good boy and I think he'd just fallen into bad company." Occasionally, there were pitched battles. While we were in Kenya, the son of Orde Wingate, the British World War II hero, was killed in the garden of a family farm by a Mau Mau gang.

There was some fear the Mau Mau might try to embarrass the British colonial government by attacking our IFAP delegates, but the only thing they did was to daub paint and put netting over a statue of Queen Victoria just outside our hotel as a symbolic protest.

On this trip I not only did my IFAP work but also some freelance work, including several radio reports for the CBC and BBC on life in Kenya under the Mau Mau reign of terror. This was my first actual "foreign corresponding." In the process, I met an editor at the Nairobi *East African Standard*, who for years had managed to be the stringer for AP, UP, and Reuters as well as individual newspapers in London, Paris, and New York. This creative fellow filed carbon copies of the same story to the various competing news organizations. When the Mau Mau terrorism broke out, he made a small fortune. But his prosperity was short-lived. Some of his clients sent in their own full-time correspondents to cover the rise of Kenyan nationalism, and they immediately discovered his activities. In the end, everybody fired him.

My brief introduction to foreign correspondence in Kenya whetted my appetite to do more reporting from abroad. That appetite was further stimulated each time IFAP held its annual meeting at the FAO headquarters building in Rome. While there I would work nights doing freelance stories for the CBC and the *Financial Post* in Toronto on everything from travel articles about Sorrento, Pompeii, Capri, or Venice to the complexities of Italian politics.

Rome became my favourite European city and Italy was and remains my favourite country in Europe. Sometimes I'd be there for a month at a time, preparing for IFAP conferences or attending other meetings. I either rented an apartment or lived in a room at a downtown Via Veneto hotel. The FAO building was practically next door to the Coliseum and the ruins of the Roman Forum and I was captivated by the sense of history all around me.

I was captivated, too, by my travels through the countryside of Europe, which provided an invaluable part of my continuing education in world affairs. Through IFAP I met such people as Pope Pius XII, the President of Italy, and cabinet ministers in Italy, France, Germany, and Britain. A particular friend was Willie Biesheuvel, a Dutch farm organization official and a future prime minister of the Netherlands.

Two men I met through IFAP especially stand out in my memory: Lord John Boyd Orr, the first director-general of FAO; and Dag Hammarskjold, the steel-willed Swede who was the second secretary-general of the UN.

Lord Boyd Orr was an exuberant idealist, a dynamic, bluff, white-haired old Scot who, with inexhaustible energy and a joy in living, led the post-war charge against world hunger. He was awarded the Nobel Peace Prize for his advocacy of a world food policy based on human needs rather than trade needs. I found his enthusiasm was equally infectious whether he was at a Saturday night dance at his farm near Aberdeen or in a United Nations conference in New York. He was a gentle man, too. He once told me of meeting in the British House of Lords a boyhood friend from his home town. The man worked at Westminster as a cleaner. They chatted for a while and as they parted, Boyd Orr said to the man, "Imagine, both of us winding up in the House of Lords."

In quiet conversations we had at his Scottish farm home or in New York or Washington, he taught me to care more deeply about the welfare of those less fortunate. I was reminded of my teen-age days when I worked after school and evenings and during the summer with underprivileged kids in Toronto. I spent many hours at the Kiwanis Boys K Club in a downtown Toronto slum area near Bathurst and King Streets and at the *Toronto Star* Fresh Air Camp in nearby Bolton, Ontario. It was enormously rewarding to see those youngsters develop and grow beyond their broken homes and bullying environment and leave behind their habits of petty thievery. We channelled their energies and talents into hockey, basketball, and baseball. We made it fun for them to study geography or history by making a game of it. I was doing then on a very localized level what I was doing later with IFAP on an international level. As Lord Boyd Orr told me, "It's the same thing on a global basis, and those youngsters of yours are just like peasants in India or Brazil, in a way, who also need help to escape their crushing surroundings."

I had been tempted as a youth to make a career of social work, and I now sometimes thought of making international social work my life. The need was so great, the cause so just, and the satisfaction so deep. But everything pulled me to journalism and I continued on my reportorial path, although occasionally looking over my shoulder at what might have been.

Dag Hammarskjold was a totally different type of person from Lord Boyd Orr, although he had the same concerns about the family of man. He called himself an "unemotional humanist" and had a fierce dedication to the cause of the United Nations, extraordinary perseverence, and a razor-sharp mind. I watched him in action many times at the UN in meetings and news conferences. Although in his early fifties, he looked younger. His face never betrayed an emotional flicker as he darted in and out of a debate, always making his points sharply, quickly, and surely. In repose on the General Assembly dais as he listened to speeches, he would rest his watermelon-shaped head in his hand, deep in thought.

I chatted with him at length a couple of times. The first time was during a visit to his thirty-eighth-floor UN office with an FAO colleague. The other time was to do an interview for an article I was writing for the *Star Weekly*. The first things that struck me walking into his office were his penetrating, twinkling gaze, his impish pale blue eyes, and his quiet assurance. He loped across the floor, quickly shook hands, and, with little small talk, got right down to business. As he spoke, his Swedish accent added emphasis to his words.

Hammarskjold was never a man for first names. I never heard anyone call him by his first name, Dag. He winced whenever he saw it in print. He himself never called any world leader by his first name, whether he was chewing breakfast steak with Eisenhower, spooning swallow's nest soup with Chou En-lai, or rowing on the Black Sea with Nikita Khrushchev.

Sometimes as he spoke it seemed his veins ran with ice water. I recalled an aide of his telling me, "He uses a rapier and he can slash very hard. That is also part of his quiet diplomacy." But at the next moment, he would become a gentle visionary, looking out his window down into the streets and saying, almost whispering to himself, "You know this is no good. I have to be down in the streets to really know what's going on."

He laughed when I mentioned to him he was known as "the oyster" who rarely came out of his shell. "My work is my life," he said.

He hated personal publicity and preferred being alone in his private life, reading poetry and philosophy or listening to Bach or Vivaldi. Reading poetry, he told me, provided him with "intellectual calisthenics," while Bach and Vivaldi provided "a beautiful way for creating order in the brain."

He had few friends. Comedian Danny Kaye, who travelled the world and worked incessantly for the UN Children's Fund, was one; another was Mike Pearson, who as president of the UN General Assembly in 1953 swore in Hammarskjold as secretary-general and with whom he shared an affinity for bow ties. With both Kaye and Pearson, he also shared a sense of commitment to the cause of world brotherhood.

Hammarskjold confused people by smoking a pipe sometimes, cigarettes sometimes, and cigars at other times. He often ate in the United Nations cafeteria, was a man utterly without pretense, and was revered by his staff, a sharp contrast from his flamboyant political predecessor, Norway's Trygve Lie.

Hammarskjold told me one of his greatest problems at the UN was language. He himself spoke German, French, English, and Swedish and read in seven languages. "So many people use the same words but mean different things," he said. He told me of how Lie, the first UN secretary-general, had a room set aside at the UN headquarters for quiet, personal meditation and prayer. "Since it was to be a restful room of personal prayer and meditation," he told me, "he wanted to have a sign outside saying 'rest room.'" Lie eventually was persuaded that something else would be less subject to misunderstanding.

Hammarskjold frequently talked of his father, who had been Prime Minister of Sweden. "His advice was good for this job," he said. "My father used to say being neutral is not a question of saying 'yes' to both sides. It's a question of saying 'no' to both sides!"

Hammarskjold dedicated his life to world peace and he died in the process. On a mission seeking to end the fighting in the Belgian Congo, his plane mysteriously crashed in Northern Rhodesia (now Zambia) on September 18, 1961. The mystery of whether it was an accident or sabotage has never been clarified.

In the six years I worked with IFAP I was introduced to the world, meeting many big and little crusaders for humanity. I learned many useful things, including the art of massaging bureaucracies: endless patience, persistence, and quiet persuasion. I also learned to seem older than my mid-twenties by wearing dark suits and projecting a relatively quiet, if persistent, demeanour. I also lied about my age. I felt people wouldn't take me seriously enough if they knew I was so young. Since I was born in 1927, I simply doctored my driver's license, passport, and other documents to change 1927 to 1921, thereby aging six years.

My time in international work also taught me to temper my youthful idealism with practicality. While I firmly believe there are causes to champion simply because they are right even if hopeless, I prefer to battle for the possible. One such hopeless battle I fought came in 1953 when I and some of my cohorts at IFAP and FAO sought to get a Canadian chosen as the new director-general of FAO. Our candidate was Herbert H. Hannam, president of the Canadian Federation of Agriculture, a progressive reformer and humanitarian. Canadians were then and still are regarded as extremely effective international civil servants, so Hannam was a candidate of wide appeal. At meetings and cocktail parties and in the hallways of Washington, London, Ottawa, Rome, and New York, we urged Hannam for this important and prestigious post. Support came from almost everywhere and we were exultant. But "almost everywhere" was not good enough. We hadn't taken politics sufficiently into account. The new Eisenhower people had just taken over power in Washington, and while they were polite and said they thought Canadians in general were awfully nice and Mr. Hannam in particular was a very nice guy, the last thing on earth they wanted as head of an important UN agency was a New Dealer in Canadian clothes.

So our scheme foundered on the rock of political realities. In fact, it had been a hopeless battle from the start, and while disappointing for me in its outcome, it was a lesson learned about battling for the possible.

My work with IFAP taught me to sharply focus my objectives, determine the limits of the authority and influence of the person I was seeking to persuade, and know who had influence on the person I wanted to influence. I learned that a person's power is what is really important, not his title. I became adept also at figuring out the trigger words and phrases that would help stimulate the desired response from a particular individual. If I knew the person had a pet project, I'd try to allude to it in the context of my proposal; if a person was very cost-conscious, I'd use phrases like "bottom line" or "budget control." I learned, too, the importance of having something to give – some piece of gossip or information or help – in return for getting what I wanted.

The lessons I was learning while working with the International Federation of Agricultural Producers were increasingly handy as my freelance work increased. It would be four more years before I would be ready to strike out on my own as a full-time Washington correspondent, but by 1954 there was now little doubt in my mind that that was the job I wanted.

3 *THE WASHINGTON BEAT*

Washington, D.C., April, 1954 . . .

On an early spring morning in 1954 I first met President Dwight D. Eisenhower. It was not a particularly intimate setting–an informal "greetings" session in the President's Oval Office with twenty or so American radio and television farm broadcasters. As director of information for IFAP, I had helped make arrangements for the meeting and it was my first chance to come face-to-face with a president in the White House.

Ike that day was at his smiling, charming best, his notorious temper nowhere in evidence. Here was the benign father figure Americans loved and even worshipped, the small boy from Abilene, Kansas, who'd grown up to be a soldier, statesman, and selfless patriot. You couldn't help being captivated by his exuberant friendliness and air of authority and the simplicity and sincerity he radiated. No wonder Americans everywhere were saying "I Like Ike!"

He spoke to us briefly as a group and then chatted amiably with individual members. After these official pleasantries were complete he ushered us out into the Rose Garden behind his office, where we had our pictures taken. I still have a print of that smiling group dominated by Eisenhower's famous grin.

As I stood on the grass smiling with everybody else, I thought of a grey-haired tourist who had stopped me not long before as I walked across the parking lot at the front of the U.S. Capitol buildings. She asked if I worked in Washington. I said yes. Her eyes glistened as she enthused, "How lucky you are to be so close to Mr. Eisenhower. Isn't

45

he just like God?" To that woman and to the country, Ike was an oasis of calm in a world of storm.

Although working full-time for IFAP, I had followed closely Eisenhower's 1952 campaign for the Republican nomination and the presidency. The election was more of a coronation than a contest–Adlai Stevenson and the Democrats never had a chance.

Then, as throughout his career, Ike took the high road and left any dirty work to his underlings. He also showed a tendency to abandon his friends and loyal colleagues when it became expedient. Already, I had begun to discern a far more complex figure than the one of the popular myth that told of the obscure colonel mistakenly identified as "D.D. Ersenbeing" in a newspaper picture in 1941, who became a brilliant war planner, then Allied Commander-in-Chief, world hero, and finally President of the United States–all in the space of little more than ten years.

The first clue to the complex man behind the grin was Ike's selection of a vice-presidential running mate in 1952. Richard Milhous Nixon, a first-term senator from California, had by then earned a reputation as a youthful, vigorous, and ruthless campaigner. In his first election, his 1946 campaign for a seat in the House of Representatives, Nixon had repeatedly implied that his Democrat opponent was a Communist sympathizer at best and at worst a traitor. In spite of media criticism, Nixon won the election. He used the same tactics in his Senate campaign against Helen Gahagan Douglas four years later. She's "pink right down to her underwear," he charged. Joseph McCarthy was certainly not the first to discover the political effectiveness of Red-baiting tactics.

Nixon's 1950 Senate victory set him on the road to the vice-presidency. But it was the Alger Hiss case that brought him to the attention of Republican power broker and twice Republican presidential candidate Thomas Dewey. Hiss, a pillar of the eastern Ivy League intellectual establishment and a brilliant diplomat, was accused of giving secrets to Communist agent Whittaker Chambers. He denied the charges and in 1950 was sent to prison for perjury for five years.

In January, 1955, after Hiss had been released from prison early because of good behaviour, I met him by chance on a train trip between New York and Washington. He'd been released from prison only a couple of months before and still had a prison pallor. At fifty-one, he was greying slightly and his shirt collar was too big. He wasn't willing to talk to me as a reporter, but he was willing to talk "man to man" and not for publication in the foreseeable future. So as the countryside rolled by, I questioned him about the charges and about his career in the State Department during the thirties and forties.

Not unexpectedly, Hiss maintained his innocence of all charges, saying he was not a Communist, was never a spy, and was not a perjurer. He was, he told me, "a rabid New Dealer," while his accuser, Chambers, was a psychopath.

Ironically, Hiss felt that he himself had helped to create the "Red Scare" environment that led to his downfall. During the post-war years, while he was a senior official at the State Department, he and many of his peers felt they had to dramatically overstate the case about Soviet military intentions in order to frighten Congress into acting. "Scare 'em, or they'll go fishing" was the motto, according to Hiss. So they "scared 'em" and in the process helped stimulate anti-Communist hysteria. To get enough money for aid to Greece to fight communism there, "We asked for twice as much as needed and frightened them to death so that we could get at least what we did need. Then, to get more action from Congress, we had to scare them even more and more and more. So the thing got out of hand and we were in good part to blame for the hysteria that followed."

So, at least, reasoned Alger Hiss.

More interesting to me than these self-justifications was Hiss's recollection of the February, 1945, Yalta Conference when Roosevelt, Stalin, and Churchill met and set the framework for the post-war world and today's East-West tensions. Hiss was an important member of the U.S. delegation to Yalta. "I was certainly not a water boy," he told me, "but also not a senior member of the conference when you think of other members, including Roosevelt, Churchill, Stalin, Anthony Eden, Andrei Gromyko, General Marshall, Admiral King, and many others."

Hiss's area of responsibility at the Conference was the development of the United Nations. He was later accused of manipulating American policy to get extra UN votes for Ukraine and Byelorussia. "A myth," according to Hiss. Gromyko had proposed a UN vote for every state in the Soviet Union. "We didn't take it seriously and felt it was simply a position from which they wanted to bargain."

At a plenary meeting at Yalta, Stalin then proposed three extra votes for the Soviet Union, for Byelorussia, Ukraine, and Lithuania. Hiss described tugging the sleeve of Ed Stettinius, the U.S. Secretary of State, and whispering, "We've been waiting for this" (meaning the Russians were now formally demanding extra votes). Stettinius then tugged Roosevelt's sleeve, had a whispered conversation, and turned to the Soviets to say "No." Roosevelt shook his head in confirmation of Stettinius. Stalin then smiled and said, "Well, then, give us two votes." He had to have at least two extras votes to "satisfy my people." Again, Stettinius said "No" and the matter was referred to the foreign ministers for further discussion.

Churchill was prepared to give Stalin his two extra votes as a trade-off for a UN vote for India, but the Americans were still adamant, according to Hiss. Stalin then met privately with Roosevelt and told FDR that an agreement had been reached in the foreign ministers' meeting "on all issues." "On the Assembly vote too?" Hiss quoted Roosevelt as saying. And without waiting for a response, Roosevelt quickly added, "Well, that's fine."

To the consternation of the U.S. delegation, according to Hiss, Roosevelt reaffirmed his acquiescence to the two extra votes to the Soviet Union at a subsequent Yalta plenary session. "It's nothing to get excited about," Roosevelt said. "It's a relatively small matter and we need to get on with other things." Hiss explained that "Roosevelt was tired and not feeling well."

Later, several senior members of the U.S. delegation, including Secretary of State Stettinius, privately asked Roosevelt to reverse himself. However, his adviser Chip Bohlen warned him not to: "The Russians will negotiate like the devil, but once an agreement is reached that's the end of it. To withdraw now would be considered a gross insult by the Soviets." But the politician in Roosevelt was wary of the political impact back home of his UN concession to the Soviets. So he wrote a note to Stalin offering other concessions if the Soviets would give up the two extra seats. Stalin refused. Sick and exhausted, FDR reluctantly agreed, but left the deal secret. It wasn't revealed until after the war.

Hiss felt professional distress at the two-vote deal with Stalin, but continued ardently to admire Roosevelt. However, he disliked his successor, Harry Truman, whom he called "the little haberdasher."

Hiss recalled a moment at the 1945 San Francisco Conference establishing the United Nations when President Truman broke into uncontrolled giggling in the midst of the signing ceremony as the very bald Brazilian foreign minister approached the platform where Truman sat. What caused the Truman giggling according to Hiss was a remark from his military aide, General Harry Vaughan, who pointed to the Brazilian's gleaming pate and whispered, "Pipe the simonize job." At a later meeting in the President's office back in Washington, Hiss said Truman recalled the incident and, amid gulps of bourbon, laughed until he almost cried, remembering "that bald-headed guy who came up the aisle." Hiss didn't think it was very funny.

Before meeting Hiss I'd thought he was guilty of lying about his friendship with Whittaker Chambers and that he had indeed passed documents to the Soviet agent. This encounter with him did nothing to change my mind. Despite his articulateness, prep-school good looks, and obvious intelligence, he protested his innocence too much and blamed everyone but himself for his troubles. He even complained to me about having no money: "I can't even afford one suit, let alone two."

He may have been guilty, but the mood of the time blew his crime out of all proportion, and it was Richard Nixon who capitalized on that mood.

Nixon was a persistent, insistent Communist-hunter as chairman of a House Un-American Activities Subcommittee. And Hiss also aroused his deep-rooted suspicions (and, I think at bottom, jealousy) of Ivy Leaguers. Nixon believed Chambers' story and saw the political benefits to himself if he could expose a key Russian spy in Washington. It was the investigation and hearings of the Nixon subcommittee that led to the perjury charges against Hiss.

Nixon's success in the Hiss case brought him nationwide fame as a youthful, conservative battler who could "clean up the mess in Washington." Recognizing the political value of complementing Eisenhower's age and his fatherly hero image with Nixon's boyish "hardball" style, Thomas Dewey persuaded Eisenhower to accept Nixon as his vice-presidential running mate in the 1952 election.

There was, however, one small problem for Nixon. He was publicly pledged to support California Governor Earl Warren for the Republican presidential nomination. But as soon as he was sounded out about second spot on Ike's ticket, he double-crossed his fellow-Californian Warren and switched his support to Eisenhower. This added to the growing Nixon reputation for untrustworthiness. It was not long after this that I first heard the joke, "Would you buy a used car from this man?" So, too, at the time, came the appellation "Tricky Dick."

Early in the 1952 campaign, Nixon made his famous "Checkers" speech. He went on television to defend himself against accusations of using a secret fund of $18,000 put together by millionaire supporters looking for favours. One of the millionaires was the father of Bob Haldeman, of Watergate fame. That early fall night he came on TV right after the Milton Berle comedy show and I remember watching him with unbelieving embarrassment. What struck me was the teary-

49

eyed way he defended himself. He spoke of his loving Quaker mother, his father, how he had to wear hand-me-down clothes as a child, had to work his way through school, and how much he loved his wife Pat.

It was true, in fact, that he did have the $18,000 fund, but the money had been given to him for travel and political expenses beyond his senatorial allowance. As such, it really wasn't much of a scandal: "every dime we've got is honestly ours," he told his TV audience. "I should say this, that Pat doesn't have a mink coat. And I always tell her she'd look good in anything." And another word about Pat. ". . . I am not a quitter. And incidentally, Pat is not a quitter. After all, her name is Patricia Ryan, and she was born on St. Patrick's Day . . . and you know the Irish never quit."

And then, his dog Checkers. "A man down in Texas heard Pat on the radio mention the fact that our two youngsters would like to have a dog. And believe it or not, the day before we left on this campaign trip, we got a message from Union Station in Baltimore saying they had a package for us. We went down to get it. You know what it was? It was a little cocker spaniel in a crate that he sent all the way from Texas. Black and white spotted. And our little girl, Tricia, the six-year-old, named it Checkers. And you know, the kids love that dog, and I just want to say this right now, that regardless of what they say about it, we're going to keep it. . . ."

Nixon's maudlin corn was a foretaste of his tortured White House farewell twenty-two years later after Watergate forced him from the presidency. It worked superbly on this occasion as hundreds of thousands of telegrams, letters, and phone calls of support poured into Republican headquarters. At an airport meeting, while reporters listened in, Ike told him, "You're my boy!", and together they continued their "Crusade for Political Purity," as the campaign was called. It was a campaign, they said, against "communism, crooks and corruption." In a statement that has an ironic ring to it now, Nixon proclaimed over and over again in the 1952 campaign, "What we need in Washington is a President who, instead of covering up, cleans up."

During the 1952 campaign Eisenhower took advantage of the skill of another ruthless streetfighter–a senator from Wisconsin named Joseph McCarthy. I didn't meet McCarthy until much later, but from the time of my arrival in Washington in 1951 I watched his progress with a mixture of fascination and horror.

To my mind, McCarthy was a tragic fake, an ego-ridden, back-slapping, alcoholic bully who accidentally stumbled into his "Red Menace" crusade. Back at the beginning of 1950, he was looking for an issue around which to focus his 1952 Senate re-election campaign.

Up until this point, he'd been just another conservative Republican from a primarily agricultural state. Occasionally he had accused Roosevelt and then Truman of "selling out" China and other things to the Communists, but he certainly had never been in the forefront of anti-communism.

McCarthy always had wanted to be "somebody." If he couldn't be important in fact, he fantasized. To himself and in his publicity, he became "Tail Gunner Joe," a South Pacific Marine Corps hero, even though he had actually been a desk-bound intelligence officer during World War II who had taken half a dozen or so "milk-run" combat flights for the experience. He talked to reporters and to the public of his "war wounds" when, in fact, he'd broken his leg falling off a ladder. Later, when he became a power in Washington, he bamboozled the Pentagon into giving him several medals for his wartime heroics.

At a dinner meeting in January, 1950, McCarthy's advisers made several suggestions of issues around which to focus his re-election campaign. One proposed housing. Somebody else suggested the importance of building the St. Lawrence Seaway as an economic boon for Wisconsin farmers. Joe wasn't excited by any of these. Then one of his friends, an extremely conservative priest named Father Edmund Walsh, suggested communism.

A couple of weeks later, McCarthy asked two reporters from the *Times Herald*, a conservative Washington newspaper, to write a speech on anti-communism for him. They and another colleague from the *Chicago Tribune*, also a conservative newspaper, pasted together a speech based on old newspaper clippings and standard conservative Republican rhetoric.

You have to remember the atmosphere of this time to understand the impact the speech would have. The Korean War was raging; Alger Hiss had just been convicted; in Britain, top nuclear physicist Dr. Klaus Fuchs had just been arrested as a Soviet spy; the "China Lobby" was at its propaganda zenith, accusing the Truman administration of "selling out" to the Chinese Communists; there were widespread accusations of an American "sell out" to the Russians at the Big Four Yalta Conference in 1945; and two days before McCarthy's speech, FBI Director J. Edgar Hoover announced that there were more than half a million Communists and sympathizers in the United States.

On February 9, 1950, McCarthy flew to Wheeling, West Virginia, to speak to the first of a series of Republican Party meetings leading up to the mid-term elections that November.

It was a thirteen-page speech heard by only 275 people, but it almost instantly made McCarthy into a commanding figure. Yet, except for one sentence in that speech, McCarthy might have become only a footnote to history: "I have here in my hand a list of 205 [persons] . . . a list of names that were made known to the Secretary of State as being members of the Communist Party and who nevertheless are still working and shaping policies at the State Department."

In one form or another, this statement would be repeated over and over again for the next four years of McCarthy terror. The irony is that he didn't have any list at all, and the number of "known Communists" changed from speech to speech. It didn't matter. The United States was ripe for a Red-baiting demagogue and McCarthy stepped eagerly into the role.

It was by no means the first time an American politician launched a "Red Scare" campaign to win votes. It started back as far as 1919 when the then Attorney General of the U.S., A. Mitchell Palmer, sought political advantage through such tactics and others continued the technique through the 1920s and then in the 1930s with the House Un-American Activities Committee, headed by conservative Texas Congressman Martin Dies. In fact, most of the McCarthy style of accusation by innuendo came from Dies, and by the late 1940s fifteen states had their own little "Un-American Activities" committees aimed at rooting out the "Reds." In 1947 there were the "Hollywood Ten" hearings, seeking to expose some movie stars and writers as Communists or "fellow travellers." The ground was well fertilized by the time McCarthy came along, stimulated by the virulent bellicosity of Stalin and his post-war grabs of Eastern Europe.

Truman, then Eisenhower, played into McCarthy's hands. Joe's friend J. Edgar Hoover fuelled the crusade with a flood of raw data leaks from FBI files. His supporters included respectable Republicans like Senator Robert Taft of Ohio and church leaders like Francis Cardinal Spellman, as well as the extreme right-wingers. "McCarthyism is Americanism with its sleeves rolled up," Joe was fond of saying. Or "I don't use powder puffs." He certainly pulled few punches.

The most inexcusable support given to McCarthy came from Eisenhower, who disliked him personally but publicly went along with McCarthy and even exploited him on occasion. During the 1952 campaign, the Senator accused General George C. Marshall of helping to "sell out" China to the Communists. As Army Chief of Staff, Marshall had headed the American military during World War II, was Truman's Secretary of State and later Secretary of Defense, and author of the Marshall Plan to help rebuild Europe. Even more important, he was Eisenhower's mentor, the man who overrode opposition to appoint Ike as Supreme Commander in Europe during World War II.

Eisenhower had planned to make a complimentary reference to his former boss in a campaign speech in Milwaukee on October 3. McCarthy demanded the reference be deleted. Eisenhower's political advisers agreed and Ike reluctantly capitulated. It was a clear case of political expediency winning out over personal integrity. The headline in the *New York Post* following the speech said it all: "HE HAS MET THE ENEMY, AND HE IS THEIRS." This would not be the only time Eisenhower abandoned a friend in a tight spot.

During the campaign and during his first term, Eisenhower distanced himself from McCarthy the man. But his public comments were so restrained as to give McCarthy more power. Privately Ike might mutter, "I won't get down in the gutter with that guy," but he waited until the senator had fatally ruined his reputation and public opinion had shifted before raising a hand to stop him.

It's hard now to recapture the terror of McCarthyism. We've had so many terrors since then. But at the time, to work for an international organization like IFAP was enough to be thrown under suspicion. To speak of "peace" in those Cold War days was to risk being called a "fellow traveller" at best, a traitor at worst. The Girl Guides were attacked as being subversive for suggesting the United Nations was a good thing. Hundreds of people refused to sign an endorsement of the Declaration of Independence because it sounded communistic.

My first secretary at IFAP had been forced out of her job in the federal government by McCarthyism. Her late husband's brother had once subscribed to the Communist newspaper, the *Daily Worker*, so she was branded as "potentially subversive," investigated by the staff of a Senate committee, and urged by her boss to resign to prevent awkwardness for her department. In confusion and embarrassment she did.

Her story was repeated thousands of times in Washington and elsewhere throughout the U.S. in the 1950s. Careers were ruined, senators and congressmen were browbeaten into silence or defeated at the polls, and the State Department was put into a perpetual state of panic awaiting the next McCarthy accusations. He had an unquestionable impact on American foreign policy–without him, John Foster Dulles could not have pursued his own hawkish diplomacy with such vigour. Like Eisenhower, Dulles personally deplored McCarthy, but he used him for his own objectives.

After Eisenhower was elected President, McCarthy was riding high. With Republicans in control, he became chairman of both the Senate Committee on Government Operations and its Permanent Subcommittee on Investigations. He held hearings in Washington and elsewhere to expose those he accused of being Communists, subversives, or traitors.

He bluffed, he lied, he altered photographs. He thought little or nothing out in advance and felt no remorse in retrospect. He just shot from the hip, using character assassination and guilt by association to expose "traitors," "spies," "Reds," "Commies," "homosexuals," and "perverts." In his simple-minded lexicon, *liberal* meant *Communist*, *progressive* meant *subversive*. Once when I questioned an accusation he'd made, he angrily told me, "If he walks like a duck, talks like a duck, then goddamnit, he is a duck." This was his standard answer to those who questioned his tactics.

In my observation, Joseph McCarthy was an extraordinarily hard worker, at least up to the beginning of his downfall in 1954. But he read little, was completely unconcerned with the accuracy of research, and was utterly reckless in his accusations. His staff was terrified of his flamboyant exaggerations of the information they gave him–but for almost four years, no one dared challenge him.

In his private moments, however, Joe McCarthy was friendly and gregarious. He drank too much, liked talking to reporters, and often played poker with them. Perhaps the most puzzling aspect of the man was this duality between the public and the private person. In the early days when I talked to him off the record, he treated the whole thing largely as a joke, laughing loudly at how some of his targets and their defenders were getting so upset, and childishly relishing all the publicity he was getting. He genuinely did not seem to understand the human impact of what he was doing. He could not understand why people hated him.

On more than one occasion I saw striking evidence of this seeming split personality. In 1953 I was covering a McCarthy committee hearing at which Truman's former Secretary of State Dean Acheson testified. When it was over, I rode with McCarthy down an elevator in the U.S. Capitol building. We stopped one floor down and Acheson got on. Just moments before, McCarthy had accused him of sheltering spies and "selling out" to the Communists, stopping just short of calling him a traitor. As Acheson got into the elevator, we all tensed at the prospect of this face-to-face confrontation. But McCarthy beamed and said, "Why, hi Dean!", as he grabbed for Acheson's shoulder. The tall, austere, former Secretary of State froze, backed away, said not a word, and icily got off at the next floor. McCarthy seemed genuinely puzzled. "Now what's wrong with that guy?" he asked those of us still in the elevator. No one answered.

On other occasions, I heard him viciously attack a reporter by name in a speech, accusing him of Communist sympathies. After the speech, he would come over grinning and slapping the astonished fellow on the back. "Don't take it so seriously," I heard him tell one of my colleagues. "It's just politics." Another time he lambasted New Jersey Republican Senator Robert Hendrickson on the floor of the Senate as "a living miracle . . . the only man in the world who has lived so long with neither guts nor brains." McCarthy then walked off the floor back into the Senate cloakroom, where he greeted Hendrickson with a broad smile and asked, "How ya' doin', pal?" Anyone who covered McCarthy in those days has similar stories.

McCarthyism affected Canadians as well as Americans. A number of Canadian names came up during the McCarthy investigations and other congressional Red-hunting activities. The long-time, respected senior Ottawa civil servant and Clerk of the Privy Council, Robert Bryce, was publicly mentioned by the Senate Internal Security Sub-committee as a suspicious individual who had associated with Communists while a student at Harvard. McCarthy didn't run that committee, but it had the same style. Julian Sourwine, subcommittee counsel, to whom I would talk when writing "Red-hunting" stories, told me the accusation against Bryce was not serious. "We're not trying to smear Bryce," he said. "Bryce was just a walk-on character, an incidental reference."

More serious were the private mutterings of Sourwine and other staff members of the various Senate and House investigating committees about Lester Pearson, then Canada's Minister for External Affairs and later Prime Minister. Based on congressional committee testimony given in secret in 1951 by self-admitted Soviet agent Elizabeth Bentley, the staffers and investigators suggested Pearson was someone to watch carefully. Bentley had claimed that Pearson gave information and documents to a Communist agent when he was the Canadian ambassador in Washington during the war and that he had close connections to a Communist cell in Washington at the time. Whenever Pearson took public positions opposed to the U.S., these Red-hunters sought to undermine Pearson's influence by telling journalists and U.S. policy-makers of Bentley's testimony and warning that Washington should be wary of Pearson. It was another form of McCarthyism, an attempt to minimize or eliminate the influence of anyone who was not an ardent Cold Warrior. Although I never talked to Pearson directly about it, his aides, including Bob Farquharson (at the time Minister-Counsellor at the Canadian Embassy), told me Pearson had indeed talked to and given material to a man Elizabeth Bentley claimed was a Communist agent, but they were public speeches and statements, and in conversations with the man he simply reiterated what he had said in his speeches or in talking to reporters.

The anti-Pearson campaign had some effect in muting Pearson's impact. He was labelled by some conservative publications as a neutralist and *Time* magazine called him "Nehru in a homburg"–Indian Prime Minister Nehru often opposed U.S. foreign policies.

The most painful accusation surfaced in 1957, years after McCarthy himself had been disgraced. It centred on Herbert Norman, the Canadian ambassador to Egypt, who was accused by the Senate Internal Security Subcommittee of having been a member of Communist cells in the U.S. in the 1930s and early 1940s and of aiding the Soviet cause. Three weeks after the accusations were made public, Norman committed suicide by jumping off the roof of the Swedish ambassador's apartment building in Cairo. To the Red hunters, this proved his guilt. To his colleagues, the Canadian government, and the Canadian media, it was murder by slander.

The day after Norman's death, I and half a dozen fellow reporters cornered committee counsel Robert Morris in a Senate hallway outside his office. A back-slapping, fortyish former judge, he seemed delighted with the news and was only too happy to be photographed smiling broadly holding up a newspaper front-paging the story. When our questioning began, his smile disappeared.

"Who's your next victim?" one reporter snarled. Equally forgetting my professionalism, I asked, "How do you feel as a murderer?" It was a vicious, bitter reportorial inquisition, and the nastiest news conference I'd ever attended. All of us, in fact, lost our sense of impartiality in a highly emotional assault on the committee counsel. Morris shrugged off our questions and stormed back into his office.

Not only the media were outraged. Pearson had complained when Morris and his subcommittee released the information a few weeks earlier. Now the Canadian government officially and bitterly protested to Washington. Ironically, the evidence against Norman had been supplied to the FBI six years earlier by the RCMP, but the RCMP later told the FBI that further investigation proved it was groundless. Nonetheless, the FBI, under J. Edgar Hoover's guidance, had leaked the accusation to the Senate subcommittee, which in turn had published it.

With Norman's suicide, Canada-U.S. relations were momentarily shattered. "There have been fights, squabbles, and bickering between us before," a Canadian Embassy official told me, "but never has there been a time when the whole country was raging mad at the United States." Canada threatened to refuse to share future security information with the U.S. Even Eisenhower was embarrassed. He told us at a news conference a few days later that he hoped the whole "incident" would be "dropped if possible." Later he apologized to Canada.

Slowly, Canada-U.S. relations got back to normal, but a bitter aftertaste was left. The excesses of Robert Morris and his fire-eating cohorts on the subcommittee, such as Senator James Eastland and Senator William Jenner, were among the last vestiges of virulent McCarthyism. In fact, it was only a few weeks after Herbert Norman's suicide that McCarthy himself died.

McCarthy reached the depth of his tactics and the height of his power with the hiring in 1953 of twenty-five-year-old Roy Cohn as his investigating committee chief counsel. A brilliant, brooding, arrogant lawyer, Cohn sought to provide substance and order to McCarthy's theatrics. He was at times alarmed at McCarthy's excesses, but, similarly obsessed with the Red menace, he nevertheless egged him on.

In 1954 I covered a number of sessions of McCarthy's investigating subcommittee. By now the subcommittee hearings were daily fodder for the media and there was a lot of demand for coverage from Canadian newspapers. Watching McCarthy and Cohn browbeating a witness was a chilling experience. At one hearing in March, 1954, they zeroed in on a middle-aged black woman, a widow by the name of Annie Lee Moss who had been fired from her $3,300-a-year Pentagon job as an Army Signal Corps clerk. McCarthy charged, based on information fed to him by the FBI's Hoover, that she was a Communist and probably a spy. Before a belligerent Joe McCarthy and a badgering Roy Cohn performing for television cameras and a huge audience, this frail, now-unemployed woman was clearly terrified and on the verge of tears. She was utterly baffled by the accusation and the hearing and could hardly speak. She'd had little education, had never heard of Karl Marx, and didn't know what the word "espionage" meant.

As McCarthy and Cohn waded deeper into innuendo, rumour, and hearsay, their case publicly fell apart. No one ever finally determined whether this was a case of mistaken identity, some kind of personal vengeance by a fellow Pentagon employee, or what. Later, Annie Moss was rehired by the Pentagon, one of the few who did get their old jobs or any decent job after Joe and Roy were finished with them. But McCarthy's humiliation in this case marked the beginning of his downfall.

A few weeks later, a running battle with the entire U.S. Army exploded in his face. McCarthy had called General Ralph Zwicker "a disgrace to the uniform" for supposedly shielding those who had promoted an Army dentist whom McCarthy suspected of being a Communist. This, at long last, was too much for former General Dwight Eisenhower. Ike was further incensed when a scandal erupted over the fact that McCarthy and Cohn had sought preferential treatment for G.

David Schine, who had just been drafted by the Army. Schine was a wealthy and close friend of both men, having worked with them on subcommittee investigations. McCarthy and Cohn demanded Schine be given extra time off, be freed from KP duties, and be allowed to sleep in.

The Schine scandal, the Zwicker accusations, and other wild McCarthy charges about the Army led to the famous Army-McCarthy Senate hearings in the spring of 1954. The Democrats forced the hearings to be held, and under heavy pressure from his Senate colleagues, McCarthy had agreed to step down temporarily from his subcommittee chairman-ship while he squared off against the Army. Starting in late April, the hearings went on until mid-June, capturing headlines and providing a riveting television spectacle.

For the first time, the American public saw Joe McCarthy day after day on live television. It was a startling, revealing, and, in the end, disgusting performance. His crude, slanderous recklessness was finally exposed. Joseph Welch, the Army's pixie-like, crafty New England lawyer summed it all up one day when he asked, "Have you no sense of decency, sir?" McCarthy laughed and didn't answer, but it was clear he indeed had no sense of decency.

Abandoned by Eisenhower and even Nixon now, deserted by his conservative Republican friends, and finally censured by the U.S. Sen-ate and shorn of all power, he slunk into isolation and loneliness, beginning to drink more heavily. As the months and years went by he became more and more of a shadow.

I remember sitting in the Senate press gallery on the first day the Senate was back to work in January, 1957, after the Christmas recess. McCarthy came clumping listlessly into the chamber. He no longer bothered to wear his toupee and his face looked sallow and puffy. He shuffled toward his place, wanly smiling at a couple of senators, then collapsing into his seat. He sat there constantly playing with his black-framed glasses and occasionally wiping a chunky hand across his face. Other senators joyfully greeted each other after their holiday, but no-body came up to McCarthy. He had become a pathetic, lonely old man. Privately, he would sob to his few remaining friends, "I can't take it anymore."

I watched him later that winter at the Senate Labor Rackets Com-mittee of which he was a member. Even knowing the harm he'd done, I found it painful to watch him. McCarthy would totter in half drunk, his blank eyes suddenly brightening when he saw the TV cameras on. He'd interrupt the testimony of a witness to interject his own questions, slurring his words. The chairman and fellow senators tried to keep him quiet but he'd whine about being cut off, about being stabbed in the back, and they would embarrassedly let him continue. All he wanted was to be noticed, to be seen on television again. After two or three incomprehensible questions, he'd smile, laugh his thin, tinny laugh, and stagger out.

After one such intervention, I went outside with him to chat. His handshake was sweaty and his glasses kept falling off. He complained of bursitis, sinus trouble, and liver problems. For the most part he was incoherent, but one thing stood out above all – he'd become a pathetic drunk wallowing in self-pity. He was only forty-eight but looked seventy.

A few months later he died of what the doctors called "acute hepatic failure." In fact, he drank himself to death. The sad irony is that with all his evil anti-Red histrionics, McCarthy never uncovered a single Communist on his own. All his exposés had been investigated before by government authorities.

The whole episode of McCarthyism exposed a dark side of President Eisenhower and his approach to his presidency. He didn't want to get involved in unpleasantness and detail, but he was susceptible to political expediency, and while he may have hated McCarthy the man, he and John Foster Dulles used McCarthy the politician to curry favour and to help them fight the Cold War.

Eisenhower, who had spent forty years as a soldier, wanted and needed the protection of a strong chain of command and efficient staff officers. His primary staff officer was New Englander Sherman Adams, his flinty-eyed, parsimonious, iron-fisted number-one assistant. The message around Washington was that to get anything from Eisenhower, you first had to "Let Sherm do it." Nothing got to Eisenhower's desk unless it was initialled "O.K.S.A." Adams was Eisenhower's "No" man and he fiercely protected the President from politicians and officials whom he felt did not have sufficiently important business to bother Ike. As a result, he was the most feared and hated man in the administration.

But it was a three-legged stool of authority under Ike. While Adams ran the White House and had the last word with Eisenhower, Eisenhower also depended on two other men. One was George Humphrey, a Cleveland steel mogul who was Secretary of the Treasury, and the other was John Foster Dulles, the evangelical, brilliant, rigid, and wilful Secretary of State. Humphrey ran the country at home; Dulles ran the country abroad. Eisenhower once let slip his dependence on Humphrey, remarking that in cabinet meetings "I always wait for George Humphrey ... I know he will say just what I am thinking." And of Dulles, he said, "He is the wisest, most dedicated man that I know of."

Much like a later Republican president, Ronald Reagan, Eisenhower let it be known that in almost all cases he wanted to initial a proposed solution, not to argue about how to solve the problem. He became the arbiter or umpire of the U.S. government, a kind of Chairman of the Board rather than its Chief Executive Officer. In fact, in wartime and in peacetime, Ike's critics had nicknamed him "The Great Hesitator" for always delaying decisions until they were fully "staffed out."

General Douglas MacArthur, who had once been Ike's superior officer, attacked his style, calling him "a batman" and "the apotheosis of mediocrity." Eisenhower retorted that in the Army he had "studied drama under General MacArthur." But there was some truth to MacArthur's characterization. It was rumoured that Eisenhower kept two folders on his desk. One was marked "Problems That Time Will Solve"; the other was marked "Problems That Time Has Solved." The President simply shuffled paper from one file to the other. Though the story is almost certainly apocryphal, it doesn't seem that far-fetched.

Eisenhower was heavily criticized for spending so much of his presidency away from his White House office. He took frequent "working vacations" that were far more vacation than work and averaged upwards of 100 days away from Washington every year. Press Secretary Jim Hagerty would store up a bundle of announcements to be doled out to reporters during these trips to give the appearance of a hardworking, even though holidaying, President.

Even when he was working in Washington, he usually managed to make it out to the lush, well-manicured Burning Tree Golf Club just outside Washington a couple of times a week as well as practising chip shots and putting regularly on the White House back lawn just behind the glass doors of his office. This, of course, led to all sorts of jokes among reporters, such as:

Press Secretary Hagerty to golfing foursome at thirteenth hole: "Would you mind letting the President play through, please."

Foursome: "Why?"

Hagerty: "We've just had word that New York City has been bombed and the President would like to finish the round as soon as he can."

Another golfing joke going the rounds was carried on bumper stickers that proclaimed: "Ben Hogan for President. If we're going to have a golfer for President, let's have a good one."

Ike's relationship with reporters was never warm. In the years I watched him from my journalistic perch, he never showed any particular fondness for members of my profession. He reluctantly tolerated us as a necessary evil, but that was all. Unlike his successors John

Kennedy and Lyndon Johnson, he was not one to exchange gossip with reporters. As a Canadian correspondent I showed up at his weekly news conferences, travelled with him on occasion, and observed him at White House functions and public speeches. He would smile, nod, and sometimes say "Hi," but he never gave any indication he knew or cared who I was. Reporters were just some of the furniture that went with the job. But even so, over time I got to know the man, especially in the course of White House news conferences.

Regular White House news conferences began with Woodrow Wilson inviting half a dozen reporters into the Oval Office, where they would cluster around his desk. Sometimes the conferences weren't very enlightening. Once Calvin Coolidge was asked if he had any comment on the presidential election. "No," he said. "What about the world situation?" "No," he said. "About prohibition?" "No," he said. Then he added, "Now remember, don't quote me."

Until John Kennedy came along, the past master of the presidential news conference was Franklin Roosevelt. Don Minifie often told me of how Roosevelt simply charmed the pants off reporters, sharing little secrets, kidding them about their stories, and in the process masterfully manipulating what they wrote. Actual quotations were then not allowed except in rare instances. The Harry Truman news sessions occasionally got more confrontational, but it was not until the Johnson and Nixon years that the presidential news conference became a cockpit opposing inquisitorial reporters and combative Presidents.

But Eisenhower was the first television President. Just after Ike was sworn in as President in January, 1953, Press Secretary Jim Hagerty took what was then a momentous decision not only to allow the President to be quoted directly on whatever he said in his news conferences, a major departure from the past, but also to allow television cameras to cover the meetings with reporters. This was, of course, in the very early days of TV, and it wasn't live.

We all worried about television. Hagerty wanted to allow cameras into the news conference because of requests from TV news departments, but more important, because he thought seeing Ike in action would strengthen his public support. It did. But most of us were against the idea. We fretted that some reporters would show off, that the lights would be bothersome, that the cameras would take up too much space.

As it turned out, TV was a nuisance at the beginning and some reporters did show off. But television very quickly became just another part of the media covering the story, and it didn't affect the substance of our coverage.

Eisenhower met us almost every Wednesday morning in the ornate, high-ceilinged Indian Treaty Room in a White House annex building. There could be as few as 100 of us and sometimes as many as 200, the overflow sitting in a kind of peanut gallery upstairs. While we waited, the current state of Ike's famous red-hot temper was a constant subject for speculation. If he walked in wearing a brown suit we took it as a sign he was in a bad mood, which meant a grumpy news conference.

Ike would come striding in aggressively, sometimes smiling, sometimes scowling, with Secret Servicemen and aides trailing along behind. He'd march up to the two microphones behind a desk and stand in front of us as his aides sat or stood to the side with the Secret Servicemen standing off in the background.

He was impatient with long-winded questions. His eyes would glaze over with boredom and then suddenly snap back to life as he cut off the reporter in mid-sentence. If Ike didn't like a question, his normally ruddy face would turn crimson and, as he got angrier, flame red. He'd chew his lips and start to scowl, his neck veins would swell, his shoulders would arch back, and he'd be silent for a moment trying to control his temper. Then he'd bark "No!" or "Yes!" or say, "Now look, I just don't want anything more about that."

Once I was sitting in the second row just to the side of Eisenhower and beside Bill McGaffin of the *Chicago Daily News*, who rose to ask if Ike "would be willing to do without that pair of helicopters that have been proposed for getting you to the golf course a little faster than you can make it by car." I sank into my seat trying to edge away from McGaffin as an electric silence took hold of the room. Looking squarely at McGaffin (and I thought me, too), Eisenhower literally shouted, "Well, I don't think much of the question because no helicopters have been procured for me to go to the golf course."

McGaffin rose to pursue his inquiry but was blasted back into his seat with a withering presidential scowl as Eisenhower snapped, "Thank you! That's all!" And that was an order ... the end of it. It was clear, we were the privates and he was The General.

In fact, the helicopters referred to had been announced by the White House a few weeks before and presidential spokesmen had said they would be used to take Ike to and from the airport and possibly also to ferry him to the golf course.

There were light moments, too. Once, in the middle of a news conference, Ike's alarm wrist watch suddenly went off, startling reporters and momentarily terrifying the Secret Servicemen. The President reddened in embarrassment and explained he'd forgotten to turn "the damn thing off."

Eisenhower himself never really understood or liked television. He thought it was a bother. In making formal television speeches, he became wooden and unsure. On one occasion, using an early type of Teleprompter that got stuck and stopped, Eisenhower stopped, too. He waited. Then he bristled. "The goddamn thing's stopped." And he waited some more. Finally, the prompter began to work again and the President continued, leaving an utterly bewildered TV audience wondering what had stopped and why Ike had just stood there in the middle of his speech.

Although the Eisenhower news conferences were fairly formal, there was much more rough-and-tumble informality to the daily briefings we'd get from Hagerty or his aide, Anne Wheaton. When Ike had a slight stroke early in his second term, the plump and confused Anne gave us a complicated medical statement and then led us on a chaotic briefing about the exact nature of the illness. I stood scribbling in my notebook at the back of her office as the following exchange took place.

Reporter: "Anne, is this a heart attack or a stroke?"

Reporter: "Anne, just so we don't get off the green here, this medical language at the top of page two, does that mean a heart attack or ..."

Mrs. Wheaton: "That is a form of heart attack, as I understand it, the heart ..."

Reporter: "Is stroke a better word for it?"

Mrs. Wheaton: "I cannot tell you that. This will have to stand by itself."

Reporter: "Let's get this straight before we leave, Anne."

Reporter: "A form of heart attack you said, Madam Secretary?"

Mrs. Wheaton: "As I understand it, an occlusion is."

Reporter: "This is of the middle cerebral artery?"

Mrs. Wheaton: "That's right."

Reporter: "Is it a heart attack or a form of heart attack?"

Mrs. Wheaton: "Both ... form of heart attack ... I think ..."

Reporter: "This is a stroke, is it not?"

Reporter: "A slight stroke?"

Reporter: "Wait a minute ... Anne is saying something different now."

Mrs. Wheaton: "As I understand it, cerebral does have a connotation of something to do with the head ..."

And so it went as I tried to figure out what had happened to Eisenhower. It finally turned out to be a slight stroke, but it took half an hour before we knew for sure.

Throughout his presidency, Eisenhower projected the image of a stern but loving grandfather who could break at any moment into that winning grin. It was an image that reassured the public while he left most of the governing to others.

Foreign policy he gave to the righteous, rigid, and arrogant John Foster Dulles. It was said Dulles had trained to be Secretary of State since the age of five, having combined his Wall Street law career with diplomacy for every president from Wilson through Eisenhower. He was the grandson of one Secretary of State and the nephew of another, had been legal counsel to the U.S. delegation at the World War I Paris peace talks, an adviser at the San Francisco founding of the United Nations in 1945, a delegate to the UN, a U.S. ambassador, and finally had achieved his life-long dream of becoming Secretary of State.

Dulles travelled more miles than would Henry Kissinger. He was forever in mid-air proselytizing his philosophy of brinkmanship. With Dulles it was his way or no way. As he once said at a Press Club luncheon I attended, "I prefer being respected to being liked." Repeatedly he was urged to let a situation simmer for a while, but he constantly sought to stir things up. Around the State Department there was a joking recommendation for Dulles: "Don't do something. Just stand there."

But that was not the Dulles style. He pursued his diplomatic whirlwind crusade with religious fervour. He was a pillar of his Presbyterian church, a stout believer in Christian charity, a man of high moral character, and an ardent and forceful believer in The American Way Of Life. He was convinced he was fighting God's war against the Communist devil. His brother Allen Dulles once said Foster had "his own line to God." His righteous wrath could be monumental, as when he felt the British double-crossed him with their Suez attack in 1956.

His Olympian arrogance and moral certainty were even more ingrained than those of one-time colleague Senator Warren Austin, who as a U.S. delegate to the United Nations once admonished other delegates in a Middle East debate, saying, "Let the Arabs and the Jews settle their differences in a good Christian manner." It was the kind of sentiment Dulles wholeheartedly endorsed, not at all from ignorance or an attempt at humour, but from the profound depth of his Christian convictions. Indeed, when his faith was confronted by the atheistic Communists and the Moslem Arabs playing footsie over the Aswan Dam in Egypt in 1956, it led to one of his worst mistakes. He reneged on a deal to help finance the dam, and in doing so he paved the way for the Egyptian-Russian deal that gave the Soviets a massive entrée into the Middle East, where their influence still plagues the West.

More than any one individual in the West, John Foster Dulles personified the Cold War. He spoke of "liberating the slave nations of Eastern Europe" and of going "to the brink" of war in order to preserve peace. He once told a Time-Life reporter, "You have to take chances for peace just as you have to take chances in war. Some say we were brought to the verge of war [by my policies]. Of course we were brought to the verge of war. The ability to get to the verge without getting into war is the necessary art .... We walked to the brink and we looked it in the face. We took strong action." In a nutshell, that was the theory of brinkmanship.

As for Canada, he didn't spend much time worrying about us, except to try to enlist our support for his policies. One of his aides told me he felt Canadians had an "inferiority complex" and an "ambivalent attitude" toward the United States. According to a private memorandum that came to light later, he felt Canada was "a very important piece of real estate to be humoured along."

He never understood John Diefenbaker, who was elected early in Eisenhower's second term, and he was a bit leery of Mike Pearson, who was External Affairs Minister in the first five years of the Eisenhower Administration. Pearson and Dulles were friendly enough to call each other "Foster" and "Mike," but whenever I saw them together there always seemed to be some distance between them, with Dulles very much acting the part of the superior being. When they met in March, 1956, at a Canada-U.S.-Mexico summit conference at a luxury resort hotel at White Sulphur Springs, West Virginia, Dulles greeted Pearson by saying, "Did you bring your golf clubs with you?"

"No," said Pearson, "but I'll be glad to caddy for you."

To me, as an occasional observer, Dulles seemed a man utterly lacking in humour or grace. For instance, I watched with fascination the way he dealt with congressional committees. He was like an impatient professor lecturing the elected politicians on U.S. foreign policy, the evils of communism, and the obvious advantages of confrontational diplomacy. While listening to the committee members' questions he'd constantly draw intricate doodles on a long, yellow scratch pad. I sat at the press table a few feet from him and sometimes I'd try to grab a few of the Dulles doodles after he testified. But as soon as he got up, his aides would sweep everything away and cart it off to be burned, fearing the doodles might reveal some state secrets.

In spite of his cold public exterior, Dulles could apparently be a captivating companion on occasion. In a conversation after Dulles's death in 1959, Livingstone Merchant, a one-time Assistant Secretary of State and former ambassador to Canada, described Foster entertaining friends with anecdotes about Roosevelt and Churchill, Stalin, and Khrushchev. "Even when he was flat on his back in excruciating pain crossing the Atlantic in a stuffy plane, he'd tell us stories," Merchant recalled, describing one of Dulles's last trips before his cancer became too much for him.

The combination of Dulles's brinkmanship and the McCarthy witch hunts scared the dickens out of most Americans. The venerable Daughters of the American Revolution (DAR) demanded more guns and bullets and atom bombs to combat the Communists, wanted no truck or trade with the "Red Nations," and opposed disarmament talks. They charged the United Nations was a front for communism and they denounced all foreign aid. At one point, they demanded that the gold at Fort Knox be recounted to see if any foreign nation had made off with some of it. They also denounced the number of foreign recipes in American cookbooks and the increasing consumption of vodka. At one meeting, Robin Hood was attacked as Communist propaganda.

The John Birch Society also flowered in this climate of anti-Communist virulence. During the fifties the group had wide membership and quite a few supporters in the U.S. Congress, numbering two sitting congressmen among their actual members. In 1961 I did a CBC documentary on the Birchers. In his Boston office, Robert Welch, the John Birch Society president, told me that Eisenhower, John Foster Dulles, Allen Dulles (head of the CIA), and Chief Justice Warren were all Communist agents or sympathizers. One chapter head in North Dakota called Eisenhower "a willing Communist tool."

The Cold War atmosphere of the Eisenhower years inevitably led to great entrepreneurial ingenuity among those involved in the business of building bomb shelters. I took a look at this subject in an article for the *Financial Post* in October, 1961. I was never able to get a precise estimate on how much money was spent on bomb shelters and radiation devices, but one government official told me the figure ran in the tens of millions of dollars. My research confirmed that it was certainly a booming business and one that involved many quick-buck artists as well as more reputable firms. I found one New England outfit that advertised a "bomb shelter" for $4.20. When I called the company an official told me without laughing that this was a small tool to be used for opening manhole and sewer covers in the event you didn't have your own shelter or were caught away from home during a blast. Much of the marketing of shelters and spin-off products had the unmistakable aura of used-car hucksterism.

There were two basic categories: the "simple fallout" shelter that went for "as low as $400" and the "blast shelter" that started at $2,000. The U.S. government recommended a blast shelter for those living in cities while simple fallout shelters were okay for small towns and rural areas. An Alexandria, Virginia, company, though, offered a "guaranteed cut-rate shelter" good for blast *and* fallout for "as low as $895."

Some companies offered a "twin pack" of a bomb shelter below and a swimming pool on top. Others proposed a shelter under your existing pool. "Your family swimming pool is the perfect spot for a shelter," one advertisement said. "Just three feet of water affords better protection against the atom bomb than a 30-foot wall." Construction companies also offered "community bomb shelters" for apartment buildings.

The more enthusiastic bomb-shelter builders talked of "individually styled" shelters, including a Cape Cod version, a ranch-style, and a bungalow. Some told me they could put in billiard and ping-pong tables so you could while away the hours of waiting after the atom bombs had fallen. And every shelter just had to have a special radiation detection device. I talked to an official of the Survival Equipment Company in New York who told me they were doing a big business selling "The Family Radiation Measuring Kit" for $24.95. He showed me one of their newspaper advertisements: "Remember," it said, "you can measure fallout radiation and SURVIVE! Don't wait! Order this life-saving equipment today!"

There was considerable discussion at public meetings and in the media at the time about what to do if the neighbours wanted to get into your bomb shelter. With space and food limited, the general consensus seemed to be "shoot them." To prevent the neighbours from knowing you had a bomb shelter, some companies disguised their workmen as TV repairmen or swimming pool construction workers. In Florida and much of the South, there were public arguments about whether blacks should be allowed to use the same bomb shelters as whites. A wealthy Washington hostess was reported in the papers to have built an elaborate bomb shelter with numerous small rooms, but none big enough for herself. "The shelter is for the servants," she was quoted as saying. "I expect to be out of town when it happens."

Among the macabre jokes going the rounds of Washington in those days was the following: "What will you do when the bombs start falling?"

"I'll join a crowd and walk slowly to the cemetery."

"Why slowly?"

"I don't want to start a panic."

Even the Society for the Prevention of Cruelty to Animals got involved in the bomb-shelter business. The society was alarmed that so little attention was being paid to the safety of pets in the event of nuclear attack. The SPCA sent me a pamphlet it was distributing in the millions across the United States urging householders to stockpile pet food, water, and, to soothe nervous cats and dogs, a supply of phenobarbital in their bomb shelters. The pamphlet was entitled "Survival of Pets After the Blast."

Through all the Dulles sabre-rattling and the McCarthy witch-hunting with its tragic and sometimes silly repercussions, Eisenhower remained immensely popular by doing very little. In fact, the most progressive and far-reaching act of his first four years in office was an unwitting one. Following the 1952 election, Ike rewarded his former rival Earl Warren with the appointment as Chief Justice of the Supreme Court. As Governor of California, Warren had proved himself to be a liberal Republican.

Two years later the bombshell exploded that has since transformed the United States. On May 17, 1954, the Warren Supreme Court ruled the idea of "separate but equal" public school facilities was unconstitutional. (They certainly had been separate, but never equal.) The Supreme Court demanded full school integration "with all deliberate speed."

At the time, I was filled with the idealism of IFAP, FAO, the United Nations, and the other international agencies with which I'd been working, and it was an exhilarating moment when the Supreme Court ruling was announced. It seemed as though the millennium had arrived. As it turned out, our celebration was about a decade premature.

I well remember the shock that swept over official Washington. President Eisenhower was jolted, the southern politicians were outraged, and Ike's answer was to move with all deliberate slowness. You could readily see Ike's exasperation when he was pressed on the subject at his weekly news conferences. On one occasion, the famous Ike grin disappeared and his face reddened as he admitted he wanted integration to move more slowly. I wondered at the time whether his reaction was in fact one of anger or embarrassment.

I was told by several people who had talked with him that Ike was deeply angry with Chief Justice Warren for putting him in such a spot. It wasn't that he was against integration as such (although he had opposed integration of black troops during the Korean War), but that he just didn't want to disturb the status quo. Eisenhower preached patience but made no clear commitment to carrying out the will of the Supreme Court. He passed a few laws and set up a few commissions, but they were tame laws and tame commissions, designed more to slow down than to speed up integration. He never heard the signal bells of the black revolution.

His only real test came in September, 1957, early in his second term, at Little Rock, Arkansas, when Governor Orval Faubus defied the courts in an attempt to prevent the integration of Little Rock's Central High School. Reluctantly, Ike sent in federal troops to enforce the court order. But he made it clear to us at his news conferences that he did it to maintain order and uphold the court, and certainly not to endorse the idea of integration.

I had the feeling from listening to him and talking with others who saw him privately during this period that he felt he was steering a moral middle course between the white supremacists and the Ku Klux Klan on one side and the blacks on the other side. The immorality of his "morality" never dawned on him. He did not and could not understand the "Negro" issue. By the end of Eisenhower's presidency in January, 1961, six years after the Supreme Court ruling, only one-sixth of one per cent of black students in the South would be integrated in schools. Most of those were in Florida and Texas.

In 1957, I talked to a leader of the American White Citizens Council, John Kasper of Little Rock, who was picketing the White House protesting against any action on the Warren Supreme Court decision. Carrying a sign in each hand calling blacks "apes," he told me, "They'll all have to be shipped back to Africa. That's where they belong."

Over in the Congress in those post-Warren Court decision years, the southerners were doing everything they could to delay even the modest proposals of President Eisenhower to enable the blacks to exercise their constitutional rights to vote and go to school. I sat in the Senate press gallery at the end of August, 1956, watching South Carolina Senator Strom Thurmond begin what was to be the longest filibuster in Senate history, up to that time, by talking non-stop for twenty-four hours and eighteen minutes. It was his way of protesting Ike's civil rights proposals. Thurmond started in his strong, deep, southern-accented voice at six minutes to nine at night and, gulping orange juice and ice water, continued until twelve minutes after nine the next night, ending in an exhausted whisper. I saw him at the start and at the end, and in between he read from the Bible, talked about Roman history, quoted poetry, and picked up books at random from a knee-high pile around his lectern. Senator Thurmond had been the 1948 southern Dixiecrat candidate for President and was the revered leader of white segregationists. While Thurmond was trying to stop the progress toward racial equality in the Senate, his southern supporters were taking concrete action to prevent blacks from voting. To register to vote, blacks had to correctly answer questions such as these ones posed in North Carolina and reported by a congressional committee: "How many bubbles in a bar of soap? How many rooms in the Court House? What is due process of law? What was the 19th State admitted to the Union?" It was the same story throughout Mississippi, Alabama, South and North Carolina, and Louisiana.

George Lee, the first black to register to vote in Humphrey County in Mississippi, was shot dead. Lamar Smith, who organized the voter registration drive in the same county, was also killed. One black witness told a Senate committee of less drastic action: a vote registrar rejected him because he was left-handed. Blacks were also discouraged from voting by threats of job dismissal, bank foreclosure on their homes, and boycotts of black store owners by white wholesalers. Membership in the Ku Klux Klan expanded during this period – the Anti-Defamation League said the KKK was growing by 50 per cent a year.

But as Ike neared the end of his first term, most of this was still off in the future. Meanwhile, the golfer President toyed with the idea of retiring to Gettysburg. He told us he'd like to sit in the front porch rocking chair at his farm for the first six months "and after that, start rocking." He seemed more relaxed whenever he went to Gettysburg, an easy seventy-five-mile drive from Washington. His farm was just out of town, and whenever reporters followed him we'd stay at the Gettysburg Inn for $8.50 a night or at a nearby tourist home for $5. He had an office at the hotel and would meet us there from time to time, joking about our "holiday" with him.

There was no way the Republican Party would let him retire to the farm. He was a priceless asset for the Republicans, a guarantee of another presidential victory. "We could run him stuffed and we'd win," Republican Senator William Jenner told me. Ike finally agreed to run and walloped Stevenson even more thoroughly than in their first encounter. Although the Republicans did not regain control of the Congress (they had lost it in 1954), it seemed like Ike could be re-elected forever.

But things didn't go so well in his second term. Apart from the first stirrings of the black revolution, his friend, Treasury Secretary George Humphrey, left the administration, Dulles died, and Sherman Adams, his strong right arm in the White House, was caught in a scandal for accepting gifts from a wheeler-dealer named Bernard Goldfine.

I sat just behind Adams at a congressional committee hearing in the late summer of 1958 as the all-powerful, white-thatched, Bible-reading "Sherm the Firm" confessed his sins. There is always something irresistibly fascinating in seeing the mighty levelled and the committee members clearly enjoyed taking their revenge on the now humble and contrite Adams for all the "No's" he'd given them during the previous six years.

As Eisenhower had done before in the case of his old friend and mentor, General Marshall, he deserted Adams, his friend and closest confidant, and let him resign in embarrassment. Adams had always wanted to be ambassador to Canada, but Ike wouldn't give him the job because it might be politically damaging. The man who had come to Washington in 1952 to "clean up the mess" once again sought to distance himself from a tainted situation.

While Eisenhower presided over a period of Cold War and brinkmanship on the international scene and relative social tranquility at home, he is more often remembered for his decisions not to involve the U.S. in a potential nuclear conflict and his final warnings about the dangers of the "military-industrial complex." On three separate occasions Eisenhower's advisers urged on him the use of atomic weapons and three times he said no, even though he initially flirted with the idea. The first occasion was during the Korean War, when General Douglas MacArthur wanted to drop the bomb on the Chinese. Later Eisenhower did agree, however, to threaten to use nuclear weapons in Korea. This was done in private messages to the Chinese and Russians as a way of accelerating the peace talks.

Then in the spring of 1954, the Chairman of the Joint Chiefs of Staff, Admiral Arthur Radford, tried to persuade the President to make a nuclear strike against the Communists in Indochina to forestall a French debacle. Even John Foster Dulles considered it, according to Anthony Eden, the late British Prime Minister. But again, Eisenhower said no. On September 12 of the same year, Admiral Radford, Air Force Chief of Staff General Nathan Twining, and Chief of Naval Operations Admiral Robert Carney urged Eisenhower to approve nuclear bombing of China during a crisis over Matsu and Quemoy, the tiny islands between China and Taiwan. Eisenhower refused.

Those three "no's" were perhaps his greatest legacy.

These decisions weren't known widely at the time, and wouldn't be until after his farewell speech as President made headlines. On his retirement from the White House, Eisenhower would warn that "the military-industrial complex,'' the powerful collusion of the big defence industries and the Pentagon, might one day dominate American policy. In the 1980s that gloomy prediction has become a reality.

Eisenhower's great strength was his genius as a co-ordinator and compromiser. This he did superbly in World War II as Supreme Allied Commander. It was the job he loved the best, as he once told a small group of us at his Gettysburg farm. And yet, to my mind, in all but the ultimate question of nuclear war, Eisenhower was a failure as President. The reality was much less than the heroic image. He could have done so much, but he did so little. When I think of Eisenhower I am reminded of Edmund Burke's comment, ''The only thing necessary for the triumph of evil is for good men to do nothing.'' Or, as Winston Churchill said of some of his pre-war political adversaries within the Conservative Party, ''The malice of the wicked was reinforced by the weakness of the virtuous.''

Ike meant well, but did little. The waves of change were lapping at his feet but he didn't notice them.

4 *THE FREELANCE LIFE*

Washington, D.C., 1958 . . .

With Eisenhower's reign coming to an end, you could somehow feel
the Eisenhower ice jam beginning to break up. Wherever I travelled in
the U.S. I sensed that people were ready for a more vibrant leadership
from a new generation of political leaders. The politicians also sensed
this as they pawed the ground waiting for the start of the 1960 presidential race. Nixon was the Republican heir apparent, and among the
Democratic hopefuls were Lyndon Johnson, the most effective Senate
Majority Leader in American history; Senator Stuart Symington, the
handsome, liberal, "good ol' boy" from Missouri; Senator Hubert
Humphrey, the ebullient, then-left-winger from Minnesota; Adlai Stevenson, the revered, eloquent, and two-time standard-bearer; and the
brash upstart, Jack Kennedy. For a political junkie it was a propitious
moment to become a full-time Washington correspondent.

In my last few years at IFAP I had begun to do more freelance reporting, not only for CBC Radio news and public affairs programs, the
occasional CBC Television program, and the *Financial Post*, but also
for several Canadian newspapers. My ambition was to be a Washington
correspondent and, also, I needed the money.

Amid all the travel and work, my marriage had collapsed in the early
1950s. The anguish of a marriage breakdown is not a unique experience
these days, but for me the agony of losing my daughter Anne was a
soul-tearing wound, especially since I was still cursed by that damnable
WASP credo of not sharing or showing my feelings.

As far back as 1954 I'd started stringing for the *Windsor Star*. In

1955 I became a regular contributor to the *Financial Post* and in 1956 for the *Vancouver Sun*. I also occasionally wrote articles for the *Family Herald*, *Maclean's*, *Chatelaine*, and the *Star Weekly*. I was a professional whirling dervish, doing both my IFAP work and an increasing amount of freelance reporting. Now, in the summer of 1958, I decided the time was ripe to leap totally into the perilous world of freelance journalism.

The transition was not as traumatic as it might have been, though, thanks to all the freelance sideline assignments I'd been building up in the previous years, but there would no longer be a regular paycheque coming in. I worried about being able to pay the rent and the alimony, as well as making a decent living. At the same time, I found the prospect exhilarating, knowing I would be paid only for specific work done.

As a full-time freelance journalist I had to maintain and expand my contact with the various editors in Toronto, especially at the CBC, the *Financial Post*, *Maclean's*, and other publications, so I drove up to Toronto every couple of months to knock on editors' doors, letting them know I was available for assignments and exchanging gossip. Whenever I travelled elsewhere in Canada to make a speech or participate in a meeting, I would drop in on editors.

As a freelancer, I quickly appreciated the value of creative recycling of the same story in order to meet the varying whims of different editors and target audiences, and to avoid competitive conflicts. A story on, say, the Democratic Party platform, could emphasize the international implications of the platform for the CBC, be slanted toward the economic repercussions for the *Financial Post*, outline the political nuances for the *Windsor Star*, and concentrate on the platform's impact on lumber and resource imports for the *Vancouver Sun*, with perhaps a behind-the-scenes view for *Maclean's* on who was manipulating whom for what purpose in the backroom fighting over the platform. I'd also do soft feature stories for the CBC's Harry Boyle. He'd pay $25 for interviews with the likes of Duke Ellington and Billie Holiday.

As a result of an interview, I became friendly with Billie in the last few years of her life. I was a jazz and blues fan and she was my favourite singer. "Lady Day," as she was known, was a gentle, sad woman whose sheer guts had taken her from clip-joint gin mills to recognition as one of the world's great jazz and blues singers. Her rendition one night in a Washington nightclub of "Stormy Weather" remains a sublime moment in my memory. When I knew her, she was struggling to break out of her addiction to heroin and two bottles of gin or vodka a day, guided by her husband Louis McKay, a tender man who always seemed worried about Billie. As she travelled, she and Louis would send me postcards signed "Billie and Louis McKay" – she seemed to be winning her battle.

Toward the end of her life, I remember doing an interview with her for the CBC radio program *Assignment*. It was barely usable because she had gone back to her old ways and was high on both booze and drugs. Louis, whom she called "my man," fussed around us in her dressing room, explaining, "She's tired and she's hurtin'. She's been working so hard and trying so hard. But things just catch up with her." In July, 1959, she died of the eroding effects of her life-long addictions.

For several years, beginning in 1958, I did a daily report for the CBC 8:00 a.m. radio news. My report was fed to Atlantic Canada at 7:00 a.m. Eastern Time. That meant getting up about five, driving a mile or so to the NBC studios where at the time we did most of our CBC feeds to Toronto, writing the script, airing the piece at seven, and often repeating it with new information at eight. I've found few things less enchanting than calling somebody to check a fact at six in the morning. A soft and gentle response is not usual. But then, at that time of day, everybody is fuzzy. Once during a live 7:00 a.m. report, to my consternation I heard the announcer in Toronto solemnly intone, "Now for that story, we go to Knowlton Wash in Nashington."

Returning home the dozen or so blocks from NBC about 8:30, I'd promptly go into the office I had set up in the basement of my home, complete with separate telephone lines, files, typewriters, and a news agency wire service. The next hour was spent organizing the rest of the day, making phone calls to politicians, diplomats, and bureaucrats, as well as to editors in Toronto and elsewhere. I was rigidly disciplined about time, organizing the hours carefully around events and assignments. Without tough discipline, a freelancer can too easily succumb to professional lassitude and consequent financial ruin.

Usually about 10:00 I'd go to a hearing in the Senate or the House of Representatives or at one of the myriad government agencies, from the Federal Power Commission to the U.S. Tariff Commission. The time-saving trick was to arrive after the principal witnesses' presentation had been made – this was always written and handed out – pick up a copy, and then listen to the questioning. Then there might be an hour or so spent going through documents and statements in search of information relating to the testimony.

The amount of work I was now doing for CBC meant that I was working not only at my home office, but also in Don Minifie's office in the National Press Building a couple of blocks from the White House. I would check in there about noon for messages. I ate lunch as seldom as possible, except when lunching with a news source. Otherwise I felt it a waste of time.

One particularly rewarding lunch, however, was when a group of us sat down with the dean of all Washington correspondents and an American journalistic icon, Walter Lippmann. His columns had enormous influence on policy-makers and we felt we were sitting at the feet of "The Master." He talked about war – specifically World War I, World War II, and Korea – and made a comment I've never forgotten. "I hate old men," he said, "who make wars for young men to fight."

Early afternoon, I'd either be doing research, attending another hearing, or visiting a news contact. At least once a day there would be a news conference worth attending, whether with President Eisenhower, the Secretary of State, a Pentagon official, or other representatives of government departments and agencies.

It was easy to get around the various buildings on Capitol Hill because they all had underground tunnel connections with each other. From the Senate office buildings to the Capitol building where Congress met, you took an open trolly car. But you had to walk through the tunnels leading from the various office buildings used by members of the House of Representatives. When I was first in Washington there was only one Senate Office Building, known affectionately as the "SOB." When a new one was built you had to tell cab drivers whether you were going to the "old SOB" or the "new SOB." In time, there was a new House office building, too, and a new facade to the Capitol. This was known to reporters and politicians as House Speaker Sam Rayburn's "last erection."

By mid-afternoon on most days, I'd be back at the CBC office preparing for our nightly television and radio feeds to Toronto. When they were over it usually would be off to a cocktail party to see what information could be picked up, to a dinner, or just a quiet drink with a source. Later at night, I would usually spend some time in my home office writing a piece or two. On Saturdays and Sundays, I generally spent half a dozen hours or so each day writing longer stories such as magazine articles. About once a week I'd have a dinner at home for a few people from the Canadian Embassy, other embassies, the State Department, government agencies, or the Congress. And once or twice a month I'd have a party for twenty or thirty news contacts and fellow journalists.

In 1955, I had married a Mexican diplomat's daughter. She had been the FAO representative at the United Nations. Her father, who had fallen out of favour with his government and was now retired and living in Washington, was in straitened circumstances and his pride prevented him from accepting my support. But his dignity was upheld by teaching me Spanish, for which I paid him. It turned out to be a valuable linguistic tool in my later coverage of Latin America, although I never became as fluent as I would have liked.

The major news stories in Washington usually broke around the so-called "golden triangle" consisting of the White House, the State Department, and the Pentagon. As a general correspondent, I found it intriguing to note the different types of reporters covering those three beats on a full-time basis. At all three locations, the news agencies, the networks, and the big papers, such as the *New York Times* and *Washington Post*, dominated the reportorial hierarchy. At the White House, reporters were generalists, picking up every detail of presidential activity, primarily doing reactive rather than analytical reporting. At the State Department it was the reverse. Reporters there concentrated on informed analysis of foreign policy and were by far the brightest journalists I knew. Those covering the Pentagon were experts on defence policy and weaponry and had far more specific, detailed knowledge of their beat than the others. They also had closer, more intimate relations with the officials they were covering. Those same differences in reporters in the "golden triangle" exist today except that there is now less reactive and more investigative and analytical journalism coming out of the White House.

Washington, more than any other capital, makes use of background briefings by administration officials and foreign diplomats to provide inside information on a particular government action or policy. There were three basic categories of briefings. A simple "backgrounder" meant you could say an unidentified State Department (or other department) official had said such and such. A briefing described as "deep background" meant you could not identify the department and you could say only that an administration official said such and such. Finally, there was the "deep deep" background briefing where no position could be attributed to any department or the administration itself and your story could only say that you understood that such and such was the administration position. Those kinds of stories we called "thumb suckers" because you were on your own with no source given to support your story.

Of course, there were leaks galore. Washington is undoubtedly the leakiest city in the world. Officials send up "trial balloons" to see what public reaction might be without being identified with the proposals. Sometimes those who have lost an argument within the administration try to win by leaking ahead of time. This gives public opposition a chance to materialize. Others, in need of ego-burnishing, leak because they want the world to know they are key figures in some decision-making. Some leak to embarrass a bureaucratic rival.

Even presidents leak deliberately. They do it, as their officials do it, to gain some public advantage over their opposition, or sometimes, as one White House official has said, "to put our spin on things." What presidents are unhappy about are leaks of information they don't want the public to have, such as arguments within the administration. Often, senior government officials think they may be able to influence an impending presidential decision by leaking information they fear he may not have seen. Politicians leak to curry favour with the media and to put themselves in a good light.

The diplomatic corps was and is also an important source of back-grounding and leaking. On important stories it was critical to hear the same information from three or four different sources to get as full a perspective as possible. That meant a lot of phoning, visiting, and buttonholing of people at cocktail parties and dinners.

The famous Washington cocktail party scene was an important part of the Washington beat. It was not that so much information was actually obtained at the diplomatic and political parties, but confirmation of stories was often made and contacts were established for a follow-up on a particular story. The French Embassy parties were always the most elaborate, with the best food and Moet Chandon as the *champagne ordinaire*. The British parties were the most informative even if the most spartan in food and drink. The Russian parties were the biggest; the Canadian parties the friendliest; and Democratic political parties the noisiest. The fare would range from smoked salmon and caviar at embassy parties to such exotica as chocolate-covered ants and dried grasshoppers at some lobbyist affairs. The ants tasted just like chocolate nibbles, but the grasshoppers had a salty, earthy taste and it was somewhat unnerving to see those bulging grasshopper eyes just as you popped one into your mouth.

Part of my job was getting to know as many senators and congressmen as I could. This was one of the more enjoyable aspects. A now forgotten senator from Ohio, Senator Stephen Young, was a favourite of mine because he brooked no nonsense from constituents complaining about his votes in Congress. He showed me some of his responses to such letters of complaint. To a union official pleading with him to support a particular bill, he wrote, "Dear Sir: Why would I do a thing like that? You are insane. Sincerely yours ..." To another complainer he wrote, "Dear Sir: Some idiot is writing me stupid letters with your name on them. I thought you should know. Sincerely yours ..." Senator Young also told me a trick he had to handle long-winded telephone complainers. He said he would simply hang up the phone while he himself was talking, leaving the caller to think he had been accidentally cut off since people didn't hang up on themselves. Except Senator Young.

Inevitably, a lot of a Canadian reporter's time in Washington is spent tracing the impact of U.S. actions on the Canadian economy. Boom there means boom here. When they stop building homes in Boston, we stop making lumber in British Columbia. When they stop making cars in Detroit, we stop mining in Ontario. Particularly my writing for the *Financial Post* led me to follow closely the decisions by the Congress, government departments, and agencies that affected good times or bad in Canada.

I've always believed that almost anything a reporter wants in Washington is available somewhere. You just have to keep digging for it, talking to sources and ploughing through documents and statements to find it. I.F. Stone, a much-revered journalist, was a good example of that. He seldom went anywhere in Washington except to libraries and archives where he dug through thousands of documents searching out facts. He became one of the best-informed reporters in town.

Most of our trade trouble with the U.S. came from the Congress, not the administration. Usually, I found the State Department was on our side in trying to stop protectionist action in the Congress. In fact, until very recently, the Canadian government felt it would be indelicate, if not improper, for Ottawa to lobby openly and directly with the Congress on some trade issue, preferring to leave it to the State Department to represent Canada's views to the congressmen.

I'd keep track of every legislative proposal that came up that would affect Canada. There would be bills to increase tariffs on Canadian bread exports to the U.S., or bills to put quotas or higher tariffs on Canadian minerals, or umbrella "Buy American" provisions in government procurement. Most of these died before getting out of a congressional committee because of State Department opposition or because they were only meant as rhetoric to satisfy some domestic pressure group. The Canadian Embassy and the Canada desk at the State Department would also track these bills, raising alarms or soothing fears as the case might be.

Political signals on U.S. trade policies also could be discerned in the platforms that the Democratic and Republican Parties prepared at their presidential nominating conventions. Some years after this period, when arch-conservative Barry Goldwater got the 1964 Republican nomination, I wrote in the *Financial Post*: "Canadian exporters had better head for the hills if Barry Goldwater is elected President of the U.S."

That was because of the strong protectionist flavour to his platform. Traditionally, Republicans have been more susceptible to domestic protectionist pressures than the Democrats. The more conservative the Republican candidate, the more susceptible. And that meant big trouble for Canadian exports to the U.S. In the end, though, very few of the protectionist measures actually became law.

Much of the credit for that went to the hard-working diplomats at the Canadian Embassy and the Canada desk at the State Department. In my eighteen years in Washington, no one ever matched the effectiveness on the U.S. side of Rufus Smith, who dealt with Canadian affairs for two decades, heading the Canadian desk for several years, and also for a time serving in the U.S. Embassy in Ottawa. With southern charm, acute perceptions, a razor-sharp mind, and real empathy for Canada, Smith was probably the most effective and important U.S. official in Washington as far as Canada was concerned. Certainly there were higher authorities, including the Secretary of State and the President, but they all took careful guidance from what Smith said.

The Canadian Embassy was, of course, a focal point for much of our Canada-U.S. bilateral coverage. Hardly ever would a day go by that I wouldn't visit the embassy or have at least a couple of telephone conversations with someone there. The official channel for reporters was through the minister in charge of information at the embassy. His job was to steer us to the right source if he didn't have the details himself. Occasionally his job was to deflect us. But more important than dealing with Canadian reporters was his job of educating and steering the American press on what was going on in Canada. That was a challenge because, although Americans like Canadians and think we are "nice" and "just like us," there is precious little U.S. reporting of what goes on in Canada.

In 1958 very few Americans had ever heard of retired Prime Minister Louis St. Laurent, fewer still of the new P.M., John Diefenbaker. Most thought Canada was still a British colony. (In 1965, when we got our own flag, Americans were startled. "A handsome bunting," the *Baltimore Sun* said. "Somehow," editorialized the *Portland Oregonian*, "it reminds us of a label on a can of lard.")

In my first years of reporting from Washington, the job of Canadian Embassy information minister was handled by Bob Farquharson, former editor of the *Globe and Mail* and minister at the embassy. Bob provided solid, reliable backgrounding for us. In 1958, the Canadian ambassador was Norman Robertson, an erudite old Ottawa hand known as "The Mandarin's Mandarin" for his long-time experience at the top levels of Canada's civil service and a man who was uncomfortable with reporters.

He also struck me as a man of uneasy grace at least on public occasions and uncomfortable in the political and diplomatic hothouse of Washington. He had the wisdom, however, to make good use of Farquharson's camaraderie and contacts to help the Canadian cause in Washington.

In addition to the work of our diplomats, individual Canadian companies, industry associations, and groups such as the Canadian Exporters Association would make the occasional foray into Washington. Their purpose was to woo the Congress and the administration. They would meet senators, representatives, congressional committee staff, confer with officials at the State Department, Pentagon, or Commerce Department, have a cocktail party and a dinner or two, and then go home. Only a very few Canadian companies had their own full-time representatives or lobbyists in Washington. I always thought Canadian business was missing a bet by not doing much more to influence the economic decision-makers of Washington. Our diplomats can only do so much and Canadian corporations then and now foolishly ignore their own best interests by not spending more time and money on the wooing of Washington.

Since I'd first started working closely with Don Minifie in 1956, I had learned a great deal about my craft. Don was a passionate, intensely curious, and meticulous reporter. He always wanted to see and hear things for himself. In his implacable search for accuracy he wouldn't settle for something second hand if he could avoid it. In those early years he became a friend, colleague, and mentor who shared with me not only his immense knowledge of Washington but impressed me with his charm and sophistication. As much as any reporter I've ever watched in action, his reports exuded integrity and style. And unlike many in the business, he agonized personally over the human implications of government policies and world events.

In the late 1950s the CBC office in the National Press Building that Don shared with me was a closet-sized room that was also shared by Max Freedman, a brilliant Canadian journalist who wrote for the Manchester *Guardian* and occasionally broadcast for the CBC.

In 1958, we had an unexpected late-afternoon visit from CBC President Alphonse Ouimet and what seemed like the entire board of directors of the CBC. Minifie, Freedman, and I were at our three desks, books spilling out of a dilapidated bookcase, reports, papers, magazines, and congressional reports scattered into the corners on the floor. It was crowded when the three of us were there, with Freedman dictating into the phone to the *Guardian* in England, Minifie rehearsing his radio report, and me banging away at my typewriter, all of us on deadline. Suddenly, into this scene stepped the CBC president and his cohorts. Somehow they all managed to get into the room, gingerly stepping over the newspaper- and book-strewn floor, literally standing cheek by jowl. Looking with dismay at the spectacle, they mumbled apologies for intruding, backed out the door, and suggested we meet later in their hotel suite. Soon after, largely, I think, because of the Ouimet visit, the CBC got a bigger office and we even got a chair for the occasional visitor.

When Minifie was away, I'd take on his freelance daily news report for *O'Stado* in Sao Paulo, Brazil, one of the world's great newspapers at the time, certainly equal to the *New York Times* or *The Times* of London.

I particularly recall my sense of triumph at the front-page treatment *O'Stado* gave to a story I'd done on the Democratic Party challenge to the Republicans leading up to the 1960 election. I couldn't read Portuguese and hence I didn't know if the Brazilian editors had cut anything, but it certainly looked impressive. *O'Stado* wanted stories on major U.S. political developments and on foreign policy actions and it was sheer professional joy working for this respected paper. As I wrote, I sometimes fantasized I was writing for the *New York Times*.

Occasionally, I'd take over on a freelance basis the work of the Washington correspondent for the *London Daily Mirror*, a vivid demonstration of going from the sublime to the ridiculous. Instead of the detailed, nuanced stories on international politics I did for *O'Stado*, the *Mirror* editors wanted Washington scandal, offbeat features, and personality pieces. I was astounded to see stories I'd file on important Eisenhower pronouncements wind up as two sentences on page three. But tabloid-trivialized as the *Mirror* was, it also paid a lot more money than *O'Stado*.

In the spring of 1958, in addition to my radio, TV, newspaper, and magazine freelancing, I began publishing a newsletter called "Washington Through Canadian Eyes." It concentrated on Canada-U.S. relations, primarily in the economic area, along with behind-the-scenes background information, reports on upcoming Washington issues and events of importance to Canada, and analysis of U.S. policies as they affected Canada. It went to several hundred subscribers, but in the end it took too much time and effort and never made it into the black, so in late 1959 I quietly let it pass out of existence.

Although based in Washington, I spent a lot of time at the United Nations covering General Assembly meetings, the Security Council, and other UN stories. Here, my IFAP experience was particularly useful because I already knew the right contacts on many of the stories. Sometimes I'd be on my own and sometimes I'd help out the CBC's regular

UN correspondent, who in the late 1950s and early 1960s was Stanley Burke, later the first journalist to anchor for *The National*. During one story in this time period when presidents and prime ministers from Khrushchev to Harold Macmillan of the United Kingdom and from Fidel Castro to John Diefenbaker all came to speak to the UN, I went back and forth between Washington and New York every morning and night for two weeks. Other times, during a running debate in the Security Council on the Middle East, for instance, I'd base in New York for the duration of the story.

Washington, D.C., February, 1957 ...

The big story for me in the late 1950s was the Senate Labor Rackets Committee investigations into the influence of organized crime on the labour movement. It had begun its investigations early in 1957 with the intent of helping develop legislation that would clean out the mob. The Teamsters Union, as the union most infiltrated by the Mafia, was the prime target for the investigating senators who included, among others, John F. Kennedy and Joseph McCarthy. It was through coverage of the Senate Labor Rackets Committee that I first got to know both John Kennedy and his brother Robert.

At the time of the hearings, John Kennedy was already a politician to watch and he was clearly using them as a political springboard. He had been first elected to the Senate in the 1952 election and my first glimpse of him had been in 1954, a year and half later. I was looking down from the press gallery at a half-empty Senate, listening to a dreary debate on agricultural policy. And there, paying no attention whatever, was the young senator from Massachusetts with one leg slung insolently over his desk. Tanned and handsome in his blue sports jacket and reading the *New York Times*, he looked the carefree epitome of "Joe College." In the House of Representatives during his terms there from 1946 to 1952, he'd been known as "The Kid Congressman," and the nickname seemed appropriate. To my eyes then, John Kennedy looked anything but a U.S. senator, let alone a future president.

But from the very beginning, Jack Kennedy had "the royal jelly." He wanted to be president and wanted it badly. On the surface he had just about everything. He was rich, a war hero, likeable, witty, street smart, and a handsome young bachelor. If he was known among the press corps for one thing when he was first in Congress, it was as a Don Juan whose sex life was envied and speculated upon endlessly. He and his friend, Senator Henry "Scoop" Jackson of Washington, were credited in those days with many more romantic conquests than legislative achievements. Kennedy was considered by most of us in the Washington press corps in the mid-1950s to be an intellectual lightweight, a dilettante who was insensitive to McCarthyism and inattentive to the portents of the black revolution.

It was not until 1956 that any of us took him seriously as a presidential possibility. That was the year he published his Pulitzer-Prize-winning book *Profiles in Courage* and then missed by a whisker being the vice-presidential running mate to Adlai Stevenson. He lost to a Tennessee backwoods clown with an undeserved image for integrity, Senator Estes Kefauver. Kennedy later came to believe he never would have been president had he won that vice-presidential nomination and gone down to defeat with Stevenson in 1956. But from that moment on, what had once been a Kennedy goal became a Kennedy obsession. "Why not me?" he told me in his Senate office in 1958. "I could do it as well or better than the other possibilities."

Since 1956, everything he had done had been aimed at the White House. He prowled around the idea of being president like a cat around a bird cage. He spoke out often on foreign and domestic policy. He curried favour with political bosses and established toeholds throughout the party organization. He cultivated the media, too, talking to us often after a day's hearings of the Labor Rackets Committee and at other times. He genuinely liked reporters and had been a reporter himself for a while, covering the establishment of the United Nations at the San Francisco organizing conference in 1945. We knew he was using us, but what politician wasn't, and anyway he was good copy, providing us with many a story and much background on a man we felt was a political comer. Besides, we liked him a lot personally. We would often kid him about his New England accent. It came across in private much more strongly than when he spoke publicly. You had to listen carefully as he spoke of "Cuber," "Canader," or something happening in the "Way-ust" or the "Ee-ust." He talked of "pow-aw" and "despayuh," and once, later, opening a Mona Lisa exhibition, referred to "Moaner Leeser." He also talked very fast, and when taking notes during conversations with Kennedy, I again regretted never learning shorthand.

As an ex-sailor, he privately used salty Navy language sprinkled with a few "fucks," "pricks," and "shits," but his swearing seemed to be for incidental emphasis rather than the deeply emotional swearing I later heard from Johnson and Nixon. He liked to tease reporters on their speculative stories, especially if the speculation was wrong. And he enjoyed making fun of himself.

In the course of a dozen or two office and corridor conversations in

1957-60, I saw a lot of the Kennedy style and philosophy. He was conversationally graceful, witty, and knowledgeable about politics and history. I learned a lot of the old Boston Irish political sayings he liked to quote: "Don't get mad, get even"; or "Never complain, never explain." As an authentic South Pacific war hero, he admired courage and was occasionally critical of the inconspicuous war record of Nixon, or of Humphrey or Rockefeller. Later he gave us all at least one of the PT-109 tie clips commemorating his South Pacific heroism in saving the crew of his PT boat, which had been sliced in half by a Japanese destroyer.

I was astonished at his fascination with how much money people had and what reporters and editors earned. As a multimillionaire himself, he never thought about such things as mortgages and car payments. He was also a bit of a tightwad. He rarely carried any cash with him. Once in his office he sent an aide for some magazines, but had to ask if anybody had any money. There was a momentary silence and I muttered that, well, I had five dollars. "Fine," he said, sticking out his hand. "That'll do." I never did get it back, nor did I ever put in an expense claim, figuring the CBC bookkeepers wouldn't allow it anyway.

I found out from talking to others that he was forever borrowing money from aides, reporters, and, later, Secret Servicemen. I was told one story that at mass while he was running for president, the collection plate came by and Kennedy, as usual without cash in his pocket, asked a friend beside him to put something in the plate. The friend put in $20 and Kennedy whispered, "Shouldn't I put in more than that?"

In those pre-presidential days, my conversations with him revealed that he not only was vulnerable about his personal cash, he was also uninspired by broad economic policies. I had the sense he barely knew the difference between monetary policy (money and credit) and fiscal policy (budgets and taxes).

During his years in the Senate he never became a "member of the club." He was never one of the boys. His fellow senators, especially after 1956, felt he was too ambitious and too young. Perhaps because he was ambitious and young, he was more open with reporters. Certainly I was able to talk to him much more frequently then than later, when he was under the constraints and pressures of his campaign and his presidency.

John Kennedy was half the tough, pragmatic, sometimes bawdy Boston Irish politician, and half the graceful, stylish intellectual. Even his friends were split in two, half of them belonging to the "Irish Mafia" and half to the cultured society of intellectuals.

While he loved to hear gossip about others and to tease and make fun of himself, I don't think I ever heard him reveal a deep personal feeling of his own. He was in frequent pain from a wartime back injury and had to wear a back support corset, but he never referred to his pain. In spite of his back, he always seemed healthy with his perpetual Palm Beach tan, his talk of football and baseball, and his rambunctious family. I think he didn't talk about his own aches and pains for fear it might dim his image. Similarly, I never heard him refer to the tragedies of his family – a brother killed in war, a sister killed in a plane crash, and another sister in a home for the mentally retarded.

When he was irritated at a long, involved, or vague question from one of us, he'd rock a bit in the padded rocking chair in his Senate office, a chair he later moved to the White House, or he'd tap his teeth with his fingernails. Sometimes as we were leaving his office, his secretary, Evelyn Lincoln, would bring in a big glass of milk, or Jackie, whom he had married in 1953, would arrive with a thermos of clam chowder. At his desk, he'd often munch a lunch-time sandwich brought by Mrs. Lincoln or by his Boston family retainer, "Muggsy" O'Leary, a lovable old Irish politico straight out of *The Last Hurrah*.

At the Senate Labor Rackets Committee John Kennedy was a sharp and persistent inquisitor. But he was always backed up by his brother Bob, who as chief counsel for the committee was the main questioner. Bob had a terrier-like approach, cajoling, flattering, scolding, accusing, and berating a witness; sometimes he babied and sometimes he bullied. His reputation for being tough and nasty really began at these hearings. During his questioning of witnesses, Bob's unruly forelock would flop down over his forehead. While listening to testimony he'd pull at his hair with a finger, perch his glasses atop his head, play with a pencil, and smile or scowl. Sometimes his personal puritanism came through. When quizzing prostitutes, his face would redden and he would become flustered and wind up laughing at himself in embarrassment.

On many a day in 1957, 1958, and 1959 I sat in the big, ornate, high-ceilinged Senate Caucus Room, fascinated by the parade of shady characters testifying before the committee and equally fascinated by the performance of the Kennedy brothers. Seldom before had such a crew passed before the public eye. There were the labour leaders, such as Dave Beck, president of the Teamsters Union, and his successor, Jimmy Hoffa; there were the "fixers," such as "Good Old Reliable" Nathan Shefferman from Chicago; and there were the Mafia hoods, such as "Tony Pro" Provenzano of New Jersey, Sam Giancana, the Chicago killer and mob leader, Johnny Dio of New York, and Barney

Baker, the terrifying 300-pound, six-foot-four-inch pal of "Bugsy" Siegel, Meyer Lansky, and Joe Adonis. Almost all of the Mafia witnesses have since been murdered, as was Hoffa.

As well as these, there was a cast of characters straight out of Damon Runyon: pimps, prostitutes, madams, gamblers, pool-hall sharks, enforcers, crooked politicians, hit men. One witness explained, "Well, I was a bootlegger, and a gambler, and subsequently went into the horserace business." All of these people, one way or another, worked with the Teamsters Union.

One winter day in 1959 I was late for a hearing, and as I rushed to my press table seat someone bumped into me. I unceremoniously pushed him out of the way and snapped, "Look where you're going, stupid." He looked long and hard at me and then moved away. Only as I settled into my seat and the first witness was called did I realize I'd just shoved around Mafia killer and mob leader Giancana. I sank down in my seat, hoping he'd not notice me again.

As it was, he didn't testify for long, just repeating over and over, "I decline to answer because I honestly believe my answer might tend to incriminate me." He always said it with a little giggle and finally Bob Kennedy said, "I thought only little girls giggled, Mr. Giancana."

In his testimony about the same time, mobster and Teamster official Barney Baker, who had served two prison terms, mentioned a man named "Cockeyed" Dunn. Kennedy asked him, "Where is he now?"

"He has met his Maker," replied Baker.

"How?" asked Kennedy.

"I believe through electrocution in the city of New York," Baker responded.

Joey Gallo, who ran an "enforcer" union in New York, refused to answer questions at the hearings but privately told Bob Kennedy he'd help his brother in the 1960 presidential election. Kennedy declined.

Altogether some 1,500 witnesses appeared at the Senate hearings, and one of the most important was Dave Beck, the Teamster union president. He was fat, florid, loud, and dumb. Shortly after his appearance before the Senate committee he was forced out of the Teamster presidency because of scandals revealed in the hearings of using union funds for his personal finances. Beck was a bald, bull-necked, pig-eyed witness who not only refused to testify by citing the Fifth Amendment on self-incrimination, but for good measure cited the First, Second, Third, and Fourth amendments as well.

Jimmy Hoffa succeeded Beck and there was gossip among those of us covering the hearings that Hoffa had secretly schemed to get rid of his boss by helping the committee. We never knew how much "help" he gave, but in any event, it didn't do him much good when his turn came to testify. Hoffa was tough, chunky, very street smart, and spoiling for a fight. In his early appearances he wore loud ties, brightly coloured socks, and suits that looked like they'd been tailored by Kresge's. Later, he donned stylish grey suits and dark ties. He always came into the hearing room with a cocky strut, tight-faced and surrounded by tough-looking aides.

Hoffa constantly dodged questions, claiming bad memory and good "forgettery," repeating endlessly, "To the best of my recollection I cannot remember." Or, as he answered one question, "I can't remember nuthin' in the chokin' department." His elusiveness drove Bob Kennedy nuts. To make it worse, Hoffa would taunt, "Now, take it easy, Bobby." Or, "Bobby, don't get so worked up." Hoffa knew Kennedy hated to be called "Bobby" by strangers.

On such occasions you could see Kennedy's eyes burning into his adversary as he tried to control his temper. Sometimes they would glare at each other for two or three minutes without a word being said. Usually Kennedy would carry on, but sometimes he would ask one of the senators to continue the questioning until he could calm down. Meanwhile, Hoffa would sit there smirking, gulping a glass of water and swilling the water around his teeth.

I found it fascinating to watch the clash of wills. I have never seen two people project their hatred for each other with such intensity. At one point, Kennedy told me he believed Jimmy Hoffa was "genuinely evil."

One night about nine o'clock and long after the day's hearing ended, Kennedy gave me and a couple of other reporters a drive home. As we headed down the hill from the Senate Office Building, we passed the offices of the Teamsters Union. The lights on the top floor where Hoffa's office was located were ablaze. "If that son of a bitch is still working, then we should be, too," he said, wheeling the car around and going back to the office. I got a cab home. A few years later, Pierre Salinger, who was then a Bob Kennedy aide and later John Kennedy's White House press secretary, told me a similar story. Apparently Kennedy would often go back to work if he saw Hoffa's lights still burning.

Most nights, Robert Kennedy worked late at his office and sometimes I and a few reporters would chat with him for half an hour or so after the day's testimony. Bob couldn't be home with his family very much during this period, so his family came to him. His wife Ethel would be on hand at the hearings and sometimes his children were there, sometimes his mother, sometimes his sister-in-law, Jacqueline.

This was the first time I saw a lot of Jackie, though I'd met her in 1953 when she was the "Inquiring Photographer" for the *Washington Times Herald* covering Eisenhower's inauguration, and later in that year I'd run into her from time to time as she prowled the corridors of Capitol Hill looking for people to question for her photographic column. In fact, long before they met romantically, she had snapped John Kennedy's picture and interviewed him for her column. At the Senate Rackets Committee hearings, Jackie would sit at the press table and we'd chat occasionally, but my initial impression of this dark-eyed, heavy-browed Dresden doll was that she was slightly snooty. Certainly she was not "one of the boys," as Ethel Kennedy was. While you could joke, argue, and talk freely with Ethel, there was a reserve, almost an invisible barrier, with Jackie.

Ethel would gossip with us at the press table and burst into applause if Bob made a good point in his questioning of witnesses. Whenever this happened, he'd look over to her with a shy little smile, then a frown and a quiet shake of his head. When the day's testimony ended, often she and Bob would walk out of the hearing room holding hands, chirping to each other and looking like a couple of newlywed teen-agers.

The hearings, which ended in mid-1959, revealed that the Teamsters hired and fired mayors and police chiefs in many cities and towns, bribed and paid off, bombed, broke arms and legs, murdered, and worked closely with small-time and big-time criminals. For a reporter, it was the best show in town. For the Kennedys, it was a political platform. They made headlines daily, gaining a nationwide reputation as youthful, hard-hitting, anti-crime crusaders who had the Teamster and Mafia bad guys on the run. Actually, the hearings didn't do much to lessen crime, but, sparked by the efforts of Senator Kennedy, new legislation was passed to lessen the chances of criminal control of union locals.

The hearings gave me a chance to get to know the two men who came to represent for me the standard of achievement for those in public service. At this point I already admired both John and Bob Kennedy; in time I came to venerate them. As early as 1957 I wrote an article for the *Windsor Star*, the headline of which was: "Young Men With Future. Inquiry Brings Fame to Kennedy Brothers." I was attracted by the quickness of their minds, their dedication and determination, and their growing sensitivity to the underdog. More than most politicians they inspired strong emotions of both love and hate. They generated a kind of excitement that is rare on the political scene.

To idealize is to overestimate, and perhaps my admiration for Bob and Jack Kennedy undermined to some extent my professional detachment as a reporter. That is a risk all of us run, and in retrospect there likely were a few occasions, especially at the end, when my admiration got in the way of reporting them dispassionately. Though both men would be central figures through the 1960s, it was Bob who particularly impressed me from the start.

Washington, D.C., 1958-60 ...

While the Kennedys were gaining fame with their probing into organized crime and big labour, Vice-President Richard M. Nixon was making the most of a thankless job. Eisenhower used Nixon essentially as a political fixer: he was sent to patch things up or to make suggestions to Senator Joseph McCarthy or to assuage conservative Republicans if Ike made a "liberal" utterance. Occasionally he would be the one to fly a political kite for the administration, such as the proposal in 1954 to give sharply increased support to the French in Indochina, a move Eisenhower subsequently decided against because of negative public reaction to Nixon's statement. Nixon also did a great deal of travelling overseas, visiting fifty-three countries in the eight years of his vice-presidency and learning a great deal about foreign affairs in the process.

But Nixon anguished over Ike's indifference to him personally. He was never a friend of the President's, never a confidant. This was never more obvious to reporters and to the public than in the mortifying moment at a presidential news conference in August, 1960, when Eisenhower was asked what ideas his vice-president had proposed that he had adopted. Sitting in a seat two rows from him, I could see Ike's face grow crimson as he paused a moment and then told us, "Well, if you give me a week, I might think of one. I don't remember." Most of us gasped; we couldn't believe our ears at Ike's putdown of his own vice-president. A few years later, Kennedy White House aides fed us a quotation from British Prime Minister Harold Macmillan. Macmillan, in conversation with Kennedy, quoted Eisenhower as telling him that Nixon had never been to Ike's presidential retreat, Camp David, in the Maryland Catoctin mountains. "I wouldn't have him on the place," Ike was supposed to have said.

But Nixon did have a couple of heroic moments during Ike's second term. He undertook a "goodwill" tour of Latin America in the spring of 1958, which climaxed in Caracas, Venezuela, with anti-American "killer mobs" battering his car, smashing its window, and endangering his life. His Secret Service guards drew their guns, expecting a final assault on the car, but at the last minute the arrival of Venezuelan troops drove off the screaming, spitting, rock-throwing mob. Eisenhower was so alarmed that he had the U.S. Marines ready to move in. This proved unnecessary, and Nixon arrived home on May 15 as a conquering hero.

I went out to the airport to see him return. In an extraordinary display of respect for Nixon's courage under fire, Eisenhower himself was there, along with the entire cabinet, most of the Congress, about thirty ambassadors, and more generals and admirals than I could count. Nixon was dumbfounded by the scene and his eyes brimmed with tears as he came down the ramp.

His other international moment of triumph came in Moscow a year later, in July, 1959, where he met Nikita Khrushchev. He had a grudging admiration of Khrushchev, calling him "a bare-knuckle slugger who gouged, kneed and kicked," a characterization not entirely unworthy of Nixon himself. This was the time of the famous "Kitchen Debate" at an American exhibition in Moscow displaying U.S. products. Touring the exhibition, Khrushchev suddenly stopped at one point near a kitchen display and in front of everyone started arguing with Nixon, who had commented that his father owned a general store in California. "Oh, all shopkeepers are thieves," Khrushchev responded, and the debate was on.

Nixon said there were thieves everywhere, including the Soviet Union. Then they argued the merits of washing machines, and before hastily scribbling reporters and befuddled Soviet and American officials, Nixon and Khrushchev compared their economies, compared military strength, and argued about ultimatums. Nixon then said they should argue no more and Khrushchev said, "Thank the housewife for letting us use her kitchen for our argument."

It was a rare public glimpse of high-level international debate and Nixon won hands down. The incident suggested his developing skill in the world arena and he fully exploited his "Kitchen Debate" in later years.

During the visit he and Khrushchev had private debates, too, which Nixon reported were "tough, forceful, and earthy." Earthy, they certainly were, as Nixon told a group of us a couple of years later. He said the Soviet leader criticized him for making anti-Soviet statements while in Moscow and told Nixon his remarks were "shit" and that "Fresh shit stinks. People should not go to the toilet where they eat."

In September, 1959, a few weeks after this famous encounter, I had a chance to observe Khrushchev in person on his official visit to the U.S. Coming as it did on the heels of McCarthyism and in the thick of the Cold War, the impact he made is even more remarkable.

Eisenhower was clearly uncomfortable with the trip even though he had agreed to allow it. Khrushchev arrived in Washington on a warm early September day and I watched him bounce down the airplane steps with the Stars and Stripes and the Hammer and Sickle flying side by side. He carried a black homburg which he continually put on and took off. When he began his airport arrival speech, he slammed the homburg on a brass pole beside him and it dangled there until he finished. The famous Ike grin became a scowl and he remained sourly correct as he watched Mr. K. upstage him.

I followed Khrushchev during part of the tour, which took him from Washington to Los Angeles, an Iowa corn farm, Chicago, and New York. Even back in those Cold War days he could have won a lot of American votes. He was a master at dealing with the public: glib, colourful, jovial, emotional, at ease when "pressing the flesh." He was on the go from dawn to midnight, and full of surprises. Had he been born an American, I'm sure Khrushchev could have become a political power in the U.S.

Nikita Khrushchev was an extraordinary man to watch at relatively close range. To put it simply, he was a ham. He was constantly kidding reporters. "Capitalist press," he would yell at us, making the most of his few words of English. "Goot morgen," he'd smile at us at the start of each day. "Vurry goot. Peace. Peace." Then he'd bustle off in his brisk waddle, joking in Russian, waving to people and sometimes shaking hands with the soft, warm hands he claimed had once worked a miner's pick and shovel.

Although Khrushchev was renowned for his drinking, I never saw him drunk as he downed wine, champagne, and vodka at almost every stop. He loved American hot dogs, and once in a meat plant in Chicago, while gulping a hot dog slathered in mustard, he saw his official guide, the very proper Bostonian Brahmin Senator Henry Cabot Lodge, awkwardly picking at his hot dog as if it were some strange, foul-tasting object. "Eat your hot dog, capitalist pig!" Khrushchev laughed at Lodge.

To reporters and sometimes in speeches when Khrushchev wanted to emphasize he was telling the truth about something, the world's leading atheistic Communist would say, "I'll swear on a Bible that is correct." Occasionally, he'd get angry with our questions. At a news conference in Washington, he bristled at what he felt were critical questions about Soviet policy, telling us, "If you're going to throw dead rats at me, I can throw dead cats at you." During the visit Khrushchev threw a "dead cat" at veteran, granite-faced Foreign Minister Andrei Gromyko, telling us, with Gromyko at his side, that he was "a good boy" because he does just what he's told to do. That may explain Gromyko's extraordinarily long career as Soviet foreign minister.

Once or twice we saw Khrushchev at the start of private meetings with U.S. government officials, businessmen, or labour leaders. There, as in public, he couldn't stay still. He'd jump up out of his chair and walk around the room, his voice rising and falling in his rapid-fire way of speaking. Sometimes he'd poke his host in the ribs or laugh at a joke on himself. He argued forcefully in those meetings for the virtues of the Soviet system. He was enormously proud of his country's scientific achievements, especially in space, and he reacted in anger to what he felt were any slights. "Do not treat us like poor relations," he would yell. But we were all taken aback when Louisiana Senator Allen Ellender came out of one session with him and told us he was convinced Khrushchev "was clearly a committed Communist."

Khrushchev was forever offering glib sayings. So much so that we told him he was known to us as "The Sage of Moscow." He liked that. He had a Russian saying for just about every situation. "He who wants to have eggs must put up with the cackle," he'd say. Or, "When you lose your head, you don't care over losing your hair." "Repetition is the mother of knowledge." "Every duck praises its own pond." And, "You won't catch an old sparrow napping."

He liked to call himself an "old sparrow," although with his more than 200 pounds bulging on his five-foot-six-inch frame, he was more like a fat pelican. In fact, at dinners his wife Nina would sometimes tap his finger as a warning to eat more slowly. He gulped his food, cramming a thickly buttered roll, a piece of meat, and a potato into his mouth all at the same time. He shovelled in his food with his head bent only a few inches above his plate. Frequently, with an elaborate flourish he would wipe his mouth with his big napkin, sometimes to a stern-eyed admonition from Nina, who worried about his table manners.

Once he had finished eating, usually well ahead of everybody else, he would start talking. At a Washington dinner with the Central Intelligence Agency's Allen Dulles, Khrushchev joshed him, saying, "I know you. I read the same reports as you do. Why don't we save a lot of money and combine our spying so we don't have to pay twice for it."

Khrushchev's American antics were embellished a year later when, in the fall of 1960, he addressed the United Nations General Assembly in New York. Among the other world leaders who spoke on that occasion was British Prime Minister Harold Macmillan. I was in a radio booth above the General Assembly while Macmillan was speaking. Angered at something Macmillan said, Khrushchev took off his shoe and began banging it on his desk. Looking utterly puzzled, Macmillan paused in mid-speech and then, with great irony, asked if he could have a translation of the Soviet premier's comment.

Later that September John Diefenbaker also spoke to the General Assembly. Ever after, during political campaigns, he claimed that the shoe-banging incident had happened while he was attacking the Soviet Union for its treatment of minorities. It was a good story, demonstrating Diefenbaker's concern for the oppressed. The trouble with the story was that it didn't happen that way. But Diefenbaker repeated it so often in speeches and private conversations that he must have come to believe it himself.

Washington, D.C., May 27, 1959 ...

One man who would have sought to prevent the Khrushchev visits to the U.S. and the United Nations was John Foster Dulles, but he had died shortly before the trip. Dulles had been plagued by many illnesses in his lifetime, including phlebitis, malaria, a slipped disc, a hernia, diverticulitis, and severe hay fever. But it was cancer that finally killed him.

Dulles's funeral was one of the major stories I covered that year and was a landmark in my journalistic career because it was my first television news assignment for the CBC.

Actually, at the time I wasn't particularly excited about doing CBC television reports because they took much longer to prepare than radio reports, were more complicated, and paid the same: $25 each. But I felt the future lay in television and I wanted to learn as much as I could about this new medium of communication. The challenge of television was irresistible.

In those days, CBC did not have its own TV camera crew in Washington so we rented a crew from UPI-Movietone for the events we covered. The crews were grizzled veterans of the newsreel days, reminding me of an old movie I'd seen as a kid called *Too Hot To Handle*. In it Clark Gable was a cynical, tough-talking, hard-drinking newsreel cameraman filming the Japanese invasion of China in the late 1930s. The Movietone crews had been everywhere and seen everything from the war in the South Pacific to the invasion of Normandy, from

FDR's first campaign to the flight of the *Hindenburg*. To my relatively innocent eyes, they were something akin to minor gods. But, of course, I never let that feeling show and in talking with them sought to be as tough and world-weary as they.

This first TV news assignment was relatively simple: direct the cameraman in shooting a hundred feet of film of the funeral cortège coming out of the church and then shoot more film of the burial at Arlington Cemetery. When it was all over, I did a "stand up top and tail" at the gravesite. This meant doing an on-camera lead into the film footage and some concluding on-camera remarks standing in the same place. I did a voice track to cover the funeral footage and then we gave the film to a motorcycle messenger who rushed off to the airport to catch the first plane to Toronto. It was a long way from today's videotape recorders and satellite hook-ups. But from now on, with increasing emphasis, television was going to be a big part of my professional life.

My most vivid memory of that day was watching in fascinated apprehension as eighty-three-year-old West German Chancellor Konrad Adenauer almost fell into the Dulles grave. He'd been watching the casket arrive and was backing up as it approached, backing straight toward the grave. No one wanted to upset the dignity of the moment by shouting out a warning from twenty yards away, although more than dignity would have been upset if he'd fallen in. At the last instant, a Secret Serviceman grabbed Adenauer's arm and steadied him off to the side. I caught a smile flicker across the face of Dulles's younger brother Allen, still CIA chief, who observed the scene. It was a hint of the chasm of difference between Foster and Allen Dulles, something I would learn more about a few years later.

Don Minifie and I collaborated on coverage of the Dulles funeral, but he was never entirely comfortable with the technical paraphernalia of television. He had worked for so many years in radio and print, and the new medium seemed alien to him. "They tell you to be natural ... be relaxed," he told me. "And yet there are all those lights pouring down on you, cameramen looking at you, soundmen checking you, someone screaming time cues in your earplug, and the bloody producer telling you what to do when he doesn't know a damn thing about the story. It's not natural at all. The whole thing is, in fact, an unnatural act."

Anchoring the Quebec results in a federal election some time later, Don showed his defiance of TV technology. While he was giving the results on air, the director spoke to him through his earplug, giving him direction on what to say next. That's one of the challenges of live programming, to keep talking while simultaneously one and sometimes two people are talking to you with instructions. But Don preferred to do one thing at a time. So he suddenly stopped giving the Quebec results and, still looking at the camera but now listening to the director's voice in his ear, started nodding, shaking his head, and talking to the director, all to the utter mystification of the unknowing audience across the country. "Yes ... yes ... no, I don't think so ... why?" he said. The director quickly realized what was happening and decided to keep quiet. Then Don went back to giving the results.

A few weeks before Dulles died he was visited by the eighty-four-year-old Winston Churchill, who had retired as Prime Minister four years earlier. I covered Churchill's four-day visit to Washington and watched the aging but still impish British statesman come wobbling down the airplane steps into the arms of Dwight Eisenhower, who said, "Hello, my dear friend. Delighted to see you." He held a gold-handled cane in one hand and made a V for Victory sign with the other. I watched his fringe of white hair flutter in the breeze, his blue polka-dot tie giving a jaunty air to the old cherub.

He didn't spend much time with reporters but at least I got to ask him one question: whether he'd be going to Canada. He wasn't, he replied, saying, "I am indeed sorry that the brevity of my stay makes it impossible for me to visit Canada and see many of my old friends." Actually, it was a useless question since I already knew the answer, but I couldn't resist asking it anyway just to be able to say I'd once talked to the great man.

Another visitor from London I covered was Queen Elizabeth, who had come to Washington in the fall of 1957. The last time I had covered her was for BUP when she was Princess Elizabeth. In Washington, she seemed nervous. As I followed her around the city, she would go through the same uneasy motions every time: tug notes out of her purse before speaking, fold them back and forth in her hands, swallow several times, and then begin. It's small wonder she was apprehensive, because the American photographers and reporters were so aggressive. "Hey, Queen," I heard one shout on a supermarket tour, "don't just stand there, do something." Or "Hey, Queen, look this way!"

Covering the high and mighty in Washington during the late 1950s was sometimes interspersed with covering less awesome but equally fascinating characters, such as baseball's legendary Casey Stengel. We met briefly before he was due to testify at a Senate hearing in 1958 on the application of anti-trust legislation to baseball. I was duly impressed until he opened his mouth. In our conversation and in his later testimony, a torrent of words flooded out, few of which had any

Photos 1 and 2: Mother and father at the time of their marriage.

Photos 3 and 4: As a pre-schooler and a high schooler.

Photo 5: Tapping out copy at an IFAP conference in Rome in 1953.

Photo 6: Arriving in Nairobi, Kenya, with delegates to the 1954 IFAP conference.

5

4   6

7

Photo 7: With President Eisenhower and radio-TV farm programmers in the White House Rose Garden in 1955. (U.S.D.A. Photo)

Photo 8: Interviewing Richard Nixon during his unsuccessful 1962 campaign for the governorship of California. (CBC Photo)

Photo 9: Interviewing Pierre Salinger during the Cuban missile crisis of October, 1962. (CBC Photo)

Photo 10: During visit with American Nazi Party leader George Lincoln Rockwell in 1963 at his Arlington, Virginia, headquarters. (CBC Photo)

8

9

10

11

Photo 11: In a Cuban sugar cane field near Camaguey with Ché Guevara and producer Don Cameron in 1963.
(Photo by Eddie Chong)

Photo 12: With young Cuban revolutionaries and CBC soundman Eddie Chong.

Photo 13: Rio, 1963.

Photo 14: With producer Bill Cunningham at the 1966 Rio Carnival.

13

12

14

Photos 15 and 16: An awkward equestrian encounter on a Uruguayan estancia while filming the introduction to our *Newsmagazine* coverage of the 1967 Punta del Este summit conference.

Photo 17: A strolling 1967 interview on the Uruguayan economy.

Photo 18: Anchoring the 1965 Canadian election with Norman DePoe.
(CBC Photo by Robert C. Ragsdale)

15

16

17   18

19

20

Photo 19: Feeding a radio news report to CBC Toronto from the Washington studio in 1966.

Photo 20: With CBC French network correspondent Judith Jasmin and soundman Richard Ayo in the CBC Washington office studio.

Photo 21: That Old Gang of Mine: CBC correspondents in 1965 gather for their *Year End Report*. From left to right: Michael Maclear; Peter Reilly; author; David Levy; Tom Gould; James M. Minifie; Norman DePoe; Phil Calder; Stanley Burke.
(CBC Photo by
Robert C. Ragsdale)

Photo 22: Norman DePoe.
(CBC Photo by
Robert C. Ragsdale)

Photo 23: Don Macdonald, CBC Chief News Editor in the mid-to-late 1960s.

22

21

23

24

Photo 24: Doing a television report from President Lyndon Johnson's Oval Office. (CBC Photo)

Photo 25: About to take a $20-a-block taxicab in the Dominican Republic Civil War of 1965.

Photo 26: Interviewing Ronald Reagan at his California ranch during his successful 1966 campaign for governor. (Photo by William Harcourt)

Photo 27: Discussing economics and philosophy with a topless San Francisco shoeshine girl for a TV documentary during the 1966 congressional elections. (Photo by William Harcourt)

26

25   27

28

29

30

Photo 28: Interviewing U.S. Marine ''grunts'' at their sandbagged outpost near Pleiku, Vietnam, 1967.

Photo 29: Having lunch in the Officers' Mess at Da Nang with cameraman Neil Davis (left) and an escort officer.

Photo 30: Coming back from a helicopter sortie with Neil Davis.

Photo 31: Walking with actor Paul Newman, who was campaigning for Senator Eugene McCarthy in the 1968 New Hampshire presidential primary.
(CBC Photo)

Photo 32: Talking with Governor George Wallace of Alabama during his presidential campaign of 1968.
(CBC Photo)

32

33

34

Photo 33: Covering Bob Kennedy's final campaign, the 1968 California presidential primary. (CBC Photo)

Photo 34: Conducting one of the last interviews Bob Kennedy gave, aboard his campaign train in California's Central Valley during the final few days of his campaign for the presidency. (CBC Photo)

relationship to the other. Only Casey knew what he meant and he wasn't telling in any language comprehensible to mankind.

During his testimony he was asked by the committee chairman, Senator Estes Kefauver of Tennessee, why he thought baseball should be exempted from the anti-trust legislation. Casey, in vintage "Stengelese," replied: "Because in what other business can you retire at the age of fifty years with a pension, and the second thing about baseball is that it is interesting to the public and the owners' own fault if they don't improve their ball clubs."

Senator Kefauver said he didn't quite understand. "Well," said Stengel, "if I was a chamber of commerce member I would not want a team to leave a city because it puts money in the city and we are drawing tremendous crowds because of our overseas broadcasting and more parking and so forth because you can't drive a car on a highway which is very hard these days if you are over forty-five. And besides baseball is cleaner than any other business in 100 years."

The senator was still puzzled. "Well," said Casey, "you take in Japan, where they put 45,000 fans in the ball park over there where the people are trying to play baseball with small fingers, that's what I mean."

A clearly befuddled Senator Kefauver gamely tried again, asking Stengel whether he thought the World Series should be made truly international with other countries competing against American teams. Casey scratched his head and said, "Well … you have a good argument there, and once I had a team in the Navy and players on the ship when they were on the land, too long I wouldn't play them. See what I mean."

The senator didn't. Neither did those of us listening transfixed. In a final burst of exasperation Senator Kefauver asked Stengel about his own background. "Well," Stengel said, "a few times I was discharged you can call it discharged, there is no question I had to leave but in the last ten years naturally the Yankees have had great success with a ball club that has got the spirit of 1776 and I have been in baseball forty-eight years and there must be something good about it."

With that, Senator Kefauver thanked Stengel and banged the gavel to end the testimony, shaking his head in disbelief. Looking at my notes years later, I realized Stengel rarely ended a sentence. He just kept on going until he was interrupted.

Washington, D.C., January 2, 1960 …

On January 2, 1960, John Fitzgerald Kennedy announced his candidacy for the presidential nomination of the Democratic Party. That noon just about every reporter in town crowded into the Senate Caucus Room to hear the formal announcement. It was the same room in which he'd gained so much attention during the hearings of the Senate Labor Rackets Committee and the same room where Joseph McCarthy's battle with the Army had finally ruined his career. The Kennedy announcement was one of the worst-kept secrets in town since he had talked relatively freely about his ambitions and had already rented a campaign office and hired a staff including Pierre Salinger as public relations chief.

During 1958 and 1959 a few of us would sometimes chat with him after a day's hearings of the Senate Rackets Committee. He'd talk to us either in the Senate Caucus Room where the committee met or in his own office. (Ironically, his office was just across the hallway from Vice-President Nixon and they would occasionally drop in on each other to exchange gossip.) Over the course of these conversations Kennedy's philosophy seemed to me to evolve, especially as he got closer to making his announcement. He leaned more to the left in world politics, only slightly left of centre in domestic economic policies, and a bit further left in social policies. But he was by no means the darling of the Democratic liberals and he viewed them with scepticism.

He made it clear to us he was impatient with what he called "liberal utopians" and criticized them for believing power compromised the purity of their philosophy. He was a pragmatic liberal-centrist who believed power should be used to improve things bit by bit. He was wary of sweeping solutions. He felt you had to "endure the gap" between what you want and what you can get.

Years later, Pierre Salinger and I discussed this in a Chicago hotel room late one night and he complained to me, "You guys all thought Kennedy was essentially enjoying only the exercise of power. He did that, sure, but there was much more. It was power he wanted to exercise to achieve things ... his New Frontier ... a new kind of liberalism building on Roosevelt and Truman. And above all, he wanted to exercise power to pursue a peaceful world. So it wasn't just for the pure exercise of power for the sake of it."

Whatever Kennedy's true motives, he was off and running. But at best, most of us rated his chances at a relative long shot. In spite of his style, glamour, and money, at forty-two he was too young, too brash – and he was Catholic. The party old guard was suspicious of him, and the liberals disdainful. So the Kennedy strategy was to get attention by winning the primaries, and then use those victories to leverage the party establishment's support as the candidate who could beat Richard Nixon for the presidency.

In March, he swept through New Hampshire in victory; in April he won Wisconsin; and in May, most important of all, he submerged Hubert Humphrey in West Virginia. West Virginia did three things for Kennedy. It made him the clear front-runner; it made him face and conquer the fear of his Catholicism in that predominantly Protestant state; and it brought Kennedy face to face with poverty.

Going with him into the tarpaper-shack homes of jobless coal miners, or going down into the mines with him, I could see him literally transformed from someone who thought of poverty in terms of statistics to thinking in terms of fellow human beings. For the first time, it seemed to me, it hit home to him that there was real human suffering as a result of unemployment or dangerous working conditions. It was the most important lesson he learned in the primary campaigns. It gave him sense of humanity that he had previously lacked.

After West Virginia, the "Stop Kennedy" campaign began. Humphrey complained, "Kennedy is the spoiled candidate and he and that young emotional juvenile [Bob] are spending with wild abandon." Lyndon Johnson referred to Kennedy as "a young kid" or "young Jack" and said a president needs "a little grey" in his hair. Harry Truman said Kennedy was too young ... "wasn't dry behind the ears yet." "May I urge you," Truman told Kennedy, "to be patient."

Patience was never a Kennedy virtue. But even we reporters travelling with him were startled when he responded to this counter-attack in a speech. Yes, he was young. So, too, was Thomas Jefferson when he wrote the Declaration of Independence, and George Washington when he commanded the Continental Army, and Christopher Columbus when he discovered America. We expected him to compare his age to Jesus Christ. In fact, according to his speechwriter, Ted Sorensen, Christ had been in the script but had been crossed out as going just a bit too far.

The other basic criticism, echoed by Humphrey and other liberals, was that Kennedy was trying to buy the presidency with wild spending of his father's money. That criticism had been made repeatedly, and a couple of years earlier he had sought to deflect it at a Gridiron Club dinner with Washington correspondents by reading a telegram he said he had received from his multimillionaire father. "Dear Jack," he quoted, "Don't buy a single vote more than is necessary. I'll be damned if I'm going to pay for a landslide."

Going into the Los Angeles convention, Kennedy was the man to beat. He had his primary wins and was gaining growing, if grudging, support from party bosses, thanks to the tough backroom organizational skill of his brother Bob. His biggest worries were Lyndon Johnson on the right and Adlai Stevenson on the left. Talking to Kennedy insiders at the time and later, I got the impression that Kennedy would have gone to Johnson if he couldn't win.

He admired Stevenson, gave the nominating speech for Stevenson in 1956, and knew of the awe in which Stevenson was held by Democratic liberals, who revered his polished eloquence and his deep liberal beliefs. What was left of the old Roosevelt New Dealers in the party, led by no less than Eleanor Roosevelt herself, supported Stevenson. But Stevenson had a fatal flaw. He had a brilliant, unmatched capacity to define, but little capacity to decide. He worried endlessly over decisions and would spend many hours writing and perfecting his own speeches instead of giving the gist of what he wanted to say to a speechwriter. He even dawdled over the decision whether he would or would not run for a third time for the Democratic presidential nomination.

This 1960 Democratic Convention was the first I'd covered on the spot and it made me a convention addict. It also was the first convention where so much beauty met so many politicians. Hundreds of stunningly proportioned blondes, brunettes, and redheads greeted delegates and reporters with "come hither" smiles and outstretched hands. The hands, however, contained buttons for Kennedy, Johnson, Stevenson, or Symington. From seven in the morning until after midnight, the girls plied their button trade in hotel lobbies, corridors, parties, dinners, and occasionally on the street. I made an extensive survey of this political phenomenon and found Kennedy girls were mainly brunettes, Johnson girls blondes, and Stevenson girls more intellectual, often wearing glasses.

It was a fascinating education in American political tactics to watch the "Stop Kennedy" forces at work. Stevenson worked primarily in the open with rallies and big demonstrations. Johnson, on the other hand, worked mainly behind the scenes, in hotel rooms, private meetings with state delegations, and hideaway get-togethers with party power brokers.

The Johnson people also fought dirty. They told us Kennedy was not only too young, too Catholic, and too snobbish, but that he was physically unfit for the presidency. He had something called "Addison's Disease," they told us. Impressed with the revelation, I scribbled it down in my notebook, not having a clue as to what "Addison's Disease" was. I and a dozen others went to Salinger's offices in the

Biltmore Hotel to ask about it. He was stunned, having heard nothing about it. We waited around until Salinger came back to tell us Kennedy had an adrenalin insufficiency that was fully under control.

Johnson's big mistake was challenging Kennedy to a debate before the Texas delegation. Kennedy agreed, provided the debate would be in front of both the Texas and Massachusetts delegations. There must have been more reporters than delegates in that big room at the Biltmore as the two entered. I could feel the atmosphere snapping with electricity. It was a political High Noon and both men knew it. Kennedy had a habit of brushing back his hair when he was nervous, and I watched his grey-blue eyes dance back and forth across the delegates' faces, nodding and smiling. Johnson was more obviously nervous, licking his lips, elaborately waving to people, and seeking to appear to be in charge.

Both were earnest, friendly, and spoke of their accomplishments. Johnson could and did claim much more than Kennedy, but he couldn't resist little jokes about age and experience and "grey" in the hair. Kennedy deflected Johnson with wit, and with the most effective weapon he had: the growing belief among Democrats that Kennedy was the only Democrat who could beat Nixon. The debate was a draw. But a draw was fatal for Johnson, and it was the beginning of the end of his 1960 presidential campaign. For Kennedy, it was one down and one to go. He was jubilant about the Johnson encounter but increasingly worried about Stevenson.

And well he should have been. Stevenson was sparking enormous demonstrations in the hotels and at the convention at the Sports Arena. Hubert Humphrey came out for Stevenson, labour unions announced their support, and so did some farm groups. The critical California delegation was dominated by Stevenson supporters. We heard reports that what little support Kennedy did have in California was melting, and his support was melting, too, among Idaho delegates. With Eleanor Roosevelt leading the bandwagon, the Stevenson people were making a lot of effective noise.

I got to the Sports Arena Tuesday afternoon, July 12, at the absolute apex of the Stevensonian bandwagon. The building was surrounded by chanting Stevenson supporters with bands, signs, and the lustiest lungs in Los Angeles. Inside, more Stevenson supporters filled the observer seats and jammed the arena with the biggest demonstration of support any candidate had had.

By an advance tip, I was standing just at an entrance to the arena when Stevenson himself arrived. He was entitled to come to the convention floor as a member of the Illinois delegation, but traditionally, candidates for the party's presidential nomination just do not come to the convention itself before the voting. So arriving like this was a daring, tradition-shattering move that set off one of the loudest, longest convention demonstrations I've ever seen.

As Stevenson arrived, the cheers could be heard in San Francisco, and a slow-motion mob scene got underway. I was suddenly propelled by pushing crowds into Stevenson's arms. I shrugged apologies, and he smiled. There was no point in talking because you couldn't be heard. Then he, I, and a couple of dozen others with him were shoved through the inner doors and out onto the floor of the arena. It was a ragtag parade as we stumbled along the floor, totally interrupting whatever business had been going on from the platform. I sensed this was a crucial moment and tingled with both fear of being trampled to death and excited anticipation.

Finally, spinning away from Stevenson and the front of the column, I escaped to the side to nurse bruised arms, legs, and ribs and to make some notes. I watched Stevenson, perspiration dripping down his joyous face, slowly make his way to the platform. There was no plan for him to speak, but it was the only way the crowd could be controlled. This was clearly the moment. A brief, stirring message filled with Stevensonian eloquence and passion would sweep the delegates off their feet. He was introduced and another frenzied roar of approval shook the rafters, the roof, and probably the surrounding parking lot.

He grinned. He waved. And then he spoke. "I know who's going to be the nominee," he said. "The last man to survive." A few people laughed. More of them gasped. You could almost hear all the air whooshing out of the suddenly collapsing Stevenson balloon.

He'd told a joke. A weak one at that. The moment demanded, indeed commanded, a Churchillian call to arms, and he might well have won the delegates' support for the presidential nomination if he had met the moment. He had them in his hands. But at that moment of truth he failed, and he lost. After that, it was a Kennedy certainty.

The only uncertainty was what state would put him over the magic winning figure of 761 delegate votes. The Kennedy people told me they figured they'd go over the top on the first ballot with the Virgin Islands' four votes.

It was after 10:00 p.m. when the voting began with Alabama going for Johnson. Arizona went for Kennedy. Arkansas for Johnson. California for Stevenson. Colorado and Connecticut for Kennedy. Tension heightened and the Sports Arena grew quiet as the roll call progressed.

I pushed my way over to the Wyoming delegation where I saw Ted Kennedy waving his arms and arguing forcefully with the delegates.

I heard him say, "You could do it ... you could make history right now, for Christ's sake! Do it ... we'll remember you." At that point, Kennedy was eleven votes short of victory. The Wyoming delegates quickly huddled together with a rising crescendo of anticipation in the arena and a hundred journalistic ears, including mine, leaning in to hear their words. "Okay, ... it's Kennedy. We'll go for it."

And then the official announcement: "Wyoming, fifteen votes for Kennedy." There was pandemonium. Teddy Kennedy hugged whomever was next to him and then jumped onto a chair, nearly fell off, laughed, waved, shouted, and cheered as John Kennedy went over the top. Kennedy's winning total was 806 votes against 409 for Johnson, 86 for Symington, $79\frac{1}{2}$ for Stevenson, and $140\frac{1}{2}$ for others.

Even before the shouting settled down to a murmur, the speculation began about who Kennedy would choose as his vice-president. At the start of the convention I'd heard from a Kennedy source that Hubert Humphrey was favoured. But when Humphrey threw his support to Stevenson, Kennedy struck his name off the vice-presidential possibility list. His old friend Senator Henry "Scoop" Jackson was a contender and so was Senator Stuart Symington. By breakfast time the next day we'd heard reports that it might be offered to Lyndon Johnson. That dumbfounded almost everyone. Reporters couldn't think of a greater mismatch of personalities and style since the pairing of Franklin Roosevelt and "Cactus Jack" Garner in 1932.

At mid-morning, I ran into Jim Patton, an old friend of mine and president of the National Farmers Union. He was fuming at the idea. Labour leaders I saw echoed Patton's disbelief. The Stevensonians were aghast. A massive coalition of anti-LBJ forces began. "It's a sell-out" was their theme, as they complained Kennedy was betraying the liberals by going to Johnson. But it was already too late. We didn't know it at the time, but Kennedy had talked to Johnson the morning after his victory and offered him the vice-presidential spot. Although Kennedy admired Johnson's political and legislative shrewdness and liked him as a kind of roguish riverboat gambler, he didn't really want him as vice-president. It was a pro forma offer Kennedy expected to be refused.

All that morning and early afternoon, while we reporters were speculating, chasing rumours, and trying to pry information from Salinger, high drama was taking place in the Kennedy and Johnson rooms at the Biltmore Hotel. As historian and Kennedy family friend Arthur Schlesinger has reconstructed those hours, Bob Kennedy said of his brother, "He never dreamt that there was a chance in the world he would accept it.'' But Johnson immediately said ''Yes,'' and a stunned John Kennedy reported back to his brother, ''You just won't believe it ... he wants it.'' ''Oh my God,'' said Bob, ''what do we do?''

What they did, as I was told later by Salinger, was for Bob to go to Johnson and tell him there was opposition to him from liberals, but if Johnson still wanted the job, he could have it. According to Schlesinger, LBJ burst into tears and said, ''I want to be Vice-President.'' That was that, and Johnson became Kennedy's vice-presidential nominee. It also began a blood feud with Bob Kennedy that lasted till Bob's death. From that moment on, Johnson blamed Bob Kennedy for trying to take the vice-presidency away from him.

As we scurried about the Biltmore Hotel trying to pick up leads, none of us knew until late afternoon what was really going on and it was years before we were able to piece together the whole story. One key player, aside from Johnson and the Kennedys, was the publisher of the *Washington Post*, Phil Graham. As a friend of both Kennedy and Johnson, he worked feverishly behind the scenes to bring about the Boston and Austin political marriage. Working with Graham on this project was syndicated columnist Joseph Alsop, who also knew both men well.

At 4:00 p.m., we jammed into a sweaty basement hall in the Biltmore Hotel to hear Kennedy's choice. Even with the speculation, it was a stunning announcement when he said, ''Lyndon Johnson.'' As I look back on my notes, however stunned I may have been it seemed to me to make a lot of political sense for what was going to be a very close election race against Richard Nixon. It almost guaranteed Kennedy would win the key state of Texas and reassured the South. The liberals and labour would swallow their uneasiness because they had nowhere else to go. It comforted the power brokers of the Democratic Party. In retrospect, without Johnson, Kennedy would almost certainly have lost the election. He never forgot that, and personally treated Johnson well.

Chicago, July 26, 1960 ...

The 1960 Republican presidential nominating convention in Chicago was the quietest I would ever attend. Over the years of his vice-presidency, there had been some ''Dump Nixon'' agitation among Republican liberals. But with powerful conservative backing and his international triumphs in Caracas and Moscow, Nixon was a cinch to be the 1960 Republican nominee.

He had been a congressman at thirty-three, a senator at thirty-seven, vice-president at thirty-nine, and, at forty-seven was the obvious presidential candidate for his party.

At the convention, in spite of a "Draft Rocky" movement, Nixon was home free over Nelson Rockefeller and all other challengers. About the only major development was a party decision not to parade a group of trained elephants onto the convention floor. There was little hoopla, few pretty girls handing out buttons, and no razzle-dazzle. It was more like a morticians' convention.

One bonus for me at the convention, though, was an introduction to René Lévesque, who was then a correspondent for the CBC French network. We were doing our television reports from the Conrad Hilton Hotel in downtown Chicago in a room that had been converted into a temporary studio.

Early every evening we would broadcast our reports and invariably René would be late. I'd go first, and then the crew would wait around for him. Sure enough, with seconds to go before he was on the air, René would come bursting into the room with a big smile, hair flying, cigarette hanging out of the side of his mouth, looking utterly dishevelled and harassed. He'd slide into the chair behind the desk as the camera lights would snap on. Never did he have a script. He'd pull pieces of paper out of various pockets, squint at his notes, mutter and shrug to himself, and then suddenly he'd be on. I don't think he ever looked at his notes. He just talked, explained, gossiped, laughed sometimes, frowned sometimes, and altogether delivered a riveting, emotional, and highly opinionated report on what was going on.

His professional style was totally different from my own factual, non-editorializing reporting and that of Don Minifie, with whom I worked at the convention, and for that matter, totally different from anybody else. Along with Don, we'd go for a drink and gossip and exchange information after the program. René was warm, exuberant, and sometimes volatile, but always well-informed. He most definitely was not a Nixon fan.

I spent the election campaign about half with Kennedy and half with Nixon. At the start, Nixon led in the public opinion polls by a comfortable margin. But in their private feelings, reporters clearly favoured Kennedy. To switch away from covering Nixon to rejoin Kennedy was like coming home. With Nixon we were manipulated, endured, and isolated. With Kennedy we were manipulated as well, but we were also stroked and given access to the candidate. Kennedy liked reporters and so did most of his aides, unlike the leery Nixon staff. One major professional help Kennedy initiated was a transcript of what he said at almost every stop. We got a mimeographed copy of his comments usually within fifteen minutes. It certainly made note-taking much easier.

We travelled much of the time with Kennedy in his family Convair, called *Caroline* after his daughter. We'd all be aboard before Kennedy, who at the last minute would come springing up the folding metal steps. He had a small private compartment at the back where he would work over speeches at a desk, catnap on a narrow cot, or guzzle clam chowder and gossip with colleagues and reporters. Often he would come up to the front of the plane to chat with those of us he didn't see privately. When working on a speech he would wear glasses, which he always was careful to take off in public. (After the campaign Kennedy sent every reporter who flew with him a cigarette box with an etching of the *Caroline* and his autograph on top. I still have mine on my desk as a prized memento.)

Kennedy started his campaign on September 3 in California and ended it there two months and forty-five states later. (It did him no good in California because the state went to Nixon.) In the first part of the campaign, Kennedy's Catholicism was a particularly critical issue since a Catholic had never been elected president and there was a strong anti-Catholic campaign.

To Canadians who have elected Catholics, Baptists, Anglicans, and Presbyterians, this may seem strange, but the U.S. was deeply divided by the religious issue. During the campaign I interviewed Dr. Ramsey Pollard, president of the Southern Baptist Convention, who gave me a copy of a pamphlet being widely distributed that reprinted part of a recent sermon of his. "Roman Catholicism," he said, "is not only a religion, it is a political tyranny ... a political system that, like an octopus, covers the entire world and threatens those basic freedoms for which our forefathers fought." He shook his head and his white hair flew as he warmed up. "Boy, the pope will run the White House if Kennedy wins."

Nixon aides sought to exploit the issue and it's difficult to believe Nixon himself didn't know they were doing it. In the end, Kennedy overcame most of the political damage on the issue with his own forthright statements on separation of church and state. As a matter of fact, he probably gained more votes then he lost. Privately, he claimed that while the nuns and priests voted for him, the bishops voted for Nixon.

Kennedy brought one totally new element to American politics, what we reporters called "the Squealers," "the Jumpers," and "the Leapers." They were young girls whose mothers had done the same thing for Frank Sinatra years earlier, but whose presence had never been seen before in a U.S. presidential campaign. Landing at an airport in the Midwest, the South, the Northeast, or the West, we'd scramble off the plane first, and then watch Kennedy walk down the sometimes shaky steps of the *Caroline*. Invariably, the squeal would immediately rise from a thousand teen-age throats. As we followed him along while he shook hands, the Jumpers and Leapers, who jumped and moved ahead at the same time, and the Squealers began some leaping and squealing simultaneously. Kennedy was at first astonished by the reaction, but quickly began to like it. He only regretted most of them were too young to vote. "If we can lower the voting age to nine, we're going to sweep the state," he said at one airport.

One Kennedy quirk was that he simply hated to wear a hat – any kind of a hat. Because of support from the hatters' union, he reluctantly agreed once in a while to carry, but not wear, a fedora. I saw him flinch when an Indian chief put an Indian headdress on his head. He took it off as fast as he could. Before speaking to the American Legion in Miami, he grimaced as he jammed on a cap when he walked onto the platform. He took it off the instant he left.

When Kennedy, or any candidate for that matter, was meeting people, shaking hands, and main-streeting his way through crowds, I liked to be close to him to hear what was said. Although at first he seemed a little uneasy about this face-to-face and "pressing-the-flesh" campaigning, he quickly came to enjoy it. Most people were tongue-tied when they met him and just smiled and mumbled "good luck." Some asked after Jackie and some wanted his autograph. I saw him sign everything from arm casts to brassieres.

When Kennedy was speaking from a platform, I liked to get away from him and stand at the edge of the crowd to get the feel of his words and the mood of the crowd. Unlike Nixon, he essentially spoke up to his crowds, not down. He wouldn't be folksy, or corny, or use slang or clichés. He never talked about his childhood, as Nixon constantly did. He always had classical quotations for contemporary problems and used them, I suspect, to project intellectualism by association as much as to illuminate a thought.

With his voice hoarse, as it was one warm night in a downtown park in Jacksonville, Florida, and with his right hand chopping the air to emphasize his points, basically he had a simple message: "I want to get things done. I want to get this country moving again." As I listened to the comments at the edge of the crowd while he spoke that night in Jacksonville, it seemed clear to me that it was his image, not his philosophy, that won the crowd. They really didn't care that much about the so-called "missile gap" or the economy or Cuba or Matsu and Quemoy. What they cared about was his spirit, his vigour, his youth, and all the new-dawn freshness they saw in him. He infused them with his own zeal. He gave them hope, and he gave them optimism.

As the campaign progressed Kennedy became increasingly sensitive to the problems of blacks and began to speak out on civil rights. Although he was a latecomer to the black cause, he learned quickly. As he travelled around the country, particularly in the South, he met with black leaders (from the flamboyant Adam Clayton Powell to a black Baptist minister named Martin Luther King, Jr., who espoused Mohandas Gandhi's non-violent civil disobedience tactics), and Kennedy was confronted for the first time by the dehumanizing reality that faced the majority of his country's black citizens.

That sweaty night in Jacksonville, Florida, his rally in the park was attended by more blacks than whites. He said, "I speak for all Americans of whatever colour and I say the same in the North and in the South." On the question of civil rights, this was certainly true.

I stayed behind in Jacksonville and travelled slowly north through Georgia, Alabama, and Tennessee to get the reaction of blacks and whites to Kennedy. The Ku Klux Klanners, the white citizens' councils, and the white supremacists hated him. "I'd kill the bastard if I could," a white segregationist Baptist minister told me in Jacksonville.

In his office in Macon, Georgia, the Ku Klux Klan Imperial Wizard, His Lordship Robert Lee Davidson, wearing golden robes, a sheet draped partly over his shoulders, and sporting a brace of pistols, told me, "Kennedy is the greatest enemy of the South since Lincoln and Sherman. But we'll get him as we got Lincoln." "We don't want mongrelization of the races ... nigras aren't good enough to have the same rights as white folks have." He claimed there were five million Klan supporters in the South.

But the blacks loved Kennedy. And many southern whites, mostly reluctant to say so, admitted Kennedy probably was right, that the "War between the States" was long over and it was time for blacks to be accepted as fellow citizens. In fact, since the election was so close, it's fair to say that Kennedy would have lost Illinois, Michigan, Texas, and South Carolina and probably Louisiana had it not been for black support.

The 1960 presidential race was the first real television campaign. It revolutionized politics in the United States and, shortly thereafter, in Canada and the United Kingdom, too. Just nine years earlier, when I'd just arrived in Washington, I had watched my TV set in fascination as Americans were for the first time linked from coast to coast by television. There was Edward R. Murrow with two big TV monitors in front of him, one showing the Golden Gate Bridge in San Francisco and the other the Brooklyn Bridge in New York. Though it was a crude, early version of "linking" the nation that's done every night now in CBC's *The Journal* and other programs, then it was breathtaking.

We take if for granted now, but in 1951 it was a miracle on a twelve-inch black-and-white TV set. Only one in ten American homes had TV back then. By the 1960 presidential election, there was a TV set in almost every home. And that was Nixon's undoing in 1960.

Nixon was an excellent debater and he had successfully used television once before in his Checkers speech. He'd had eight years as Vice-President of the United States. So he just knew he'd wallop Jack Kennedy in their TV debate.

That September 26 night I watched the first debate with a group of correspondents gathered in front of a TV set. At 9:30 p.m. a Maybelline mascara commercial faded from the screen and up came Nixon and Kennedy. Nixon could have used some of the mascara. Within seconds, you could hear the intake of breath among the reporters and a sudden babble as we all asked the same question: "What's wrong with Nixon?" He looked like a "wanted" poster in the post office. Perspiration dribbled down his five-o'clock shadow. He seemed thin and frightened as his eyes darted back and forth and he licked his lips. By contrast, Kennedy looked dynamic, youthful, healthy.

If you listened only to the substance of the debate, however, Nixon did very well. On the words alone, I felt he won the contest, and those who listened on radio thought so, too. But seeing Nixon killed him. We live in a world of perceptions, and Nixon was perceived poorly by the TV audience. Seventy-five million people watched that debate and that was the moment Kennedy took the election lead. Nixon looked so bad his press aide, Herb Klein, had to issue reporters a news statement saying, "Mr. Nixon is in excellent health and looks good in person."

But Nixon learned a lot from that first debate. For one thing, he never again only put on "lazy shave" to cover his heavy beard; thereafter he slapped on heavy professional makeup. For another, he started wearing dark suits for TV, unlike the light one he wore on that night, which contrasted with Kennedy's elegance and reinforced his "used-car huckster" image. For a third thing, he tried to have a very cool studio to minimize his nervous perspiration.

The last point led to a fascinating little minuet I witnessed at the NBC Washington studio a couple of hours before the second Nixon-Kennedy debate. While touring the studio at NBC after feeding a couple of radio reports to CBC, I saw Kennedy's news aide, Pierre Salinger, looking over the studio, too, and turning up the thermostat to 75°F, presumably to make Nixon sweat more. Ten minutes later I saw Herb Klein come in to inspect the studio and he, too, examined the thermostat. He turned it down to 65°F. Pierre was outfoxed, I thought. But I was wrong. He came back into the studio about fifteen minutes later and, glancing furtively around, quickly turned the thermostat back up to 75. And there it stayed through the debate. Sure enough, Nixon sweated heavily throughout.

With the campaign nearing its end, Nixon grew worried, and when he was worried he fought dirty. At a Pittsburgh rally he said, "Here we go. From now on, I'm going to nail 'em every time." As we whistle-stopped with him in these final days in Pennsylvania, he warned us at news conferences and declared in speeches that Kennedy might well lead the United States into war. He said the price of everything would go up if Kennedy were elected. He said Kennedy would raise taxes and would give in to the Communists. Nixon said Kennedy was guilty of "lies, smears, and innuendoes."

In a conversation with one of Nixon's aides, several of us joked that Nixon must be getting desperate since he was getting so dirty. "Dirty?" the aide exclaimed. "Not at all. It's just the traditional earthy substructure of American politics." Nixon shovelled that "earthy substructure" for the rest of the campaign.

One thing I couldn't understand was why Nixon didn't unleash Eisenhower on the electorate early in that 1960 campaign. His aides kept saying privately that Nixon wanted to win "on his own" and not be tied to "Ike's" immensely popular apron strings. But eight days before the election, Ike finally was unleashed. It gave Nixon an enormous push. But not quite enough.

I was at NBC in New York on election night where the CBC was anchoring its election coverage. I was doing radio while Norman DePoe and Don Minifie were doing television. Early on, it looked like a Kennedy landslide. Connecticut reported first and overwhelmingly went for Kennedy. We began projecting a Kennedy triumph. But soon after, it was a different story. Through the night, we reported Kennedy's lead constantly shrinking or disappearing altogether.

It was a cliff-hanging night, decided in the end by a tiny handful of votes. Somewhere around four in the morning we were all dead tired, and more from exhaustion than wisdom I decided to flatly forecast Kennedy was the winner. After this was done, we quickly ended our broadcast and tottered back to the hotel for a couple of hours' sleep. In fact, however, it wasn't until half a dozen hours later that it became clear Kennedy was indeed the winner ... by a mere 118,000 votes out of nearly 70 million. Nixon didn't concede until one p.m. and even then he didn't do it personally, assigning press aide Herb Klein to read his concession.

Immediately there were accusations of skulduggery. Chicago Mayor Richard Daley was accused of voting the cemeteries as Kennedy won Illinois by 9,000 votes out of 4.7 million. In Texas, the Lyndon Johnson machine won the state for Kennedy (thereby proving the wisdom of Kennedy's LBJ choice in Los Angeles) by 46,000 votes out of 2.3 million. But some strange counts later came to light in Texas. In precinct 27 of Angelina County, for instance, there were eighty-six registered voters who, the count showed, voted 148 for Kennedy and 24 for Nixon.

To his credit, Nixon decided against legal appeal. "Our country can't afford the agony of a constitutional crisis," he told reporters. Besides, there may well have been just as much isolated political flimflammery among Republicans as among Democrats. Privately, Nixon told me a couple of years later during the California governorship campaign that any appeal would have taken "at least a couple of years" to go through the courts.

I went to the Senate to watch Nixon preside over his own political death when, as president of the Senate, it was his duty to declare officially that Kennedy had been elected President. In this case, Nixon was at his best. No matter how it must have killed him inside, he made a gracious, witty statement congratulating his former opponent.

Nixon's last official duty as Vice-President was to watch on the Capitol Hill steps as John F. Kennedy was sworn in on that frosty January day of 1961. Nixon seemed a forlorn, lonely, and exhausted man. Occasionally, he would look over to see the outgoing President Eisenhower and the incoming President Kennedy. In contrast to Nixon, Ike and JFK beamed under their silk top hats, at seventy the oldest-ever President (before Reagan) fading into memory and at forty-three the youngest-ever elected President beginning his brief, incandescent march across the pages of history.

By all odds, one might have thought that Eisenhower would be an exhausted volcano after his wartime leadership, eight years as President, a heart attack, and a stroke. But there he was, smiling and positively bouncing with vigour, his cheeks ruddy and his eyes bright. What made it all the more remarkable was the worn, care-ridden, taut-faced look of so many of his senior aides, including Nixon, who stood on the platform beside him after having shared his presidential and, for some, his wartime years.

As Kennedy read his inaugural address, my eyes flicked from the young man to the old man. Eisenhower's veteran colleagues on that platform let their eyes glaze over or wander through the crowd into the snowy Capitol Hill grounds. But not Eisenhower. He listened intently to every word. And then it was over. Ike shook hands with Kennedy, went off to a small private lunch, and, in the fading sunlight of a late winter afternoon, drove off to his Gettysburg farm. As I watched him leave the platform, he turned his back to go up into the Capitol building and it seemed to me the turning of his back was the turning of the last page in a chapter.

5 *THE NEW FRONTIER*

Washington, D.C., January 20, 1961 ...

It began snowing the night before the inauguration, and blowing and freezing. It was more snow than I'd ever seen in Washington and by the time it was over, eight inches blanketed the city, stopping traffic and making everybody late for everything. I had to hitchhike since taxis were impossible and buses took hours. But the snow brought an effervescent mood and people happily stopped to pick me up. Stalled cars littered the roads and ladies in minks hitched up their party dresses and staggered through the drifts to the pre-inaugural festivities. It seemed like New Year's Eve as the city celebrated the end of one era and the beginning of a new one.

President-elect John Fitzgerald Kennedy and his wife Jacqueline started out the evening at a party at the home of their old friend, *Washington Post* publisher Phil Graham, who had done as much as anyone to put Kennedy in the White House, then they went on to an inaugural concert at Constitution Hall, and finally they attended a gala organized by Frank Sinatra at the National Guard Armory.

Although I wanted to follow him as closely as possible on this "night before," because of the snow I decided to go only to the Sinatra gala. It turned out to be the biggest, noisiest, fanciest, and most liquid of all the inaugural parties, including the five formal inauguration balls the next night, with white-tie Democrats and their ermine- and mink-clad wives drinking gallons of free champagne. It was a lollapalooza of a party. The place was packed with Hollywood stars and TV personalities. The dance floor was a madhouse and at one point I saw two mink stoles

113

lying on the floor trampled by passing dancers. Policemen gave up trying to unsnarl the snow-clogged traffic jam outside the Armory and came inside to enjoy the party. One high-flying officer grabbed my tuxedo lapel, asking, "Where ish the free champagne, Charlie?"

As the evening wore on and the arrival of the Kennedys grew imminent, the Democrats were not so much drunk on the California champagne or the Scotch they brought with them as they were intoxicated with the presidential triumph, the Kennedy magic, and their first inauguration since 1948.

The Kennedys left the inaugural concert at intermission and, with police outriders and Secret Servicemen, drove the three miles through the snow, past a floodlit Washington Monument and on to the Armory. When they arrived, those of us inside could hear over the dance music and din the roars of greeting from the crowd outside and then the echoing shouts, "He's coming! He's coming!" And suddenly, there they were, Jack and Jackie walking to their box, beaming and waving at the dancers on the cavernous floor below and joking with a score of Kennedy family members and friends: his father Joe and mother Rose, Bob and Ethel, and other sisters, brothers, cousins, nephews, and in-laws.

I was always fascinated to see the Kennedys together because, among other things, they loved to chew gum with great gusto. A dozen Kennedys all in a row, their jaws moving up and down as they chewed in rhythmic unison, had the same effect as heads swivelling at a tennis match. I'd seen it at political rallies, at congressional hearings, and now, here, too, at the inaugural gala. Jackie, of course, didn't chew, and on this occasion the President-elect didn't either, although most of the others did.

As they watched the pandemonium on the dance floor below them, the Kennedy family and friends passed Scotch around and kept slapping each other on the back. In the box along with the Kennedy clan were singer Eartha Kitt, whom I watched arguing animatedly with her hosts, and Hollywood siren Angie Dickinson clinging to "Red" Fay, a South Pacific wartime pal of Kennedy's. On the dance floor I noticed playwright Arthur Miller with a bottle of champagne under one arm and a blonde under the other. Ethel Merman was there, as were Jimmy Durante, Tony Curtis, Janet Leigh, Frederic March, and others.

Midway through the evening, Kennedy and Jackie walked down the steps from the box to the dance floor, followed by Secret Servicemen and relatives and friends. They whirled past the dancers, constantly nodding, smiling, and calling out to friends. Jack would single out reporters who were dancing nearby and shout introductions to Jackie.

For the President-elect, the night ended about four in the morning after a post-midnight supper his father gave him at Paul Young's, a downtown restaurant. The guests included Gene Kelly and Nat Cole as well as family and friends. Four hours later, Kennedy was up and practising his inauguration address.

I covered him going to mass at a church near his Georgetown home and later followed him as he drove to the White House – carrying his top hat – to have coffee and a chat with Eisenhower. They spent a little less than an hour together and in that time I walked the mile-long parade route from the White House to the Capitol, where the inauguration ceremonies would take place.

It had stopped snowing toward dawn and the sky was blue with the occasional puff of white cloud, but it was still bitterly cold. Apart from the snow and the crowds, what I noticed most was the security – 5,000 soldiers and police were on hand. That doesn't seem such a large number now, but back in 1961 it seemed a veritable army. Flame throwers had been used to melt the snow in some areas and something called ''Roost No More'' had been sprayed on trees and buildings along the route to get rid of the starlings.

Walking gave me a chance to get the feel of the crowds. Among the men, women, and children waiting for the inaugural parade, an unusually large number of young people lined the route, which was packed ten deep. Many wore parkas and ear muffs because of the cold but their spirits were high as they laughed and beat their hands to keep warm. By the time I got to the Capitol, even with a sweater under my jacket and coat, I was frozen stiff and my fingers were too cold to scribble more notes.

Kennedy was about twenty minutes late arriving for his inauguration. This was appropriate since he was always late for everything else. As we stamped our feet and massaged our hands to keep warm, he kept putting on and taking off his top hat. Finally he put it aside and all of us in the press stand a couple hundred yards away took out our notebooks.

Richard Cardinal Cushing of Boston, an old Kennedy family friend, began with an endless invocation in what I thought was surely the most grating, twanging Boston Irish voice in all Christendom. At one point, I noticed blue smoke curling up from under the lectern and I felt certain it was a sign that the Cardinal should stop. It turned out to be a short-circuit in the electric wires of a heating system under the lectern and for a few moments there was fear the whole lectern would go up in flames.

Then New England poet Robert Frost began reading but stopped to complain that the sun was in his eyes and he couldn't see to read. Over the address system, we heard him mutter, "I'm not having a good light here at all. I can't see in this light." Lyndon Johnson quickly stuck out his hat to shield Frost's eyes. He then continued.

Contralto Marian Anderson, who had been the first black to perform in the White House, sang and then finally, at nine minutes to one, John F. Kennedy took off his overcoat, placed his hand on an old family Bible, and was officially sworn in as the thirty-fifth President of the United States.

As the young President gave his historic inauguration address, his Boston Irish accent added an unforgettable flavour and urgency to Theodore Sorensen's rolling cadences. Earlier, we'd been handed the text of his speech and while he spoke I scribbled notes with my be-numbed fingers. I noted his style of delivery, the reactions of the crowd and the dignitaries, and I watched to see if he was following the printed version of the text. He spoke for only a dozen minutes, then walked up the steps of the Capitol and went inside for lunch. I ran into the Capitol building, too, to the nearest typewriter in the Senate press gallery to write my stories, phone in a report to the CBC in Toronto, and at last try to get warm. The gallery staff helped us do that with some warming alcoholic liquids in honour of the day.

"The torch has been passed to a new generation of Americans," Kennedy had said, with puffs of frosty air popping out of his mouth and his finger jabbing at the air. The new generation he spoke of was the precise opposite of the one F. Scott Fitzgerald had written of forty years earlier, a generation, he said, that had "grown up to find all gods dead, all wars fought, and all faiths in man shaken." John F. Kennedy's new generation was proud, confident, and anxious to start "making things better."

The catch phrase of the new administration was the New Frontier, recalling FDR's New Deal while striking just the right tone of modernity. In the days following the election, as I had watched Kennedy assemble his team, his campaign rhetoric about a new generation of leadership had taken on real meaning.

Between the election and the inauguration two and a half months later, Kennedy flitted between the family compound at Hyannisport on Cape Cod, his father's cream-stucco mansion at Palm Beach, the thirty-fourth-floor penthouse at the Carlyle Hotel in Manhattan, and his own red-brick home in the fashionable Georgetown area of Washington. All the while he was choosing his cabinet, organizing his government, and studying a fifty-page takeover blueprint prepared for him by former Truman aide and future Johnson Defense Secretary, Clark Clifford.

The stories I did for CBC, the *Financial Post*, and other Canadian newspapers concentrated on who would be in the Kennedy cabinet and on the young couple who would live in the White House. After her 1953 high society wedding, Jackie had said, "I married a whirlwind ... people who try to keep up with him drop like flies." That was certainly true for those of us trying to keep up with Kennedy in those post-election days. Through December and into early January, I spent endless chilled hours waiting for announcements in front of Kennedy's home, a five-minute drive from the White House. Some neighbours took pity on us and invited us inside or passed out coffee and cocoa.

Together with other reporters, I waited and watched as would-be New Frontier officials walked up the porch steps, or as Pierre Salinger (who would become White House press secretary) or sometimes Kennedy himself would come out and tell us of new appointments.

The single most controversial appointment he made was naming his brother Bob as Attorney General. Years later, Bob told me he didn't want to be Attorney General and had told his brother "no," because it would be politically embarrassing. But Jack insisted; he said he needed his brother. He was certainly aware of the political criticism he'd get for such an appointment. He told his friend and neighbour, *Newsweek's* Washington bureau chief, Ben Bradlee, "I think I'll open the front door some morning about two a.m., look up and down the street, and if no one's there, I'll whisper, 'It's Bobby.'" He didn't quite do that, but he did open the door one cold day to tell us simply "It's Bobby." I later heard he had whispered to his brother just before the door opened, "Damn it, Bobby, comb your hair!"

In spite of the cold, you could sense a rising excitement in anticipation of the Kennedy takeover. New Frontiersmen were pouring into town. There had been nothing like it since the FDR New Dealers came to town in 1933. With the exception of Robert Kennedy as Attorney General and Robert McNamara as Defense Secretary, it was a relatively safe and quiet cabinet. The sparkle came from those who filled the lesser jobs ... the policy coal-shovellers on the Kennedy train, not the engineers.

These New Frontiersmen were young, bright, activist, articulate, and tough and had a confidence bordering on arrogance. They were hot-eyed, brainy enthusiasts, ready to go, and they offended the retiring Eisenhower appointees with their disdain of the past eight years and their anxiety to take over. You ran into them all over town that January, as they lined up at the starting gate.

At noon-hour on January 20, they began moving into their offices as assistant secretaries, deputies, legal counsels, and special assistants in every department from Agriculture to Defense.

This is one of the big differences between the American and Canadian systems. When we change governments, we change the politicians but few of the bureaucratic mandarins. When the Americans change, there is a whole new face to government from the cabinet officers right down to departmental bureau heads. It means the Americans can make significant policy changes much more quickly than we can. What they lose is continuity and experience.

As well as filing stories about the political transformation of Washington, I did a half-hour CBC *Newsmagazine* program on how Jack and Jackie met and what they were like privately. To this end, I spent a good bit of time chatting with and interviewing his secretary, the friendly and talkative Mrs. Evelyn Lincoln. "I knew he was going places when I first met him when he was a congressman," she told me, "and I wanted to go with him."

Much has been written about Kennedy's penchant for wenching. I certainly was aware of the gossip during his congressional days, but I never saw any first-hand evidence. As a presidential candidate he did seem especially interested in his beautiful, brunette stewardess-cum-assistant on the *Caroline*, Janet des Rosiers.

During any brief conversation I had with her, she was always friendly and very protective of Kennedy. The same was true of Pamela Tunure, another aide about whom much Kennedy gossip centred, especially when he had her appointed as Jackie's news secretary.

Although Evelyn Lincoln loved to talk about her boss, she was very protective about Kennedy's personal life. When I asked her once about all the stories of Kennedy's lady friends, she smiled and said, "Well, he certainly has a good eye." I always had the feeling Mrs. Lincoln didn't mind his female friendships too much and that she slightly resented Jackie.

Charles Bartlett, Washington correspondent for the *Chattanooga Times*, and his wife Martha had introduced Jack to Jacqueline Bouvier at a dinner party. "Their eyes met over the asparagus," Bartlett once told me. "And that was that."

Jackie brought class to the Kennedys. She was a cultured, shy, reflective society blueblood whose fierce independence enabled her to survive the rough and tumble *nouveau riche* Boston Irish Kennedys. On family picnics, they'd munch peanut butter sandwiches and guzzle Cokes while she'd eat *oeufs en gelée* and sip *vin rosé*. They liked touch football. She preferred ballet.

One afternoon back in 1958 I went over to interview Jackie in her Georgetown home. In private, she was warm and eager to be friendly. The apparently snooty air I had noticed at the Senate Labor Rackets Committee hearings turned out to be more a reflection of her fear of crowds and unease in a strange public environment. At home, she displayed an offbeat piquancy and a charming irreverence toward politics. Accused by her husband's political opponents of spending $30,000 a year on clothes, she had said, "I couldn't spend that much unless I wore sable underwear."

Altogether, Jackie was probably the most decorous, stylish First Lady since Dolley Madison held sway as White House hostess during the terms of both her husband James Madison and Thomas Jefferson, who was a widower.

Jackie didn't add brain power and political savvy as Eleanor Roosevelt had. (Robert Kennedy once commented, "Jack knows she'll never greet him with 'What's new in Laos?' ''). Nor did she melt into the background as had Mamie Eisenhower and Bess Truman. Instead, she gave an elegant sheen to the Kennedy White House and the New Frontier with her parties, her clothes, her artistic interests, her fox hunting and travelling.

Five days after the inauguration, Kennedy began the first of the live television news conferences. Thanks to Jim Hagerty, Eisenhower had given television equal place at presidential news conferences, but that was edited film. Now, there was to be live coverage.

There was great debate among the Washington correspondents as well as government officials about "going live" instead of having the news conferences recorded and vetted by the White House before being released. The argument against it was that the President could inadvertently reveal state secrets or make a mistake that would have major political, economic, or diplomatic reverberations. The news agencies, such as UPI and AP, were against going live, as were most newspapers, on the grounds that it would give television and radio an advantage since they would get the news first. They also argued that live television would encourage the more exhibitionist reporters to become carnival performers. James "Scotty" Reston of the *New York Times* thought the idea of live TV presidential news conferences was "the goofiest idea since the hula hoop."

But Pierre Salinger and most other White House aides disagreed. They thought it was a good idea, and so did Kennedy. They believed, as he did, that Kennedy could effectively exploit live television. So Salinger moved the news conference out of the old, cramped, so-called Indian Treaty Room in the White House Annex, where Eisenhower held his meetings with the media, to the spanking modern, spacious, blue-backgrounded State Department auditorium.

For that first Kennedy news conference on January 25, 418 of us were sitting in the State Department auditorium, marvelling at the relatively plush seats compared to the hard, folding chairs at the Eisenhower sessions. Promptly at 6:00 p.m. we all stood as Kennedy strode across the stage to a lectern, smiling broadly and followed by Salinger. "Good afternoon, and be seated," he said.

As 60 million Americans watched him, Kennedy announced the Soviet Union was releasing two American airmen who had been imprisoned and whose release Khrushchev had saved for a Kennedy announcement. "As a present," the Soviet premier later told the new President. Kennedy talked about Laos, the Congo, and domestic affairs with assurance, quickness, and wit. It certainly was very different from the stumbling Eisenhower syntax that we'd been used to for eight years.

Aware that he was living on a bull's-eye, Kennedy rehearsed each news conference carefully, with Salinger and other White House aides grilling him with the questions they expected to be raised. But he still had to be quick on his feet on many occasions. Kennedy held a total of sixty-three news conferences and rarely was caught off guard. He was also sharply aware of how to dress for television, how to use the lights and the camera angles to his best advantage, and what gestures were most effective. He always screened his news conference performances and passed his evaluations to Salinger, which ranged from "I could have done better with that one," to "That camera angle murders me." The time he spent in preparation and evaluation was time well spent. It was the principal way the public saw him and a good impression gave him important political clout in dealing with Congress.

There were usually about 200-300 of us at the Kennedy news conferences. Most of the questioning was done by correspondents whose regular, full-time beat was the White House. These White House regulars, representing the news agencies, the U.S. networks, and major newspapers, all had designated places in the front row while the rest of us scrambled for the closest seats we could get. Kennedy might also recognize a few other reporters at random. It was rare for any foreign correspondent to ask a question except for those from Reuters, which was such an important worldwide news agency.

Canadians and other foreign correspondents felt the news conferences were basically for the American media and that we shouldn't intrude too often with bilateral questions. Overall, I have always felt that presidential coverage by Canadian reporters is among the best balanced, perhaps because we are not as preoccupied as some of our U.S. colleagues with following a particular angle. With Kennedy we concentrated more on foreign policy than the American reporters and sought to put into perspective what the President said rather than simply regurgitating his words, as the U.S. news agencies tended to do. It was a good example of the importance of having Canadian reportorial eyes on Washington (and elsewhere for that matter). We provided Canadian readers, listeners, and viewers with a Canadian perspective on the news instead of simply parroting American-oriented stories.

In spite of earlier fears about television, reporters seldom misbehaved, although Kennedy was sometimes impatient with long, complicated, pontificating questions such as those that occasionally came from the thoughtful CBS newsman Martin Agronsky, now with PBS. Kennedy was amused by a very large, floppy lady with a heavy southern drawl named Sarah McClendon, who represented a number of Texas newspapers and who would identify herself as being with a different paper every time she asked a question. While it had utterly mystified Eisenhower, it made Kennedy laugh and he sometimes congratulated her on her growing list of newspaper employers.

Kennedy, like Eisenhower, always started with a wire service or network correspondent and the conferences were ended after half an hour or so by the dean of the White House reporters, the gruff, sharp Merriman Smith of UPI. Smith concluded each session on his own or on a nod from Salinger with "Thank you, Mr. President." In fact, "Smitty" had written a book on his White House years covering Roosevelt and Truman and entitled it, *Thank You, Mr. President.* Despite his privileged status, Smith pulled no punches and asked tough questions.

No matter how tough the questions, Kennedy usually controlled his temper, but he could be coldly sarcastic. The only times I saw him truly angry during news conferences were once when he was asked a question about Vietnam and once during a crisis with the steel industry. In both cases, his eyes tightened and his face froze in barely controlled fury. In the spring of 1962, two American military advisers were killed in Vietnam and a reporter asked if there soon might not be many Americans fighting and dying there. With a withering look, Kennedy barked "No!" and for a moment I thought he was going to come down off the platform and punch the reporter.

The other occasion was also that spring. Kennedy felt he had been betrayed by the steel industry when it raised prices in defiance of a presidential request and in spite of earlier agreement not to do so. Instead of his usual slight wry grin, his jaw was set and his face was grim as he practically goose-stepped to centre stage of the State Department auditorium and slapped down some papers on the lectern. The steel price increase, he said, was "irresponsible," "unjustifiable,'' and done with ''utter contempt'' in a ''pursuit of power and profit.'' He called it an almost traitorous act in view of the crises in Berlin and Southeast Asia where Americans were risking their lives. He left as grim as he came in. Later we heard he'd privately said, ''My father always told me that all businessmen were sons of bitches, but I never believed it till now.'' He told us at a subsequent news conference that the quote was substantially correct. A short time after this, Big Steel rolled back its price increase.

There were 1,200 of us with White House credentials, but these included cameramen, soundmen, and other technicians as well as many out-of-town reporters. In fact, less than 100 were around the White House with any frequency. Press Secretary Salinger held briefings for reporters twice a day in his office, dressed in shirt sleeves, puffing a cigar, and wisecracking his way through questions as we crowded around his desk. We had an unwritten rule that no one could leave his office until an important briefing was over. That way, nobody could be scooped. For special briefings, we often met White House officials in Salinger's office or in a room off the lobby called ''the Fish Room'' because of FDR's penchant for hanging there stuffed fish he'd caught.

We gave Salinger a nickname after he successfully wiggled out of an order from Kennedy to lose weight by going on a fifty-mile hike. ''I may be plucky,'' he said, ''but I'm not stupid.'' Ever after, he was ''Plucky Pierre.'' He was well liked by reporters not only for his personality, but also because he was a good professional and we could trust him.

Outside Salinger's office there was a large waiting room known as the West Lobby, through which visitors came to meet the President and in which reporters lounged for hours waiting for news. We slouched in chairs or on a big black sofa, coats, hats, and cameras piled atop a large, round Philippine mahogany table in the middle of the lobby and newsreel and TV equipment piled in the corners. At times, I had the feeling the place looked like a high-class flophouse. Over the years, I suppose I spent hundreds of hours sitting in those big black leather chairs or typing away in the tiny paper-littered press room, just off the lobby, that was furnished with spittoons, typewriters, and telephones. The media facilities have improved greatly since then, although they have lost a good deal of character.

Waiting is one of the less exciting parts of being a reporter. You wait for statements to be released, for speeches to begin, for briefings to start, and for meetings to open. You simply wait for something to happen. At the White House and elsewhere some reporters passed the time playing gin rummy, gossiping, or reading the *Daily Racing Form*.

Because I always hated to waste time, I'd usually spend the waiting hours going over some research or planning coverage of other stories.

Many of Kennedy's closest friends were news people, such as *Newsweek's* Ben Bradlee, later editor of the *Washington Post*, Charles Bartlett of the *Chattanooga Times*, and Joe Alsop, the influential, acerbic syndicated columnist at whose home he dined the night of his inauguration. But while Kennedy's personal relations with reporters remained good throughout his presidency, he, like most presidents, became increasingly disenchanted with some of the media for reporting him unfavourably or misrepresenting his views and actions. "I am reading it more but enjoying it less," he told us at one news conference.

The glamour of the Kennedy arrival at the White House seemed heightened by the invasion of Washington during his first few months in office by a Hollywood crew filming the movie *Advise and Consent*. That spring Walter Pidgeon, Henry Fonda, Charles Laughton, and a host of popular movie stars came to town for a few weeks and we reporters were asked to play extras and some even got speaking parts in news conference sequences of the movie. In 1959, a *New York Times* congressional correspondent, Allen Drury, had written the book on which the movie was based, so we all felt a certain kinship to it. My own claim to Hollywood fame is a brief flash of myself in a reportorial crowd scene at the Senate.

Any time I was in President Kennedy's office, whether shooting film when he was away or with a group of reporters clustered around his desk in some impromptu conversation with him, or at a small ceremony, I always had a sense of history. I knew I was in the office where Franklin D. Roosevelt, Woodrow Wilson, and Abraham Lincoln had worked.

Going into the office, you walked in the door past Secret Service guards, who were there even when he was out of town, and stepped across the thick blue rug into a big oval room 35 feet by 28. In Kennedy's time, you quickly saw it was an ex-Navy man's office. There were ship models on shelves and over the fireplace two huge paintings of an 1812 naval battle between the *Constitution* and the British frigate *Guerrere*. Kennedy's desk had been found by Jackie when she was exploring the attic and basement when they first moved in. It was a sturdy old piece of furniture given by Queen Victoria to President Rutherford B. Hayes, and was made from the timbers of a famous frigate called *H.M.S. Resolute*, which had been wrecked off North America.

Once when Kennedy was away, I did a CBC *Newsmagazine* documentary on decision-making in Washington and we filmed several segments in his office. The desk itself was untidy when we were filming and his secretary, Mrs. Lincoln, told me he usually had a messy desk, littered with papers, phone messages, clippings, magazines, and newspapers. I couldn't resist sitting down in the big leather presidential chair as well as plunking myself into the famous white-padded rocking chair.

Huge windows were behind the President's desk overlooking the rose garden and the rolling south lawn of the White House with its majestic magnolia trees and the Washington Monument in the distance. Eisenhower used to step outside his office and practise golf shots and putting. If you looked carefully, you could still see the marks of his golf shoes on the floor by the window.

Unlike many of his predecessors, Kennedy was happy in the White House. "I have a nice home, the office is close by, and the pay is good," he said. Harry Truman had called it "The finest prison in the country." Thomas Jefferson said it was a "splendid misery." Other presidents referred to it variously as "a place of extinction" or "a crown of thorns." But not Kennedy. He never complained about it being "lonely at the top." He had none of the black moods that Nixon and Johnson would have, and as he told us at one news conference, "This is a damned good job." Perhaps part of the reason for this was that he had a young family and they made the White House home.

When Canadian Ambassador Charles Ritchie was presenting his credentials to Kennedy he was startled when the President suddenly rose from his rocking chair, calling out, "Shoo! Shoo!" Writing of his alarm in his diary, Ritchie said, "For a moment I was frozen in my place ... I might be the first Ambassador in history to be shooed out of the White House." Then Ambassador Ritchie looked beyond Kennedy and saw Caroline leading her pony Macaroni into the Oval Office, and he realized the President wasn't talking to him. In the early days of Kennedy's presidency, Macaroni wandered around the south lawn freely, but eventually he was banished because he became such a nuisance.

Oxford, Mississippi, September 30, 1962 ...

One of the first challenges Kennedy had to face as president was the increasing importance of the civil rights movement. For several years Martin Luther King, Jr., had been organizing a kind of peaceful guerilla warfare against the segregation that still was widely practised throughout the South. He led marches and boycotts of restaurants and bus terminals.

JFK had learned the lessons of his campaign and narrow victory,

124

which would have been impossible without black support. On coming into office, he appointed more blacks to high government office than any previous president in U.S. history: ambassadors, judges, senior civil servants, assistant secretaries of departments. He introduced new legislation to move blacks closer to the realization of equality. But while he was moving more quickly than any past president, it wasn't fast enough for many in the black community.

On the very day Kennedy was sworn in as President, the biggest racial confrontation during his time in office began. A nine-year Air Force veteran, James Meredith, sat down on that day and wrote a letter to the University of Mississippi seeking admission. He stated his qualifications and the fact that he was a Negro. The university said "no." Mississippi Governor Ross Barnett said "no." But after more than a year of hearings and waiting the courts said "yes." And Kennedy said "yes" and used federal troops to enforce the court decision.

When registration time arrived, I flew to Oxford, Mississippi, to see the classic confrontation. At Ole Miss, I saw thousands of white students, Ku Klux Klansmen, and ordinary citizens marching around the campus singing "Glory, glory, segregation" to the tune of "Glory, glory, Hallelujah." There were screams of "Go home, niggers. Go home, Communists," "Barnett Yes, Castro No," and "Kill the apes."

Federal troops had been sent to restore order, and eventually, with the help of tear gas, horses, and clubs, an uneasy calm was restored. But not before the first of the major race riots that would rock the U.S. in the 1960s and culminate with King's death in 1968. Ole Miss was my first experience with a race-mad mob, and it was terrifying. I had never before seen such blind hatred on people's faces or heard it screaming from their mouths, or seen it lashing out as white fists, clubs, and tire chains smashed into the skulls of blacks. In the years to come I would see much more of that, but this time it was all new.

A reporter is never safe in a race riot. This was made horribly clear at Ole Miss when one of my Washington colleagues, Paul Guihard of Agence France Presse, was shot and killed. The troops stayed for several weeks and federal marshals accompanied Meredith to every class for months. His family was threatened, his home shot up, and he was subjected to physical threats and verbal abuse. But he stayed, and two years later he graduated.

A few years after the dramatic confrontation at Ole Miss, when Ross Barnett was no longer governor of Mississippi, I spent an afternoon with him in his law office in Jackson. So far as the public was concerned, he'd been a defiant, fire-eating, white supremacist throughout the confrontation at Ole Miss.

The contrast in our private meeting was stunning. Instead of the frothing bigot who had stirred up so much emotion, he was a courtly, solicitous, smilingly pleasant elderly gentleman of the Old South. He quietly explained to me that he "really liked 'culuhed fokes' but they had to go slower on this integration thing." He wasn't against them, he said, he wanted to help them, and he felt all the trouble was started by "uppidy" northern blacks and Communists.

I was confused about Barnett's role at the Ole Miss riots and some time later I asked Bob Kennedy about Barnett. He told me the Mississippi governor had pleaded in private with President Kennedy to "help me out of this mess." He had offered to pay for an education for Meredith anywhere in the world, if only Meredith would give up the idea of going to Ole Miss. Then he suggested Meredith just delay a year or two, after which Barnett said he'd guarantee admission to the university. Finally, according to Bob Kennedy, Barnett said, "Send in your soldiers and I'll say that I'm forced by superior federal forces to bow to a military occupation and the will of the federal government." In other words, he wanted out, and he wanted to save face.

Unhappily, in contrast to his private pleading, his public stance was so ferociously anti-black and anti-Washington that he did much to incite the riots before any deal could be made.

Washington, D.C., February, 1961 ...

As with most U.S. presidents, Canada was a bit of a mystery and a bit of a nuisance for Kennedy. To Kennedy, as to most Americans, Canadians were "just like us." And yet, we weren't. When we criticized the U.S. or didn't respond in the way the Americans thought we should, there was puzzlement or anger. And Kennedy was mystified by our French-English issues. He genuinely liked Canadians, but I was always taken aback, at least in the time before he became president, by his lack of knowledge of our system of government and of the leading Canadian personalities.

Prime Minister John Diefenbaker came to Washington one month after Kennedy was sworn in and this was considered a great honour since Diefenbaker was Kennedy's first visiting foreign dignitary. (JFK made his own first foreign trip to Canada three-and-a-half months later.) I remember the intense apprehension about the first Kennedy-Diefenbaker meeting among Canadian Embassy and State Department officials. Everyone wondered whether the two would get along, fearing they would intensely dislike each other at first sight. The aging prairie populist and the young Boston sophisticate didn't hate each other at first sight, but they did very soon after.

Kennedy knew the political usefulness of publicity both for himself and for Diefenbaker, and when their meeting ended he took Diefenbaker for a stroll on the White House front lawn to the delight of photographers, reporters, and TV cameramen. I watched them chatting, smiling, and walking about. It was the first and last time there would be such a happy scene.

Years later Robert Kennedy told me, "You know, my brother really hated only two men. One was Sukarno [dictator of Indonesia] and the other was Diefenbaker." According to Bob, the President felt Diefenbaker was a grandstanding, insincere, sanctimonious bore. In time, he came to believe he was also a liar, a blackmailer, and a betrayer. President Kennedy felt Diefenbaker consistently misrepresented U.S. policies and used anti-Americanism for his political advantage.

An entirely accidental unpleasantness for Kennedy in connection with Diefenbaker occurred during a tree-planting ceremony on Kennedy's first visit to Ottawa in 1961. As Kennedy shovelled earth over the roots of two red oaks to commemorate his visit, he strained his war-injured back. Six months later, when he met Harold Macmillan at their Bermuda conference, I noticed Kennedy still occasionally winced with pain. He obviously couldn't blame Diefenbaker for that, but it nevertheless unpleasantly reminded him of the Canadian Prime Minister.

But the Diefenbaker action most hurtful to Kennedy personally was when the Canadian Prime Minister kept a copy of a private, one-page U.S. government memorandum on what the U.S. should seek from Canada. It had been prepared for the same Kennedy-Diefenbaker meeting in Ottawa in mid-May, 1961. The document had been accidentally left behind by a U.S. official at a meeting and was picked up by a Canadian official and given to the P.M. Two years later, in the heat of an election campaign and with Diefenbaker facing defeat, his aides leaked to reporters the story that the memo had "SOB" scribbled into the margin in JFK's handwriting. Aides suggested that the Prime Minister might release the memo as proof Kennedy was trying to manipulate Canada. Apparently they hoped the "SOB memo" would win Diefenbaker votes since he had labelled Liberal Leader Mike Pearson as "Kennedy's candidate."

Kennedy thought it was blackmail. So did his staff. He vigorously denied writing "SOB" on any memo. He told his friend Ben Bradlee, "At the time, I didn't know he was an SOB. I thought he was a prick." He told Bradlee that the controversy over the document was at the root of much of the Canada-U.S. differences at the time on nuclear arms, NORAD, NATO, and Cuba.

Prime Minister Diefenbaker was only one cause of presidential stress. There were the inevitable picketers for one cause or another who would parade back and forth in front of the White House. When scientist Linus Pauling led an anti-nuclear march outside the White House gates, we were told Caroline asked her mother, "What's Daddy done now?" Caroline provided a number of useful quotations for us, and Salinger was anxious for us to have them because he felt they humanized the presidency. He told us, for instance, of a remark by Caroline to a White House guest who had asked where her father was. "Oh," she said, "he's upstairs with his shoes and socks off doing nothing."

Cocoa Beach, Florida, February 20, 1962 ...

Kennedy really brought the United States into the space age with his proclaimed goal of putting a man on the moon within a decade. It was during his presidency that the first American was launched into space. Alan Shepard made the first sub-orbital flight a few months after Kennedy's inauguration and from then until nearly a year later, I spent a lot of time at the space base at Cape Canaveral near Cocoa Beach. It was an exciting, romantic story then, the challenge of a new frontier and the brave men facing the mysterious unknown. In 1961 and 1962 I was at the Cape more than half a dozen times. In December, 1961, and on into January, 1962, we started doing stories on John Glenn's preparations for his flight and on his early abortive attempts. It was a long wait until, finally, he was launched successfully in late February.

In those pioneering days, you couldn't help being swept up in the emotion and excitement of the launches, even of unmanned rockets. When astronaut Glenn, or Shepard or Gus Grissom, was sitting in that little bird cage thing atop the rocket, your emotions were all in your throat. Even to us hard-bitten reporters, those guys were indeed heroes. Each rocket would rise on lift-off with such agonizing slowness, you'd find yourself screaming at the thing to get off the ground. The screams would turn into cheers as it rose majestically over the beach and headed into the sky over the Atlantic Ocean. Then suddenly, you'd fall silent, embarrassed at the yelling but realizing that everybody else had been yelling, too.

Shepard was much more the typical American "hot jock" pilot than Glenn. Darkly handsome, with twinkling, mischievous eyes and clearly looking for action, Shepard was fascinating to watch off duty. The space-age groupies fell all over him. He'd arrive at the Holiday Inn bar with some friends and leave half an hour later holding hands with a bronzed blonde whom he would whisk away in his Corvette. A running gag you'd hear from groupie girls was "four down and three to go," meaning they had wooed and won four of the astronauts and were zeroing in on the other three. So many made the claim that, if true, the astronauts wouldn't have had time to train.

Cocoa Beach in those days was a raucous, low-rent resort that had suddenly became a space-age boom town. In January and early February, if we couldn't do stories on Glenn's launch, we did stories on the neon-blazing, horn-honking strip of Highway A-1-A that was Cocoa Beach. Motels sprung up overnight and looked like it. The place was crowded with men and women on the make, entranced by the phallic symbolism of the rockets.

Reflective of the mood of the place is a letter I wrote to my editors at CBC Toronto at the end of one abortive "Glenn watch." "It's been a little adventuresome down here at Cocoa Beach," I wrote. "Doug Skene our cameraman was robbed of $200 plus, some others in our hotel were also robbed, there have been three rapes down the road and just the other night there was a murder in the bar. Some fellow came in, pulled out a gun and pumped six shots into a waitress. Doug Skene was sitting half a dozen feet from the girl. Now there's a major manhunt on for the fellow.... "

John Glenn, the freckle-faced, red-headed "Presbyterian pilot," was never around the girls or bars, and when reporters were able to talk to him at news conferences he was all business. No wonder he was known as "Goodie Two-shoes" and "the Preacher" by his colleagues. He was the perfect All-American hero, modest, articulate, self-confident, and God-fearing. He was also a pain in the ass for most of the other seven original Mercury astronauts.

Glenn had a hard time getting off the ground on his historic first flight into space. I must have covered four or five aborted attempts to launch. I'd get up about 4:00 a.m. and go out to the news area, which was a few hundred yards from the launching pad. Then it was wait, wait, wait. "Shorty" Powers, the hard-drinking, tough-talking public relations officer, would keep us posted on what was happening. It was cold in the early Florida winter dawn and sweaters and hot chocolate were the order of the day. Mostly because of weather and sometimes because of technical problems, Glenn's launch was repeatedly called off and we'd all troop back to our motels and bed. It was a happy day when he finally made it.

As exciting as the space program was, it couldn't match Cuba for news copy. Both the greatest disaster and the greatest triumph of the Kennedy presidency centred on Cuba. He inherited the CIA "Bay of Pigs" invasion plan from Eisenhower, learning about it in a briefing from CIA head Allen Dulles a few days after the election. He could have stopped it, but he didn't for two reasons. All through the campaign he'd spoken out for a tough line against Castro; and once elected, he was persuaded by the CIA and the generals that the invasion by 1,400 Cuban exiles trained and orchestrated by the CIA had a good chance of success.

The plan was flawed, however. Among other things, it assumed an uprising by anti-Castro Cubans within Cuba itself, an assumption born of wishful rather than realistic thinking. It was doomed for certain when Kennedy refused to authorize extensive U.S. air attacks. When the whole thing collapsed, he took full blame, saying, "Victory has a hundred fathers and defeat is an orphan." Mystifyingly, his popularity as registered by the Gallup Poll shot up to an astounding 83 per cent.

In spite of this, the Bay of Pigs was his worst humiliation and it became a national trauma in the early months of his administration. Perhaps its most damaging result was the encouragement it gave to Khrushchev in his mad Cuban missile adventure a year and a half later.

I was on assignment in Tokyo for the *Financial Post* at the time of the Bay of Pigs invasion, but the story did have one beneficial consequence for me as a journalist: it gave me an opportunity to interview Allen Dulles. As a result of the Cuban fiasco, Kennedy removed Dulles from his post as director of the CIA.

As American master spy since 1953, Allen Dulles was not someone who easily granted interviews, although he was very visible in Washington throughout the 1950s as a social gadabout and urbane bon vivant. I saw him at theatre openings, baseball games, and embassy parties. His life had been devoted to spying and he clearly relished all its danger, excitement, and romance. He had a reputation as a lady's man and as an amiably ruthless and unscrupulous operator with a vast network of personal contacts in the underworld of espionage. He had been called by Soviet writer Elya Ehrenburg "the most dangerous man in the world" with his army of secret agents, scientists, psychiatrists, economists, soldiers — even his own secret air force. In the Eisenhower years he had operated with little interference.

About a year after his dismissal by Kennedy I visited him in his Q Street home in Georgetown. We were doing a CBC *Newsmagazine* report on the craft of espionage and I wanted to film an interview with him. He wouldn't agree to appear on camera, but on the phone he told me in an almost mischievously conspiratorial voice, "But let us talk anyway, just privately."

When I arrived, he met me at the door wearing an old cardigan sweater, a bow tie, and slippers. Pouring me a Scotch and motioning me to sit down in his study, he smilingly told me the things he didn't want to talk about. These included the Bay of Pigs and his relationship with Kim Philby, the famous Soviet spy Dulles had known when Philby was stationed with the British Embassy in Washington. But he did want to talk about spying.

His eyes twinkled through rimless glasses and he puffed away on his pipe as he talked of running spies in Germany near the end of World War II from his base in Switzerland and how he had secretly met with emissaries from the German generals who plotted against Hitler and had encouraged their plan. In fact, his "spy game" work had started in Switzerland during World War I and he laughingly told me he once interviewed Lenin before Lenin returned to Russia in 1917, but had dismissed him as relatively unimportant. "So you see you can be too quick to dismiss a seeming nut," he told me. It was clear that he had simply loved the thrill of the spy game.

As I looked at this handsome, effervescent old fellow smoothing down his white moustache, sipping whisky, and chuckling over some remembered anecdote, it was hard to imagine that here was the Master Spy himself, who had overthrown dictators and undermined governments, who had bribed cabinet ministers and sent agents out to kill and to be killed. This cherubic old man in his slippers and cardigan could hardly have done all that. But he had, and much more.

During the Cold War his CIA had built the "Berlin Tunnel" under East Berlin to tap the Communist telephone system; he'd had the U-2 spy plane built and developed satellite espionage. Left-wing dictators that Eisenhower and John Foster Dulles wanted to get rid of, such as Mossadeq of Iran and Arbenz of Guatemala, were overthrown. He had a plan to assassinate Patrice Lumumba of the Congo because he considered Lumumba "a Castro or worse," but the plan was never implemented. He bribed Communist leaders to get a copy of Khrushchev's famous secret speech denouncing Stalin. His hands were in everything, but his fingerprints were seldom seen. He'd taken U.S. espionage a very long way from the day in 1929 when U.S. Secretary of State Henry Stimson disdained the whole idea of spying when he sniffed, "Gentlemen don't read each other's mail." Unlike the British, most American leaders had felt spying was an unsavoury business unfit and unnecessary for a democracy. Only during World War II and after did espionage become a fully accepted tool of U.S. policy.

As well as the Bay of Pigs, Dulles had his list of failures. He had failed to assassinate Castro and there was the affair of U-2 pilot Francis Gary Powers, who didn't use his suicide needle when he was shot down by the Russians on May 1, 1960.

Powers did all the things a spy is not supposed to do. He failed to destroy his secret plane and failed to use his poison suicide needle hidden inside a hollow coin, later telling a Senate committee hearing that he was told to use it only if he wanted to. I covered that hearing and was struck by Powers' preoccupation with his needle. He said that while parachuting from the U-2, he worried the Russians would find it. "I got to thinking," he said, "that when I got on the ground if I were captured they would surely find this coin. But maybe with just the pin lying loose in the pocket it would be overlooked. So I opened up the coin, got the pin out, and just dropped it in my pocket." The Russians, however, found it when they searched him.

Powers later claimed that he was supposed to destroy the plane only if it were in danger of falling into Soviet hands, but he said he wasn't sure he'd be able to do that without hurting himself. So he didn't push the destruct button. After he was captured, he apologized to the Russians for the U-2 operation and became a propaganda pawn of the Soviets. Khrushchev used the incident to embarrass Eisenhower and destroy a Paris summit conference.

Eisenhower's press secretary, Jim Hagerty, when asked what the U.S. had learned about the U-2 catastrophe, said simply, "Don't get caught."

And yet, in February, 1962, after he was released in exchange for Soviet superspy Colonel Rudolph Abel, the discredited Powers was welcomed back as a hero. When he came to Washington to testify about his experience, I sat in open-mouthed astonishment as senators fell all over themselves congratulating Powers for his "courage," "patriotism," "bravery," and being "a fine American citizen." Dulles was no longer CIA director when Powers appeared before the committee and did not share the senators' opinion of the pilot's bravery, but he kept quiet about it.

As we chatted, Dulles told me the CIA used to prepare lengthy reports every day for President Eisenhower, but Ike seldom read them. So, he said, the CIA began summarizing the world in 500 words along with some graphics and put that on Ike's desk every morning. Apparently, Ike would read that.

We talked briefly about his battles with Senator McCarthy's Red hunters who, he said, were "barbarians helping, not hurting, communism." He was as strong in opposing McCarthy as his brother at the State Department had been weak. Allen Dulles also didn't think much of FBI Director J. Edgar Hoover, whom he regarded as a nincompoop, but one who, nevertheless, was a brilliant bureaucratic infighter. "He knew what bodies were buried where," Dulles said.

As we shook hands when I stood to leave, I felt Allen Dulles was a tired and rather bored old man who now only really came to life with recollections of his remarkable and raffish spy career. He died a few years later.

Washington, D.C., October, 1962 ...

The Cuban missile crisis had been predicted by Republican Senator Kenneth Keating of New York as early as August, 1962. Since then Keating had been saying the Russians were building missile sites in Cuba. When I interviewed Keating about it in early October, he told me his information came from Cuban refugees, and he said the sites were for offensive weapons. I checked his warnings with Pentagon and State Department officials who ridiculed the idea. They told me they, too, had heard those reports, but saw no evidence to support them. "Besides," one official told me, "this is a congressional election year and Keating and the Republicans are just playing politics."

U.S. spy planes had seen sites for defensive missiles being built, but not for offensive missiles. The first military reports of Soviet offensive missile sites in Cuba came from a U.S. U-2 spy plane flight over Cuba on October 14. Kennedy demanded immediate and totally secret evaluation and further U-2 flights for verification. Although we reporters knew nothing about it, the real crisis had now begun. For the next two weeks, the superpowers moved closer and closer to the brink of nuclear war.

In the first week of the crisis Kennedy imposed utmost secrecy on his aides. He demanded that they maintain all their normal schedules, go to cocktail parties, receptions, and dinners as usual, and act as if nothing unusual was happening. He didn't want to alarm the American public too soon; he didn't want to alert the Soviets just yet that he knew what they were doing; and he needed more evidence.

So, while feverish secret activity was going on to verify the existence of offensive missile sites and evaluate the implications and consider possible responses, Kennedy went off campaigning in the mid-term congressional elections. He travelled first to Connecticut, and then to Cleveland, Ohio, Springfield, Illinois, and finally Chicago. In the middle of all this he made a quick visit back to the White House to meet Soviet Foreign Minister Andrei Gromyko. Kennedy listened carefully to every word and nuance in Gromyko's comments but said nothing about the missile sites.

By the night of Friday, October 19, the end of the first week, most reporters had begun to scent that something was up. We didn't know what, but there were too many unusual things happening. Cabinet members were seen slipping into the White House through the back door, too many senior people were too often observed whispering to each other at cocktail parties, and too many big black limousines gathered daily outside the State Department buildings in the Washington area known as Foggy Bottom.

Kennedy resumed his campaigning on Friday and flew to Chicago, but already reporters were chasing Press Secretary Salinger on the "something" they sensed was going on. Suddenly, Saturday morning, Kennedy announced he had a cold and a fever, cancelled the rest of his Chicago politicking, and flew back to Washington.

Reporters travelling with him thought this odd because he seemed fine to them. When I chatted with some of them on their return to Washington, our mutual suspicions grew. Through the weekend, we all wrote and broadcast stories about the "secret crisis," speculating on Berlin, Laos, and Cuba. By Monday morning, most of us had guessed it was Cuba. All signs pointed there because of reports of U.S. troop movements in Florida and the comments by Senator Keating and others. But what the specific problem was with Cuba, we didn't know.

All day Monday, October 22, I and hundreds of other reporters spent a hectic day chasing down rumours. Kennedy met a congressional delegation at the White House at 5:00 p.m. to tell them about the crisis and then at 7:00 he went live on television and radio to tell the world of the Cuban missile crisis.

In his speech he revealed the existence of the offensive missile bases, announced increased air surveillance of Cuba, and asked for an immediate meeting of the Organization of American States (OAS) and an emergency session of the UN Security Council. More important, however, was his announcement of a blockade of Cuba effective Wednesday morning to prevent the passage of offensive military equipment. Eighteen Soviet ships were then on the high seas heading for Cuba. He warned the Soviet Union that any attack by Cuba on the United States would be regarded as an attack by the Soviet Union requiring full U.S. retaliation against Russia.

It was clear to us from the outset that Kennedy's position was one of iron determination: the Russian missiles in Cuba had to be removed. But his strategy was to apply the minimum force needed to achieve that objective, raising the ante slowly and carefully. We later discovered he had scrupulously kept the lines of communication open to Moscow both officially and unofficially.

We saw him only briefly during the next few days, but to us and to those we talked to who did spend a lot of time with him, Kennedy exemplified throughout the crisis that Hemingway quotation he so liked: "grace under pressure." As he said to friends at the beginning of the crisis, "I guess this is the week I earn my salary."

For reporters, the rest of the week was a whirlwind of on-the-record and off-the-record briefings at the White House, the State Department, the Pentagon, the Organization of American States, and, for Canadian reporters, the Canadian Embassy. We were shown maps, U-2 photos, pictures of Soviet ships heading for Cuba. We were given facts and figures on the missiles and what cities they could hit, on U.S. military preparations, and on diplomatic manoeuvring. The Pentagon told us of 100,000 U.S. troops assembled and "ready to go" in southern Florida, and of sixty-eight squadrons of aircraft on alert along with 900 U.S. warships from aircraft carriers to frigates. The Strategic Air Command was at the ready, as was the Polaris nuclear submarine fleet. We heard third-, fourth-, fifth-hand reports that some officials had urged a Normandy "D-Day" invasion of Cuba. Some wanted a "surgical" air strike on the missile sites. Others wanted to sink the Russian ships carrying the missiles to Cuba. But we also heard more authoritatively from White House aides that Bob Kennedy, his brother's most influential adviser throughout the crisis, had said the U.S. would never launch its own "Pearl Harbor."

From that and other similar comments from Canadian and other foreign diplomats and from State Department aides, I assumed along with most of my colleagues that there would be no American first strike at the Soviet Union, even though we heard of Pentagon generals urging this approach. This meant that if the Russians hit first, Washington along with other key U.S. cities would be wiped out before the massive American retaliatory strike would hit the Soviet Union. The American approach, as my sources told me, was to make sure Moscow knew the U.S. retaliatory strike would destroy Russia. The U.S. government might be badly damaged, but the Soviet government would be obliterated. Kennedy told his aide Ted Sorensen at this point that he believed the chance of World War III was between "one out of three to even."

The Cuban missile crisis literally brought the world to the brink of nuclear war. It's the closest we've ever come. For anybody living in Washington at the time, it was quite simply terrifying. A number of wives and children left the city, and bomb-shelter salesmen did a brisk business. I imagine the feeling must have been similar in London in the days just before World War II. All the theoretical thinking I'd done before about what nuclear war might be like suddenly became palpably real.

On Wednesday at 10:00 a.m. the naval blockade of Cuba went into effect. In keeping with his firm but cautious approach, Kennedy issued instructions to his Navy to, if necessary, "disable, but don't sink" any Russian ships that tried to break through the blockade. In the past, a blockade like this would almost certainly have led to a declaration of war. No response came from the Russians, but their ships kept on coming closer to the American destroyers and other naval vessels ringing Cuba.

By the morning the blockade became effective, I was spending most of my time at the Pentagon, where we were getting faster reports on what was happening. The Pentagon briefings, normally attended by a couple of dozen regular Pentagon reporters, swelled to over 100 journalists clamouring for information. That morning we were told some of the Russian ships had stopped. Then we were told some had turned around. A few hours later, we were told the missile-carrying Russian freighters were again heading for Cuba. On Thursday we continued to get jumbled and conflicting reports from the Pentagon, from foreign diplomats, and from the Soviets. Would the Soviet ships turn around and go home? Would they try to break through the blockade? Would the Russians launch an attack on the U.S.?

While we speculated all that Thursday, the President, his brother, Secretary of State Dean Rusk, Defense Secretary McNamara, and others were in intense meetings evaluating information, planning the next moves, and, like us, asking themselves questions. Should the blockade be tightened? Should propaganda leaflets be dropped over Cuba? Should there be an air strike on Cuba? Should there be an invasion?

At a briefing Friday noon, Lincoln White, the State Department press officer, warned us that "further action may be justified." This set off renewed speculation about U.S. invasion or air attacks against Cuba and the White House quickly advised us that such speculation was going too far. Years later, Salinger told me that Kennedy feared Moscow might misread U.S. intentions because of White's unauthorized "escalation" warning and that this, in turn, might cause Khrushchev to listen more carefully to the "warhawk" advisers in the Kremlin. At one briefing, a somewhat embarrassed admiral told us that the first Soviet freighter had been stopped and boarded by the crew of, of all destroyers, the *U.S.S. Joseph Kennedy, Jr.*, named in memory of Kennedy's older brother killed in World War II. They found no missiles.

As the week waned, the Russian freighters carrying missiles drew closer to the blockade line and tension mounted. But, unbeknownst to reporters and even to Press Secretary Salinger, the unofficial lines of communication with Moscow were humming. Bob Kennedy had been talking to Soviet Ambassador Anatoly Dobrynin; lower-level diplomats had been talking and passing messages back and forth through third parties. One of the most important unofficial channels of communication was contact between veteran ABC reporter John Scali and Soviet Embassy Counsellor Alexsandr Fomin, whom most of us knew and assumed was a senior KGB agent.

That Friday, Fomin called Scali, who specialized in foreign affairs, to make a lunch date. At lunch, to the reporter's amazement, Fomin outlined a proposal to settle the crisis and asked him to get it to Kennedy. Right after lunch, Scali sent a memorandum on the proposal to Secretary of State Rusk, who in turn gave it to the President. The proposal was agreed to in principle and Scali was instructed to meet immediately with Fomin. They met in the lobby of the Statler Hotel a few blocks from the White House, and Fomin said he would transmit the U.S. response to the Kremlin.

At one point during this unusual bit of unofficial diplomacy, Pierre Salinger ran into Scali just outside the President's office. Salinger knew nothing of Scali's involvement and also knew that the ABC reporter was where no reporter should ever be. He was quickly reassured by Dean Rusk, who was with Scali, that it was all right, but he also was consumed with curiosity. Only later did he find out what was going on.

That Friday night, a secret letter from Khrushchev arrived at the White House. It proposed essentially the same terms that Fomin had outlined to Scali. In the letter, Khrushchev made an eloquent plea for peace, wrote of the horror of nuclear war, and implied that he would withdraw the missiles under United Nations supervision provided that Kennedy gave a guarantee of not invading Cuba. The White House was surprised and relieved. Kennedy told his colleagues he would agree to Khrushchev's proposal, subject to verification of the missile removal, and he began drafting a response.

The next day a second Khrushchev letter arrived. It read as if the first letter had never existed. Its tone was belligerent and it demanded, among other things, that the Americans withdraw their Jupiter missiles from Turkey. Instead of the crisis being over it was now worse. The Russian ships were still coming and Moscow was making impossible demands. Scali was mortified and thought he'd been the pawn in some elaborate ruse. He angrily called Fomin and they again met in the

Statler lobby. The Russian told him he was mystified by the second letter and that he would check with Moscow. Scali reported back to Rusk and the tension mounted.

That Saturday morning, while Kennedy and his aides were meeting at the White House to ponder the now sharply escalated crisis, they were handed a report that a Cuban SAM missile had shot down an American U-2 overflying the island. Later that day they got a report that an American U-2 had flown over Siberia by mistake. Washington quickly apologized to Moscow, realizing that with both sides so close to war, a mistake or an accident could be misread and set off World War III.

The White House wasn't sure how to respond to the second letter. On Bob Kennedy's suggestion, the President ignored it entirely and responded late that Saturday only to the first letter.

Saturday night was the closest the world has ever come to nuclear war. Officials in London, Paris, Bonn, Rome, and Ottawa and other Western capitals waited nervously for the next move, frustrated at their inability to do anything significant to affect the impending catastrophe and praying that Kennedy was doing the right thing. In Washington the tension was extraordinary. Many families had left town, people had stocked up on food for their bomb shelters, and reporters waited anxiously in the White House lobby or the State Department or Pentagon newsrooms.

I'd swung back to waiting it out at the White House because it now seemed to me the first news was going to come from the President. I had had only about four hours' sleep a night since the crisis broke and hardly time for more than sandwiches and beer for meals. I was exhausted, and as I sat in the White House lobby I thought of the similar weariness of the men a few yards away who were deciding the fate of the world. They hadn't had any more sleep than most of the reporters covering the story and I wondered if World War III might be started by men too tired to think straight, either here or in the Kremlin.

I also mused about how my professional determination to be where the news was conflicted dramatically with my personal well-being. If a nuclear attack was coming tonight, I thought, I'd be among the first to know and among the first to die, since the White House would be target number one. We had been told that within minutes of the firing of the missiles from Cuba, 80 million Americans would be dead. A number of us grimly came to the conclusion that we'd have almost no warning at all, and probably just enough time for one phone call to our offices so they could at least get out a bulletin. I thought about calling my wife, and my daughter who lived with her mother in nearby

138

Alexandria, Virginia, but dismissed the idea because it might alarm them even more. Somebody poured Scotch into paper cups and we all toasted our fates.

That night my CBC colleague Don Minifie had been chasing down information from State Department officials and diplomats while I waited for something to happen at the White House. Every couple of hours I called him at the office or at his home so we could pool our information. Every couple of hours he and I would phone in a brief report to CBC radio and talk to our TV editors as well.

Finally, long after midnight, I gave up and went home because Don and I had to do an early morning CBC radio program on the crisis. After four hours of sleep, I was up at the crack of dawn (grateful, in fact, to see a new dawn at all) and began preparing for our program. I drove over to NBC and we went on the air at 9:00 a.m. Just as we began, Moscow radio started broadcasting a new Khrushchev letter. Khrushchev was sending it in the clear, he said, because time was so critical. Only by going public with their communications could Kennedy and Khrushchev be certain of getting their final messages across to each other in the shortest possible time.

Khrushchev said work on the missile sites had stopped; the missiles were being dismantled, crated, and returned to the Soviet Union; and that it all could be done under UN supervision. He asked Kennedy to lift the blockade and agree not to invade Cuba. It was a stunning moment. Minifie and I reported the story as it was breaking and then, while we were still on the air, I ran into the control room to call Salinger. He'd heard something on his car radio just as he was arriving at the office. I gave him what information we had taken down from Radio Moscow. He couldn't believe his ears, and I got a few quotes from him and he rushed off to see Kennedy.

When Khrushchev ended the crisis that Sunday morning, it was essentially on the basis of his first letter, which was largely the same as Fomin's proposals given to Scali and transmitted to the White House. Later that Sunday, Fomin called Scali to say he had been instructed to say the information provided by Scali was very helpful to Khrushchev in making his final decision. But Fomin offered no explanation about the baffling second Khrushchev letter. Most diplomats I talked to later felt it must have been written by bureaucrats in the Kremlin and that it in fact had been written first, not second, but got delayed in transmission. Khrushchev had second thoughts and sent along his conciliatory letter, which, as fate would have it, actually got to the White House before the other letter. Throughout his frenetic two days as a key player in the missile crisis, Scali, of course, could report nothing of his own activities. But he had a reporter's dream of a story to tell when it was all over.

The Sunday morning message from Khrushchev came just in time. It seemed inevitable that within the next few days the Americans would have escalated the crisis by bombing the Cuban missile sites or invading the island. And then the world might have stepped over the brink. Summing it up, Secretary of State Dean Rusk said to reporter Charlie Bartlett, "We were eyeball to eyeball. The other fellow blinked."

Kennedy had won. But he warned his aides not to gloat and to give the Cubans and Russians time and room to retire as gracefully as possible.

For his handling of the Cuban missile crisis it seemed to me Kennedy well deserved the comment made by Prime Minister Harold Macmillan, who told the British House of Commons, it was "one of the great turning points in history." It seemed to me, too, that Khrushchev earned a place in history for having the courage to back down when he recognized his reckless gamble was not going to work.

Nassau, December 19, 1962 ...

One side effect of the missile crisis was a sharp deterioration in Canadian-American relations. At the height of the crisis Diefenbaker refused to put the Canadian NORAD group on as high a level of alert as the Americans requested. Kennedy saw this as a betrayal of past promises and commitments under NATO and the Canada-U.S. NORAD agreement. The situation was not helped two months later by Dief's behaviour at the Bahamas conference of Kennedy and Harold Macmillan in December, 1962.

Kennedy was to confer with Macmillan and a day or so later Macmillan was to meet separately with Diefenbaker. But the Canadian Prime Minister "horned in," to use Bob Kennedy's phrase, and Kennedy and Macmillan were reluctantly forced to meet with Diefenbaker on the last day of their conference.

I covered that conference and it was clear from the American and British briefings that Diefenbaker was not exactly welcome. Then, when the conference was almost over but before any formal concluding statement was issued, Diefenbaker called his own news conference and revealed all the major decisions taken. The British and Americans were furious but could do nothing.

At the end the three leaders sat together for a joint photograph, and Kennedy later told Rufus Smith, who was still in charge of Canadian affairs at the State Department, "There we sat like three whores at a christening."

The Nassau conference did give me an opportunity to observe for the second time the warm relationship between Kennedy and Harold Macmillan, which I had first observed at their December, 1961, Bermuda conference. Of all contemporary world leaders, Kennedy liked and admired most the British Prime Minister. Their pleasure in each other's company was always evident from their mutual bantering. At one Washington Correspondents' Annual Dinner, the two stole the show with a witty comedy routine that put to shame the professional comedians who preceded them. They joshed each other, poked fun at reporters, and delightfully joked about the American Revolution against the British.

Kennedy enjoyed Macmillan's Edwardian style and the way he camouflaged a steely determination behind an affable patrician manner. Macmillan could also be flippant or cuttingly witty, as the occasion demanded. He could be infinitely patient, too, as I discovered during his arrival at the Bermuda airport. I'd ridden out to the airport with Winston Churchill's ne'r-do-well son, Randolph, then a correspondent for a London paper. I have never known a louder, more abusive and offensive individual than Randolph, and he was in top form on this occasion. As Macmillan climbed into his waiting limousine a belligerent, drunken Churchill staggered over to him, waving his arms and shouting something quite imcomprehensible. The only thing I heard Macmillan say was, "Now, now Randolph ... later ... later."

I saw Churchill again distinguish himself at Nassau at the Macmillan-Kennedy conference a year later by vociferously refusing to abide by the rule that no reporter could leave the news briefing until it was over. After much alcoholic pushing and shoving with guards at the door, Randolph suddenly backed away and ran hell-bent for the door, which he missed, crashing with all his overweight bulk through the wall.

Those incidents, along with a couple of occasions when I observed Churchill in a bar, endorsed for me Evelyn Waugh's comment. Upon hearing that doctors had removed a non-malignant tumour from Churchill, Waugh exclaimed, "What a triumph of modern science to find the only part of Randolph that is not malignant and remove it."

At the Nassau conference, Macmillan took time out one evening to join a media barbecue. He sat at the end of a long table, gulping large glasses of beer and watching along with the rest of us while scantily clad girls did an extraordinarily acrobatic limbo act. I was struck that night by Macmillan's astonishing capacity for beer and I still remember the cry that went up every ten minutes or so, "More beer for the Prime Minister!", as we'd pass up a large jug to his end of the table.

The Nassau conference also gave me new insight to the distinguished Southam columnist Charles Lynch, whose journalistic career went back to World War II and who had reported not only the Normandy invasion and post-war Europe, but also from Brazil and the United Nations. He was now based in Ottawa for Southam papers. One evening after our reporting had been done, we all gathered in a watering hole called The Junkanoo in downtown Nassau. During the course of liquid refreshment and calypso music, somehow a young lady by the name of "Peanuts" Alberta attached herself to us. She seemed particularly attracted by Charlie's charms, dancing with the most incredible manoeuvrability in her hips combined with extreme closeness.

As we left the nightclub, somehow Charlie had acquired a zippy red sports car, and we watched him and "Peanuts" roaring off into the night, laughing and waving at an envious group of Canadian reporters. We jumped into taxicabs and chased him to a nightclub in an area known as "Over the Hill," where we all danced the night away.

As a journalist covering a major international summit like the Nassau conference, my pattern was usually the same. I would visit the meeting site and inspect the room, chairs, and tables. Then I'd retreat to a nearby bar to gossip and exchange information with fellow reporters. Once the meetings were under way there were briefings two or three times a day and private talks with sources in an effort to glean whatever "inside material" I could get. At the end of the conference there was always a chance to see the great men themselves and perhaps ask a question at the news conference.

Almost always the talks would be officially described as "full, frank, and friendly." One high-level British Foreign Office official once provided the most inventive way I ever heard of describing what was going on without revealing a thing. Following a meeting of President Eisenhower and Prime Minister Eden, he told us, "We are in the middle of a river chewing asparagus stalks contained in a potpourri." In a TV interview I did with Diefenbaker in Nassau, he told me his presence had significantly helped the Kennedy-Macmillan meeting. When I asked him about ill-feeling between himself and Kennedy he paused, set his jaw, and said slowly, "No, not really .... "

What he said privately, however, was something else. On visits I made to Ottawa both before and after the Nassau conference, he spoke to me off the record several times about Kennedy, saying he thought the President was a "young hothead" and that he was a dangerous man whose inexperience and adventurism could "lead to trouble" between East and West. He also petulantly told me in his office on one visit that he had been the first to use the phrase "New Frontier" in reference to Canada's North and he claimed that Kennedy had taken the phrase from him.

In his book *Presidents and Prime Ministers*, the best book ever written on the subject, Lawrence Martin has graphically detailed the painful Diefenbaker-Kennedy relationship. Kennedy, with his New England accent and some poor advice from Rusk, at first mispronounced the Canadian Prime Minister's name as "Diefen-bawker." This angered the Prime Minister, who had always been extremely sensitive about what he considered personal slights. The Prime Minister also claimed Kennedy made fun of his fishing ability and his French, and Dief complained that he was too young and too brash. "That young man has got to learn that he's not running the Canadian government," Martin quotes Diefenbaker as saying. Diefenbaker is also quoted as calling Kennedy a "boastful young son of a bitch."

Diefenbaker resented also the continuing underground American attacks on his pious, well-meaning External Affairs Minister Howard Green. However "nice" a man they thought he was otherwise, State Department and White House officials privately ridiculed Green for being "naive and parochial" in international affairs. Over and over again, various U.S. authorities told me Green knew little of the world, had travelled nowhere outside North America since World War I, and in preaching disarmament was making statements that bore more relationship to wishful thinking than to reality.

They even made jokes about Green's naiveté. One official told me a story he'd heard in Ottawa when Congo leader Patrice Lumumba was visiting the Canadian capital. After a meeting Lumumba asked Green to send a girl around to his Chateau Laurier suite. Green, in his innocence about such things, assumed Lumumba wanted a secretary and dispatched one of his own to the hotel. After a hotel-room contretemps with the insulted secretary, the Congolese leader left Ottawa confused and angry. The idea of Howard Green acting as a pimp for Patrice Lumumba was something to boggle the imagination. Later, I heard other versions of this same story, including one in which Lumumba, who had been smitten by Secretary of State Ellen Fairclough, sought unsuccessfully to acquire her company for the night after Green let him down.

In the period leading up to the April 8, 1963, Canadian election, with Diefenbaker's minority government clinging to power, his last dispute with Kennedy came to a head. The issue was whether or not

Canada would accept American nuclear warheads on Canadian soil. Washington said we were committed to do so under NORAD and NATO agreements. The situation was made more difficult because of a split in the Diefenbaker cabinet. Some ministers agreed with the Americans and used the issue as a way of rebelling against the leader and his style of managing the government. Canadian Air Force officers, who also felt Canada had a commitment to accept nuclear warheads, were lobbying both in Ottawa and in Washington against Diefenbaker's position.

The warheads crisis reached the breaking point on January 30, 1963. The State Department called Canadian reporters early that evening to advise that it would be issuing a statement at 6:15 p.m. on the matter. I grabbed a cab from my CBC office in the National Press Building and arrived just as the release was being handed out. It had been given to the Canadian Embassy only half an hour before. The Canadian correspondents and even some of the regular American State Department reporters were stunned by the wording. It was an extraordinarily blunt attack on the Canadian government, virtually accusing Diefenbaker of not telling the truth and reneging on his commitment to accept the warheads. Nobody could recall Washington making such a public accusation against a friendly government.

I called CBC Toronto to file a quick radio report and then started preparing a television piece and newspaper stories for filing to Windsor and Vancouver. In Ottawa, there was outrage. Diefenbaker was apoplectic. As I checked with various officials, it was agreed the statement was an astonishing repudiation of a normally friendly ally.

A few years later I was flying with U.S. diplomat George Ball between Washington and New York and we discussed the incident. Ball was Undersecretary of State in 1963 and happened to be in charge of the State Department on that day. He authorized the statement's release on his own authority without checking with the President, although he had talked to presidential aide McGeorge Bundy. "The next day, Kennedy called me over and gave me absolute hell," Ball remembered. "I've seldom seen him so angry. He asked me, 'Why in hell did you do it?' In no uncertain terms it was clear I had made a mistake by not clearing the statement with him first. I accepted the blame because I knew I was wrong. But," he added, "the substance of our complaint was right. Canada had a commitment to take the warheads."

Kennedy agreed the complaint was justified, but he knew the statement would make life with Diefenbaker even worse. It certainly did.

Diefenbaker was so angry he recalled Ambassador Charles Ritchie. We heard in Washington that Dief thought the statement was part of a Kennedy plot to help his friend Mike Pearson and the Liberals. That wasn't true, but I've always thought that at least some people in the State Department had to be aware of the political implications in Canada of such a statement. A year earlier, Kennedy had invited Pearson to the White House along with a large number of other Nobel Prize winners. Pearson not only came to dinner but met privately with JFK beforehand. The invitation came shortly before the 1962 Canadian election and it inevitably gave Pearson considerable publicity. U.S. officials had to be aware of the political benefits to Pearson of such attention. Certainly, when the Diefenbaker minority government was finally defeated on April 8, 1963, the Kennedy White House could barely conceal its pleasure at the prospect of Lester Pearson as Prime Minister.

Washington admired Pearson partly because of his gregarious personality, partly because his attitudes were attuned to those of most officials in the State Department, and partly because of the simple fact that they had known him for so many years. Kennedy admired Pearson as an intellectual equal and a thoughtful statesman. In 1959 Kennedy had written a highly complimentary review of Pearson's book, *Diplomacy in the Nuclear Age.* The two leaders thought a lot alike and liked many of the same things. Bob Kennedy later described Pearson to me as "a really nice man. He's smart. He's understanding. And he knows an awful lot about baseball." When Jack and Mike were together they sometimes talked about their favourite sport. Pearson, a baseball addict, knew more than Kennedy. Whether they were talking about baseball or bilateral issues, Kennedy felt comfortable with Pearson in a way he never did with Diefenbaker, and they could disagree without rancour.

Pearson once told me that while he was stationed at the Canadian Embassy in Washington he had organized a rather special brand of baseball with the State Department. Embassy and State Department officials would play on Saturdays and Sundays, and in addition to bringing bats and balls, they brought along a vast vat of martinis. The martinis were a way of making things even ... a sort of handicap as in golf.

Pitchers of martinis would be placed at first, second, and third base. If you got to first base, you had to drink a martini. If you got to second, it was two martinis. At third base, three. And a home run meant four martinis. Needless to say, the heavy hitters were less sure on their feet as the game progressed. "A good time always was had by all," Pearson told me. "Especially in the high-scoring games. Sometimes we weren't sure we were playing baseball or cricket."

One thing Pearson did not have in common with Kennedy, however, was a love of sailing. Visiting Kennedy on Cape Cod after he became Prime Minister, Pearson was invited to confer with him aboard the presidental yacht on a cruise of Nantucket Sound. Pearson told me later he said "No," his stomach couldn't take it. "Touch football, baseball, basketball, tiddlywinks, or anything else, but don't take me in the water," Pearson moaned.

Washington, D.C., August 28, 1963 ...

Kennedy was two and a half years into his first term in the White House when the civil rights movement staged what to my mind was its greatest triumph, the historic March on Washington.

Since the confrontation at Ole Miss, Kennedy had been developing legislation on civil rights, but in Congress he was facing an increasing "white backlash" that threatened his plans. There was more than a little subterranean support for the kind of thing George Lincoln Rockwell of the American Nazi Party was saying: "The time has come for the white man to make a stand in the streets against the race mixers and their Communist leaders."

Kennedy looked to support within the black community to calm down those blacks who were listening to the bitter, vitriolic militants, such as Elijah Mohammad and Malcolm X. He invited to the White House leaders of such established black organizations as the National Association for the Advancement of Colored Peoples (NAACP), the Congress of Racial Equality (CORE), and the Urban League. He sought both to cool down passions and to elicit their support for his civil rights legislation.

The white backlash was coming on the heels of the campaign of the "Freedom Riders," led by CORE's James Farmer, who was seeking to move faster on integration in the South. There had been violence in the spring of 1961 and again in the spring of 1963. In Birmingham, Alabama, in May of 1963, 500 blacks were arrested by Sheriff Bull Connor and the famous picture of one of his dogs lunging at a black woman had been flashed around the world. That picture probably did more good for the civil rights movement than any other single incident, arousing the sympathy of much of the white community with its graphic portrayal of vicious racism.

A few days later Medgar Evers, a Mississippi black civil rights leader and friend of both James Meredith and Bob Kennedy, was shot to death outside his home in Jackson, Mississippi. In an important symbolic act, Kennedy arranged to have him buried at Arlington National Cemetery.

Black leaders wanted to show their support for the Kennedy civil rights bill and to demonstrate that a massive march could be peaceful. So, in the wake of Birmingham and Medger Evers' death, they organized a rally that would gather at the Lincoln Memorial on August 28 just over a hundred years after Abraham Lincoln's Emancipation Proclamation.

A quarter of a million people marched to Lincoln Memorial that day, peacefully, quietly, confidently, and happily. I was standing high on the steps of the Lincoln Memorial and watched them coming up the mall flowing toward me. There had been fears of more riots, fears that a quarter of a million people out of control could produce the worst racial violence in American history. But the marchers were imbued with King's philosophy of non-violence. As I stood there looking out over that sea of black and white faces, chills ran down my spine and tears streamed from my eyes as 250,000 voices of hope, determination, and pride sang from the depth of their collective soul the words of their protest song, "We Shall Overcome." There would be, of course, more violence and destruction in the years to come, but it seems to me, in retrospect, that at this moment at the Lincoln Memorial white America finally awakened from its long sleep of benign neglect and, at worst, murderous racism.

When King came to the microphone it was, beyond any question, his finest hour. It was perhaps the finest hour of the black revolution. "I have a dream," he said. "I have a dream that on the red hills of Georgia, the sons of former slaves and the sons of former slave owners will be able to sit down together at the table of brotherhood. I have a dream that even the State of Mississippi, a state sweltering with the heat of injustice, will be transformed into an oasis of freedom. I have a dream ...."

After covering the riots at Ole Miss and the funeral of Medgar Evers and after seeing first hand the racial hatreds that poisoned the South, it was simply wonderful to hear King's words. They seemed to wash away so much of the filth of racial injustice that had stained the United States.

That night, as I anchored a news special from Washington, our producer Don Cameron and all of us in the CBC bureau felt we had captured a moving, historic moment. We wanted to show the passionate gentility of Martin Luther King's speech and the peaceful singing and marching. But errant technology destroyed our particular dream. We were feeding our program live to the CBC network from the studio of a Washington TV station. As it happened, the station was also doing a program on the march at the same time and airing some historical footage of other marches in Washington, some of them violent. Inadvertently, the station sent out their pictures with our sound. What viewers in Canada heard was my voice describing a peaceful march; what they saw was film of riots, soldiers, machine guns, police charging on horseback, demonstrators being clubbed, and lots of blood. It was seven or eight minutes before we knew what was happening and were able to get our pictures on along with our sound. By that time, Canadian viewers were undoubtedly hopelessly confused.

Their confusion was nothing compared to our high-voltage outrage. Don Cameron reached new levels of apoplexy as he screamed at the Washington station technicians and then at the idiots at our network in Toronto who had let the wrong pictures go on the air for so long without telling us.

Actually, things had started to go wrong for us earlier in the day. As part of our program, we interviewed Marlon Brando at the top of the steps of the Lincoln Memorial. At that point I was halfway up the stairs and had the only microphone available in that area. So I tossed it up to reporter Kingsley Brown who was to do the interview, but my aim was bad and it struck Brando on the side of the head. Brown looked aghast and apologized while Brando massaged his head, slowly smiled, and still did the interview.

The March on Washington did have a considerable effect on public opinion for it was a march without violence and a powerful, peaceful plea for racial equality. It contrasted sharply with the images of Bull Connor's dogs and softened somewhat the effects of the white backlash, helping prepare the way for passage of the civil rights legislation in 1964.

By mid-1963, manoeuvring had begun for the 1964 U.S. presidential election, and Kennedy looked forward to the race, especially since it began to seem likely his Republican opponent would be arch-conservative Senator Barry Goldwater. Kennedy spoke to a business group where he said "it would be premature to seek your support in the next election, and inaccurate to express thanks for having had it in the last one." But he looked even beyond his second term, wondering what he might do after leaving the White House. His brother Bob told me he thought Kennedy might have taught at a university. He also talked of running a newspaper. I heard him say in one speech that after his second term he would be at "the awkward age. Too old to begin a new career, and too young to write my memoirs."

By now he had more flecks of grey in his hair and he'd grown a bit fat. In the third year of his presidency the lines around his eyes had deepened. At news conferences, speeches, and ceremonies, we'd check to see how big his jowls were getting and occasionally a reporter would make some kidding remark as he passed by.

Kennedy was sensitive about his appearance and Salinger told us that when he hit 190 pounds he went on a diet, limiting his intake of potatoes, clam chowder, and daiquiris. But with all the burdens of the presidency and its physical toll, Kennedy maintained his own understated elegance. Even by the fall of 1963 the White House, the administration, and Washington itself still had much of the verve of the New Frontier.

In a thousand days, Kennedy had changed the face of the country. There had been many dramatic world crises to be dealt with, from the Vienna confrontation with Khrushchev to the building of the Berlin Wall and his electrifying "Ich bin ein Berliner" visit to that city. But with the Cuban missile crisis behind him, the test ban treaty, the space program, and racial integration well underway, and the Peace Corps, the Food for Peace Program, and the Alliance for Progress in Latin America all a reality, Kennedy looked ahead enthusiastically to his second four-year term in the White House. There certainly was no doubt among reporters that Kennedy would defeat Goldwater. And in that second term, his big project was to get out of Vietnam.

There were 700 American soldiers in Vietnam when Kennedy assumed the presidency and 15,000 when he died. Although he encouraged the Green Berets in their advisory role in Vietnam and sought victory, I remain convinced he would have gotten out of the war long before the end finally came more than a decade after his death. The U.S. had 500,000 troops in Vietnam by 1966. Three years earlier, when Undersecretary of State George Ball warned Kennedy that he might have to send as many as 300,000 soldiers to Vietnam in order to win, Kennedy told him, "George, you're crazier than hell. It is not going to happen."

Washington, D.C., November 22, 1963 ...

He never had a chance to get out of Vietnam because he went to Dallas. Dallas was "nut" country, a combustible combination of easy access to guns, high emotions, and far-out political fanaticism.

Hatred for Kennedy ran high in some parts of the city, as in other parts of the South. There was a report in Washington that I was never able to confirm directly, of a theatre in Georgia advertising the movie *PT-109*, based on Kennedy's South Pacific exploits. The theatre owner put up a marquee saying, "SEE HOW THE JAPS ALMOST GOT KENNEDY." The right-wing chairman of the board of the *Dallas Morning News*, E.M. Dealy, had written to the President accusing him of being a "weak sister," adding, "We need a man on horseback to lead this nation and many people in Texas and the southwest think that you are riding Caroline's bicycle."

The hatred was spun of many threads: his racial integration policies aroused the white supremacists; his pragmatic liberalism angered the extreme conservatives; his Catholicism infuriated the religious bigots; his popularity outraged the malcontents. But in Dallas, there seemed to be more fanatics per square foot than in any other city in America. Three years earlier, Lyndon Johnson and Lady Bird had been spat on, pushed, shoved, and hissed even though LBJ had done as much for Texas as any politician ever did. Four weeks before Kennedy's visit, Adlai Stevenson visited Dallas and was met with a screaming, spitting mob, incited by retired, extreme right-wing General Edwin A. Walker. "Are these human beings or are these animals?" Stevenson said, wiping the spit off his face with a handkerchief.

General Walker, who lived in Dallas, exemplified the far right-wing thinking of the time and was a darling of the extremists. When Kennedy came to office, Walker was commanding officer of the 24th Infantry Division in Germany. Kennedy soon dismissed him from his post for seeking to indoctrinate his troops in Europe with extreme right-wing propaganda. I covered the Senate hearing where he testified after his firing. He bluntly told the senators that Secretary of State Dean Rusk was disloyal and Secretary of Defense Robert McNamara was suspect. He said the "highest levels" of the U.S. government were "selling out to the Communists."

As we reporters scribbled furiously, he said the CIA was a "den of iniquity, a no-win collaborationist, soft on communism with a commissar system." He charged that the late UN Secretary-General Dag Hammarskjold had been a Communist and that the UN itself was a Communist plot to get the United States to surrender to the Soviet Union. He attacked all kinds of books that he admitted he had never read, mumbling and stumbling inarticulately from one far-fetched accusation to another.

When Walker finished, we rushed over to talk to him. A reporter beside me started to ask him what evidence he had for his assertions.

General Walker's face reddened, his eyes blazed, and suddenly he reared back and slugged the reporter with a right cross to the eye. Then he stomped off, fuming and muttering.

We were left shaking our heads and ministering to our comrade, who said it was only a "light jab." What was disturbing was that this character was a general in the U.S. Army who until recently was a very senior officer in Europe and in charge of thousands of men and tactical nuclear weapons. It made us wonder if there were any other such people still in command.

In the spring of 1963, less than a year after Walker's testimony, Lee Harvey Oswald had tried to assassinate the general, firing through a window of Walker's home and just missing him as he sat in a chair. Oswald had used the same mail-order rifle that he later brought to work in Dallas.

Another nut stirring up American emotions with visions of traitors was the leader of the American Nazi Party, George Lincoln Rockwell, a self-styled fuehrer who idolized Hitler and sported all the Nazi paraphernalia from swastikas to brown shirts and black belts.

I interviewed Rockwell several times at his headquarters, a two-storey white-frame house in Arlington, Virginia, only a fifteen-minute drive from Washington. He lived there with a dozen of his brown-shirted "storm troopers." To enter the house was to be transported back to a scene reminiscent of the early 1930s in Germany. A huge red Nazi flag covered one entire wall in the main room. The other walls were emblazoned with swastikas and pictures of Hitler, all illuminated. He insisted that his brown-shirts stand encircling us, all wearing their broad black belts and holstered guns. Shotguns were propped up against the walls and live shells lay scattered over a coffee table. His men ended all conversation with "Sieg Heil!"

Then in his forties, Rockwell, a one-time Navy commander, was sour, surly, and stupid. His men followed suit – most were slightly fat, blond, and tall.

"We've got guts and we'll get the 'Reds' and the Jews," he told me, pointing to a banner with the party motto "The Jews Are Through in '72." During our first interview, Rockwell pulled the party program out of his desk drawer and read the first plank: "We shall investigate, try, and execute all Jews proved to have taken part in Marxist or Zionist plots of treason ...."

"How many would be executed?" I asked.

"About 90 per cent, I would guess," he smiled. "And we'd use gas chambers." As he said that, his brown-shirted bullyboy claque burst into laughter.

It's always hard to judge how seriously people like Rockwell and his American Nazis should be taken. He told me, "There are thousands of us in this country and millions around the world." I didn't believe his membership claims, but I did believe the Nazis could cause a lot of trouble.

The FBI watched them closely and they seemed to have a secret source of money aside from the $5-a-month membership fees. At the time, there were party offices in Detroit, New York, Chicago, Birmingham, Los Angeles, Philadelphia, and Dallas "and several other cities including Montreal," according to Rockwell. "Our man in Montreal doesn't want publicity so I can't tell you who he is but he's a good man. We work with a newspaper up in Canada, too." They held rallies regularly in Washington and Rockwell flew to other Nazi rallies in cities across the U.S.

Some universities even invited Rockwell to speak and other groups sent invitations. "I have my troops," he told me. "If anybody wants violence, we'll give it to 'em. We train every day here, boxing, wrestling, and we know how to hurt." A great many people did get hurt at Nazi rallies. The Nazis also held private "trials." At one such proceeding, the Washington correspondent of the Jewish Telegraph Agency was found "guilty in absentia" as a "traitor" and "sentenced" to death. Warning signs and swastikas were plastered over his house, but he was never physically harmed. The Nazi organization lost much of its force when Rockwell was murdered by one of his own "troopers" some years later.

General Walker would have been right at home with the Nazis and so, it seems, would many of the citizens of Dallas that November, 1963. Stevenson had warned Kennedy not to go to Dallas, recalling his own recent experience. But the President felt he had to go to try to patch up a political quarrel among his Texas supporters. The irony is that Kennedy was killed not by a right-wing fanatic, but by a left-wing nut swept up by the atmosphere of hatred who wanted to impress his estranged wife.

UPI got the story first, sending the dreadful news clattering from tickers across the world. "FLASH ... KENNEDY WOUNDED, PERHAPS FATALLY, BY ASSASSIN'S BULLET ... " UPI's Merriman Smith, the dean of White House correspondents, was in the car carrying news agency correspondents; it always travelled immediately behind the presidential car. Smitty grabbed the car phone and got out the first FLASH on the Kennedy shooting and then hung onto the phone to keep it away from his AP competitor by asking the operator at the other end to read back what he'd dictated, an old news agency trick.

That Friday, November 22, I was in Miami on my way back from an assignment in Latin America. When I heard the news, I grabbed the first flight to Washington and the next three days were a blurred whirlwind of chaotic emotions and non-stop work.

On Friday night as I was en route to Washington, Kennedy's body was brought back in the presidential plane, Air Force One. At about 4:30 a.m. Saturday he was brought to the White House and the casket was placed in the same East Room where Abraham Lincoln had lain almost 100 years earlier. After a family mass and a few officials and friends paid their respects, the reporters who had covered the President were allowed into the room. As I went by, four men of the Green Beret Special Forces stood at attention by the casket. There was a deafening silence in the room. Nobody spoke or even whispered. Around me many of my journalistic co-workers, hard-bitten veterans who had seen everything from wars to hangings, stood there with silent tears streaming down their faces. Mechanically, I moved out of the room, still too stunned by what had happened to be able to absorb fully the reality of the tragedy, emerging from the White House into a downpour that continued all day. One of the most painful sights that Saturday was to see Kennedy's Oval Office furniture being moved out. Somehow that brought home more dramatically than anything else the aching reality that Kennedy was dead.

I spent the weekend filing reports to Canadian papers, preparing a major piece for the *Financial Post*, and doing innumerable radio and television reports for CBC. The CBC carried continuing American network programming on the assassination and aftermath, and my CBC colleagues and I would do inserts from time to time as well as work on major CBC news specials, which we aired that weekend.

All through Friday, Saturday, Sunday, and Monday, the U.S. television networks did a magnificent and critically necessary job of non-stop coverage. In a way, television was a pillar of strength for the nation, a vehicle through which all Americans simultaneously could share their grief with each other. A University of Chicago study later reported the average American watched TV that Saturday for ten hours.

I didn't see much of the lying-in-state ceremonies on the Hill. Having walked with some of my fellow journalists in the funeral march to the Capitol, I was at the rear. The speeches in the Capitol rotunda where the body lay seemed achingly long, but actually the whole ceremony lasted only fourteen minutes. When it ended, the public was allowed to pass by the casket covered with an American flag. All day and all night, Americans paid their respects. Even after midnight they came.

I returned to the rotunda about 2:00 a.m. Tens of thousands were lined up for blocks waiting to go in. I saw long-haired kids with guitars, soldiers, sailors, people on crutches and in wheelchairs, black and white, men and women from every stratum of society. Finally, at 9:00 a.m. on Monday, the doors closed in preparation for the state funeral. A quarter of a million people had passed by the casket and when the doors were closed 50,000 more were still waiting outside.

Jackie Kennedy insisted on walking the eight blocks from the White House to St. Matthew's Cathedral, where the funeral service was to be held, and that meant all the other official mourners had to walk, too. I took up a position just across the street from the White House to watch. A choir was in Lafayette Park directly in front.

At 11:30, the White House doors opened and the walk began. As they passed me, Jackie, holding for dear life onto Bob Kennedy's hand, led the marchers. Then came President Johnson. And behind him, the most impressive grouping of world statesmen I had ever seen or will ever see. It was one of history's most spectacular ceremonies, attended by more world leaders than had attended the funeral of Edward VII in 1910.

Towering over everybody and ramrod straight was General De Gaulle. Around him were King Baudoin of Belgium, Prince Philip and British Prime Minister Sir Alec Douglas-Home, German Chancellor Ludwig Erhard, Eamon de Valera, President of Ireland, the Queen of Greece, the Crown Prince of the Netherlands, the Crown Princesses of Norway and Denmark, Emperor Haile Selassie of Ethiopia, the Presidents of Germany, Israel, Korea, and the Philippines and the Prime Ministers of Turkey, Jamaica, and Canada. There were Anastas Mikoyan, first Deputy Premier of the Soviet Union, Prince Sihanouk of Cambodia, British Labour Leader Harold Wilson. Altogether, the official representatives of ninety-two nations walked with Jacqueline and Robert to the cathedral, along with the cabinet, the Joint Chiefs of Staff, and friends of the family.

The funeral was a security nightmare; there had been several reports of assassination plans, including one on General De Gaulle (passed to the Secret Service by the RCMP). Scores of agents and bodyguards marched with the leaders while 4,000 armed police and military watched for trouble. We, too, were watching for trouble because the march to the cathedral surely offered more targets for assassination than had ever before been gathered in one place at one time. But there had been enough killing that weekend and there was no trouble. The only sound as the mourners walked up the street past me was that of church bells, shuffling feet, and those horrible drums.

After the casket, again lashed to a gun carriage, arrived at the church,

154

I skipped the ceremony in order to get a front-row place at the gravesite at Arlington Cemetery. There I waited for more than an hour in a roped-off area a few feet from the grave. The grave was on a gently sloping green hill, just below a building that had been the home of General Robert E. Lee. Ten days before, Kennedy had been almost to this very spot to honour the Unknown Soldier.

As I waited, I looked about. As far as I could see were the thousands of simple white crosses marking the graves of America's military dead. All about us were barren dogwood trees, though the grass was green and the birds twittering. Beyond the grave, down the hill and into the distance, lay all of official Washington. I could see the Lincoln Memorial directly across the Potomac River, the Washington Monument, and over to one side in the distance, the dome of the Capitol. Meanwhile, the reporters talked quietly and edged and pushed ahead to get the closest position. Having arrived early, I had staked out a position perhaps ten yards from the gravesite and didn't move from there.

Across the Memorial Bridge leading from the Lincoln Memorial to Arlington Cemetery, I could see the long black line of limousines slowly approaching us. When they arrived, fifty jets streaked overhead, followed by Air Force One. I noticed Prince Philip hurrying up the hill using his ceremonial sword as a cane. Lyndon Johnson seemed almost lost, lonely and hidden in the crowd.

The coffin was taken from the caisson and the riderless horse Black Jack, who had been so jumpy earlier, was now quiet. An Air Force bagpipe band played as the coffin was carried by the casket team to the grave with honorary pallbearers walking behind and an honour guard of Green Berets on either side. As the coffin came to the gravesite, Jackie started to move toward it but was restrained by Bob. Cardinal Cushing, his mournful face even more pained than usual, began his final words and then sprinkled holy water on the casket. A twenty-one-gun salute banged out behind us and then three volleys of M-1 rifle fire cracked in salute and a bugler played a spine-shivering taps. Through it all, I watched Jackie. Her face hidden behind her black veil, she seemed dazed, almost as if hypnotized. She moved here and there as she was told, saying nothing, and mostly hanging tightly to Bob Kennedy's hand. He was granite-faced, but I felt he might collapse at any moment. The only thing holding him together seemed to be his fierce determination to take care of Jackie.

Finally, eight white-gloved servicemen folded the flag atop the coffin into a triangle and, gently pushed by Bob, Jackie stepped forward to accept it in the time-honoured tradition of the military widow. She clutched that red, white, and blue triangle as if her life depended on it, and perhaps at that moment it did. Then she lit the eternal flame at the grave and it was all over.

But not quite.

While the funeral was the final formal farewell to John F. Kennedy, there was one last emotionally charged moment nine months later at the Democratic National Convention in Atlantic City. The delegates had just watched a film tribute to the murdered President. Then, with tears in his eyes, a wan Bob Kennedy stepped to the rostrum. For fifteen minutes the convention hall shook with cheering in a wrenching, uplifting salute to what was and what might have been.

And then, as the cheers finally subsided, Bob Kennedy softly, gently, with his throat catching from time to time and his face damp with tears, read a quotation from Shakespeare:

When he shall die
Take him and cut him out in little stars
And he will make the face of heaven so fine
That all the world will be in love with night
And pay no worship to the garish sun.

No finer tribute was ever made to John F. Kennedy.

John F. Kennedy was a memorable president not so much because of his specific achievements, except perhaps his handling of the Cuban missile crisis. His legislative successes were, in fact, comparatively few. What made him special was the excitement he generated and the style he brought to the White House, the sense that anything was possible. Because of his example, tens of thousands of Americans went into politics and many thousands of others in Canada and elsewhere around the world were inspired to enter public service and continue what they saw as his quest for excellence. He was a symbol for those who wanted, as he so often said, "to make things better."

So he is remembered not for what he did, but for what he might have done. He is remembered because he made us feel good about ourselves and hopeful about the future.

6 *ONE MINUTE TO MIDNIGHT*

Havana, Cuba, February, 1963 ...

John F. Kennedy's assassination was still an undreamt nightmare when I set off on my first major journalistic trip to Latin America. I had travelled to Mexico several times for IFAP meetings, once to cover a Mexican visit by Prime Minister Diefenbaker, and once to get married in the Ensenada town hall, meet my wife's relatives in Mexico City, and holiday in Acapulco and Cuernevaca. But this was the first of half a dozen trips to try to understand the problems of the world below the Rio Grande.

It's an area that Canadian journalism generally ignores. The CBC and Southam News Service for a brief time had full-time correspondents stationed in Latin America and, more recently, the Toronto *Globe and Mail* has established a correspondent based in Mexico City with a roving beat. But in the fifties and sixties CBC made regular journalistic forays below the Rio Grande, as it still does.

In 1963, Cuba still obsessed the Americans. When I went to Havana it was only two years after the Bay of Pigs fiasco and just four months after the Cuban missile crisis. By now Washington had persuaded the other Latin countries (except for Mexico) to break diplomatic relations with Cuba, as it had done in January, 1961, when Fidel Castro seized U.S. holdings in Cuba and publicly proclaimed his allegiance to the Communist camp. Castro hadn't always been public enemy number one for the Americans. In fact, before he seized power on New Year's Day, 1959, and for a year or so after, he was regarded by most Americans as a kind of Latin American Robin Hood ridding Cuba of Fulgencio Batista, the extreme right-wing and murderous dictator who had ruled Cuba since a coup d'état in 1952.

Ironically, Batista, as a young army sergeant in 1933, spearheaded his own liberal coup that overthrew another dictator, Gerardo Machado. Later Batista was leader of a military and student group that ousted another president. In 1940, he became a left-wing power behind the new president. Soon after, with the support of the extreme left, he was himself elected president, launching a massive plan of economic and social reform. He was defeated in 1944 but when he seized power again in 1952, the former liberal democrat turned into a fascist, bullying dictator just like those he'd earlier overthrown.

Batista never really ran the economy of Cuba; he simply gave out licences for others (many of them Americans) to run it, somewhat along the lines of a franchise system, collecting fat bribes in return. Under his regime Havana became a whore of a city, the playground of rich Americans looking for a dirty weekend. A number of people had told me stories of flying down to Havana from New York or over from Miami, picking up fourteen-year-old prostitutes, gambling at the Mafia-run slot machines and roulette wheels, guzzling quarts of daiquiris, and, for fun, sometimes throwing quarters into the street to watch the Cubans scramble for them on their hands and knees. As has been said, "every revolution is the kicking in of a rotten door," and the Batista door was just waiting for Fidel Castro.

As a young lawyer he had openly criticized Batista and on July 26, 1953, he led an unsuccessful attack on the Moncada army barracks in Santiago de Cuba, his home town at the eastern end of the island. He was imprisoned but then released in 1955 in an attempt to appease public opinion, which had been galvanized by his courtroom speech, "History Will Absolve Me." He then went to Mexico to organize his revolutionary group, which he called the 26th of July Movement. In Mexico, he met an Argentinian doctor and revolutionary, Ernesto Ché Guevara, and together with Fidel's brother Raul, they gathered around them a core of what would become one of the most dramatic political events of the twentieth century. In December, 1956, the three led a small group of supporters in a landing in Cuba. They were met by the Cuban Army and were attacked and defeated. But Castro, with eleven others including Raul and Guevara, survived and escaped into the Sierra Maestre Mountains where they recruited new supporters, planned their revolutionary tactics, and began guerilla warfare against Batista. They burned sugar-cane fields, attacked isolated Army posts, blew up bridges, and successfully converted many peasants to their cause. Two years later, Fidel, Raul, and Ché marched into Havana at the head of a victorious army while Batista fled with his millions to the Dominican Republic and the protection of its dictator, Generalissimo Rafael Trujillo. He ended up in Franco's Spain where he died in 1973.

Castro was almost universally hailed in those early, exultant days and even in Washington he was greeted as a hero when he visited the city. I covered him on that trip and he took the city by storm, kissing babies, shaking hands, and signing autographs. He wowed the senators and disarmed the hard-boiled journalists at a meeting of the American Society of Newspaper Editors where he smiled shyly and laughed at his awkward English. As he walked through the halls of Congress to a meeting with the Senate Foreign Relations Committee, I watched as secretaries, typists, and messengers squealed, "Oooo Fidel ... Fidel ... Fidel." Hundreds of them jostled each other, eager to see and if possible touch the dashing young revolutionary. I was standing beside Senate Committee Chairman Senator William Fulbright, who whispered to me, "My God ... you'd think he was Elvis Presley!"

But the honeymoon didn't last long. The Eisenhower administration was highly suspicious of Castro and, when he began arresting and executing large numbers of Batista supporters, seizing U.S. property, and denouncing Yankee imperialism, it began plotting to get rid of him. The Americans stopped buying Cuban sugar and barred most trade and began to squeeze Cuba economically in every possible way. They also began planning the Bay of Pigs invasion.

Castro was thus forced to look to Moscow for help. I've always wondered if Castro would have become so enmeshed with the Communist bloc had he not been economically pushed into its open arms by Washington policies. Without the Eisenhower squeeze, he might have become a Latin version of the independent Communist Tito of Yugoslavia. But by the time I got there in February of 1963, Cuba was a Communist state fully dominated economically by the Russians, although retaining its own special zestful Latin spirit.

Don Cameron, the executive producer of the CBC documentary program *Newsmagazine*, wanted to do a program reflecting Cuba four years after the successful revolution, now in the arms of Russia and threatened by the U.S. It was a tricky assignment because hardly any non-Communist reporters were allowed into Cuba at the time. We had endlessly and fruitlessly sought visas to get into the country but finally were told by Cuban officials in Ottawa that if we went to the Cuban Embassy in Mexico City we might be given visas there. Other than via Prague, Mexico City was the only way to fly to Havana. We took the chance and flew to Mexico with cameraman Wally Donaldson and soundman Eddie Chong. The Cuban Embassy issued the precious documents and we were set.

The Cuban airline flew twice a week and we grabbed the first plane available. Before we lugged our camera equipment on board, the Cubans examined it suspiciously and meticulously. On board, we were surprised to see armed guards walking up and down the aisle of the plane. When we landed we stepped into what seemed like a military camp. Cameron, who had been a Navy pilot and an NBC news editor, led us off the plane and straight into a lengthy interrogation by security police. They were clearly uneasy and unhappy with our arrival but eventually allowed us in for our three-week assignment.

As we drove through the streets of Havana to our hotel, we were struck by the sight of so many guns and so many Russians. Almost half the people seemed to be carrying pistols and rifles. Our hotel doorman packed a stubby Czechoslovakian burp gun and the room clerk laid his pistol on the check-in counter as we registered. It seemed like the American Wild West with a Spanish accent. On the streets, four-teen- and fifteen-year-olds proudly carried pistols. I noticed one teen-age girl carrying a rifle almost as big as she was. How she'd ever fire it, I couldn't guess. Shortly after our arrival, we went to a Russian movie and many of the boys and girls on dates carried a gun in one hand while holding the other. The guns clearly seemed to be a sign of machismo and of independence as well as a reflection of the siege mentality induced by the Bay of Pigs, the Cuban missile crisis, and the still much discussed and feared American invasion expected at any time.

The Russians were everywhere. Coatless and wearing open-necked shirts, the hundreds of Soviet technical experts seemed right at home, probably delighted to be away from the Soviet winter. Even after the humiliation of the missile crisis the previous October, in which many Cubans felt Moscow had sold them out to Washington, Cubans I talked to were grateful for all the economic aid and technical expertise the Russians were providing. A dozen Soviet freighters were in the Havana harbour unloading trucks, wheat, clothing, and factory equipment, all coming in at the rate of a million dollars a day. Everyone I talked to told me that without the Russian help, Cuba's economy would have utterly collapsed. So the Cubans were grateful. Even so, it wasn't enough as shortages of spare parts stopped hotel and office building elevators and air conditioning, slowed down factory production, and left hundreds of cars sitting idle. One striking sight was the hundreds of abandoned or barely working American cars vintage 1950s. This was because no new U.S. cars had come into Cuba since 1960, nor any spare parts. Those automotive skeletons are there in Cuba to this day, many of them still functioning.

Even with all the Russian aid and consequent Soviet influence on the Castro government, Fidel fiercely retained his own independence. While he generally supported the Moscow line, he certainly was no meek puppet and I was told by diplomats there was constant fighting with Soviet officials.

After we checked into the hotel and carried our bags along dimly lit corridors to our rooms, Cameron and I called the CBC in Toronto to let them know we had successfully gotten into Cuba and to discuss our desire to get film of Castro at work. Soon afterwards we got a vivid demonstration of the way the Cuban secret police work and a taste of what life is like under a dictatorship. During the conversation with our Toronto editors we spoke of "shooting" Castro in his office and perhaps getting more "shots" during a speech.

Almost before we put down the phone, police were banging on our hotel room door, alarmed that we were counter-revolutionaries planning Castro's assassination. A couple of hours of nervous explanation in our hotel room about the language of television proved grudgingly satisfactory, although we were watched closely ever after and were given a "guide" who was almost certainly a member of the secret police. In fact, it was a bit of a relief to have the secret policeman with us because he helped explain to dubious officials what we were doing, thereby saving us a lot of time.

In the Cuba of the early 1960s, "Big Brother" was always watching. Hotel rooms of visiting foreigners were routinely bugged and people called "Block Captains" presided over each local Committee for the Defence of the Revolution and kept watch on their neighbourhoods, reporting anything suspicious. Youngsters were encouraged to report on neighbours, friends, and family if anything suspicious was said, and propaganda was unremittingly pumped out of radio, television, and the papers. One of the very few non-Cuban reporters stationed in Havana told me he had so many police taps on his telephone that it frequently went out of order.

A couple of days after our arrival, I strolled over to a park where a Soviet exhibition displayed the latest Russian cars, tractors, and trucks while loudspeakers incongruously blared out such American tunes as "Ballin' the Jack" and "A Pretty Girl Is Like a Melody." As I walked about, Cubans gleefully shouted "Tovarich" at me, assuming I was one of the Russian technical experts or a sailor off one of the Soviet merchant ships. I paused to watch some Russians and Cubans playing chess on a card table in the park and to watch a pick-up soccer game between some Cubans and Soviets. Hammer-and-Sickle flags fluttered from poles in the park and throughout the city and were emblazoned on posters hanging in hotel lobbies and plastered on the sides of buildings. I even saw a red hammer and sickle embroidered on the rear ends of the white shorts worn by a team of girl track athletes.

With all the surveillance and phone tapping, during the first few days in Havana I was still able to talk to scores of opponents of Castro's regime. But it was only when no one else was around and always on streets or in parks, never inside a room where "bugs" could be planted. Castro was the adored "Fidel" to most Cubans, but his opponents ridiculed his six-foot-two-inch 200-plus pounds by calling him *El Caballo*, "The Horse."

Before I had left Washington for Cuba, I'd heard endless loud and lunatic talk from many congressmen and even some administration officials about the anti-Castro rebel armies in the hills just waiting to swoop down on Havana to the joy of a rejoicing population anxious to be rid of Castro. It was sheer nonsense. Diplomats told me privately that there were a few isolated bands of counter-revolutionaries in the Escambrey and Sierra Maestre Mountains. They occasionally burned a sugar-cane field but had very little support among the people and constituted no threat whatever to the popular Castro.

Cuba may not have had much intellectual freedom under Batista, but there was less under Castro. Because of this and because they felt they had no real future in Cuba, in the early years of Castro many professionals and middle-class people fled. When I was in Cuba, this exodus had left the country with a critical shortage of engineers, doctors, lawyers, and teachers. One veterinarian told me that before the revolution there were 600 veterinarians in Cuba, but now there were only 150. He, too, was thinking of leaving because he was so frustrated with the bureaucracy that had been brought to the economy. He said that he'd been pushed into half a dozen different jobs by the government over the previous eighteen months. "I can't even settle down to work in one job because of all the bureaucracy," he told me. "How can I get my job done?" One well-educated middle-class young woman in Havana complained about the lack of freedom, telling me, "It makes you feel so very old and so very hopeless." At least a couple of dozen people I talked with quietly asked me if I would take money or jewels out of the country for them, which they would get back when they had fled. I declined, but it indicated the desperation of some to get out.

In those days of Castro's trial-and-error economic plans and isolation by Western countries, the Cubans were very short of food. In travelling

162

to several cities and through some of the countryside, I didn't see one egg or one pat of butter, except in a special restaurant in Havana for visiting dignitaries. Beef was almost never seen, and the pork and chicken that we did eat was elderly, stringy, and in short supply. Nobody starved, but just about everybody complained about the food. Some restaurants didn't even bother with menus. You just ate what they had. An elderly Havana housewife showed me her ration card that allowed her one quart of milk every five days, five eggs a month – although she could rarely find any eggs at all – one chicken a month, one-eighth of a pound of butter a month, three-quarters of a pound of fish a week, one-and-a-half pounds of beans a month, six pounds of rice a month, and one bar of soap a month. The rest, as many a housewife told me, you got on the ever-present black market.

The Cubans who did eat well, though, were the students. In fact, the student was king in Castro's Cuba. Free clothes, free food, free housing, free education. By far the biggest and best meal I had was at the student cafeteria at the University of Havana, where I'd gone to talk with the students. For the equivalent of forty cents, I had soup, beef, rice, tomatoes, potatoes, sweet potatoes, beans, banana, orange juice, and a roll.

It was also hard to find razor blades, headache pills, gum, and a thousand and one things we take for granted. In fact, twenty years later, many of those items are still in short supply in Cuba. My cab driver in Havana actually cried in gratitude when I gave him a pack of twenty razor blades. I asked an official at the foreign ministry about the shortages, the sense of oppression felt by some, and the lack of free elections. "What did free elections ever do for us?" he replied. "They got us Batista. What have we to gain from free elections?"

Even with all the shortages of food and spare parts, the flight of professionals, and the lack of freedom, under Castro, Cubans did see big improvements in some areas. I talked to Canadian diplomats and other foreign observers on the scene who all agreed the very poor, the workers, the blacks, and the students were much better off than ever before. The gamblers and dirty weekenders were gone from Havana and the prostitutes were also gone. We were taken one day to a former Havana residential area of the very rich to see the mansions converted to homes for the rehabilitation of prostitutes, who were eating well, playing ping-pong, and going to school to learn skills useful to the revolution.

The emphasis on youth was not only obvious in the universities. Hotels and most business enterprises were run by men in their twenties. Government departments were often directed by people under thirty. I talked to the officer in charge of North African affairs in the foreign ministry; he was nineteen years old. There were other teen-agers running government agencies and in positions of influence.

I was told by diplomats in Cuba that Castro had set up several schools for Latin American revolutionaries, teaching them how to blow up bridges, infiltrate labour unions, and fight guerilla wars. I saw none of these schools on my trip to Cuba, although I did visit schools teaching Marxism-Leninism to sixteen-year-olds. Both students and teachers were proud of their communism. "Only through communism can we achieve for Cuba what we want; only through communism can we feed the people and give them freedom," one sixteen-year-old co-ed told me. "Everything in Cuba is the best," said a seventeen-year-old girl who had lived in the U.S. "We've got the best teachers in the world. The best weather. The best motion pictures and the best books." Then she smiled shyly, looked a bit furtive, and added, "But I'm dying for American cigarettes and Chiclets. Have you got any?" Echoing her sentiments, her boy friend standing beside us said, "Man, I'd give anything for a cheeseburger and a malted."

The students and the young leaders also led the way in demonstrating to Cubans that idealism and hard work should go together. For three months each year they left their schools and government offices to go out into the countryside to cut sugar cane. Equipment frequently broke down and the parts shortages meant more human hands were necessary. Even the renowned Ché Guevara went out cutting cane. Trainloads would leave Havana in somewhat the same way trainloads of youngsters would leave Canadian cities during World War II to harvest wheat and help on farms.

We were unsuccessful in getting an interview with Castro, so we decided to try for one with Guevara, the number-two man in the government and the boss of the Cuban economy. Along with our ever-present secret policeman guide we flew from Havana to Camaguey roughly in the middle of the island, where we heard Guevara was working in the sugar-cane fields.

As we checked into the Plaza Hotel off Camaguey's main square, I was startled to see a huge picture of John Diefenbaker plastered on the wall right up there beside Castro, Marx, and Lenin. The room clerk had also pinned up above the check-in counter the front page of the newspaper *Revolucion* with blaring banner headlines reporting Diefenbaker's refusal to take American nuclear warheads. The Cubans were making a big fuss over Diefenbaker's quarrel with the Americans.

"You must refuse the bombas atomicas," the room clerk told me. "Your Mr. Diefenbaker is a great man. It's a shame the Americans are trying to throw him out of office. Mr. Diefenbaker, I think, is a lot like Fidel.'' Which would have surely surprised Mr. Diefenbaker. Even our guide joined in the discussion, expressing his admiration for the Canadian Prime Minister although he had a word of advice for him. ''He must be tougher with the Americans, you know, fellow,'' he told me. ''He should be more like Fidel or else Canada will lose her freedom.''

The conversation reminded me of the time I covered Diefenbaker's arrival in Mexico City for a formal visit in April, 1960. His ability to speak Spanish was even less than his ability to speak French. Nevertheless, he felt it appropriate to deliver part of his arrival speech at the Mexico City airport in Spanish. While Mexican President Lopez Mateos listened intently, and we reporters listened in confusion, Diefenbaker spoke briefly in a language clearly unknown to mankind. When he finished, the President of Mexico said how nice it was that the Canadian Prime Minister had spoken in his native French language.

After settling into the Plaza, we started to hunt for Guevara. We visited the police headquarters, went to various cane-cutter union offices, and simply drove about the countryside asking people if they knew where he was. For two days we searched without a lead. On the second night, Cameron and I split up. He took cameraman Wally Donaldson and our secret policeman while soundman Eddie Chong and I struck out on our own. Along a road a few miles from town, we stopped at a roadblock and asked some soldiers if they knew where Ché was. Instead of getting answers, we got arrested.

We were led away at the point of burp guns and put into a room in an old schoolhouse. For four or five hours Chong and I sat on the floor encircled by young boys pointing black, nasty-looking guns at us. We were questioned and requestioned, accused of being American spies, threatened, and yelled at. All, in a Spanish which I understood fitfully but certainly enough to get their message. Finally, an officer arrived who checked with Havana and reluctantly believed our story. The problem, he explained, was that Guevara was cutting sugar cane nearby and they were worried about protecting him.

At least we had located our quarry, and with a little more negotiation by Cameron, whom we met back at the hotel, we arranged to meet Guevara the next day in the cane fields. As we jeeped through the dusty cane fields the next morning, Guevara's guards were everywhere, evidence of continuing tensions and fear of assassination. An outer perimeter of armed guards encircled the field in which he was working. There were guards in a middle circle and then more guards in a close circle. All were armed with burp guns, machine guns, rifles, pistols, and machetes. Guevara himself was wearing what he told me was a "machine gun pistol," which fired twenty shots at a trigger squeeze. "Very good, very accurate, very fast," he said. He also carried five twenty-shot refills.

Guevara was not only the number-two man in Cuba, he was a worldwide idol for the young and rebellious. His revolutionary history went back to his early medical student days in Buenos Aires where he joined riots against Juan Peron. In 1952 he organized guerilla bands in Bolivia and later worked as a doctor in a leper colony and helped left-wing Guatemala leader Jacobo Arbenz before Arbenz was overthrown by a CIA-backed coup in 1954. He then fled to Mexico where he first met Castro.

Having heard so much about Guevara – his bravery, his fierce determination, his radical beliefs, his ferocity in argument, and his dominating, ruthless style of leadership – I was totally unprepared for the man. Not surprisingly, he was wearing faded army fatigues and a big white straw hat, but I was surprised to discover that he was my own age – thirty-five – and that he was charming and gentle of manner. He had soft brown eyes and a shy smile on his bearded face, and when we talked he revealed a delightfully self-deprecatory sense of humour. He looked to me like a twinkly-eyed Clark Gable with a cigar in his mouth. In fact, Guevara was always puffing something. He smoked eighteen cigars and three packs of ciagarettes a day.

A diplomat in Havana had told me, "What Guevara thinks today is what Castro says three months from now." So getting an interview with him was an important scoop for us, and as I grasped his big, rough hand in greeting, he smilingly agreed to the interview.

He took off his straw hat, wiped perspiration from his brow, and asked where we would do it. We wanted to film him cutting cane in order to create some atmosphere. Since Guevara understood only a little English, I explained what we wanted in Spanish with the aid of our secret policeman guide – he was almost overwhelmed to be speaking to the revered Ché. I asked the questions in English, our guide translated into Spanish, and Guevera answered in Spanish. Later, in editing the film, we cut out the guide's Spanish questions and added a translation for Guevara's comments.

For the introduction to the interview, we asked Ché to drive his Russian-made cane-cutting tractor over to one side of the cane field and then drive slowly in our direction in an arc, cutting cane as he went, arriving finally where I would be standing. As we gave him these instructions, he nodded smilingly and drove off in his tractor to do what he was told.

Now you have to know that Don Cameron is a producer who sometimes got excited in his work, especially if something went wrong. And something did. Guevara turned his tractor away from the camera instead of toward it, causing Cameron to explode with indignation at his stupidity. The producer charged madly into the cane field after the retreating tractor, waving his arms and screaming at Guevara. "This way! This way, you idiot!" Cameron shouted.

The forty or fifty armed guards encircling us were momentarily stunned by what seemed an unbelievable scene. Then they raised their guns and I heard some ominous clicks. Even Cameron paused. Then Guevara looked up, smiled, stopped his machine, listened to Cameron, nodded, smiled again, and took off once more in his machine. This time he made the correct turn. "Good boy," said Cameron. And we conducted the interview without further incident.

Our secret police guide had turned white with fear as the scene unfolded. He later said he thought Cameron was trying to kill Guevara and had visions of all of us, himself included, mowed down by Guevara's guards. As it was, he wasn't entirely sure of the future advancement of his career.

In the interview, Guevara admitted he had made many mistakes in his economic planning for Cuba. He had tried to swing the country's economy too quickly away from its one-crop dependence on sugar. He was proud, though, of vastly expanding trade with Russia and Eastern Europe and he even hoped there would be a resumption of trade with the United States. To my astonishment, he spoke admiringly of John Kennedy. He identified I think with Kennedy's youthful zest and progressive rhetoric just as, privately, Bob Kennedy expressed admiration for the verve and style, if not the philosophy, of Guevara and Castro.

He clearly knew a good bit about Canadian problems and had followed Diefenbaker's battles with Kennedy over nuclear warheads. He told me he thought Diefenbaker a "good man" and supported his position against Washington. He said, too, he wanted to see more Canadian trade with Cuba, adding, "But the Americans might try to stop you."

The day after the interview with Guevara, he came into Camaguey to speak to a meeting of farmers. Wearing the same army fatigues and carrying the same straw hat, he told them that the past fascism was over, that the present might be hard because the country was in transition, but that the future would be golden. He spoke of more food and clothes, hospitals, homes, and schools, and future opportunities to serve the country. He was a magnificently spell-binding orator, much as Castro was, and like Castro, he could speak forever. He described Fidel as a modern-day Simon Bolivar, a contemporary saviour who would bring democracy to all of Latin America.

Guevara, like Castro, wanted not only to consolidate the Cuban revolution but also to export it to the rest of Latin America. Two years after our interview, he grew weary of the bureaucratic battlefield and left Cuba to take the lead in spreading the Cuban example and fostering revolution elsewhere in Latin America. In 1967, while directing guerilla activity in Bolivia, he was wounded in a battle with government troops, captured, and executed.

After a couple of days in Camaguey, we flew back to Havana and I spent a few more days soaking up the atmosphere, talking to people in the streets and in their homes, and interviewing officials in government offices and diplomats in restaurants. Cameron and the crew stayed a few days after my departure to get some more footage. I flew back to Mexico and home to Washington. A week or so later, I was in Toronto working with Cameron editing the film and writing the script for our documentary. After it was aired I had a letter of complaint from the Cuban Embassy, which objected to my characterization of Cuba as a "Communist" country.

In an article I wrote for the *Financial Post* summing up my Cuban trip, I started out by saying;

> Facts to get straight about Cuba:
> 1. There is no chance of anybody overthrowing Premier Fidel Castro in the near future.
> 2. Castro is not a Russian puppet. He stands strongly on his own legs.
> 3. Cuba has become a 100% communist state.
> 4. Food is short, but nobody is starving.
> 5. The economy is in chaos.
> 6.The poor probably are better off than they were before, but Cuba is an intellectual prison.
> 7. Hysteria in the U.S., as well as in Cuba, could lead to war.

Over time, the hysteria in the U.S. and in Cuba has calmed down. American tourists are now going to Cuba, as well as Canadians, and Castro said recently that he had always admired President Kennedy and felt the Bay of Pigs was a mistake inherited from Eisenhower.

A quarter of a century after Castro's revolution, Cuba remains a beacon for the far left and the Communists of Latin America, who see the "Big Stick" diplomacy of Teddy Roosevelt making a comeback in Washington and who think the democratic process of reform is simply too slow for the region. The sad reality for Cuba was that there was no viable middle ground between the fascism of Batista and the communism of Castro. It's a gap that continues to plague much of Latin America.

Mexico City, September, 1963 ...

My most ambitious trip to Latin America was another *Newsmagazine* documentary assignment, this time with producer Bill Cunningham, Cameraman Jean Bisson, and soundman Ron Wegoda. Our itinerary would take us on a month-long 10,000-mile journey to Mexico, Colombia, Venezuela, and Brazil. Our aim was to focus on the tragic disparity between rich and poor that is at the root of so many of the region's problems.

Early in September, just seven months after my trip to Cuba, I met the crew in Mexico City, just in time to cover the annual celebration marking the Mexican Independence Day of September 15. There have been only two profound revolutions in Latin America in this century, the Cuban and the Mexican. So Mexico seemed a logical place to start our trip, a country trying to solve the problem of wretched poverty and economic underdevelopment through peaceful and democractic means, in sharp contrast to Cuba's harsher Marxist-Leninist approach.

We filmed the festivities marking the anniversary of the revolution: parades, fireworks displays, and a massive bell-ringing, flag-waving public meeting led by President Adolfo Lopez Mateos in the square in front of the Presidential Palace in downtown Mexico City. At that event, I learned the fierce pride Mexicans have in their flag. I had been sitting on the curb watching the festivities and had put a paper replica of the Mexican flag under me. An angry soldier came over to me, poked me with his bayonet, and indicated very clearly that I was insulting Mexico by sitting on the flag.

In the last century and the first decade of this one, Mexico had seen presidential assassinations, civil wars, and coups, but since 1920, under the rule of the Institutional Revolutionary Party, relative calm had persisted as its leaders sought social and economic reform essentially through a relatively democratic, one-party system of government, with presidents serving a single six-year term. As President, Lopez Mateos had expanded Mexican industrial production, spread land reform, introduced tax reforms, and built roads, hospitals, and schools. After capturing the exuberant Mexican mood of celebration, we travelled with the President north to the industrial centre of Monterrey where we followed him as he opened a new steel mill, a new car factory, a section of highway, and a school.

With all the progress, however, poverty still almost overwhelmed the region and in our filming we sought to contrast that progress with the often primitive living conditions. On a highway just outside Monterrey we stopped at the dirt-floor shack of a Mrs. Lupita Caballon. From her home we filmed President Lopez Mateos and his caravan whizzing by in their big cars and then zeroed in on Mrs. Caballon. She told me she paid the equivalent of $2 a month to rent her home and spent $5 a week to feed a family of ten, mostly with tortillas, the flat, thin Mexican pancake.

We then flew back to Mexico City to watch the poor people's extraordinary devotion to the church in this 96 per cent Catholic country. During a Sunday Mass at the Church of the Virgin of Guadalupe, the patron saint of Mexico and the best-known church in Latin America, I climbed up to the rooftop to see the thousands of worshippers jamming the square in front of the church. I watched the ragged, barefoot Indians crawl two miles on their hands and knees up to the church door, hoping for a miracle cure or simply thanking God for life. When I came down I talked to several of them because I wondered what on earth they had to be thankful for. "Because I can breathe, sir," one told me. "For my children," another said.

Later that Sunday, I observed the crowds flocking to an afternoon bullfight. After God in the morning it was blood in the afternoon; many of the same people who had gone to the Church of the Virgin of Guadalupe in the morning were at the bullring now.

In our last few days in Mexico City, while Bill Cunningham and the crew continued to film, I split away to talk privately to diplomats, government officials, and business, labour, and farm leaders. From my IFAP days, I had retained a number of contacts, including the president of the Mexican farm organization; these people were able to give me an insight into the Mexican struggle for progress.

The Mexicans had been quite successful in making social and economic reforms without the dictatorial strains of Cuba. The reason, I came to believe as I listened to officials and private citizens, was the early development of a sizable middle class. Unlike in most Latin countries, it was able to grow and flourish, and as it grew in economic and political strength it provided a social and economic stability for the country and, among other things, encouraged the military to accept total civilian control.

Even with the growing middle class, however, the poor are still there in Mexico, mostly the Indians who pour in from the countryside into the crowded streets and slums of Mexico City or Monterrey or Guadalajara. They pour so rapidly into Mexico City that by the end of this century Mexico City will likely have the biggest population of any city on earth. The Mexicans, therefore, will clearly have to continue to struggle to keep ahead of their population growth and migration to the cities. But as one of the few Latin American countries with a strong democratic tradition, Mexico remains the envy and the model for many of the moderate forces of the region.

We flew out of Mexico City via Panama to Bogota, the darkly moody, isolated capital of Colombia, perched 8,600 feet up in the Andes with four mountain peaks hulking over it. After clearing customs with all our TV equipment, which in most Latin American countries was accelerated by a healthy bribe to the customs inspector handed over attached to a letter saying we were doing a documentary for Canadian television, we drove into town. Following the verve and vitality of Mexico City, it was a shock to meet the dour, grey, rain-coated citizens of Bogota, where it is perpetually cloudy and rains almost every day. Two-thirds of them were Mestizos of mixed Spanish and Indian blood; the rest were mostly European. The whole country was plunged into something called "La Violencia," a civil war that had lasted fifteen years and killed upwards of 300,000 people out of a population about the size of Canada.

Our first assignment was an interview with President Guillermo Leon Valencia. As we drove up a narrow, rundown street to the unimpressive Presidential Palace of San Carlos we were briefly held up by a parade of goose-stepping, blue-uniformed presidential guardsmen. The dull palace exterior gave way to an interior of gold-painted furniture, marble statues, and elaborately costumed guards. We lugged our equipment up a broad staircase to a reception room dominated by a portrait of Simon Bolivar, founder of Colombia and known as the liberator of Latin America. Bolivar is Latin America's greatest hero because of his leadership of the early nineteenth-century wars of liberation against the Spaniards in Colombia, Venezuela, Ecuador, Panama, Bolivia, and Peru. Latins to this day, including Castro, talk dreamily of his efforts to unify the entire continent.

It had been difficult to arrange the interview with President Valencia, involving weeks of delicate negotiations between the Colombian Embassy in Ottawa, the Presidential Palace, and our own embassy in Bogota. But finally it had been agreed to. Conscious of the effort we'd made to get the interview, we were particularly careful to be polite and respectful.

The impeccably dressed fifty-five-year-old President came across as a precise, cautious shopkeeper. In fact, he was a conservative serving a four-year term in a system of alternating liberal and conservative presidents. As Bill Cunningham and I engaged him in light banter to get him into a relaxed and talkative mood, Jean Bisson, whose camera was set up and ready to go, suddenly joined in. "Say, do you know where we can find some girls?"

The President looked blank. We looked stunned. A presidential aide coughed. I asked if it always rained in Bogota. Not to be denied, Bisson smiled broadly and again asked, more loudly, "Yeah, well, don't you know any girls?"

The President moved from puzzlement to cloudiness and we decided we'd better do the interview without further ado.

But it wasn't our day. As Bisson plugged in the TV lights to start the interview, we blew every fuse in the place, plunging the palace into darkness and bringing the well-armed guards running into the room. After half an hour of confusion, we got the lights back on. By now President Valencia was tapping his fingers on his desk in noticeable irritation so I very quickly began the interview.

He talked about "La Violencia." It had begun fifteen years previously with the assassination of the left-wing mayor of Bogota, Jorge Elicier Gaitan. Soon the violence spread into the countryside. There had been massacres in which whole mountain and jungle villages were wiped out, with children impaled on pitchforks and the ears, noses, and lips of the victims cut off. So-called "Bandit Kingdoms" sprang up in several remote areas and "La Violencia" seemed to evolve into a curious mix of politics, personal vengeance, and simple crime. "Our Army has found proof," President Valencia told me, "of the connection between Fidel Castro and La Violencia in Colombia ... I believe that not only are the inspiration and orientation coming from Cuba, but that Cuban funds are financing these anarchistic revolutionary attacks."

After our interview, I thanked the President and we left the palace. A few hours later, however, in graphic validation of President Valencia's worries about "La Violencia," several bombs exploded inside the palace. Fortunately, little damage was done.

We decided we had to take a look at what the President had called "Los Bandidos." The bandit leaders had nicknames ranging from "Black Blood" and "The Little Rat" to "The Claw" and "Revenge." There was even one incongruously called "B.B.C." Huge rewards were offered for them dead or alive.

The Colombian Air Force offered to fly us out to a military patrol in the jungle. And so we went. On the way, one of our plane's two engines conked out. "If we're not killed in the crash, we'll be killed by the bandits," a smiling captain taunted us. But we safely limped into a small airfield and jeeped our way to a jungle patrol.

We didn't find any live "bandits" but saw several dead ones and a shot-up village where another patrol had driven bandits out a few minutes before we arrived. The villagers were terrified of us and of the bandits coming back. They just wanted to be left alone by everybody.

We flew back to Bogota and, while Cunningham and the crew filmed street scenes, I spent a couple of days chatting with Canadian Embassy diplomats and government officials getting background on Colombia's political and economic problems. Like those in all of Latin America, the slum kids of Bogota didn't seem to have a chance unless there was a miracle. We found one such miracle when we visited a small school for slum children being built and paid for by Canadians. It had one big classroom and a playground with swings and teeter-totters.

After the poverty I'd seen in Mexico and in rural Colombia and on earlier trips to Latin America, it was downright thrilling to see the children in the school and to know that Canadians had made it possible. The "Parque du Canada" was a school for eighty children run by a happy Bogota policeman named Leopoldo Tiria. Toronto businessmen had put up most of the money and help also had come from the Canadian Embassy. Without our help, those eighty youngsters would never have seen a school. For them, it was a rare privilege to learn to read and write.

The youngsters at the "Parque du Canada" reminded me of my own teen-age after-school work with underprivileged kids in the Toronto slums. Watching the smile on the face of that Bogota policeman, I recognized the sense of fulfilment I had experienced.

Caracas, Venezuela, October, 1963 ...

Continuing our Latin American odyssey, we flew from Bogota to Caracas, Venezuela, and into yet another country torn by political violence. Arriving in Caracas reminded me of arriving in Nairobi almost ten years earlier at the height of the Mau Mau crisis, or in Havana seven months before. Guns were everywhere. Each time we entered a downtown Caracas building, we were checked at the door to be sure we weren't carrying guns and bombs. I was told that a favourite trick was for a woman terrorist to carry a bomb in her purse, go into a bathroom, leave the bomb in a toilet, and rather quickly leave the building.

The tension was particularly high because we arrived in the midst of a presidential election campaign and the Communists were trying to embarrass the government and encourage the public to boycott the election. President Romulo Betancourt, one-time leftist student leader and long-time activist social democrat, was just ending his five-year term as the first constitutionally elected president in the history of Venezuela to complete his term without being overthrown or assassinated. He had overcome six military uprisings, battled constant terrorism from the far left, and been shot at, wounded by a bomb thrown at his car (which killed two of his aides), and survived several other assassination attempts. Things were so tense that we were told the Canadian ambassador was unenthusiastic about being invited to accompany President Betancourt to public meetings. An honour it was, but it also was a risk. If a would-be assassin missed the President those near him might be hit.

We had arranged an interview with Betancourt but it took several days to pin down exactly when and where we would film it. Finally chasing down his press aide in a beach hotel, we arranged for the interview to be done in the President's office at Miraflores, the Presidential Palace in old Caracas.

As we lugged our equipment through the palace corridors, we passed lines of soldiers bristling with rifles and sten guns and squatting down beside machine guns. At one point, cameraman Jean Bisson tripped over a machine gun, sending both his camera equipment and the gun clattering noisily down the hallway.

In the President's office, we set up our camera, sound equipment, and lights and a few minutes later he strode in, shook hands with all of us, and sat down. He was a short, fat, fifty-five-year-old with heavy black-framed spectacles and a pugnacious and impetuous manner. He'd spent twenty-one years of his life in prison for his left-wing political views, jailed by brutal dictators such as the barbarous Marcos Perez Jiminez, who had incredibly been honoured by the Eisenhower administration with a medal but who was overthrown by the Army in 1958. Betancourt had been President in 1945-47 but was ousted by the Army, who feared his reforming zeal. By 1959, however, he was back in favour with the Army and was elected President. This time he combined his fervour for social and economic reform with a cultivation of the military that helped to ensure his presidential longevity.

As we began the interview with him, there was a strange clanking sound on the neck microphone we'd put on him. It turned out to be caused by a gun he had hidden under his shirt.

Like the conservative President Valencia of Colombia, the liberal President Betancourt attacked Castro and the Communists for fomenting murders, bombings, and general terrorism. But, he told me, "The influence of communism and Castroism has sharply diminished.... Out in the country, the followers of Castro have tried to wage guerilla war, but the peasants themselves have given their co-operation and their support to the armed forces in order to rout the guerillas." Betancourt told me of the reign of terror that had assaulted Venezuela from both the right and the left, including the "ghost cars" that roamed Caracas streets, indiscriminately machine-gunning innocent passersby. Their aim was to create instability and undermine the government.

One subject that particularly worried Betancourt, as it worried all Latin American leaders, was the phenomenal birth rate, which created a demand for housing, schools, food, and hospitals at a pace faster than economic growth could satisfy. "Venezuela, like every country in Latin America, faces the problem of a population explosion," Betancourt said. "Our population is increasing at an annual rate of three and a half per cent, one of the highest in the world.... There is a vast number of people whose diet is insufficient, who are without schools, without land to farm, and without economic development." He suggested we visit a Caracas maternity hospital intriguingly called "the Palace of Conception." There we would see what he meant about the population explosion.

A couple of days later, we arrived at what we were told was the busiest delivery room in the world, delivering a new baby every twelve minutes of every day of the year. It was exclusively for the slum women of Caracas and provided full delivery and baby care. I walked into a room where about forty women were in varying stages of giving birth, with a deafening cacophony of motherly shrieks of pain or joy and the persistent, insistent crying of the newborn. The floor was slippery, awash in all manner of liquids. Sanitary conditions would have horrified Canadian doctors. But it was far better than the straw mattresses and dirt floors of the mothers' make-shift homes crawling in flies, rats, and cockroaches that we had visited in the Caracas slums the day before. As we filmed the birth of one baby, it became too much for Cunningham, who had enjoyed a vigorous and lengthy night on the town. He retreated rapidly, throwing up as he went, and sat out the rest of our "shoot" in the car.

Almost everyone born in the Palace of Conception was illegitimate. One Venezuelan couple had thirteen children and then, to their consternation, had quintuplets. After a total of eighteen youngsters and all the publicity of the quints, they finally decided to get married.

I was told by several officials that perhaps half of all of Latin America was illegitimate. Honduras, for example, was called "the 70 per cent country": 70 per cent illiterate; 70 per cent rural; and 70 per cent illegitimate. Partly the problem was the Catholic Church's proscription of birth control devices, but even if that weren't the case, condoms, IUDs, diaphragms, foams, jellies, and the pill were simply not available to most Latin Americans.

From the Palace of Conception we drove back through the slums of Caracas to our luxurious Hotel Tamanaco and plunged into the brisk water of the Olympic-sized swimming pool, after which solicitous, smartly dressed waiters brought daiquiris and smoked salmon to our lounge chairs while soft music wafted over a loudspeaker. The hotel was high above the city and I walked over to the low wall to contemplate the view. I saw a teeming mass of horn-honking traffic jams, tall buildings, and ramshackle slums. I was repelled by the contrast of the elegance of my hotel and the dirty, dusty poverty and urban chaos below the hill.

Recife, Brazil, October, 1963 ...

In Venezuela, the slums are called "ranchos"; in Colombia they're called "barrios"; in Chile, "callampos"; and in Brazil, "favellas." But whatever you call them, the Latin American slums are the worst in the world – worse than Hong Kong, Saigon, Nairobi, Bangkok, or Calcutta. For most of the slum dwellers, there is no such thing as a toilet or running water, and the nauseating, suffocating smell is simply overwhelming for any Canadian nose.

The worst slums of all Latin America are in Brazil, and after a few more days in Caracas we flew overnight to Rio de Janeiro. We wanted to clear customs at the airport more quickly than the usual hour and a half that it took with all our television equipment, so along with the usual bribe we told the inspector that we were doing a documentary of Péle, the great Brazilian soccer hero. With swelling Brazilian pride, the inspector smilingly cleared us through at once.

We headed straight for the Ouro Verde Hotel on Copacabana Beach, had a quick swim, and then, with the help of a colleague from NBC, began organizing our filming schedule. A few days later we flew up to Recife, a city on the Atlantic in the northeast corner of the country. Our hotel there was beside a wide, sunswept beach with Atlantic waves rolling in, and we frolicked in the water briefly before going to work. Those refreshing and relaxing breaks helped us cope with the horrors we were filming.

On tourist postcards, Recife was called "the Venice of Brazil," but what we saw was considerably less romantic. We went to a slum in the heart of the city built on stilts above dirty, bug-infested water over which clouds of mosquitoes and flies circled. A sewer would be too gentle a description for this scene of subhuman squalor. But the locals were delighted when we arrived. They were bursting with pride over their new water pipe. For the first time, they had water piped in – one faucet for 2,000 people. Until a couple of months before, there had been no running water. Those who could afford it bought about a gallon of what we were told was "relatively clean" water for three cents.

The floors of their homes were dirty boards, the roofs were made of palm leaves, and the walls of old whisky crates. One woman told me with pride and, if possible, with dignity, that she actually owned her own home. She'd paid $30 for it. Most of the others rented their hovels from the city for $1.50 a month. Almost everybody in that slum was illegitimate, and most of the fathers had deserted their families. The women sent their children out begging every day and they washed clothes or scavenged for their existence. They grew old long before their time; a woman of thirty looked sixty.

Yet, in spite of the crushing oppressiveness of their shanty-town squalor, the people retained a certain dignity and generosity. A woman named Maria invited me to share her big meal of the week: a few beans, pork fat, a couple of tomatoes, and a lot of watery soup. I took a deep breath, thinking of all the bugs and germs that must be floating around in that broth, but she seemed so pleased and proud that I just had to take half a spoonful. Amazingly, it tasted delicious and I suffered no ill effects.

As we teetered along narrow planks between the houses, I couldn't help but be moved at the sight of spindly-legged, swollen-bellied children splashing about in the smelly, brown water, giggling and pushing each other as kids do everywhere in the world. Since they knew no other life, I suppose they were happy in their ignorance. I, however, inwardly cringed at the advantage of kids at home ... even those in the slums of Toronto or Vancouver who lived in luxury compared to these youngsters.

For these Brazilian children life was short and cheap. We went to a cemetery in a town called Cabo just outside Recife. A young couple, José and Ira Simon, were taking their six-month-old son to be buried. The casket was an orange crate wrapped in blue and white paper. The grave was rented. Two dollars for two years, after which the bones would be dug up and the grave rented to somebody else.

While in Cabo, I met the first of three men who made a deep impression on me because of their efforts to do something about the soul-tearing poverty around them. Each in his own way was obsessed with this mission.

I met Father Antonio Melo in his neat little village church one morning. He was about thirty, with a black crew cut, fiery eyes, and a throbbing voice. Melo was representative of a large number of activist priests throughout Latin America, men who had devoted their lives to fighting poverty with a revolution of their own. They were tolerated by the church hierarchy but were seldom supported and sometimes censured.

Father Melo told me he had become a focal point for agitation against the privileged classes in Brazil, the "stupid reactionaries" as he called them. To the rich he was known as "The Red Priest." And no wonder. He was leery of Americans and, though he claimed to be a vigorous anti-Communist, he had organized tens of thousands of farm workers into unions demanding land reform, education, food, and housing. He insisted that a starving child is not interested in democracy, communism, fascism, socialism, or any other "ism," only in eating, having clothes to wear, and learning. He even preached "selective violence," but only as a last resort. In his view, land reform was the key to Brazilian progress and indeed survival.

At a street rally one night in Recife we filmed a crowd of farm workers who had left their mud homes in the bleak, stagnant interior and had come to town to demand land reform. They wanted land of their own to farm. They wanted an end to their subservience to the rich landowners. On the back of a truck haranguing the crowd stood the leader of the Peasant League of Northeast Brazil, a forty-five-year-old rabble-rousing spell-binder named Francisco Juliao. He was a country lawyer who professed proudly to being a Communist and a disciple of Castro. "The people want beans ... the people want land," he shouted, preaching bloody revolution as the only answer to their oppressive poverty. I listened at the edge of the crowd as he electrified his audience, which continually interrupted him with shouts of approval. After his speech, we shook hands and I spoke briefly to him. I kept no notes on the conversation, but I will never forget the fierceness of his eyes.

The third man was a bureaucrat named Celso Furtado, the head of a government organization called SUDENE, the Superintendencia do Desenvolvimento do Nordeste. It was the principal government agency for development in the northeast. It was, in fact, the most promising experiment in economic aid anywhere in Latin America and was heavily financed by President Kennedy's Alliance for Progress. Furtado had met JFK in Washington in 1961.

In our interview in his office, Furtado told me, "The revolution is a fact. There is a real revolution, but a peaceful one. In five more years, I think, this area will be changed, will be completely different." I asked him why, unlike most officials, he felt the aid experts under him should involve themselves in politics. "We could not be aloof from the political problems because the people are so impatient and asking for action. Real development, you know, means giving man at least the possibility of being happy. We can't just give them food. We have to change their way of life and give them hope."

"What do you need most of all?" I asked.

"Will power. Decision capacity for acting."

What he wanted and even demanded was the will in those with money to make things happen. And will among the poor, too, in demanding food, clothes, homes, and schools.

The priest, the revolutionary, and the bureaucrat all warned that time was short. They echoed the warning of former Costa Rican President José Figueres that "It is one minute to midnight in Latin America." If anything, it's even closer to midnight now, and in spite of the efforts of people like these three, the hungry and the homeless still overwhelm Latin America. The recent upheavals in El Salvador, Nicaragua, and elsewhere result from that painful reality.

In Brazil, a year after I'd been in Recife, the Army overthrew the democracy and banished most of the left-wing activists and liberal reformers. Juliao fled to Mexico; Furtado fled to Paris to teach in the Sorbonne. I never did find out what happened to Father Melo.

We flew back to Rio after about a week in Recife, as we neared the end of our broad swing through Latin America, to do some final filming and interviewing. If Brazil's northeast was a microcosm of Latin American economic development problems, then Rio itself was a classic example of its urban crisis. I spent some time with Canadian Trade Commissioner Bill Jones and his wife Heidi, who not only gave me facts and statistics but showed me a human side of the economic problems in Rio. I watched them one morning standing at the gate in front of their home handing out bread and little cakes to the young beggars. Every morning, children would come down from the mountainside to beg, and every morning Bill and Heidi would be at their gate with food, as they said, "to help just a little." The food would last those youngsters until dinnertime. They all came from a slum known as "The Amazing Favella" up on the mountainside in the middle of Rio with one of the best views of the city. To see such splendour below and such squalor above was truly amazing.

Two and a half years later, I came back to Rio in February with producer Bill Cunningham and we spent a couple of weeks in and around "The Amazing Favella." In our documentary Bill brilliantly contrasted the grinding, demoralizing wretchedness of this slum with the gaudy rich exuberance of Carnival in Rio. In our filming on that trip we spent a lot of time with Aristarcho da Conceicao, his common-law wife, Neusa, and their son, Jorge. They lived in a home built of whisky crates and old boards teetering on the edge of the mountain high over Rio. In the 110°F humid heat of Rio's midsummer we tramped up and down that mountainside a score of times. We were often stopped at the bottom of the 168 concrete steps leading into the favella by the local cocaine salesman who offered two sniffs for about $7. Up on the favella were the homes of Rio's poor, the drifters, the unemployed, and a few lucky ones with jobs as labourers, cab drivers, waiters, and shoeshine boys.

The Conceicao family paid $3 month to rent their shack. Twelve-year-old Jorge was not allowed to jump inside the house for fear it might topple over the cliff. In his dreams, Jorge wanted to be a soccer player or a clerk in an office. In reality, he'd be lucky to end up as a pick-and-shovel labourer like his father. Every day he went down to Copacabana Beach to shine shoes for eight cents a shine. In a twelve-hour day, he earned anywhere from eighty cents to a dollar and a half, which he gave to his mother and which often bought the family dinner of beans, rice, and pork. His only escape from his depressing, de-grading shanty-town existence was to splash into the waves at Copacabana in his underwear and once a year to lose himself in the fantasy of Carnival.

Throughout the year Jorge's mother worked on his costume and he practised his samba dancing. Accompanied by the "Amazing Favella" pick-up samba band, Jorge and scores of neighbourhood youngsters would go into downtown Rio to dance through the streets. Then, on the four nights of Carnival, Jorge and thousands of other costumed, dancing, singing children along with thousands more adults, simply took over the city. The shoeless ones of the favella wear costumes, dance, and sing, even if they have to go without food to pay for their costumes.

During Carnival, everywhere you look people don't walk, they samba along the downtown streets from which all cars are banned. It's utterly disorganized pandemonium as costumed samba bands and dancers take over the city dancing to the squeaking, high-pitched echo of a cueca, a catskin drum with a hole in the middle through which a stick is rubbed up and down. Carnival is surely the world's wildest party, a tumultuous explosion of rhythm. Carnival is a moment of contagious, collective joy, snatched from a life of grinding poverty. The 1966 Carnival theme song says it in a nutshell: "Sadness please go away. I want to sing again." At the first Carnival I attended, police announced that "kissing between sweethearts is not forbidden during Carnival." I never noticed the practice being ignored at any other time either.

Filming the Carnival balls was a physical challenge. You had to fight for sheer survival in the jammed ballrooms of Rio. These were not tea dances, but a raucous, milling, dance-crazed mob of up to 7,000 dancing in utter abandon to the point of oblivion in their wilted, dripping costumes. There were many different Carnival balls. There was the huge Municipal Ball for the very rich, but also there were the Golden Rose Ball, the Children's Ball, the Copacabana Ball, politically oriented affairs such as the Gay Left Ball and the Miserable Left Ball, and, for homosexuals, one advertised as the Queers' Ball.

When Carnival is over, reality returns in the form of aching muscles, throbbing heads, and red eyes. The rich go back to their mansions and estates, the poor to their favellas, all apparently happily ignoring the insurmountable, insufferable poverty because, what the hell, they had a good party.

The Cariocas, as Rio residents are called, are simply unique. Rich or poor, they seem to have the same philosophy. They are proud, selfish, pleasure-seeking, exuberantly friendly, totally disorganized, and with the ultimate mañana complex. The Cariocas like to say, "God made the world in six days and the seventh day he devoted to Rio." Probably the only way you could set off a revolution among the Cariocas would be to ban Carnival or charge admission to the beach. I was told a story of a Communist organizer who called a mass protest march in Rio, but nobody came. Asking why, he was told, "It was raining." He called another mass protest march on a sunny day and again nobody came. Asking why again, he was told, "It was such a nice day, we all went to the beach."

Vinicius de Morais, poet and author of Brazil's famous book, *Black Orpheus*, wrote, "We don't brood over dried-up faucets. We are surrounded by the world's most beautiful scenery and the world's most beautiful women. We have the sea to wash off our worries and the sun to dry our tears."

Brazil, unlike the rest of Latin America, was settled by the Portuguese and, to my mind, Brazilians have a softer, sunnier personality than their Spanish-speaking neighbours. The original Portuguese settlers were no angels, however, and even today among the aristocracy there is some validity to the old Brazilian saying that "the Portuguese used white women for marriage, mulattoes for sex, and Negroes for work." For the most part, though, there is relatively little discrimination in the country.

In contrast to the overwhelming domination of the Catholic Church in Brazil is the devotion to Macumba, a weird combination of Catholicism and voodoo. One black night during our 1963 visit we drove half a dozen miles out of Rio to film a Macumba session. We went into what I took to be the living room of an old frame home, lit by candles and suffused with incense. An altar sat in the middle of the room, which was crowded with fifty or sixty worshippers. We filmed in fascination as the white-gowned, cigar-smoking high priestess literally scared the hell out of us. Part way through the ceremony, she swigged some potent firewater from a bottle with a live snake curling about the inside. She then passed the flames of a candle back and forth across her face a couple of dozen times, and, amid screams of support from her congregation, she and some of her aides went into a trance to chase away the Devil, or Exu, as he's called. He must have gone away because a quarter of an hour later, after much bell-tinkling and drum-beating, the high priestess came out of her trance and joined her followers in talk and drink.

The 1963 trip to Latin America, with its month of fourteen-hour work days and dizzying succession of new experiences, meant I worked more closely than ever before with Bill Cunningham. As a result, we became good friends and I came to regard him as one of the best documentary-makers in the world. I watched him build a cohesive program of enormous emotional impact from the thousands of feet of film shot in a hundred different locations. I gained new respect, too, for the artistic skills of cameraman Jean Bisson and soundman Ron Wegoda. In spite of their penchant for dinnertime conversation about their bouts with "tourista" and "Montezuma's Revenge," they gave us film and sound that sensitively and sometimes brutally captured the reality of Latin America. To the immense satisfaction of all of us, one critic, Jon Ruddy of the *Toronto Telegram*, called the *Newsmagazine* report on our trip "The most remarkable documentary I've ever seen on CBC."

Punta del Este, Uruguay, April 14, 1967 ...

My final trip to Latin America – at least as a foreign correspondent – was in 1967 to cover the Hemispheric Summit Conference called by

President Lyndon Johnson in a grandiose effort to resuscitate Kennedy's Alliance for Progress. On this occasion my producer was my old friend Don Cameron. As we flew from Rio (where we'd stopped off for a brief Copacabana interlude) to Montevideo, Uruguay, we discussed the perennial problem of how to make our coverage of this summit attractive in visual terms. You can only show so many excerpts from speeches, shots of experts arguing fine points of international relations, and presidential and prime ministerial comings and goings.

Fortunately, Cameron was and is a genius at creating an exciting visual canvas as a backdrop for the dull but vitally important international economic stories such as Punta del Este. He had an unmatchable ability, as well, to work out some of his best ideas through the smoke and alcoholic haze of noisy nightclubs. My initial reaction to some of his suggestions often was that they were truly preposterous. Most were, but in the end, most also worked.

Following up on our airplane discussions while sitting in a crowded Montevideo bar, Cameron fell in love with a musical trio whom he insisted we use in our coverage. In addition, a new-found drinking pal turned out to have a friend who owned a huge *estancia*, a ranch in the rolling Uruguayan countryside. Somebody else he met had a truck. So he put together the trio, the truck, the ranch, half a dozen gauchos, several hundred cattle, a horse, and, to my consternation, me.

"It will make a terrific opening sequence ... it'll grab people's attention and set them up for the conference," he enthused. "In just a couple of minutes it can set the scene beautifully, convey the problems of Latin America, and give visual excitement and vibrancy to a bloody complicated story." By the time the nightclub closed, Cameron had his opening sequence scribbled over three table napkins.

After a few hours of sleep and before dawn even cracked, a truck was at the hotel picking up Cameron, me, cameraman Eddie Higginson, soundman Eddie Chong, and reporter/producer Tom Leach. First stop was to pick up a bleary-eyed costumed trio. Then off we rode into the pre-dawn blackness to the *estancia*.

First, Cameron put the trio (no member of which knew what the hell was going on except that they were being paid more money than they'd earn in a week) alongside a tree and told them to rehearse anything they wanted. Then he rounded up the ranch foreman and a horse for me – a horse that seemed to be seven-feet high at the saddle. I should say at this point that I had not ridden a horse since childhood, but in an excess of alcoholic zeal the night before I had grotesquely misrepresented my horsemanship. Cameron apparently thought I was born to the saddle. He, along with the foreman, then rounded up six or seven gauchos and organized about 300 head of cattle.

His idea was to start on a wide shot of me astride the giant horse off in the distance, the gauchos driving the cattle across a shallow river, while in the foreground the trio played their little hearts out beside a huge tree behind which the Uruguayan plains stretched off into the distance. It was a scene that would have daunted Cecil B. DeMille, let alone a single, uneasy cameraman, a hesitant trio, laughing gauchos, bewildered cattle, and your terrified correspondent.

First I had to get up on top of the damn giant horse and pretend to look comfortable. Then, at Cameron's primordial scream, the scene began. First, the trio struck up, then the gauchos began shouting, singing, and cracking whips, sending the cattle splashing across the river heading for the trio at their tree. Simultaneously, my monster horse and I cantered toward the trio, me hanging on for dear life. To my sudden horror, the horse spurted into a gallop. I grabbed the reins for dear life and, to my surprise, he slowed down.

Meanwhile, I and the 300 head of cattle were thundering toward each other, the trio was strumming madly, and the gauchos shouting. Everything had to be at the tree at precisely the same time for the scene to work. That was manifestly impossible! And yet, as my horse reached the tree, I again pulled the reins, he shook his head, looked around curiously, and, amazingly, stopped.

The cattle were thundering by the tree about twenty feet away from me; the gauchos were racing alongside them; the trio was strumming. It was at that exact moment, when I was to deliver my opening introductory minute or so to the program, that I was seized with an unimaginable paralysing fear that I'd forget my words and we would have to do the whole scene over again. That's probably what brought me to my senses and I instantly recited my sixty seconds of introduction without a pause or a mistake. Then I wearily climbed down from my horse, both of us, I'm sure, hugely relieved and both convinced of our lasting incompatibility.

And Cameron was right, as usual. The scene made an impressive opening for the Punta del Este summit. It captured people's attention and drew them into the more complicated elements of the story that followed.

Since the early 1960s, the Americans had been pouring a billion dollars a year into Latin America – to build schools, roads, and hospitals, and for irrigation, teacher training, and other projects. The money came from Kennedy's Alliance for Progress, originally envisioned as a kind of Marshall Plan for Latin America. It was supposed to stimulate the Southern Hemisphere in the same way American aid had helped rebuild Europe after World War II.

Kennedy was a hero to most Latin Americans not only for his New Frontier image, but also for his moral and financial commitment to helping them. His approach was a far cry from the "Big Stick" diplomacy of Teddy Roosevelt at the turn of the century, a policy that more or less had characterized U.S. treatment of Latin America since then. Americans have generally seen Latin America as a place to make money, and they have had a nagging tendency to make trouble in the process. Eisenhower and Dulles, for instance, had heard of Celso Furtado's ideas of developing northeast Brazil and had dubbed him a Communist. This, in spite of pleas for more sensitivity from Milton Eisenhower, Ike's university president brother, and from Nelson Rockefeller, who had a particular sympathy for Latin American aspirations.

American interventionist policies were never better summarized than by General Smedley D. Butler of the U.S. Marines, who said back in 1931: "I helped make Mexico safe for American oil interests in 1914. I helped make Haiti and Cuba a decent place for the National City Bank boys to collect revenues in. I helped purify Nicaragua for the international banking house of Brown Brothers. I helped make Honduras right for American fruit companies. Looking back on it, I might have given Al Capone a few hints."

Aside from Kennedy, the other U.S. hero in Latin eyes was Franklin Roosevelt. His "Good Neighbour" policy of non-intervention, enunciated when he came into office, reversed decades of U.S. policy of exploitation and neglect.

On March 13, 1961, when Kennedy gathered Latin American ambassadors in the East Room of the White House, he electrified Latin America by announcing the Alliance for Progress – "Alianza para Progresso," he said in heavily New England-accented Spanish – "a vast co-operative effort, unparallelled in magnitude and nobility of purpose, to satisfy the basic needs of the American people for home, work, land, health, and schools ... [to] transfer the American continent into a vast crucible of revolutionary ideas and efforts ... an example to all the world that liberty and progress walk hand in hand."

Kennedy pledged $20 billion to the Alliance to bring about land reform, tax reform, and fair pay for workers, to eliminate illiteracy, and to improve health, housing, and education. Only Cuba refused to participate, claiming it was "Yankee imperialism." But Kennedy had to fight Latin conservatives who feared losing their power, and on the first anniversary of the Alliance, he warned, "Those who make peaceful revolution impossible will make violent revolution inevitable."

With a Latin American population of 300 million – 50 per cent illiterate, 30 per cent dead before the age of forty – multiplying faster than any other area of the world, the Alliance for Progress had a daunting challenge. Seventy per cent of Latin Americans lived in abject poverty while 2 per cent owned 50 per cent of the wealth. But the Alliance began to work. The democratic left started turning away from Castro. while the Americans and, slowly, the Latins themselves poured money into Alliance projects. Then came Kennedy's assassination and the Vietnam War, which soon obsessed Washington, alienated many Latin liberals, and began to squeeze U.S. financial resources so that money for Latin America was slowing down as money for the war was speeding up.

In 1967, Lyndon Johnson sought to revive the flagging Alliance, partly in an attempt to win back U.S. liberal support and divert attention from the war in Southeast Asia and partly because he was genuinely challenged by the enormity of the problems of Latin America. He imagined he could help in much the same way he had helped develop rural Texas. So he called together the democrats and the dictators of Latin America to meet at Punta del Este. At the Uruguay summit he offered them $1.3 billion a year; some new trade concessions; a plan for continent-wide co-ordination of highways, television, and communications; and a proposal for a Latin American Common Market. He wanted them to launch widespread programs of land reform and tax reform and to stimulate co-operatives, student groups, and unions.

But the Latins said it wasn't enough. Even worse, they were profoundly split themselves. The dictators, primarily of the right, wanted more U.S. money but weren't interested in such dangerous things as tax reform and land reform. The democrats were suspicious of Johnson's motives. While they revered Kennedy, they reviled Johnson, the warmonger.

In a way, LBJ's attempt to revive Kennedy's dream collapsed because of an unholy alliance between the extreme left, who viewed Washington efforts as American imperialism, and the extreme right, who feared it would destroy their wealth, power, and property. The 11,000 flowery words of the conference's final communiqué did not hide the collapse. Nor did Nixon, Ford, Carter, or Reagan do anything to bring it back to life. And that is a tragedy. For without profound, peaceful social democratic advances, Latin America likely will echo for generations with the bombs of the dictators of the left and right, and run with the blood of the people.

"The real problem here in Latin America," a Canadian diplomat in Caracas told me, "is not communism, or Castro, but it is poverty. If Castro and communism disappeared tomorrow, the problems would still be here." His statement is as true today as it was then. The enemy was and is not communism or Castro, but the ocean of bare-back, empty-stomach depravity surrounding the islands of callous, vulgar opulence.

Robert Kennedy, as a senator in 1964, told a group of Peruvian students in Lima that there must be a revolution in Latin America, "a revolution which will be peaceful if we are wise enough, human if we care enough, but a revolution which will come whether we will it or not." And a year later when he came back from another Latin American trip, he warned, "If we allow communism to carry the banner of reform, then the ignored and the dispossessed, the insulted and injured, will turn to it as the only way out of their misery." It is too bad that such perceptions never made their way into the White House Oval Office.

Among the scores of Latin diplomats I talked to on half a dozen trips south of the Rio Grande, the question always came up about whether Canada would or would not, should or should not, join the Organization of American States. Would we just be American puppets in OAS, or would we be a middle ground between the U.S. and the Latins? Certainly the Latins then, as now, wanted us in OAS. The Canadian hesitancy at joining has always been born of a distressing lack of interest, and the reality that we would have to make choices on issues between the U.S. and the Latins. The Latins think we would favour them. The Americans think we would favour them. Not being a member of OAS, we are courted by everybody. As a member, we would have to take sides.

For decades, Ottawa has preferred the comfort of being a well-courted neutral, offending no one. And for decades, they have been expecting us at the Organization of American States. There has even been a "Canada chair" literally waiting for us in the storage room of the Pan-American Building in the Washington headquarters of OAS for more than a generation. But we've never sat in it.

"It is a real pity that Canada does not participate in our hemisphere organization," Colombian President Guillermo Leon Valencia told me. "We need you and we want you," Venezuelan President Romulo Betancourt told me. That was twenty years ago, and we're still not in.

Paul Martin, as Minister for External Affairs, tried vigorously but vainly to persuade his colleagues in the cabinet and in his own department to join OAS. Mark MacGuigan fought but failed in the same battle when he was Minister of External Affairs. The External Affairs mandarins and our political leaders give lip service to Latin America but their lips don't move very much. They're simply preoccupied by other matters. I suspect, too, that our apparent disdain for Latin America is also a product of a sense of smug superiority among our decision-makers who feel they are a class above what they consider to be the banana republic emotionalism of the Latinos.

But they're wrong. We should be in OAS. We are, after all, part of the Americas. We can help in many ways, and we can be of real value as a bridge between Washington and the Latin Americans and as a leader in the hemisphere. We could provide the sympathetic understanding that the proud and sensitive Latins look for in vain from Washington. We both have to live next door to rich Uncle Sam. And we both run the danger of catching pneumonia whenever Uncle Sam sneezes.

Canada, by not participating as a full member of the Western Hemisphere through OAS membership, simply sits back, clucking unhappily from time to time but making no real effort to try to put out the flames in our neighbour's house. We just don't give a damn, simply swinging between amiable ignorance and callous indifference.

7 *HELLO LYNDON*

Washington, D.C., November 1963 ...

Lyndon Baines Johnson had hated being Vice-President. He was a man who craved power, languishing in "the most insignificant office that ever the intention of man contrived or his imagination conceived," to quote President John Adams' late-eighteenth-century description of the job he had held under George Washington.

Johnson had begun to drink more heavily and to whine self-pityingly about his unhappy fate. He sometimes invoked the memory of Franklin Roosevelt's first Vice-President, John Nance "Cactus Jack" Garner, another Texan. Garner was supposed to have said that the job was "not worth a pitcher of warm spit." Johnson, with his fondness for earthy bluntness, once told me Garner actually used the word "piss," not spit.

As Senate Majority Leader during the last two years of Ike's first term and all of his second term, Johnson had been one of the most powerful men in the United States. Now, quite simply, he was out of the action and bored to tears. You could see it in his dulled eyes, his long, mournful, and grumpy face, and his slumped shoulders as he went about Washington and presided over the Senate – his principal constitutional function other than succeeding a dead president. JFK did give him a fair bit of work, often on diplomatic missions abroad or supervising the U.S. space program, and he had issued orders that any significant report or policy paper from all government departments must be sent to LBJ. Johnson came to admire his boss, though he never stopped warring with what he regarded as the Kennedy clique.

He was deeply suspicious and resentful of Ivy Leaguers, polished easterners, and what he called the "in-tel-lec-shuls," including most of the New Frontiermen. "To them," he later said, "my name is shit and always has been and always will be. I got their goddamn legislation passed for them, but they gave me no credit." He called them "overbred smart alecks who live in Georgetown and think in Harvard."

Johnson was a raw-boned product of the dirt-poor, dusty dry Hill Country of Texas and had a Texas-sized cultural inferiority complex, not comprehending and hating the poets, the writers, the classical musicians, and the ballet choreographers who adorned many of Kennedy's White House evenings. His preference was to "bullshit with the boys" over political schemes with a Cutty Sark Scotch, his tie loose, and his feet up.

He had hoped he could recast the vice-presidency as he had other posts he held earlier in his career and turn a job of admittedly limited power into one of expanding power and influence. But he failed and he blamed his failure not on Jack Kennedy, but on Bob Kennedy and the other New Frontiersmen whom he felt were laughing at him behind his back and frustrating his every move. Worst of all, the summer of 1963 saw a liberal movement to "dump Lyndon" from the 1964 Democratic ticket and Johnson's fears were eased only when Kennedy assured him he would stay as Vice-President. Ever since the 1960 convention, when he felt Bob Kennedy had tried to prevent him from being Kennedy's vice-presidential nominee, he had hated him, and in private he characterized Bob as "that little runt" or "a shit ass," the epitome of the eastern Ivy League intellectual. And Bob Kennedy was a constant threat to Johnson's power since he had his brother's ear.

But Dallas changed everything. Suddenly and brutally, Lyndon Johnson was President and he flew back from Dallas on Air Force One a new man; the sad, shambling Vice-President was reborn. While everyone else was overcome by shock, misery, or chaotic confusion, LBJ almost alone knew exactly what to do. On his way back he whispered to the UPI's Merriman Smith, "God knows the last thing I wanted was to become President in this way. But I'll tell you one thing. Now that I am President, with God's help you're going to live long enough to write that I was the best President this country ever had ... because I'm going to try like hell."

In the weeks that followed the assassination, I watched him at news conferences, at meetings with politicians or diplomats, making speeches, and in quickie informal news conferences. He was unmistakenly a man in charge, the anchor of stability through those perilous, nerve-wracking, unsure days when so very much changed forever. "Everything was in chaos," he later said to his biographer Doris Kearns. "We were like a bunch of cattle caught in the swamp, unable to move in either direction, simply circling round and round. I understood that. I knew what had to be done. There is but one way to get the cattle out of the swamp. And that is for a man on the horse to take the lead, to assume command, to provide direction. In the period of confusion after the assassination, I was that man." This was Johnson at his best.

The word I kept hearing at the White House and all over Washington in those days and weeks was "continuity." To take hold of the presidency, Johnson told everyone he met he wanted to continue the Kennedy mandate and even though he instinctively hated the Kennedy men, he knew that for a while he needed them. "I need you," he told Pierre Salinger, Ted Sorensen, and every principal Kennedy official. "I need you more than John F. Kennedy ever needed you." "Without them," he said later to Kearns, "I would have lost my link to John Kennedy and without that I would have had absolutely no chance of gaining the support of the media, or the easterners or the intellectuals. And without their support, I would have absolutely no chance of governing the country." At the same time, he brought his own people into the White House, and so for a while there was a two-track stream of presidential advisers. In time, when he felt confident enough, he began shedding the Kennedy people one by one.

Johnson brought to the presidency the same combination of gritty determination, base cunning, unctuous charm, and brute force that had made him such a successful Texas politician and U.S. senator. Having been weaned on his politician father's Texas populism, he left his teacher's job in Texas in 1932 to come to Washington as executive assistant to a Texas congressman. In those early days he was a cyclone of political action, making friends of the rich and powerful and getting himself appointed three years later as the Texas director of Roosevelt's National Youth Administration. He idolized the author of the New Deal, and he used the job to get himself elected to Congress in 1937 as a staunch FDR supporter. But he was defeated in his first try for the Senate in 1941, spent a year in the Navy, and returned to Congress in 1942. When he was first elected to the Senate in 1948 he became known as "Landslide Johnson" – he had won the Democratic nomination for senator in a hotly contested, highly controversial primary race by eighty-seven votes out of one million cast, his margin of victory coming from a late count of a ballot box in the hamlet of Alice on the Mexican border.

In the years after he became Majority Leader of the Senate, I sat in the press gallery above the Speaker's chair watching Johnson in action. He had a heart attack in 1955 but in the late 1950s his energy seemed undiminished as he scurried about the Senate floor, flinging an arm around one senator, whispering to another, walking in and out of the glass doors at the back where he wheeled and dealt in the so-called Senate cloakroom. When he spoke, we reporters had to lean over the edge of our balcony seats straining to hear his mumbled words. But he loved talking to reporters in small groups, always milking us for tidbits of information and always talking, walking, waving his arms, and grabbing hold of people.

He was the most effective Majority Leader in the history of the U.S. Senate. He could manipulate and massage the senators to get legislation passed as no one else could. With his large, ruthlessly overworked and underpaid, but highly effective staff, his own tireless searching for every scrap of useful information and gossip, and his encyclopedic memory, he knew more about the private needs and desires of the senators than anyone ever did. "I knew the Congress as well as I knew Lady Bird," he once said.

He would save cigars he was given at banquets for elderly but helpful Senator Carl Hayden of Arizona; he would go to marriages and funerals of senators' relatives; he would do a multitude of little favours for his constituents, and anyone who might later be able to help him, from getting tickets to sit in the visitors' gallery in the Senate to procuring airline tickets or hotel rooms. He understood the back-home constituencies of other senators as well as or better than they did. And since, as Majority Leader, he controlled which senators served on what committees, he could make life easy or unpleasant for his colleagues. He used his favours to get the legislation he wanted passed. He rarely got into philosophical discussions with them or with reporters and concentrated on, as he told us, "gettin' things done." Until LBJ, the U.S. Senate had almost always worked a genteel 10:00 a.m. to 5:00 p.m., but he forced it into a pattern of nighttime sessions in his unremitting drive to get laws passed.

My most memorable encounter with him in those years was in the spring of 1959 in his huge green-and-gold-painted Capitol Hill office (as distinct from his "Texas office" across the street in the Senate Office Building) that he'd recently had refurbished by a New York interior decorator and which we reporters called the "Taj Mahal." One evening, after a Senate session, I and several other journalists walked through the big outer office where, along with several girls, his future Presidential Press Secretary Bill Moyers worked, and into the garish inner sanctum. There he sat in shirt sleeves behind a huge, paper-strewn desk. Unlike the barely audible voice on the Senate floor, the private Johnson was loud, flamboyant, and overwhelming both in personality and physical stature – he was six-feet-three-inches tall.

I have long forgotten the subject of his rambling discourse on that occasion; what I do remember is his seemingly inexhaustible supply of obscenities. But the words alone would not have made such an impression. It was the ferocity of his style, the way he used language to shock, intimidate, and finally conquer.

As he strode back and forth in front of us on that spring day of 1959, I could feel the raw power and magnetism. While talking he would reach into one of the deep wire baskets on his desk to pull out some document he said was "confidential," and in a conspiratorial voice he would read a snatch of it to us while picking his nose, scratching his huge ears, or massaging his bottom. His long arms flailed in the air to emphasize a point when they weren't picking, scratching, or massaging.

He was the crudest man I've ever known. If he had persuaded someone to his point of view, he would tell us, "I got his pecker in my pocket." He referred to his own instrument of sexuality as "Jumbo." When he felt he was being bamboozled, he'd shout, "I may not know much, but I know the difference between chicken shit and chicken salad." One night during the 1960 presidential campaign, he angrily told a small gathering of reporters in his hotel room that Nixon's vice-presidential candidate, Henry Cabot Lodge, was so dumb "the goddamn sonofabitch can't find his ass with both hands." On another occasion and of another politician, Johnson commented, "He doesn't know enough to pour the piss out of his boots." Prime Minister Lester Pearson, who heard Johnson at his primitive worst, described his language as "sulphurous," "strong," and "unconsidered." "He was," said Pearson in characteristic understatement, "certainly a very earthy and vigorous man."

Johnson's style remained the same when he became President. As the United States' Chief Executive, he liked nothing better than to discuss high policy with some official from the State Department or Treasury while sitting on the toilet. He once complained about "one of those delicate Kennedyites who came into the bathroom with me and then found it utterly impossible to look at me while I sat on the toilet. You'd think he had never seen those parts of the body before." I'm sure Johnson enjoyed his bathroom conferences because he felt the shock of the location gave him leverage over visitors. One of his secretaries told me she had taken dictation from him in his bedroom while he was simultaneously on the telephone, watching three TV sets, and lying naked on his side getting an enema.

Above all, the Johnson style was based on fear, and it was terrifyingly effective. In talking to his aides, his secretaries, his political allies, and his enemies, I heard the same theme over and over again; they all were afraid of Johnson. They feared his volcanic temper, his animal energy, and his awesome revenge. When he was angry, he launched into a blistering, obscenity-filled assault on his victim.

His temper was mercurial and could be sadistic. His Assistant Press Secretary Malcolm Kilduff told me of the day Johnson came striding through his office, looked at Kilduff's messy desk, and snapped, ''I hope your mind is not as cluttered as your desk, Kilduff.'' Mac hastily cleared everything off his desk and, as luck would have it, later in the day Johnson again strode past Kilduff's desk and, looking at its now bare top, snapped, ''I hope your mind is not as empty as your desk, Kilduff.''

Johnson demanded total loyalty from his staff – anything less than adoration was treason. ''When you see an ambitious assistant thinking more of his own future than the President, you know at once you're in trouble,'' he told biographer Doris Kearns. He dominated his staff by giving them overlapping jurisdiction and by keeping them offbase, praising them to the skies one day and freezing them out the next. He'd bawl them out for not turning out the office lights when they left at night and so became known to his staff and to reporters as ''LBJ – Light Bulb Johnson.''

He insisted not only on loyalty and even obsequiousness from his staff, but he also demanded their instant availability to him. Presidential Press Secretary George Christian strolled outside his White House office one day and while away from his desk the President called him.

''He's not here now, Mr. President,'' Christian's secretary replied.

''Where is he?''

''He's outside and away from the phone for a few minutes.''

''Honey, I want you to get this phone fixed so it will ring wherever he is.''

Bill Moyers was a young Baptist preacher whom Johnson befriended and hired while he was Senate Majority Leader. Moyers was the one of Johnson's four press secretaries over his White House years who sustained an independent spirit in spite of the LBJ onslaught. He later quit because he could no longer take it. As reporters at the White House we heard that one day Moyers was saying grace at the President's dinner table in a very low voice.

''Speak up, Bill! Speak up!'' said Johnson.

''I wasn't addressing you, Mr. President,'' Moyers replied.

One official, though, had a power base that was impregnable even to Lyndon Johnson. That was FBI Director J. Edgar Hoover, whose manipulative talents and cupboard full of secret files made Johnson leery of getting rid of him no matter what Hoover did. "I'd rather have him inside the tent pissing out, than outside pissing in," he told aides.

With all his coarseness, Johnson could be charming, too, particularly with women, whether they were reporters, secretaries, or wives. At a party or even sometimes at a political rally, he'd give them a big bear hug, a great flirting smile, and a soft, sweet drawl. He loved to dance, and as one female NBC reporter told me, "He danced real close, too."

But Johnson couldn't stand criticism or even a pause in adulation, and this attitude extended to the media. He wanted reporters not just to be sympathetic to him but to be sycophantic. Being a sycophant had rewards of sorts. Max Freedman, a friend of mine and a brilliant journalist who wrote for the Manchester *Guardian*, succumbed and wrote outrageously flattering stories about LBJ, defending his policies in private conversation and in public speeches. At one informal news conference in Johnson's office in 1965, I was astounded to see Max repeatedly pose set-up questions for the President, asking him to explain his popularity and wisdom. I found it embarrassing, all the more so because Max was a friend and a fine professional. But I suppose he found it a worthwhile tradeoff for the reward he got of hours alone with Johnson for exclusive interviews.

LBJ was not afraid to share his earthier side with visiting foreign dignitaries as well as with his cronies and reporters. This was clearly evident on visits to Johnson's LBJ Ranch in the Texas Hill Country fifty miles from Austin. If he was earthy in Washington, he was a wild cowboy on the Pedernales River that ran through his property. In his presidential days, there was a regular parade of politicians, officials, and foreign leaders to the ranch, including West German Chancellor Ludwig Erhardt, British Prime Minister Sir Alec Douglas-Home, and Prime Minister Pearson. They all got the same full Johnson country-boy treatment.

Johnson would often insist on driving his white Lincoln Continental while the visiting dignitary sat in the back seat and the media and the Secret Service cars followed along in a kind of mechanized safari. With a Stetson on his head and gulping from a paper cup of beer that sat perilously on the dashboard, he'd careen over the hilly terrain at speeds up to ninety miles per hour, all the while turning his head to talk with his terrified guest. In the midst of this performance, he sometimes would grab the car phone to talk to his wife Lady Bird back at the ranch about dinner, or he would talk to the Secret Serviceman following him.

Without warning he would jam on the brakes to point out some grazing Herefords just off the road and describe their life history. Behind him, Secret Service cars and media cars would bump into each other as they stopped to see what the President was up to. At some stops, he would sometimes leap out of the car and pace around.

One story I had heard of a visit to the ranch by Mike Pearson and External Affairs Minister Paul Martin in January, 1965, had a ring of truth to it, although it was probably apocryphal. Johnson, Pearson, Martin, Secretary of State Dean Rusk, and White House Adviser McGeorge Bundy, and an old LBJ friend from Texas, were jammed into a car on a typical speeding ride through the ranch. Martin, who was notorious for having a bad bladder and who hadn't had a chance to go to the bathroom for hours, was simply desperate to go. As the story went, while Pearson and Rusk were discussing Vietnam, Martin blurted that he just had to go to the bathroom, whereupon Johnson shouted, by God, he "had to have a piss too," so the car was stopped and LBJ and Martin got out to stand at the side of the road peeing into a ditch.

During the same visit Martin got a chance to be with Johnson privately. Martin got up early the next morning and went down to the Johnson kitchen to get a glass of milk. In came Johnson looking for a cup of coffee and the two of them chatted for an hour in their pajamas and sipping coffee and milk.

Pearson had a slightly more hair-raising experience on that trip when Johnson insisted that the P.M. join him on a fifteen-minute helicopter flight over his ranch. Pearson was still wearing his homburg and dark suit while LBJ was in ranch clothes. Johnson had a bar in his helicopter and he and Pearson guzzled Scotch while they whizzed over the scrub trees, rocks and dusty hills, and tiny deer and armadillos.

At ranch barbecues for his guests, Johnson would introduce them to his "kissin' cousins," including the folksy Cousin Oriole, an elderly Johnson relative whom he allowed to sass him. During the parties, he'd sometimes get up on a horse, show off his cattle, and almost always serve mammoth amounts of deer-meat sausages, ribs, fried catfish, pinto beans, cole slaw, and his favourite desert, tapioca pudding – all this washed down with alcohol and beer to a loudspeaker serenade of "Deep in the Heart of Texas."

It is difficult to reconcile the public Johnson, whose television image was that of a kindly, caring, soft-spoken, but sometimes stern uncle, with the private man we reporters knew. And this difference raises a perennial issue that faces journalists who spend private moments with public figures. What is truly off the record? Where do I draw the line between the public's right to know and the public figure's right to privacy? Johnson once told Helen Thomas of UPI that he didn't want reporters writing stories about how many drinks he had or "when I go into a strange bedroom." He wasn't alone among presidents in wanting his own self-image reflected in the media and in seeking a little conspiracy with reporters to shield some of his personal habits. Until recently, most reporters generally joined the conspiracy. There was little reported at the time on Roosevelt's confinement to a wheelchair because of polio, Truman's bourbon-loving and poker-playing, or Kennedy's wenching.

The contemporary journalistic wisdom is that anything goes. Personally, I question that. If the past or present personal life of a public figure has a direct bearing on the performance of his or her job, then it seems to me to be perfectly legitimate and even necessary to report it. If it has no bearing, however, and is only an interesting curiosity, then I think it becomes a judgement as to whether or not the public interest is served by its revelation, and a matter of good taste. With the seemingly insatiable public curiosity about the personal lives of public figures, I suspect I'm fighting a losing battle.

In the wake of Kennedy's assassination, Johnson's drive and decisiveness and his ability to get what he wanted overcame the morbid terror of those awful late November days of 1963. Two days after the funeral, I watched Johnson tell the Congress and the nation, "Let us turn away from the fanatics of the far left and the far right; from the apostles of bitterness and bigotry; from the defiant of law and those who pour venom into our nation's bloodstream...."

Johnson was a tornado of activity in those early weeks. He held informal news conferences in White House hallways, in his office, or outside on the lawn, and he moved the formal news conferences into the White House itself. In his first ninety days, he called a stream of influential people to the White House to seek their support – leaders of Congress, governors, mayors, businessmen, farm and labour leaders, civil rights activists. They all got what became known as "the Johnson Treatment," an emotional combination of pleading for help, appeals to patriotism, and lapel grabbing, nose-to-nose persuasion. "I don't have charisma," he said, "but I get things done." LBJ was able to pass into law earlier Kennedy proposals on everything from health care for the aged to new money for schools. And civil rights legislation.

Johnson, who was a late convert to the black cause, was nevertheless an ardent and total convert. Seeking to get Congress to pass the Kennedy civil rights proposals, he said, "We have talked long enough in this country about equal rights. We have talked for 100 years or more. It is now time to write the next chapter and to write it in books of law." He turned his back on his southern roots and on his Texas friends to become a champion of civil rights. He cajoled, pleaded, threatened, and manipulated to finally persuade Congress to pass the 1964 Civil Rights Act, the most significant civil rights legislation in about a century.

As a southerner, he had voted against all civil rights legislation from 1937 to 1957. He had called Harry Truman's 1948 civil rights proposal, "a farce and a sham ... an effort to set up a police state." He rationalized later that these proposals didn't have a chance anyway. But then came the famous May 17, 1954, Supreme Court decision on school segregation. As Senate Majority Leader, he successfully steered Eisenhower's modest 1957 civil rights bill into law. As Vice-President, he increasingly spoke out for stronger laws to protect black rights. Finally, as President, he succeeded where Kennedy had failed by passing legislation guaranteeing those rights.

Dallas, Texas, February, 1964 ...

A weird and wonderful interlude in those early days of the Johnson presidency was the trial of Jack Ruby, the man who shot and killed Lee Harvey Oswald on national television. I have covered a lot of strange court cases in my time – from sensational divorce trials to complex bankruptcy hearings. But this was the most unusual and the most entertaining. It was a circus, pure and simple.

The setting was a Dallas courtroom in February, 1964, and the cast of characters seemed straight out of a comedy by the Marx Brothers. The judge was Joe B. Brown, an affable character who got the case because of the court rotation system – the leading citizens of Dallas were appalled when they learned he would be representing Texas justice. Ruby's defence lawyer was the silken-voiced Melvin Belli, a well-known, brilliant, and flamboyant San Francisco bon vivant who had taken the case because he loved lost causes and revelled in publicity. He was aided by a mountainous Texas lawyer with a heavy drawl named Joe Tonnahill. The district attorney was Henry Wade, a cigar-chomping, spittoon-spitting refugee from a B-grade western. And of course, there was the fifty-two-year-old Ruby himself, a ferret-faced Dallas strip-joint operator who told me in an interview that he now had found God and was reading the Bible every morning. "I can't magnify my impression and attraction to the Bible," he added.

The day the trial began it was like a Hollywood opening. There were about 100 reporters on hand, including correspondents from Australia, Japan, Czechoslovakia, Sweden, and Britain, along with several from Canada. One of the American reporters was famed sob sister Dorothy Kilgallen, who impressed me with her determination to get herself into every television shot and still picture being taken.

At one point before the trial got underway, Judge Brown was giving a news conference in one part of the courtroom, the district attorney was doing the same thing in another part, defence lawyer Tonnahill was talking to reporters, and Ruby himself was surrounded by journalists. The foreign reporters were flabbergasted by the extreme informality of the court.

Into this chaotic scene marched Melvin Belli, sporting cowboy boots and a Saville Row suit under a black cashmere topcoat with a scarlet silk lining. He strode through the mêlée and up to the defence counsel's desk, slapped down the red velvet carpetbag he used as his briefcase, and took off his coat. At this performance the noisy courtroom became silent.

"Boys," he cheerily announced, "my hotel room is bugged and my briefcase has been gone through." Noting his legal adversaries, he said, "I'm going to eat six cloves of garlic every morning. Then all I have to do is advance on them." Then he opened his carpetbag and took out some medical reports on Ruby and a book entitled *The Living Brain* (he never did explain what it had to do with the case). He informed us as we waited for the proceedings to formally begin that he enjoyed whisky and women, adding, "You can't trust a guy who gives up booze and women."

With some difficulty, the trial began. Belli's strategy was to claim Ruby could not get a fair hearing because any jury selected in Dallas would want to send him to the electric chair as a way of "cleansing" the city of the whole Kennedy tragedy. The judge dismissed this argument. Ruby, when asked if he thought he'd get a fair trial in Dallas, ignored his lawyer and said, "Of course I will."

When he couldn't get the trial moved elsewhere, Belli sought a jury made up of members of minority groups, believing that they would be more sympathetic to a man charged with killing Kennedy's assassin. "Any day in the week," he told us, "I'll take a good jury of Jews, Mexicans, and Chinese."

Belli was absolutely frustrated by Judge Brown. The basic problem was that Belli knew the law inside out and Judge Brown didn't. Belli could argue rationally, logically, and effectively all the fine legal points, but it didn't do much good. Often he would cite a legal precedent to prove his argument and Judge Brown would simply say, "Yeah ... well ... I don't think so anyway."

Joe Brown was an overly amiable, dumb, heavy-set caricature of a Texas judge. Once, when a stripper was before him, he had adjourned the case and invited the lady into his office for a private demonstration. During the Ruby trial it was revealed that four years before he had sponsored Ruby for admittance to the Dallas Chamber of Commerce. Despite this, Judge Brown refused to disqualify himself.

He adored the publicity he was getting in the case and during testimony would sometimes interrupt to tell us to "get that down" because the point was important. Or he'd say, "Can you fellows hear everything okay?" He told me during one lunchtime break that he learned "the judging business" by carefully watching the judges in the then popular TV series *Perry Mason*.

Throughout the Ruby hearing Brown constantly interrupted the proceedings, argued and joked with lawyers, made asides to reporters, and chatted with officials. At one point, he loudly said to an assistant, "Go get me some branch water. I'll need it for this." From time to time he puffed his pipe and occasionally used one of the two spittoons on either side of him. Once, confused by the evidence, he muttered aloud, "You know, the harder I go, the behinder I get."

Even while the court was in session, the courtroom was in constant bedlam as the judge and lawyers shouted at each other, electric fans whirled on the ceiling, the defence lawyers whispered to their client, and everyone milled around gossiping and laughing. At one point there was a jail break in the building and the trial was recessed; on two other occasions spectators at the trial had to be disarmed, one of them a former stripper in Ruby's nightclub.

District Attorney Wade chewed up four six-inch cigars every day – more when he was angry. He never smoked them, just chewed. I'd watch in fascination as he'd start chewing and spitting. Within an hour, the last morsel of cigar would pop into his bulging cheeks. He had a green spittoon at his feet but he had a notoriously bad aim and the floor around his seat was exceedingly slippery.

Belli was accused by Wade of making a circus of the courtroom by trying to get publicity for himself. Shouts of "liar," "insulting," and numerous incoherent rantings echoed through the court, from the lawyers and onlookers.

"You can't talk to me like that," Belli would shout back.

For some inexplicable reason, much of the shouting involving accusations of communism. The two sides accused each other of being "Communist agents": "The district attorney doesn't deserve to live as an American in this country. He wants to exercise the laws of Communist Russia in this court!" screamed Tonnahill at one point. That was too much even for Judge Brown, who said, "Now you are all treading on dangerous ground Be careful and let's not have any trouble."

To complete the scene, policemen and Texas Rangers sporting pearl-handled revolvers were everywhere. Everybody seemed to be carrying guns. There had been fear that Ruby, too, might be assassinated and the Dallas cops didn't want to lose him as they had lost Oswald. So Ruby was accompanied everywhere he went, even to the bathroom, by armed guards. Every trip he took from his cell to the courtroom, the guards were there. Several times, I went down to Ruby's cell to talk with him and accompany him and his guards back along the corridors to the courtroom. It seemed to me that in spite of all the precautions, anybody could have got him. In fact, on the first day of the trial a man was found wandering the halls of the building mumbling about the assassination of President Kennedy and carrying a loaded .22 calibre automatic pistol.

In court the sallow-faced defendant sat nervously crossing and uncrossing his legs, scratching his ear and his rear, his eyes constantly leaping about the room. He'd cough, shiver, and scratch away at his perennial five o'clock shadow. He'd rub his hand across his balding head and pat his belly. He seemed unable to sit still.

One night I went over to the Carousel, Ruby's striptease nightclub, but found it empty. The owner of the strip joint next door told me, "He never was any good. He used to give away turkeys to try to get people to go to his club. I never gave turkeys away." The Carousel's marquee advertised "Girls! Girls! Girls!" and inside I found the kind of place you'd expect in Tijuana or Tangiers, a dive catering to the dregs of society. Paint was peeling, rats skittered about, and half the garish neon lights weren't working.

The trial lasted a month, but I only covered the first couple of weeks of the legal charade. On March 14, 1964, Ruby was found guilty of murdering Oswald and sentenced to death. Three times while he languished in jail awaiting his appeal, he tried to commit suicide. In October, 1966, the Texas Court of Criminal Appeal reversed the conviction because of judicial errors by Judge Brown and ordered a new trial. Before it could begin, however, Ruby died of cancer.

Five months after Ruby's trial, while I was in San Francisco to cover the 1964 Republican presidential nominating convention, Melvin Belli invited those of us who had covered the proceedings and were at the convention to come to a party at his home in the hills just south of the city. Belli's party provided a brief respite from my coverage of the convention. Aside from several ladies attired in topless dresses, the most memorable thing about the party was the bathroom. The toilet seat in Belli's master bathroom was gold-plated and moulded to the contours of his own ample rump.

Nelson Rockefeller, the liberal Republican governor of New York, was the conservative Barry Goldwater's principal adversary for the nomination. Rockefeller had first sought the presidency four years earlier, but had no chance against Nixon. This time, the Republican conservatives dominated the party and wanted nothing to do with the liberalism of Rockefeller. He was also hurt by his recent divorce and remarriage to a much younger lady named "Happy."

"Rocky" and "Happy" were, however, an attractive couple to reporters and Rockefeller himself was the most gregarious of all politicians I have known. Although in private he had a ferocious temper and an imperial style, in public he was always "one of the boys" with a big, fat smile on his face and saying "Hi, fella" to everybody. He had a peculiar habit of saying "Thanks a thousand." Maybe he felt it softened his multimillionaire status. Sometimes he'd joke about his family wealth. He told one audience "Both my grandparents left school at fourteen, but somehow they made out." Rockefeller loved meeting people – main-streeting and shaking hands and slapping backs, kissing babies, munching corn on the cob and hot dogs, and donning Indian headdresses. He ballyhooed his way through the primaries winning friends, but not votes.

By the time the candidates and the delegates got to the convention in San Francisco, Goldwater was a cinch in spite of last minute and futile efforts by perennial presidential aspirant Harold Stassen and former liberal Republican Pennsylvania Governor William Scranton. The convention, however, was uproarious as the triumphant conservatives launched repeated and bitter attacks on both party liberals and the media, whom many of the delegates lumped together as "Commies and beatniks." I heard one delegate shout inexplicably, "Down with Walter Lippmann."

During one tumultuous session, NBC reporter John Chancellor was grabbed by police and hustled off the floor while still actually doing a live report for NBC. With incredible aplomb, he described his arrest, being hustled out of the convention hall by the cops, and, with the camera following him every moment, finally signed off with the words, "This is John Chancellor reporting from somewhere in custody."

On the second day of the convention when Nelson Rockefeller got up to speak, the roof fell in. Catcalls and boos, cowbells and horns echoed through the Cow Palace. When he attacked the "hawkers of hate and purveyors of prejudice" I happened to be on the floor immediately below the podium and I thought the delegates were going to rush the platform and string him up. If I was alarmed, he wasn't. But platform officials, all of them Goldwater supporters, momentarily enjoyed the spectacle and then got worried.

"It'll be okay. It'll be okay," they told Rockefeller.

"Well, they're your people and you'd better cool them down," I heard Rockefeller say. "I'm entitled to five minutes. You control your audience and I'll make my five minutes."

He stood there, smiling grimly throughout the whole demonstration until it finally petered out and he was allowed to make his statement. "This is still a free country, ladies and gentlemen," he said to renewed catcalls and boos.

They didn't want to hear Rockefeller but Goldwater later gave them exactly what they wanted: "Extremism in the defence of liberty is no vice. Moderation in the pursuit of justice is no virtue." His victory at the convention marked the first time Republicans had voted for a nominee with their true hearts since Calvin Coolidge was chosen in 1924. The next time they did it would be sixteen years later when Ronald Reagan was nominated.

During the San Francisco convention I was impressed not only with all the political hoopla but with another demonstration, this one relatively private. One evening for dinner, I joined about a dozen Canadian reporters in going across the Bay to Sausalito. Much liquid flowed and the highlight came when prize-winning editorial cartoonist Duncan Macpherson of the *Toronto Star* decided to demonstrate his favourite trick of pulling the tablecloth off our table without disturbing glasses, dishes, or cutlery. Nobody believed it possible and wagers were made. He took off his jacket, rolled up his sleeves, and while we watched in fascination and the waiters in horror, Macpherson gave the table linen a great yank. Off it flew, and to the absolute astonishment of all concerned – most especially Macpherson himself – not a glass fell or a dish rattled.

During the convention, I met the celebrated columnist and broadcaster Walter Winchell, who was doing his broadcasts from the Mutual

Broadcasting System booth next to ours. He had been a journalist of enormous influence, a man catered to by Roosevelt and whose opinions swayed millions. I had previously been impressed with his impact, although appalled by the frequent inaccuracies and "show biz" emotionalism of his reporting. As we munched hot dogs at a stand near our booths, I asked him how he double-checked his facts in some of his exclusive stories. "Oh," he replied, "if I took the time to check the facts and rumours before writing them, I'd never have time at all to write or broadcast or do the other things I do." His was not my idea of journalism and in this and other conversations I found him to be one of the most egocentric, loud, and unpleasant persons I'd ever met.

When the convention ended, I flew out with a CBC French network colleague, Jean Grand-Landau, for a few days' relaxation in Las Vegas and then he and I drove a rented convertible through the deserts, valleys, and canyons of Nevada, New Mexico, Utah, and Arizona. On that trip I came to better understand the fiercely independent self-reliant conservative philosophy behind Barry Goldwater and his supporters. They were taking into contemporary times the gun-carrying, pioneering spirit of their frontier forefathers who faced the dangers of the harsh terrain, extremes of weather, and hostile Indians, relying only on themselves, their guns, and occasionally their neighbours, but seldom the government. And they had tamed the West with that attitude of fearless independence.

Atlantic City, August 24, 1964 ...

There was a very different philosophy at work across the country in Atlantic City where the Democrats met that year for their nominating convention. It was a late August political "love-in" for Lyndon Johnson.

H.L. Mencken once wrote that an American political convention is "as fascinating as a revival or a hanging." For the Democrats, 1964 was a "revival," a gaudy, garish, slapstick affair. Atlantic City in those days was the faded, jaded ex-mistress of holidaying Americans – Coney Island on the cheap or a poor man's Blackpool. And it was on the boardwalk of Atlantic City that delegates spent most of their time, walking along the beach, munching saltwater taffy, drinking beer and booze, and singing and laughing. Occasionally they indulged in a dollop of serious business in the convention hall.

On the boardwalk, delegates were diverted by mind readers and diving horses, roving bands playing "Hello Lyndon" to the tune of "Hello Dolly" and the perennial Democratic theme song, "Happy

Days Are Here Again." Parties were thrown by fan dancer Sally Rand, who twirled her fans, and by rich Democratic supporter and party-giver Perle Mesta, whom Truman had made ambassador to Luxembourg. She was the "Hostess with the Mostest," bringing along a butler, two maids, a cook, a chauffeur, and a party arranger. Occasionally I'd glimpse that magnificent political faker, self-annointed black leader Adam Clayton Powell, driving about with a blonde in his pink Cadillac.

The reporters covering the convention spent more time outside than inside the convention hall, and my CBC colleagues and I tried to find ways to make a television program on it interesting. In the process producer Don Cameron had me interview a crystal-ball fortuneteller named Madame Edith, who held forth on the boardwalk in her "Temple of Knowledge," I also scampered over rooftops to interview a sixty-two-year-old flagpole sitter named Dixie Blandy, a bartender who planned to sit up there for seventy-eight days to set a world flagpole record.

The only political suspense at that convention was who Johnson would choose as his vice-president. He was secretive about it as always. The choosing of a vice-president is a tricky business because while he's only a heartbeat away from the presidency itself, the choice invariably is based not on talent but on things like balancing the ticket by appealing to all the groups the presidential candidate doesn't. In making the choice there are considerations of geography, philosophy, age, religion, and ancestry. To balance Johnson, probably the best candidate would have been a liberal from the Northeast born of an Italian father and a Polish mother who also happened to be a black named Cohen.

The best possible vice-presidential candidate I ever heard of, but who never made it, was one-time New York City Mayor and Congressman Fiorello LaGuardia. He was half Italian and half Jewish, an Episcopalian who first married a Catholic and then later a Lutheran of German descent. And he spoke seven languages. He was a balanced ticket all by himself.

In the end, Johnson chose Hubert Humphrey, a one-time flaming liberal from the Midwest whose flame had faltered and whose great attraction to Johnson was his loyalty, not to say obsequiousness.

Once Atlantic City was over, the Johnson-Goldwater race was on. It was the nastiest, dirtiest American presidential campaign in generations. There were charges of corruption, sexual perversion, and even insanity. Goldwater had billboards across the country proclaiming, "In Your Heart You Know He's Right." Democrats countered with anti-Goldwater signs saying, "In Your Guts You Know He's Nuts." At rallies, news conferences, and speeches, Goldwater called Johnson a "faker," a "fraud," and a "wheeler-dealer." He said Johnson encouraged hoodlums to run loose in the streets, was responsible for racial violence, and supported sexual promiscuity. "Go Gay with LBJ" read one Goldwater sign I saw.

In response, Johnson and his supporters claimed Goldwater was a "trigger-happy nut" who would cause nuclear war and dismantle Social Security. They claimed Goldwater was so conservative he refused to travel around the world for fear he'd fall off the edge. They said his strategy to prevent nuclear attack on the U.S. was to "get all those wagons in a circle." One time at the LBJ Ranch, Humphrey accidentally stepped into some cow dung, grinned, then smiled and told us he had just stepped on the Goldwater platform.

For a reporter, the jokes and the vitriol provided the only break in an otherwise steamroller triumph for Johnson. Goldwater never had a chance. On the campaign trail he was his own worst enemy. In covering his off-the-cuff remarks at news conferences or in informal conversations, we hesitated to quote him because what he said was so often factually wrong, stupid, or self-wounding. He turned off millions of Republican voters at one point by calling President Eisenhower's administration "a dime-store New Deal." As a westerner he said he hated the East and once warned me against being "bamboozled and hornswoggled by eastern sons of bitches." Another time he said publicly it might be a good idea to "saw off the eastern seaboard and let it float out to sea."

In public he was impossible; in private, he was a very nice man, witty and gregarious. He enjoyed being with reporters, sometimes arguing, joking, and drinking with us, especially as the campaign wore on. Aware of his reputation for Cold War recklessness and how Johnson was exploiting it, Goldwater had a sign pinned up on a bulkhead of his campaign plane saying, "Better Brinkmanship Than Chickenshit." Reporters covering the two candidates vastly preferred Goldwater to Johnson as a travelling companion, although I suspect their votes went to LBJ.

One of the most interesting aspects of the 1964 primaries had been the candidacy of Alabama Governor George Corley Wallace for the Democratic presidential nomination. In the aftermath of Ole Miss, his confrontation with the federal government on the steps of the University of Alabama, and the passage of the civil rights bill, Wallace parlayed his racist rhetoric into frightening national political support. In the Democratic Party primary in Wisconsin, he got 34 per cent of the vote; 30 per cent in Indiana; 43 per cent in Maryland. Those figures sent shock waves through the body politic. But the party organization rallied behind the sitting President and Johnson urged Wallace to withdraw from the nomination race. His popularity, however, encouraged him to make another presidential try in 1968.

In the November showdown between Goldwater and Johnson, LBJ won one of the great landslide victories in American political history. He got a bigger majority than ever before and his coattails swept hundreds of Democrats across the country into the Senate, the House of Representatives, the state legislatures, and the offices of mayors, sheriffs, and county governments. In the Congress, he all but wiped out the old conservative coalition of Republicans and conservative southern Democrats. At last he was out from under the Kennedy shadow.

Selma, Alabama, March, 1965 ...

In the early days following the 1964 election, before Vietnam began to sink his presidency and obsess the President, Lyndon Johnson put his Great Society rhetoric into legislative action.

He had been searching for a catch phrase to characterize his presidency as Kennedy had with the "New Frontier," Truman with the "Fair Deal," and Roosevelt with the "New Deal." The previous March he'd tried out "Better Deal" and spoken of a "Glorious Society" and in April had begun using "the Great Society." Ironically, the phrase had come from a young Kennedy aide, Richard Goodwin, whose vision inspired Johnson but whose independent, abrasive style killed their relationship. Unbeknownst to both men at the time was a book entitled *The Great Society* written in 1914 by an English Fabian Socialist named Graham Wallas, a fact with which Goldwater Republicans had tried to portray LBJ as a wild-spending socialist.

With the election triumph making him President in his own right and not just an accident of history after Kennedy's assassination, Johnson began putting a distinctive LBJ brand on the country. No longer did we reporters hear him referring to the need to pass laws to fulfil the Kennedy legacy. It was now, as his campaign slogan had put it, "All the Way with LBJ."

His Great Society war on poverty was designed to complete Roosevelt's New Deal. He introduced more major legislation in the first few months of 1965 than the White House had sent to Congress since the heyday of FDR. He wanted and got new laws on federal aid to education at all levels, more money for a multitude of programs to feed, clothe, house, and care for the poor and the elderly, to improve Social Security, to establish a domestic peace corps. His monumental Voting Rights Act of 1965 would provide new safeguards for black voters, guaranteeing them the right to vote, especially in the South, in practice as well as in principle. Altogether he sent Congress sixty-three major and separate documents demanding legislative action and he got most of what he wanted.

The first big challenge to Johnson's civil rights legislation came in Selma, Alabama, in March, 1965, and it became the turning point for the black revolution in the United States. Dr. Martin Luther King, Jr., president of the Southern Christian Leadership Conference whose "I Have A Dream" speech still echoed through the country, was leading a campaign to get blacks to register to vote throughout the South. He was concentrating on Selma and by mid-February the town's bully-boy sheriff, James Clark, had jailed 2,000 blacks and liberal whites who were helping the King campaign. One black youngster had been fatally shot.

King called for a march to protest the arrests and to draw more attention to his campaign. His supporters would walk the fifty miles from Selma to Montgomery, the state capital. They left on Sunday, March 17, but the march was broken up by state police using tear gas and billy clubs. Two days later, 1,500 marchers left Selma but again were stopped by state troopers. That night, a white Unitarian minister, James Reeb, thirty-eight, was beaten to death by white thugs. Johnson then federalized the Alabama National Guard and ordered 2,000 of them along with regular Army soldiers to guard the route of a new march to Montgomery. I flew down to Selma to cover it.

I watched the nervous marchers start out from a Methodist church in Selma and walk across the Edmund Pettus Bridge en route to the capital in their, at last, successful march. I could hardly believe my eyes as I watched the Alabama State Police actually leading the marchers as they came across that bridge. These were the same policemen who'd used clubs and tear gas two weeks before. The police protection, however, did not prevent violence.

That spring the whole town of Selma reeked of hatred. It was dangerous to interview black leaders or cover meetings. The "good ole boys" of Selma not only beat and killed blacks, but whites, too, and reporters were a special target for abuse. I carried around a tiny Canadian flag and lots of CBC insignia to identify myself as a Canadian and a reporter, but that made no difference. "You're all the same," a hawk-faced, foul-mouthed little runt shouted at me one night outside my hotel. "Get out of town, you slimey, nigger-lovin' ... you, you, Commie, pinko liberal."

Before taking their advice to leave town, I interviewed Sheriff Clark. Fat, jowly, and snarling, he told me in an interview, "Nigras are the lowest form of humanity ... they's only good for beatin', fuckin', and pickin' cotton.''

It was the same atmosphere all over Alabama. In Birmingham, the city's director of public safety was a bigot named Eugene "Bull" Connor who loved his work of jailing demonstrating blacks. At one point, he hauled 3,300 blacks into jail, including Martin Luther King, Jr. He was a big-city version of small-town Selma's Sheriff James Clark. With billy clubs, fire hoses, horses, and dogs he broke up sit-ins, pray-ins, demonstrations, and marches. Northerners, professors, liberals, Communists, and blacks were all the same to Bull Connor. "Scram," he'd tell us in brief street interviews. "You're trying to cram niggers down our throats and we won't take it.''

And yet, ironically, Bull Connor probably did more for civil rights than almost anyone else. Newspaper and television pictures of Bull Connor's dogs snapping and snarling at blacks dramatically told the story. Those pictures generated more public sympathy and political support for integration than almost any march or sit-in. Three years later I talked with Bull Connor on the floor of the Democratic presidential nominating convention in Chicago where he was a delegate from Alabama. He was the same virulent, black-hating man. For Bull, nothing had changed.

It was King's activity in Selma, the dogs of Bull Connor, and the terrorism of Sheriff Clark that galvanized Johnson into action on his Voting Rights Act of 1965. In the middle of the Selma crisis, he went up to Capitol Hill to deliver what I've always believed was the greatest speech of his life. To heighten the drama of a Presidential Address to a Joint Session of Congress, he spoke on prime-time television. I listened to him on my car radio as I was en route to the airport to catch a plane to Montgomery and then drive to Selma. His deeply felt, emotional oratory in a moment of crisis was so affecting that I drove onto the shoulder of the road to listen to the speech.

"Their cause must be our cause, too," he said. "Because it is not just Negroes but really it is all of us who must overcome the crippling legacy of bigotry and injustice. And we shall overcome....

"This great, rich, restless country can offer opportunity and education and hope to all – all black and white, all North and South, sharecropper and city dweller. These are the enemies – poverty, ignorance, disease. They are enemies, not our fellow man, not our neighbors, and these enemies, too, poverty, disease, and ignorance, we shall overcome....''

Johnson paused dramatically and raised his southern-accented voice in a kind of hoarse shout of daring, defiance, and determination as he said, "We shall overcome!" I still get spine tingles remembering his emphasis and his words, words that even John Kennedy had never dared use in public.

In contrast to his domestic policy, LBJ's foreign policy was disorganized and ultimately catastrophic for his country and for him personally. It played on all the themes of U.S. moral superiority and the need for hemispheric hegemony. The inexorable escalation of the war in Vietnam is the most notorious result of this policy, but there is much additional evidence. As early as the spring of 1965, only a few months after his inauguration as President, Johnson sent the Marines into the Dominican Republic.

Santo Domingo, May, 1965 ...

Not since Calvin Coolidge sent the U.S. Marines into Nicaragua to put down a liberal insurrection against a conservative government in 1925 – they stayed until 1933 – had American troops intervened directly in a Latin American country. For thirty-one years, the Dominican Republic had been run by the ruthless dictator Generalissimo Rafael Trujillo. While he became a millionaire, most of the country's three and a half million people remained dirt poor. Then in May, 1961, he was assassinated and, after a series of transitional governments, a democratic election put into the presidency short-story writer and liberal politician Juan Bosch, who had returned to the Dominican Republic after twenty years in exile. Kennedy supported Bosch strongly, but his government faltered – I was later told by diplomats in Santo Domingo that it was because of his own ineptitude. He was overthrown by a military coup in September, 1963, and once again fled into exile. Bosch was succeeded by a wealthy and conservative aristocrat, Donald Reid Cabral, but within a year and a half a civil war broke out.

Army officers who supported Bosch tried a coup d'état. They failed, but the President was forced out and "Loyalist" Army generals took command. The rebel officers trying to restore Bosch to power continued to fight, seizing parts of Santo Domingo. The Loyalist generals then appealed to Washington for military supplies and diplomatic support. They got the support of the U.S. ambassador, who warned President Johnson that the rebels were Communist-infiltrated Castro supporters and that U.S. troops should be sent. Johnson, quoting his ambassador, said "blood will run in the streets" without U.S. intervention, and on April 28, 1965, he sent in 400 U.S. Marines and shortly thereafter several hundred members of the crack 82nd Airborne Division. By mid-May, 22,000 U.S. Marines were in Santo Domingo, opening up a so-called International Zone between the two sides.

Officially, the U.S. troops were there as a neutral force supporting neither side. In fact, Washington supported the Loyalist generals and opposed the rebels, whom LBJ labelled "A bunch of Communist conspirators." White House officials privately told reporters of stories of "1,500 bodies in the streets," "heads on lamp posts," and a whole array of accusations about rebel atrocities that turned out to be inaccurate.

Early in May, 1965, I flew into Santo Domingo via Puerto Rico on a U.S. military plane. With cameraman Jack Judges, I climbed into a U.S. Marine truck at the San Ysidro airport and headed for the Embajador Hotel in town. As we left the airport, five Loyalist Army planes took off for a strafing attack on the rebel-held sections of the city. Some Marines started firing at the planes, but U.S. officers screamed out to their men, "Stop! Stop! They're ours! Don't fire." Later, Washington officially denied our stories on what we had seen. So much for U.S. neutrality. We bumped into town aboard the truck, and as we entered the seventeen-mile-long corridor dividing the rebels and the Loyalist forces we crouched to the bottom of the open-backed truck as we heard the "Whap! Whap!" of rifle fire and the staccato of machine guns sending bullets over our heads. Nobody was hurt, but it was a nerve-wracking introduction to Santo Domingo.

As soon as I checked into the Embajador – all tourists had fled as well as most of the maids and bellboys – I headed straight for the hotel telephone switchboard operator. Getting out telephone calls to the CBC was both expensive and time-consuming. The first thing a broadcast journalist does on arriving in such a situation is to bribe the hotel switchboard operator. In Santo Domingo $50 a day did wonders. It got me near the top of the list for the limited time the phones were operating. Still, I sometimes had to wait four or five hours for a call to come through. Several times, my call got cut off going from the CBC switchboard to the newsroom and another four or five hours of waiting ensued. When the power was off in the hotel I had to read my report for radio and television news by candlelight. On a couple of occasions I held my script too close to the flame, with the inevitable result.

Most days I'd skip breakfast and go out early to see what was happening, checking first with U.S. military officials for the formal reports on casualties and movements by the two sides and on any new U.S. actions. Then, with cameraman Judges, I'd go looking for "bang-bang," trying to get action footage of the fighting. This meant going

211

through checkpoints along the International Zone into rebel or Loyalist territory.

On the second day in Santo Domingo, Judges and I found a skirmish going on between Loyalists and rebel forces and I decided to do a report on the fighting. It's always a triumph for a correspondent in the middle of a war to be able to stand up straight, look grimly into the camera, and start a report by saying, "That gunfire you hear is a battle raging just behind me...." This is the sort of report we all seek to send in to our editors to demonstrate our on-the-scene courage. Judges obligingly set up his tripod and camera in front of a brick wall a couple of hundred yards away from the shooting and I stood up to do my thirty or forty seconds to camera beside two bodies, civilians hit a few minutes earlier.

Actually, the person in most danger in such reports is not the correspondent but the cameraman. In 1965 we were using film instead of tape, as is generally the case today, and setting up the tripod and putting a camera atop looked to any unsophisticated teen-age rebel like a machine gun being mounted. As Judges signalled me to start, I saw a puff of smoke pop out of the wall on one side of him and then another puff on the other side of him. We both knew those puffs were sniper bullets. Jack looked at the spot where one had hit, then the other, and then at me, and slowly, but very firmly, he shook his head and wisely got the hell out of there. I crashed to the ground and lay there with my two dead neighbours until darkness came about half an hour later. After that, Judges never again trusted my judgement in choosing locations for my reports.

As usual in wartime, costs went sky-high in Santo Domingo. I once hired a cab to go three particularly dangerous blocks and the charge was $20 a block. The usual rates, though, were about $55 a day. What with $20-a-block cabs, $50-a-day bribes for the hotel telephone operator, and the high cost of food and drink, it was a very expensive war, and when I did a report on it for CBC Television, one of my editors accused me of seeking to justify my expense accounts in advance.

Being a Canadian can be very helpful to a foreign correspondent, as I again discovered on this trip. Canadians are liked around the world, perhaps because people like what they think we stand for in global politics or perhaps because we are beneficiaries of anti-Americanism. I think more the latter. For instance, a cab driver took Jack Judges and me to a Santo Domingo checkpoint called, as so many are, "Checkpoint Charlie." When we told the driver we were Canadians, his face lit up, he turned around, shook my hand (leaving a knee to do the steering), and shouted "Aiee. Que magnifico. Viva Canada. Damnable Yankees." His friendliness didn't alter his costliness, though. To go through the most dangerous part of the city he still wanted $20 U.S. for every block.

Whether in Santo Domingo or Vietnam or Brazil, or during the Paris riots of 1968, I found it always paid to fly the Canadian flag on our car and tell people: "We're Canadians." Peter Jennings of ABC, Morley Safer of CBS, and most of our Canadian colleagues working for the U.S. media found it helpful to display their Canadian origins.

What was unique about the war in the Dominican Republic was the ability to cover it from three sides: the Loyalists or the Junta, as they were called; the rebels; and the Americans. You could spend an hour or so at a machine-gun outpost with the Marines or paratroopers, ducking sniper shots and watching the U.S. soldiers return the fire, then say good-bye, walk a block or two through the lines during a lull, and go talk to the snipers who moments before had been firing at you and the Americans. Most of us reporting from the scene had the unique experience of not only being shot at by one side, but being shot at by all three sides.

A still photographer was setting up his equipment in a window of a building near the Ozama River to get a sniper's-eye view of the U.S. paratrooper lines. Suddenly two shots crashed through the window, narrowly missing him. He quickly took down his equipment, left the building, and went across the river to the paratroopers. After diligent search, he found a private first-class who had shot at the window, mistaking the photographer for a sniper. He proceeded to give the private hell for nearly killing him. The private apologized profusely.

There was one rebel sniper who apparently worked on a part-time basis. He would go through a paratrooper checkpoint in downtown Santo Domingo about 4:00 p.m. every day, chat amiably with the Marines, go into a house a block away, go up to the fourth floor, pick up a .22 rifle, and fire ten rounds at the Marines on the checkpoint. Then he'd leave his rifle, calmly walk downstairs and back to the checkpoint, check his damage, talk to the Marines again, and be on his way. He did it once too often, though. The Marines finally caught on and the next time he went to that fourth-floor window, a 50-calibre machine gun let loose and he was never seen again.

While the war was deadly serious, it certainly had its comic aspects. Both the Junta forces and the Dominican rebels were incredibly bad shots. On one occasion I watched a Junta tank crew become furiously frustrated at repeatedly missing a house filled with rebel snipers. In a black rage, they rolled the tank up to the house, swung the turret around, poked the gun right through a window, and fired. I don't know if they actually hit anybody, but at least they did hit the house.

Not only were they bad shots, but the Dominicans must have been the world's sloppiest soldiers. Standing outside rebel headquarters one day I watched a black sedan screech to a stop and a senior rebel officer leap out. As he came out of the car, three gas bombs he was carrying fell to the ground and rattled along to my feet. Then he stumbled and his bandoleer came off, crashing to the pavement and scattering his bullets all over the place. He and I and several others got down on our hands and knees to retrieve the scattered bombs and bullets.

Perhaps because they were such lousy shots, the Dominicans had an almost fatalistic unconcern about being hit. Women with laundry perched high on their heads constantly wandered about in the middle of the fighting.

One day, carrying a tape recorder and going out on my own to try to get some "bang-bang" battle noise for CBC Radio, I found myself trapped on a side street in the International Zone about a mile from the hotel. Rebel snipers opened fire at a U.S. machine-gun post where I happened to be talking to some American soldiers. I fell to the street and crawled behind a little ridge of rock. As I lay there spreadeagled in the dust and dirt wondering why on earth I'd got myself into this mess, the sniper fire poured in and the ear-splitting responses of the U.S. machine guns shook the street. I was quite frankly scared to death. My tape recorder had fallen to the ground and, unknown to me at the time, the thing had been jarred into starting as it fell.

As the bullets flew over my head and smacked into the earth around me and into a nearby U.S. tank, suddenly I heard children's voices. I looked up to see two ten-year-old boys banging on the side of the tank with a stick and shouting at the Marines. "Empties! Empties!" they screamed. A marine corporal atop the tank paused in firing his 50-calibre machine gun, looked down incredulously, and shouted, "What?" "Empties!" they cried.

Simultaneously it dawned on me and the corporal that these kids, amid all the shooting, were demanding the Marines give them back the "empties" from the Coca-Cola they'd brought earlier. The corporal was thunderstruck, shouted "Fuck off!" and returned to his machine gun. The two kids screamed back a string of Spanish obscenities and angrily wandered away, seemingly oblivious to the bullets whizzing around them.

After I had lain shivering on the ground for three hours, a lull came – probably time out for rebel dinner – and I crawled away unbloodied but still shaken.

Back at the hotel I went straight to the bar to grab a triple rum and water (the Coca-Cola had run out) and shared my story with Peter Jennings, an old friend who was then at ABC in New York. We went up to my room to play the tape recorder that had been accidentally jarred into operation while I was pinned down. Between the crackling of gunfire we listened to a totally unusable outpouring of bizarre and obscene comments about the editors who had sent me to Santo Domingo. I hadn't even realized I'd said a word out loud.

Jennings, too, had gone through a frightening day, having covered a Loyalist and U.S. paratrooper capture of a rebel-held radio station. He, too, had been pinned down by sniper fire. We went back down to the bar to join other colleagues who had similar stories and we all soothed our nerves with rum as everyone tried to talk at once.

One of the chief incongruities of Santo Domingo was being in the midst of the bloody fighting most of the day and then, at the 6:00 p.m. curfew, going back to the Embajador Hotel, having a drink in the bar, and dining by candlelight (the power was often off) under crystal chandeliers while guns crackled outside.

There was no place totally safe in the city. Our hotel was shelled a couple of times and was the target of occasional sniper fire. But the building was not seriously damaged and it was about the most comfortable place in town. Often at night we would go up to the rooftop and watch the bright red and white tracers streaking through the sky. A few years later and half a world away, I would do exactly the same thing, standing on a rooftop of the Caravelle Hotel or the Majestic in downtown Saigon.

My stay in the Dominican Republic brought home vividly to me the occupational hazards of my profession. Not only did I stand a good chance of being wounded or killed as I made my journalistic rounds, it was on dangerous assignments such as these that we correspondents most often overindulged in alcohol.

One colleague and I regularly wound down at the end of the day over more than a few drinks in the hotel bar. On one particular night I finally left him in the bar and didn't see him again until four days later, when I finally went to his hotel room. The room stank of sweat and vomit, and he lay unconscious on twisted bedsheets soaked with perspiration and urine and soiled with excrement. Broken glasses and dozens of empty rum bottles littered the floor and tables.

I opened the windows and splashed cold water on his face. He groaned into trembling consciousness, alternately pleading for more rum, screaming about "things" crushing in on him from the ceiling, and crying about his fears of failure as a correspondent, as a husband, and as a father. I spent several hours holding his hand and his head, listening to his torment and spooning soup into his mouth. When the civil war calmed down, I took him out, back home to Canada and to his family.

Such a brutal confrontation with the black hole of alcoholism, and later similar ones, were more than enough to make me swear off hard liquor not long after I had ended my correspondent career.

Apart from this unhappy incident, my life in Santo Domingo continued much as before. I wanted badly to talk to the rebel commander, Colonel Francisco Comaano, so I could balance his side of the story against what we were being told by the Americans and the Junta. By offering a nervous cab driver double his normal fee, Judges and I persuaded him to take us through the checkpoints into rebel territory and on to the rebel headquarters at the other side of town.

The headquarters turned out to be in the same building that housed the Canadian Embassy. Though the embassy staff had prudently moved out, some still came back from time to time to talk to rebel officials and find out what was going on. The building itself was undamaged but, except for the rebels, deserted.

We talked to the balding and burly Colonel Comaano in his cigarette-butt-littered office while men armed with machine guns, burp guns, rifles, pistols, and gas bombs rushed in and out shouting requests and instructions amid the constant jangling of telephones and the popping and belching of nearby gunfire. Comaano wore an open-necked shirt and had a pistol tucked into his belt. He was a career Army officer who had headed Trujillo's anti-riot squad. He had been named provisional president by the rebels.

"No soy communista," he calmly told us, denying American claims that this was a Communist-controlled revolution and that he was another Castro taking his lead from the island only 150 miles away. The Americans had identified the names of fifty-eight Communists among the rebel leaders but these included some teen-agers, some who were not even in the country, and, according to Col. Comaano, none who were Communists so far as he knew. "There may be some Communists fighting with us," he said. "I don't know how many, but maybe a few. But they don't give me orders or supplies or anything. This is a revolt of the people against the generals." He did tell me that he couldn't control some of his troops or stop them from shooting at the Americans. When the civil war ended, Colonel Comaano was sent into

216

exile by the provisional government, but he returned a few years later and was eventually assassinated.

The Junta leader, General Antonio Imbert, was a pugnacious, wily intriguer who boasted to me in an interview that he was the coup-de-grâce trigger man, one of the team that had assassinated Trujillo. But no matter how much he tried to trade on this with the public, he remained unpopular among the people. That probably was because he had for years been a good friend and supporter of the dictator. They had a falling out and he had turned on his boss only at the very end.

After I left, the fighting began to calm down, essentially because of less rebel activity. At first the Americans thought Imbert should be the new president but they later abandoned him as being too unpopular and it was months before the leaders could be found to form a provisional government that satisfied the Americans. The rebels finally acquiesced in its establishment and the American Marines and paratroopers then withdrew.

It had been a bloody civil war with heavy casualties on both sides, although not nearly as heavy as President Johnson had originally feared. The biggest casualty, in many ways, was the credibility of the Johnson administration. LBJ sent in the Marines before consulting the Organization of American States and lied about American conduct. U.S. troops were told the rebels were Communist enemies and that the Junta troops were "friendlies." The U.S. government made extensive loans of money to the Junta while nothing went to the rebels. The U.S. forces cut the rebel side in two through establishment of the International Zone, making the Junta's job easier. U.S. troops allowed Junta forces to go through U.S. checkpoints, but held back all rebel efforts to reinforce their beleaguered northern side.

The official line was that there were no U.S. troops in the area of Radio Santo Domingo when it was captured from the rebels by the Junta troops, but, in fact, reporters were with U.S. paratroopers at the station. We were told the Marines and paratroopers never fired unless fired upon, but they did and any reporter who went out to the battle area knew this.

Seldom has there been a more graphic example of the need for an independent media than the Dominican Republic civil war. Without reporters on the scene seeing for themselves, people would have had only the untruths and half-truths of government propaganda. In this instance, the LBJ administration acted as if it agreed with the philosophy of the rulers of the Soviet Union and dictators everywhere who view the media as instruments of the state to be used to further the objectives of the state.

217

Reporters are often accused of cynicism and sometimes they succumb to this occupational hazard. Given the difference in so many instances between the official line and what we see with our own eyes, whether it is in military or political fighting, this attitude is easy to understand if not support, and Santo Domingo's dirty little war certainly encouraged the cynics among us.

The end result of the U.S. intervention in the Dominican Republic was a gain for the Communists, who used the U.S. intervention as evidence of American support for the right wing. It was a blow to U.S. prestige and trustworthiness among educated Latin Americans. On the other hand, the Americans eventually did wind up with a "safe" neighbouring country and Johnson marked it down as a success. (The Reagan administration did something similar in 1983 in Grenada.) The post-civil-war interim government staggered through until June of 1966, when an election was held. Juan Bosch ran for the presidency but was beaten by conservative politician Joaquin Balaguer.

The sour aftertaste in the mouths of American liberals following the Dominican Republic intervention was the real beginning of the liberal desertion of LBJ, in spite of his Great Society. It planted the seeds of Johnson's destruction, which came to full bloom in Vietnam over the next three years.

Toronto, November 8, 1965 ...

Being so soaked in American politics as a Washington correspondent, it was refreshing to get home from time to time for speeches or meetings and especially to be assigned by the CBC to cover Canadian elections during the early 1960s. In 1962 I was moderator of a panel on election night; in 1963, my assignment was to cover the Ontario results; and in 1965, I co-anchored the CBC election night programming with veteran political reporter and old friend Norman DePoe. Criss-crossing the nation that fall following Diefenbaker and Pearson gave me not only a broader political perspective, but also revived my sense of Canadian nationalism. The politics may not have been quite as large-scale as that of our American neighbours, but I could get so much closer to the political leaders than I could in the United States.

In election campaigns Pearson usually travelled with his wife Maryon, who clearly found politics less than appealing. On platforms, she usually was frowning or scowling and looked bored. She once commented, "Behind every successful politician there is a surprised wife." She was, however, an after-hours pillar of strength for Pearson.

Their relationship was distinctly unlike that of Olive and John Diefenbaker. "The Chief," it seemed to me in the campaigns I covered and on his foreign travels, was utterly dependent on Olive. On platforms he was forever peeking over at her, seeking support and guidance, and he'd get a reassuring look that he was doing well, or a head-shaking frown to be careful.

Diefenbaker was certainly one of the most colourful politicians I ever covered. With his evangelical fervour and soap-box passions, he was part William Jennings Bryan, part Lyndon Johnson, with a dash of Harry Truman and Richard Nixon thrown in. On the platform he was a Shakespearean actor, shouting, whispering, his arms flailing, his curly grey hair leaping out, and his eyes blazing while denouncing the "mess" in Ottawa or the "iniquity" of his opponents. Many of his accusations were, to put it prudently, terminologically inexact, and he seldom dealt in policy detail while on the stump. Campaigning, he was all emotion and he always gave one hell of a show.

Diefenbaker had been under attack for poor health during the 1965 campaign, with suggestions that, because of his shaking, he had Parkinson's disease or some other palsy. Trying to refute these charges at a home-town rally in Prince Albert, Saskatchewan, one night, Diefenbaker's local campaign manager vociferously denied there was anything wrong with Diefenbaker's health. "Why," he cried, "I've known and worked with John for forty years and he has been shaking like that ever since I first met him!"

Diefenbaker loved "helloing" and handshaking his way down the main streets of small-town Canada and most of all in his home town. I walked with him in Prince Albert a few times through the years, including near the end of his life, and found he knew just about every person in town by name, even the dishwashers in the Chinese restaurant.

With Diefenbaker in his home town I also found a phenomenon that haunts journalists with any public profile, especially television reporters. As we walked along, Diefenbaker would ask me to shake hands with people, making me part of his entourage. He, like some other politicians running for office, often sought to exploit high-profile journalists on such handshaking campaign occasions, thus implying without saying so that you are supporting them. As a reporter you simply want to cover the story, not be part of it, and yet if people recognize you it's next to impossible to be an anonymous note-taker observing from the sidelines. The higher the public recognition of the reporter, the harder it is, and in some cases you just have to give up covering these kinds of stories.

The 1965 election also gave me my first glimpse of Pierre Elliott Trudeau, who was running for office for the first time in the Montreal riding of Mount Royal. I followed him around for a couple of days because he was billed as a new kind of politician, beholden to no one, irreverent, brilliant, and brash. His independence and impatience are what I most vividly recall and he made little effort at the usual political glad-handing and baby-kissing. We once entered a CBC TV studio where he was to take part in a debate. As usual with television, there were delays in getting things set up and his face clouded at the delay until he finally said, "Ah, if they're not ready, I'm going," and he did, slinging his black leather coat over his shoulders like a cape and storming out the door.

Other travel through Canada that gave me an enriching and growing awareness of current Canadian attitudes included taking a couple of publicity tours for the CBC. In midsummer 1965 I travelled throughout the West for a week and the next summer I went to Atlantic Canada. I also flew up from Washington on major news stories from time to time, covering the doctors' strike in Saskatchewan in mid-July, hosting programs on the Gerda Munsinger sex scandal in 1966, and covering early FLQ stories in Quebec.

One particular FLQ story almost literally fell into my lap during an assignment at the United Nations. I was at the CBC office at the UN one afternoon in September, 1966, when a phone call came in for me. A gentleman from Quebec was on the line saying he and his colleague had been hiding out in New York but now wanted to surrender to the authorities through me. "What are you wanted for?" I asked. He explained that he and his friend were wanted by the RCMP, the FBI, and the New York City police for non-capital murder and bombing, and in connection with a plot to blow up the Statue of Liberty. The callers were writer Pierre Vallières and sociology professor Charles Gagnon, leaders in the separatist FLQ group. I didn't know too much about their story and checked with Toronto for details. What Vallières and Gagnon wanted was CBC coverage as they picketed the UN for their cause and then were arrested.

I said I'd have to notify the police and they agreed to be arrested while picketing, but not before. I persuaded them to come down to our studio for an interview to be aired that night. They agreed, and in the interview quite openly admitted to me what they'd done. After the interview they popped into the UN press area to promote the cause of Quebec separatism. We arranged to meet the next morning on the street across First Avenue from the UN. And, as agreed, I had our office advise the police of what was happening.

That night suddenly it seemed every policeman in New York City was chasing me. I moved to a different hotel for the night to escape their calls. The next morning I arrived early with a camera crew and chatted with the waiting detectives, who warned me, "Those guys had better show or you're in a hell of a lot of trouble." That I knew.

But right on time the Quebecers showed up with signs and flags. We filmed their marching back and forth for ten or fifteen minutes and then the police moved in to arrest them. It was all very pleasant and the Quebecers went off smilingly into custody.

Toronto and Washington, D.C., 1965-66 ...

During the 1960s, the number of Canadian correspondents in Washington grew from three or four to more than a dozen, representing major Canadian papers, Canadian Press, the CBC, and even some private radio stations. However, Canadian journalists often got lost in the information shuffle in Washington – often being left out of U.S. and British briefings. So, to achieve a measure of recognition and clout, we formed the Canadian Correspondents Association. I was elected president and we had regular background briefings and lunches with key officers in the administration as well as with various diplomats. As an organization we were able to get busy officials more readily than any of us could individually.

Our Canadian Correspondents Association was a relatively junior supplement to the big-league associations for Washington reporters, such as the Overseas Writers, the State Department Correspondents Association, and the National Press Club. The Overseas Writers and State Department groups had frequent off-the-record lunches and meetings with various authorities. I was a member of both and found it extremely valuable to be privately backgrounded in question-and-answer sessions with the likes of the secretary-general of NATO, the U.S. Secretary of State, King Faisal of Saudi Arabia, Adlai Stevenson, Hubert Humphrey, Dean Acheson, Harold Wilson, or Bruno Kreisky, then Foreign Minister of Austria.

At the National Press Club our lunches were on-the-record and therefore less revealing. They were more eclectic, too, with our guests ranging from South Korean President Chung Hu Park to Alfred Hitchcock, to West German Chancellor Ludwig Erhart and Maurice Chevalier.

With the growing complexity of news reporting in Washington and elsewhere and with the explosive growth of television news, life got increasingly peripatetic for the CBC correspondents. On assignment each of us was doing daily radio and television reports, preparing for Sunday radio programs summing up the major events, and working on TV programs like *Newsmagazine*. These days there are three or four people doing the job one did then, but the difference now is a demand for much higher production values than we had then. During the 1960s we were forever on planes and trains going somewhere on a story for *The National, Newsmagazine*, or a news special or radio news. We plunged into wars and political crises, chased interviews with the high and mighty of the world, covered elections, and searched out the offbeat.

When I look back on it now, my travels were breathtaking. A typical one-year period from the fall of 1963 to the fall of 1964, for example, found me travelling to Toronto eighteen times, to New York twenty-one times, to Ottawa four times, London, England, twice, San Francisco twice, Montreal twice, the Bahamas, Vancouver, Penticton and Kamloops in British Columbia, Paris, Tokyo, Mexico, Colombia, Venezuela, Brazil, and in the following American States: Delaware, New Hampshire, Michigan, Oregon, California, Nevada, New Mexico, Arizona, New Jersey, Florida, Mississippi, and Louisiana. To places like New Hampshire and California, there would be two or three trips and in each state I'd visit up to half a dozen different cities.

During a typical period in October of 1966, I flew up to Toronto on Monday the third for program-planning meetings. On Wednesday I flew to New York to spend the day following Nelson Rockefeller in his campaign for re-election as governor. The next day I flew to Michigan to spend the day with the gubernatorial campaign of Governor George Romney, a presidential aspirant like Rockefeller. Friday it was back to Washington; then on Saturday I flew with Senator Bob Kennedy to Iowa for a couple of days as he campaigned. Then it was back to Washington for a day, and on the following Tuesday, October 10, I went to Pennsylvania with Vice-President Humphrey. On Wednesday I was in Massachusetts with Senator Edward Brooke. Friday it was back to Washington and then a flight out to California on the weekend to cover the gubernatorial race between Ronald Reagan and Pat Brown.

Another trip about this time took me on a wild goose chase to Guatemala to find Martin Bormann, Hitler's former henchman. Don Cameron and I were following up a report that Bormann had been found on a farm in Guatemala. Outside police headquarters in Guatemala City, police and government officials led out before us a wrinkled, flustered old man. He looked nothing like any pictures of Bormann I'd seen, but the Guatemala police thought he was. He didn't seem to know what on earth was going on. His fingerprints were sent to Germany and within a couple of days a message came back saying he wasn't Bormann. The old man was sent back to his farm, and we did a story on the man who wasn't Bormann.

Newsmagazine was the cause of much of our travel, a weekly prime-time TV program on the major stories of the week. The program began with the launch of television in Canada in 1952 and was the cradle of much of subsequent TV journalism in Canada. At the start of TV, newscasts were short and simple, mostly consisting of an announcer reading copy supplemented by a few filmed reports from correspondents around the country and the world, similar to the ones you see today. The first host of *Newsmagazine* was Lorne Greene, its first editor, Harry Rasky (now an award-winning documentary producer), and later editors included Michael Maclear and Morley Safer, now of the CBS program *60 Minutes*. Over the years "Newsmag" was the alma mater of many of Canada's best TV reporters and producers, and probably reached its heyday in the 1960s with Don Cameron as executive producer. In those days we did not only the weekly program, but also more news specials than ever before. I started contributing to "Newsmag" in 1959 and for a couple of years in the late 1960s I anchored most of the programs, flying up from Washington. At other times, veteran Norman DePoe anchored the program, as did Peter Reilly. Cameron and Bill Cunningham, known as the "Gold Dust Twins" for their frequent assignments to exotic places, were the most memorable producers in the program's history. The program did have a brief hiatus off the air in the early 1970s when, as Director of News and Current Affairs, I foolishly replaced it with another. The error was later rectified. In 1981 *Newsmagazine* gave way to *The Journal*.

The first program, on September 12, 1952, had featured a story on the fighting in Vietnam, Laos, and Cambodia, a story that would last almost as long as *Newsmagazine* itself. On January 3, 1954, in fact, *Newsmagazine* did a program on the fighting there entitled "War Without End." From late 1952 to mid-1981 *Newsmagazine* trained its camera lenses on everything from the 1954 tent-raising of the Stratford Festival in Ontario and the Hungarian and Suez crises of 1956 to the revelations of Watergate and the drama of the Iran hostages; from Truman to Eisenhower to Kennedy to Johnson to Nixon to Ford to Carter to Reagan. Sadly, the program went off the air without airing a final salute to its illustrious history because of a strike at the CBC.

It was enormous fun being a CBC correspondent in those days, as well as being enormously demanding and low paying. At the time, the CBC was paying abysmal salaries to its correspondents: $8,000 to $10,000 a year in most cases. The rate was okay with me because I had continued my work with the *Financial Post, Vancouver Sun, Windsor Star*, and *Maclean's, Chatelaine*, and other magazines. I also was still preparing the IFAP newsletter for $300 a month. With rental and living allowances from the CBC, it still wasn't a lot of money, but certainly I was comfortable.

However, my extracurricular work began to fall away as the demands of television increased, and most of my colleagues didn't have my access to extra freelance work. So, as a group, the CBC foreign correspondents decided our lot needed improving and in late 1965 we formed the CBC Foreign Correspondents Association.

Romeo LeBlanc, the French network correspondent in Washington, became president and I was elected vice-president. (Later, when Romeo went to Ottawa to become Pearson's press secretary, I replaced him as president. Still later, Romeo became a Trudeau cabinet minister). Our first objective was to improve the terms of the contracts under which we worked, including an increase in salary, better benefits, and the option to join the CBC staff, which would give us pension rights.

In late 1965 and early 1966 Romeo and I met with CBC management in Ottawa and Washington to pursue our objectives. The negotiations with the corporation were tough but occasionally lightened by farce. At a critical point in one set of negotiations in the winter of 1966, CBC officials came down to Washington from Ottawa, Toronto, and Montreal to bargain with us. Romeo and I thought it might be enjoyable and tactically useful if we entertained our visitors as lavishly as possible the night before the bargaining began. We reasoned they might think us good fellows and perhaps be less agile in the morning when we met to negotiate. As host for the occasion, Romeo (a light drinker) poured extraordinarily generous drinks for our guests. As the evening turned into early morning, it was clear from their raucous singing, shouting, and merry incoherence that our guests were enjoying themselves. It was a very different scene the next morning.

Sharp at nine our talks began with surely the greenest, sorriest-looking, most pained negotiators the CBC management ever fielded. Two of them were actually able to sit down at the table with us, gulping large cups of coffee and frequently excusing themselves. The third could only make it to a couch nearby where he lay with eyes closed and an occasional moan gurgling from his throat. When we had convinced the other two corporation officials of a point, we waited for the third to react. If there was silence, we assumed agreement. But once in a while this poor soul would rise slightly from the couch and croak "No!", whereupon he would collapse again, exhausted from the effort.

With this meeting and others, we finally were able to negotiate almost a 50 per cent increase in salaries plus many of the benefits we had asked for, and we did get the option to go on CBC staff. We had achieved what everyone felt was a fair agreement, if not a model negotiation.

Although technically not a foreign correspondent, Norman DePoe went on many foreign assignments and was recognized as a leader of what some regarded as a group of unrepentant anarchists. Don Minifie, my Washington friend and mentor, was known as "the father of us all."

Minifie had a temper that occasionally burst out, usually with producers who, he felt, were trying to get him to say something he didn't think was accurate. "The dishwashers of television," he called producers. On one such occasion, he thumped his desk so hard it totally collapsed in front of him. Apart from Romeo LeBlanc and our French network members, our colleagues at various times included Morley Safer, Michael Maclear, Stanley Burke, Tom Gould, Doug Lachance, David Levy, Bob Evans, Donald Gordon, Peter Reilly, Tom Leach, Gordon Donaldson, Bill Stevenson, Ron Chester, Peter Daniels, Ab Douglas, Phil Calder, Ron Collister, and, latterly, David Halton. We were all, in a sense, descended from the intrepid CBC correspondents of World War II, such as Marcel Ouimet of the French network and Matthew Halton of the English network (the father of David Halton).

CBC Chief News Editor Bill Hogg was the commander-in-chief of the English news service who tried to bring some order to our operations from his desk in Toronto. Hogg was a journalistic traditionalist – old-fashioned in style and attitude. He may have been a fussy, quiet soul, but he had a keen eye for journalistic talent, even if no eye at all for the rambunctious nature of the CBC correspondents of the day.

He once entertained some of us at his north Toronto home with half a case of beer, which he doubted we'd consume but thought would help him appear to be one of the boys. Needless to say, the party was over quickly. When wooing a potential correspondent, he would take him out to lunch at Bowles, which was barely one step up from a soup kitchen. He was horrified at our off-air antics, but through a stream of gentle memos he prodded, admonished, and encouraged us to become a highly professional corps of correspondents.

In 1965, Don Macdonald succeeded Bill Hogg as chief news editor. Much of the credit for the CBC's journalistic expansion and increasing excellence in those days must be credited to him. He nurse-maided many a correspondent through trying times. While Hogg never really understood us, Macdonald did, and furthermore, with his endless patience, he forgave us our excesses. Don is one of the unsung background heroes who humanized CBC bureaucracy for us. Both Hogg and

Macdonald had their hands full, for we were often a pretty unruly bunch, jealous of our independence and fiercely proud of both our eccentricities and our professionalism.

Norman DePoe had a mad love affair with the gin bottle yet was the brightest, sharpest, most knowledgeable, and best communicator among us. Before a news special or *Newsmagazine* program he was hosting, Norman would almost always have his nose in a science fiction book and his hand on a glass of gin, seemingly oblivious to all the technical activity going on around him. He could explain in ninety seconds of simple colloquial language the most complicated federal budget. He had a more detailed knowledge and love of Canadian politics than any reporter I've ever known, and no matter how many demons were chasing him, he would appear on camera as a relaxed, rumpled, and reliable reporter, the antithesis of many a modern-day blow-dried, button-downed reportorial TV personality. The audience knew they could trust Norman. Columnist Dennis Braithwaite wrote in 1965, "When DePoe comes on in his rumpled seersucker suit and five o'clock shadow, hoarse of voice, short of wind, he has the smell of news on him."

I had first met DePoe in 1953 when he was editor of a program called *Radio News Roundup*. A few years later I was inadvertently responsible for his going to Ottawa as the first CBC television correspondent there. Bill Hogg had asked me to go, but I preferred to stay in Washington. Hogg then asked DePoe to go to Ottawa. He became, in fact, the first broadcast journalist allowed to have membership in the parliamentary press gallery, which hitherto had forbidden the upstarts from the electronic media belonging to the gallery. It turned out to be one of the best reportorial appointments the CBC ever made.

Mind you, Norman could be a problem, for he loved to argue, sing, and drink, and he could be mercurial in friendships. After a night of comradely carousing with one young reporter, they met in a Toronto bar the next night. The young reporter came up to him and said "Hi," and Norman responded. "Get away, kid, don't bother me."

He hated bureaucrats of any and all kinds and they in turn tended to have limited sympathy for him on hearing endless tales of his alleged indiscretions. Norman's temper occasionally was directed at colleagues as well as bureaucrats. He was incensed when the CBC National News did only a fifteen-second report on the death of veteran magazine writer and editor, the brilliant and sensitive Blair Fraser. DePoe fired off this telegram to his senior editors:

I would just like to put on record my appreciation of the fact that

226

you found time even to mention the death of Blair Fraser on the National News.

I was moved and touched by hearing for the 95th time a chorus of "we shall overcome" on the standard cliche civil rights story from Washington. Was so impressed that there was room for that cliche of all cliches 'the breakaway state of Biafra' and all the political crud.

But still you found those 15 seconds without even a picture of a Canadian who was greater than any of you shits will ever be.

Thank you from the bottom of my heart.

Norman DePoe.

Anchoring a federal election program and listening on his earphones to the director in the control room, DePoe angrily snapped to the TV audience, "I'm now listening to the instructions from the producer and if he'd speak up, we'd know where we're going."

In Paris in early 1964, I came round to Norman's hotel room to chat before he went off to a formal reception for General De Gaulle and Prime Minister Pearson at the Elysée Palace. I arrived to find Norman sound asleep in his bathtub, surrounded by empty brandy bottles and clutching a brandy snifter.

The head of the CBC London news bureau, Larry Duffy, arrived shortly after and together we got Norman out of the tub and into his formal attire, clanking with his World War II medals. As he left for the reception, he could barely stand, let alone walk. I didn't go, but heard the following story later that night.

To the horror of Prime Minister Pearson and his aides, all of whom knew Norman well, at one point during the reception General De Gaulle began moving in DePoe's direction. Everyone feared disaster. Suddenly De Gaulle was in front of DePoe, pointed to one of Norman's medals, and said something. DePoe snapped to attention, crisply said, "Oui, Mon General ..." and carried on an animated, respectful two- or three-minute conversation with De Gaulle in fluent French. De Gaulle moved on, and Norman returned to his previous state.

Norman loved London above all cities and when in London he often switched his drinking habits from gin to port. Once another correspondent remarked on this one night in a BBC bar. He replied, "It's port, damnit! I'm in London now!"

His face, with its deep worry lines, a neat military mustache, and mischievous twinkle in the eyes, reflected his life. He also was a man who worked best alone. He hated producers and, as I can attest, woe betide any co-anchor on a major live news special. When Norman and I co-anchored the 1965 Canadian federal election we were forever tripping over each other as each of us tried to speak first. Norman had to be in charge and when he was, he was unbeatable, unflappable, and incomparable.

That 1965 election coverage provided an insight into the creativity of producer Don Cameron, as well as the stressfulness of live television. Norman and I had just finished our run-through of the big pre-election special when Cameron stomped into the studio from the control room bristling with changes. The trouble was, we were two minutes to air.

"Won't work," he said. "Won't work at all. You gotta make page 8 page 1, page 1 page 4, page 3 page 7, page 7 page 2 ...." He was ripping the program apart with now one minute to air.

Norman and I looked at him incredulously as we shuffled pages madly. The control room thought Cameron was insane. The director was having apoplexy and, as the seconds ticked down to air time, all was chaos.

Cameron wheeled around and marched back up to the control room, hollering over his shoulder, "and make page three the last one," just as we were cued to go on. It was breathtakingly risky, but it worked and was a very much better program as a result, even if Norman and I were very much older when it was over.

Norman's pleasure in barroom singing entertained his colleagues, but that – and his constant smoking – caused his voice to get raspier with each passing year. Sometimes it disappeared altogether. However, I never heard him sing more lustily than at a 1966 New Year's Eve party in his Toronto apartment as we were ushering in Canada's Centennial year.

Always a fierce patriot, as midnight arrived Norman's pride and sentimentality took over. He insisted we all herald this auspicious occasion not with "Auld Lang Syne" but with "O Canada." He stood at attention at the stroke of midnight and, amid tears from some members of his chorus, led all of us in singing "O Canada." All, that is, except a relatively newly arrived British journalist who thought the scene was funny. Norman suddenly glared, red-faced and ramrod-stiff, broke off the singing, and shouted shame on the incredulous Briton. A brawl was narrowly averted, and the offender escaped in confusion.

There was, however, one occasion when, in spite of talent and determination, alcohol almost got the upper hand with Norman. He was unexpectedly called away from a lengthy visit to the Press Club bar in Ottawa to do a live report into *The National*. He made his way to the Chateau Laurier where the CBC had an unmanned, automatic camera focused on a desk, but controlled back at the station some miles away. The reporter would sit behind the desk and deliver his report without seeing a soul. I did it a few times myself and it was an eerie feeling. It had its advantages and, in this case, its disadvantages.

Since no one saw Norman in person, no one back at the station or at the network control room in Toronto knew the extent of his lack of sobriety. *The National* came on, Norman was introduced, and the audience saw a man staring glassy-eyed at them. The second he began to speak it was clear Norman was in trouble. As he proceeded with his report, his head was slowly sinking to the desk and he barely got to the end of an admittedly slurred report when his head thudded onto the desk an instant after he signed off. The editors in Toronto sent someone around to the Chateau to steer their weakened colleague home.

Of somewhat similar character and brilliance was Peter Reilly, who, among other postings, was UN correspondent for CBC during this period. Like DePoe, Reilly was a romantic. He could be as moodily Black Irish as they come, high in spirits one minute and low the next, a man of deep sensitivity and sentimentality which he tried almost desperately to hide behind a tough, raucous exterior. I think he felt he had to have a tough front to get ahead in the news business. He was mortified one night when I ran across him in a Toronto bar, tears coursing down his face as he cried away some personal problem. For some reason, he never wanted his colleagues to see his gentle side. In many ways, at bottom, Reilly was more poet in spirit than reporter.

We all moved about the globe, but none more than Michael Maclear, who had gone into the Sierra Maestre Mountains to interview Fidel Castro just before he launched his successful final battle for power in 1958 and into the marble halls of the Indian government to interview Jawaharlal Nehru. Maclear had the advantage over most of us of possessing not only the determination and insight of a superb journalist, but also a rare creative genius as a producer. He could capture the mood of events as well as report the facts. His work in Vietnam certainly proved that, especially in the early seventies when he was in Hanoi and other northern cities reporting on the American bombing.

Territorial prerogatives were always dear to a correspondent's heart and we were all uneasy when a fellow worker came into our area on a reporting assignment. The warmest of personal and professional relationships could suddenly chill during such territorial invasions. On one occasion, Far East correspondent Tom Gould found his territory invaded by Peter Reilly when Reilly and *Newsmagazine* producer Bill Harcourt were assigned with Gould to a Vietnam story.

Gould and Reilly worked together uneasily, not to say testily, as each sought to demonstrate his own expertise. In fact, it was a highly combustible arrangement and Harcourt found himself increasingly running interference between the two, seeking peace in the CBC family. Almost every morning Harcourt would arrive in the lobby of the Majestic Hotel to see the two either feuding or writing separate telegrams of resignation and outrage. Irate cables flew from Saigon to Toronto, although Harcourt managed to prevent a couple of them. Some were even dispatched directly to CBC President Alphonse Ouimet who, sitting in Ottawa and worrying about other things, must have been mystified by the contretemps. As the assignment ended, however, the resulting program showed that both correspondents could put aside transitory personal rivalries and produce a first-class report on the war in Vietnam.

There were examples of more intense rivalries, too. In a Paris bar once, "Newsmag" producer Bill Boyd was slugged and knocked flat by Paris correspondent Doug Lachance, who had mistaken him for Don Gordon, the London correspondent who Lachance thought was poaching on his journalistic territory. Lachance was then living on a houseboat on the Seine but later rented a house in Paris, which he shared with his brother-in-law, Peter Ustinov.

Given the frenetic pace we all set and the amount of alcohol consumed, it's no wonder that some health problems occasionally cropped up. But they seldom held us down for long. The prize for best determination not to let a thing like a heart attack deflect a lifestyle was clearly won by one of our number who was hospitalized in Toronto. I visited him a couple of times in hospital and noted he had a particularly stunning nurse. His heart may have been physically damaged, but its romantic beat was as strong as ever. In fact, too strong for the stern propriety of hospital morality.

One night as the nurse and my colleague were cuddling under the blankets and under the oxygen tent, the head nurse inopportunely popped into the room. It was clear that what was happening should not have been happening with a heart attack patient under an oxygen tent. The stunning nurse left her hospital job forthwith, but shortly thereafter she found a haven as a live-in companion to succour my recovering co-worker at home. And they lived happily ever after for a month or two.

Romantic hearts beat strongly among most of the correspondents most of the time. But there was one of my colleagues who really went too far. He had taken his bride on their honeymoon to Paris where I encountered the newlyweds at a small party at a colleague's apartment. During the course of the festivities, the bridegroom drew the hosts aside to ask a personal favour. Would they mind if he left his bride with them for a few days because he had a rendezvous with an old flame in Germany? The hosts reluctantly acquiesced and off our colleague went to frolic on the Rhine with his old ladylove. After a week of this extracurricular activity, he returned to Paris, picked up his bride, thanked the hosts, and continued on his honeymoon.

There was also the correspondent who had a passionate predeliction for ambassadors' secretaries. He claimed it was journalistic research, but it seemed simpler than that. Whatever the motivation, ambassadors' secretaries from Rome to Paris, from Bogota to Caracas and elsewhere, certainly seemed to inspire him.

A number of the correspondents had a particular appreciation for the wiles of oriental femmes fatales. Some were serious encounters that resulted in marriage; others were more transitory. One colleague used to save up his energy for prodigious nights in Bangkok and Hong Kong after some rigorous assignment. A couple of times I arrived with him at the Hong Kong Hilton to see him greeted with open-armed exuberance by the bell captain, who had been instrumental in arranging previous nocturnal encounters. Ever after, whenever I checked into the Hong Kong Hilton, I'd be greeted by the same broad-grinning, gap-toothed Chinese bell captain, shaking his head in hilarity and saying, "Ahhh. How's our clazy flend? He some fella! My! My!"

Another romantic "fella" was perhaps a bit naive. While in Rio once, he fell madly in love with a Copacabana beach beauty improbably named Lulu. Blonde and long-tressed and bursting out of everything from bikinis to men's shirts, Lulu was a knockout. She also was a professional in the business of romantic encounters. Unfortunately, this particular colleague was an innocent abroad and he thought he'd found true, everlasting love.

After two weeks of midnight trysts and morning splashes at the beach, our assignment ended and it was time to leave. A tender moment of parting turned into a traumatic shock for my friend when Lulu demanded to be paid. But pay he did and remained so entranced with her charms that, notwithstanding her professional status, he went to Rio several times to visit her. The last I heard they still exchanged Christmas cards.

There was one Don Juan among us who had three girl friends living in the same Toronto apartment building. On his visits back to Toronto from overseas he had to juggle his visits very carefully to avoid mayhem.

On one memorable occasion, his juggling failed utterly. Upon leaving one lady after an afternoon dalliance, he ran into another of the three in the lobby. He quickly said he was coming to see her and they playfully trotted up to her apartment. A few hours later, he bade her adieu and, also in the lobby, ran smack into his third inamorata as she was coming back from dinner. With a wan smile and a tired wave of his hand, he offered the usual explanation and together they trudged back up to her apartment.

At midnight he emerged, an extinct volcano of passion, and repaired to a nearby hotel bar where I greeted him with the innocent query: "Anything new?"

Every December we were brought home from our posts around the world to do a year-end wrap-up program for radio and television and to get reacquainted with Canada. This was especially important for those who weren't able to get back during the year. At these times we also would be briefed on new CBC policies and organization, which changed with unremitting regularity. It was also an opportunity to catch up with our fellow workers and share tales of our exploits. Given our collective wisdom of the back streets of the world, several of us repeatedly proposed a special series we called "Fleshpots of the World," but CBC management never agreed to it.

Every year-end get-together would also see an evening out for the correspondents' annual dinner. To say such dinners were raucous is to say the atom bomb makes a loud noise. We would usually reserve a private room in some unwitting dining establishment, but we were never allowed to go back the next year. There were times when we unwisely invited senior CBC officials to join us; they usually left shaking their heads in disbelief. Our bosses Bill Hogg and Don Macdonald had the good sense never to come.

At each dinner we awarded to one of our members "The Bull's Pizzle," an elaborate red plastic corkscrew. It was given to the correspondent who committed what we voted to be the most outrageous act of defiance during the preceding year. This might include such expense account claims as those of Stan Burke, who one year earned the award for the breathtaking size of his expenses in moving from New York to Paris. Don Minifie won another year for an especially vigorous attack on CBC management for failing to put the news programs in colour. "To shoot news in colour film would be distracting," declared a management official. "Blood is red, you know," Minifie had thundered back at the conclusion of a most impressive tirade. Other awards were given for vigorous letters of resignation sent off with disquieting regularity, for telling off a producer in the most flamboyant fashion, and for many other acts of organizational anarchy and sabotage.

At one particularly active dinner in a downtown Toronto Chinese restaurant, there were a dozen of us in a private dining room, downing large glasses of rum, rye, and Scotch along with our bird's nest soup, egg foo yong, and sweet and sour pork. When it came to the fortune cookies, we began to get especially frisky.

One correspondent began berating another for the way he was treating a young lady of their acquaintance. The other, feeling insulted, took a wobbly poke. To create a diversion and end the fracas, another of our number poured a bowl of (fortunately) cooled soup over my head. A friend on my left took umbrage at this and while I sat there soaked and stunned, he grabbed my assailant by the throat. At this point, I slid quickly to the floor and looked up benignly, not to say astigmatically, as arms flailed wildly everywhere amid shouted obscenities, much laughter, chairs turning over, and dishes smashing into walls and onto the floor. During the mêlée the doors burst open to reveal three Chinese waiters proudly carrying a tray of sweets. They took one look, let out a Cantonese shriek, and scuttled out the door.

When the police arrived, they took a look inside, recognized a face or two, and quietly locked the doors and let us continue until exhausted. After paying for the food and broken crockery, and being warned never to return, we trickled away into the night.

Our 9:00 a.m. meeting the next morning with CBC officials was slow getting underway as we groped to our places one by one, a bruised arm here, a scratched face there, headaches everywhere. One of our number even had his neck in a brace.

The annual visits to Toronto also provided a chance to catch up on expense accounts. We were forever late in submitting these, a situation we blamed on our busy schedules, but which we and our bosses knew didn't get done on time because we hated to do them.

When finally complete, some were marvels of inventiveness. I'm not aware of anyone actually cheating on his expenses, but by the time the accounts were prepared, often many of the receipts had been lost and memories faded. That demanded a certain creativity. If ever a Governor General's Award for fiction was deserved, it was for some of our expense claims. There would be expenditures listed for such things as "piranha repellent," "Gaucho Airlines," "wharfage fees," and "secretarial assistance." One daringly inventive soul put down "Lunch with General De Gaulle" on one occasion, and on another, "Snack for Baluba Tribesmen."

There was the producer who carried several thousand dollars for his crew on a trip to Latin America but neglected to keep a single receipt, preoccupied as he naturally was with the story he was doing. In a spurt of creativity, he wrote a memo saying he had dutifully kept all the receipts and had so many of them, in fact, he had to buy a briefcase. Unhappily, he wrote, the briefcase was stolen in Rio. Then, he put down the total money expended, plus the cost of the briefcase, which, miraculously, added up to his advances.

Someone once took things to unacceptable excess, covering the cost of taking a girl friend along on an international trip, listing her as "excess baggage." (Ever after she was nicknamed Miss Excess Baggage.) That, we felt, was going much too far. The corporation thought Stan Burke was going too far when he included his sailboat and a nanny among the family effects being shipped from New York to Paris.

Correspondents would occasionally spend a few days in Seoul while on assignment in Korea, staying at the General Walker Hotel and routinely submitting expense accounts based on the hotel's "Korean Plan." It was only when a sharp-eyed news executive named Ron Johnson was reading *Playboy* magazine one day that he discovered "Korean Plan" covered room, meals, and a young lady. He issued orders forthwith that American and European Plan would be all right, but "Korean Plan" was now out.

But the corporation could be understanding in smaller things. At the 1964 Democratic Convention in Atlantic City, I gave five dollars to the fortuneteller named Madame Edith we had used to forecast the winner. On my expense account I simply put down "Madame Edith, $5.00." There were no questions asked by the bookkeepers. Sometime later, after doing a story in Japan, I put on my expense account, "$25.00 for 'Increasing Joy Forever,' " which was the name of a geisha girl who had been helpful in research. Again no questions.

The CBC budget was severely depleted by one assignment to Cuba. Bill Poulis was sent from Toronto as a contract cameraman to be paid a certain amount for every day he was in Cuba. Although the trip was to be a brief one, as a freelancer he was paid extra for his own special equipment he took with him. As luck would have it, Poulis was arrested by Cuban authorities and kept under house arrest for about two months. He didn't mind in the least because the Cubans treated him well and he made a mint on his daily fees from CBC. But it took a long time for the CBC news budget to recover.

The only correspondent who gave the Correspondents Association a problem on expenses was London-based Ron Chester. As president of the association, I was requested by our members to admonish Ron for being excessively prudent with his expense accounts. He was, we felt, letting down the side somewhat with the modesty of his claims. As one member commented, "Ron is a damn good reporter but not arrogant enough to be a correspondent."

At our year-end reunions we loved to tell each other stories of on-air mishaps as well as boast of our prouder moments. One of my most embarrassing experiences on air was while doing a live interview with Senator Wayne Morse of Oregon during a CBC news special. Our time, as always, was limited, so I told him that I would signal him when he had thirty seconds left by tapping his knee under the table. He nodded absently. When the moment came, I reached under the table and tapped him. He broke off in mid-sentence, looked at me in amazement, and said to me and a couple of million watching Canadians, "Why are you grabbing my thigh?" With a mortified look, I mumbled, "To tell you your time is up, Senator. And now, back to Toronto."

One of the more memorable on-air gaffes was made by Stan Burke when he was CBC correspondent at the United Nations. During a live news special linking Toronto, Ottawa, Washington, and the United Nations, things began to go wrong. Cues were missed and tempers flared. Especially at the UN end. When the program was thrown to the UN, Stan, having received several previous wrong cues and thinking "here's another," looked at the floor director and said to him and to the nation, "Christalmighty, don't throw cues at me!" We all thought it pretty funny, but we didn't reckon with the public. In those days, "Christalmighty" was pretty strong stuff in the swearing department on air. Letters, phone calls, and telegrams of protest poured in. Stan had to apologize and it made all of us more aware of the impact of what we said on television.

Another awkward on-air moment occurred when Kingsley Brown was pacing atop a hill overlooking the twinkling lights of Birmingham, Alabama, just before he opened a live news special on one of that city's race riots. A hilltop opening shot gave a sense of the city, but the location lacked studio conveniences such as a clock. Worse still, neither Kingsley nor his cameraman had the right time on their watches. As a result, when ten o'clock arrived and the program was on the air what the nation saw was Kingsley walking up and down and peering into the camera, saying, "One minute to go, eh Ed?"

Ed said "Yup," and then more pacing by Kingsley. He turned away from the camera, looked out over the city, and very elaborately and carefully scatched his behind in front of what must have been a couple of million astonished Canadians. He looked again at his cameraman and said, "Nearly time." Then, "O.K. I'm set." Finally, one minute after actually going on the air, with the audience in confusion and the control room at the Birmingham station in chaos, Kingsley smiled and said, "Good evening ..."

That particular edition of *Newsmagazine* had more trouble. Don Minifie was doing a report for the program from the studio at the Birmingham station, got confused, and read the same page of his script three times as producer Don Cameron paced up and down behind Minifie in helpless exasperation and was seen doing so by the TV audience. Altogether it was a disaster and Cameron and Brown later claimed the local station had sabotaged them.

As correspondents, we loved doing exotic or unusual sign-offs to our reports. Stan Burke detoured out of his way once on an African tour so he could sign off, "This is Stanley Burke in Timbuktu." Another colleague took a 200-mile detour so he could sign off from Katmandu. Once while travelling with Richard Nixon, I couldn't resist stopping off in a town slightly off our route so I could report from Knowlton, Wisconsin. And I also gave in to temptation in a Canadian election report once by signing off "Knowlton Nash, in Knowlton, Quebec." Nobody, however, can top Ottawa reporter Bill Casey, who more recently signed off, "This is Bill Casey in Punkydoodle Corners, Ontario."

Greener American pastures occasionally entranced us then, as they do now. In 1964, Morley Safer left CBC to join CBS in New York. It was, however, an unintended departure. Stan Burke was being wooed by CBS and they asked him to send down a tape of his work. Stan sent along a tape of one of our year-end programs. CBS sent back a message of thanks to Stan, but no offer. However, they did make an offer to Safer, whom they saw on the tape and liked. Morley went on to his highly successful career with CBS news.

At the time, one senior CBS news executive muttered, "That's no loss." A short time later, when Peter Jennings was interested in joining CBC TV news, the same executive told his staff, "No, he'll never make it in television." Safer at CBS and Jennings at ABC have more than made it.

In those early years, Jennings had had a hard time getting recognized as a journalist instead of a pretty-boy announcer. One of his co-workers at CJOH in Ottawa was the urbane Peter Stursberg, a well-known one-time CBC correspondent at the United Nations who was outraged when told Jennings was covering a NATO meeting going on in Ottawa. "Why," said Stursberg, "he doesn't know NATO from Jello!"

Stursberg got his own comeuppance years later. The writers of his evening newscast on CJOH were unhappy with his habit of arriving late in the newsroom, grabbing his script, and sometimes going on air without having read it beforehand. One evening they changed the traditional opening line and Stursberg went on the air with the salutation: "Good evening. I'm Peter Rabbit and here is the news ...." His writers said he didn't even notice.

For all the fun and adventure, we paid a heavy price, some heavier than others. Home life, as most people know it, was largely non-existent for most of us. We were, indeed, married to our jobs of being correspondents with wives and children too often taking second place to the demands of the news. For some, perhaps it was guilt about that which led us to drink too much. Guilt, and the frenetic pace we set skittering about the world chasing wars, revolutions, diplomatic crises, and political battles. We drank, too, for comradeship. Us against the world. And we drank for fear – fear that someone would beat us on a story, or that we'd miss a good angle. And worst of all, fear that we'd lose self-confidence. The biggest drinkers among us, I think, had recurring nightmares of failing to match their own high demands of themselves with their actual performance. We drank to escape these fears of failure and we drank, too, to escape the frustrations and pressures of our chaotic lives. A few slid into alcoholism.

As time went on, increasingly I resented bitterly the waste of talent caused by surrendering to the bottle. I knew too many brilliant reporters who suicidally sought to drown their fears of failure in alcohol. For them, and for all of us, it was a stupid loss.

The pressure faced by TV correspondents in those days was dramatically different from their print counterparts. The TV correspondents were, in effect, using a two-ton pencil to cover their stories with all the technical paraphernalia of television, and they faced the often infuriating frustrations of TV – fighting and bribing your way through customs, helping to lug the equipment on and off planes, trains, and buses, being plagued by equipment that sometimes didn't work, and the panic of time to make a plane schedule for shipping film, or the tensions and demands of live on-air work. For television and radio, we rarely had the luxury of time to cogitate and savour the writing of our stories, preoccupied as we were by the pressures of time. We were journalistic fire brigade commandos in a high-wire act with no net, and it's no wonder some took solace in the bottle. What intrigued me in later years was that some of the hardest-drinking correspondents and producers grew out of their dependence on alcohol as a relaxant when they moved on to other jobs.

Malibu Hills, California, October, 1966 ...

In 1966 I got my first close-up look at Ronald Reagan. It was at a political barbecue at his 300-acre ranch in the Malibu Hills being held for his supporters and the media who were covering his campaign for the California governorship.

As I drove up from Los Angeles north into the hilly country of scrub trees and bare, brown hills, I was extremely sceptical about Reagan's run for the governorship. He faced tough opposition from Governor Pat Brown, the father of Jerry Brown, the man who succeeded Reagan as governor in 1974. From a distance Reagan seemed to me to be a washed up, middle-aged movie actor.

But I had forgotten his proven effectiveness as a political speaker, a skill I'd seen graphically demonstrated during the 1964 presidential campaign of Barry Goldwater in a televised appeal for funds to aid Goldwater. The speech wasn't thought-provoking or even well-written. But it was the most financially successful speech ever given up to that time. A million dollars cascaded into the Republican treasury from viewers stimulated by his half-hour plea for money, entitled "A Time For Choosing." In retrospect, it was that speech that was the start of Reagan's reputation as "The Great Communicator," and it set him on the road to the presidency of the United States.

On that occasion, as I watched him speak, he seemed to make genuinely persuasive the corny, simplistic, boiler-plate script he read about law and order, opposing communism, and fighting big government. Reagan was the nice guy next door who made "Goldwaterism" sound comfortable, friendly, and plausible – something Goldwater himself never could do. Reagan simply communicated believability. Almost as soon as he was off the air a group of southern California millionaires decided he was their ideal candidate for Governor of California and who knows what else.

When I arrived at the ranch, I greeted several British, French, and American reporters and saw old actor friends of Reagan's such as Andy Devine, Robert Taylor, Buddy Ebsen, and Walter Brennan, all, like Reagan, right-wingers.

CBC *Newsmagazine* producer Bill Harcourt and cameraman Eddie Higginson were with me on the assignment and we got the Reagan friends together for a group discussion about his qualities. They all agreed Reagan would be a good governor. "Maybe one day even president," Robert Taylor added. Listening to them, I privately scoffed at their admiration. When we finished filming the discussion I walked over to Reagan. The moment we shook hands and started talking I was reminded of the effectiveness of the Goldwater speech. Reagan was, and is, a very nice guy. A genuine man. A believable man.

No matter how you judge his arch-conservative rhetoric, you feel that he at least believes it deeply, that he just knows those old-fashioned values of self-help, good neighbourliness, and stick-to-itiveness will triumph over even the most complex and difficult national or international issue. His approach has been described by columnist George Will as "Carnegieism": one-half Andrew and one-half Dale. It is now. And was then.

As we talked we walked away from the ranch house to his corral to look at some horses. He pushed back his cowboy hat, his leathery face crinkled into a smile, and his eyes danced with pleasure as he said softly, "You know, I just love this land ... the horses ... the sky." Then with his arm around the waist of his wife, Nancy, he mused about his acting career, then under political attack. With a defiant pride, he said, "Damn it, I was not such a bad actor. Really not bad at all. Anyway, who says an actor should be barred from being governor?"

We chatted for a while and we persuaded him to get on his horse and ride around the corral for a few minutes so we could film him. Then with Nancy adoringly gazing on, we did a TV interview. Afterwards, he went off to greet other guests at the barbecue.

While all of us were guzzling beer or drinking harder stuff, I noticed Reagan sipped only a bit of wine, and nothing more. The explanation, I found out later, was that he was turned off alcohol because his father was a drunk. In his autobiography, he wrote of coming home one day as a child and finding his father on the porch "drunk, dead to the world."

A few days after the barbecue, Harcourt, Higginson, and I were up in San Francisco, where it was clear not everyone endorsed Reagan for governor. In what became a bit of a CBC cause célèbre, I interviewed a topless shoeshine girl who clearly disliked his old-fashioned moral values. "If Reagan gets in," she told me as she slapped and slicked my shoes, "there goes topless right out the window, and there goes a lot of jobs." We went next door to follow this up with someone described on a marquee as a "topless lady psychiatrist." But fortunately perhaps, she wasn't in. (In fact, after Reagan was elected Governor, topless did go out. But bottomless came in, not a clear net gain in moral values.)

Back at the CBC in Toronto there was quite a commotion about showing my interview with the topless shoeshine girl. Some prudish executives felt it was too risqué to air. But Eddie Higginson had shot the interview with special care so that the inevitable mammary swaying that accompanied the shining was seen primarily as a shadow on the wall. As the topless young lady swayed and shined, she and I had a serious discussion of Reagan's conservative philosophy and its implications, all done with relative discretion, thanks to Eddie's creative filming. It made an intriguing juxtaposition: attention-getting packaging of a serious subject.

My next real encounter with Reagan would not be until fourteen years later, long after Reagan's two terms as Governor of California and his near-miss for the 1976 Republican presidential nomination, and ten years after I myself had left Washington. This time it was only a perfunctory smile and a nod at me as he arrived back at his old alma mater, Eureka College near Peoria, Illinois, for a campaign stop during the 1980 presidential election campaign.

It was a scene of cloyingly pure Hollywood sentimentality in the festooned Eureka gymnasium when a grinning "Dutch" Reagan walked onto the platform as the star graduate of the class of 1932. And yet, that's the problem with Reagan for most sceptical, if not cynical, reporters. We see about him an aura of corny sentimentality and a simplistic, trite attitude. We tend to think it so phony. But he, in fact, is all that: unabashedly corny, sentimental, simplistic, and utterly genuine.

Eureka means as much to Reagan as his ranch. It's part of his soul. "Everything started for me here on this campus," he told the crowd. As he stood on the platform he accepted a football sweater with number 80 on it, slipped off his jacket, and pulled the red-and-white jersey over his head without mussing a hair.

There were no overt politics this night. It was a night for memories. He was a boy again. He told of working his way through college washing dishes in the girls' dormitory. "Best job I ever had," he joked. His old football coach, Ralph "Mac" McKinzie, spoke of Reagan as "a plugger" when he played guard for the Eureka football team. Actually, Reagan wasn't all that great a football player, but he loved the game, the atmosphere, and the college.

Reagan spoke of old football triumphs at Eureka, of how the field was so badly sloped when he played that the safety man had to wait for a kick to come up over the hill in the field before he saw the ball. To the disbelief of the reporters present he emotionally urged the team to win tomorrow's big game, echoing Vince Lombardi's words that "a team that won't be beaten, can't be beaten." He even invoked Knute Rockne to encourage his alma mater to victory against the dreaded Concordia University the next day. Unhappily, in spite of Reagan encouragement, Eureka lost 14-7.

And then he walked out of the gym into the clean, crisp mid-October night to light a huge pep rally bonfire. Suddenly everybody broke into song and there, still wearing his red-and-white football sweater, with a misty, dreamy grin on his face, the soon-to-be fortieth President of the United States of America held hands with Nancy and joyously sang the old school song, " 'Neath the Elms." It was surely the most exhilarating moment of his 1980 campaign.

It was unbelievable to the cynical, seen-it-all, world-weary eyes of reporters and political hangers-on. But it was a pure, sweet slice of middle America. And suddenly, I understood the source of Ronald Reagan's faith. He thinks the world is Eureka College. And therein lies his strength as well as his weakness. No matter how many factual stumbles he may make, no matter how simply he sees the most complex problems, Reagan is a happy man in his own certainties. The values and lessons of Eureka College and small-town middle America can, he believes, overcome any challenge.

It was those values he took to the White House. But even though they are imbedded in his psyche, his presidency, as was his California governorship, has been marked by pragmatism. His rhetoric is much more conservative than his actions, which is certainly just as well. Reagan's long-time aid, Ed Meese, once commented, "Today's hard-liner is yesterday's liberal who was mugged last night." In some ways, that's the story of Reagan's life. He was an ardent supporter of Franklin Roosevelt, and campaigned for President Truman in 1948 and supported Helen Gahagan Douglas against Richard Nixon in his Senate race of 1950. He knew the aching poverty of the depression. But as he got richer in the movies and television, he was "mugged" by high taxes and he gradually moved to the political right. His is also the quintessential American success story: a poor, small-town boy who, through luck, pluck, and a bit of talent, became rich, famous, and eventually President of the United States.

Washington, D.C., May, 1967 ...

Throughout his presidency, Lyndon Johnson displayed an intense need for secrecy – a trait somewhat at odds with his garrulous nature and his habit of calling in reporters for a chat that usually became a harangue. The presidency must have secrecy in some of its business, of course, but Johnson took this to ridiculous extremes.

I suppose he felt it gave him political leverage. Men would be told they were to be appointed to senior jobs in the administration, but days before the announcement there would be a leak to the news media and

Johnson would be furious, rescinding the appointment before it was announced, often after the astonished near-appointee had already resigned from some other job.

He once decided to appoint black leader James Farmer as director of a special project on literacy, but killed the appointment and the entire project when the news was leaked a few days before the announcement. He decided on a new Food for Peace plan, but then cancelled it two days before the announcement when he read about it in the *Baltimore Sun*. In 1965, *New York Times* correspondent James "Scotty" Reston saw an advance copy of a Johnson speech to the UN that proposed a solution to the organization's financial crisis. When Johnson read the story in the *Times*, he was so mad he dropped the proposal and made another speech altogether.

Johnson also liked to keep reporters guessing on his travel plans. We would be told by White House aides, "It's a prudent man who'd bring a suitcase tomorrow." That would likely, but not necessarily, mean Johnson was going to travel somewhere the next day. But we wouldn't be told where or when. You had to make a guess as to whether or not you wanted to go with him to wherever he was going.

One night in May, 1967, I got a call from the White House saying, "It would be prudent if you came to Andrews Air Force Base at 7:00 a.m. tomorrow."

"Why?"

"I can't say."

"Is the President going somewhere where I'd want to be with him?"

"Well, depending on your interests, he might or might not be."

On the basis of that kind of a conversation I generally had to decide whether to spend the several hundred dollars on air fare I'd be charged for the flight with the President and whether to risk the time involved.

Sometimes, though, there were clues. Normally, the White House didn't call Canadian reporters on trips. So, in this case, chances were it involved some Canadian interest. There also had been some speculation he might visit Expo '67 in Montreal. He had planned a trip to Expo earlier but cancelled it when word leaked out that he was going. After making calls to Canadian Embassy and State Department officials who knew little more than I did, or at least weren't saying, I got a call from Sheila Skelley, our CBC Washington producer who, in turn, had a tip-off call from a friend at the White House that Johnson was going up to Canada. So, with Sheila's confirmation, I decided to be "prudent" and turn up at 7:00 a.m.

In fact, after much hemming and hawing, Johnson had decided the night before that he would not fly to Canada. His current press secretary, George Christian, figured, however, that it would be wise not to cancel the press plane he'd ordered up just in case LBJ changed his mind again. At 6:30 the next morning, Johnson called Christian to say he now was thinking of going. At 7:00, he called again to say he was going.

Some reporters got only half-an-hour notice to get to the airport and Christian was assaulted with complaints. "The scene at Andrews," he said later, "was one of a raging volcano." At the air base in the early dawn, we still didn't know for sure if we were going anywhere at all. When we saw Johnson arrive at 9:00 a.m. and get aboard Air Force One, we at least knew we would be travelling. Even after take-off we weren't told, and there was speculation we were flying to the LBJ Ranch in Texas, which certainly would have been bad luck for me. Some thought we were going to Chicago for a speech.

Finally, after I'd had a healthy Bloody Mary breakfast, the public address system crackled: "Welcome aboard. To end your suspense, we're going to Montreal to see Expo '67 and then to Ottawa to see the Canadian Prime Minister." I, and several Canadian colleagues who had made similar guesses, heaved a sigh of relief.

We tramped around Expo with Johnson and then flew on with him to Ottawa where he conferred with Prime Minister Pearson. They met at the Prime Minister's summer residence at Harrington Lake, Quebec. While LBJ was at Expo, U.S. Secret Servicemen had flown to Ottawa to check out security arrangements for Johnson. Pearson complained about all the burly, arrogant U.S. agents who invaded his house and squatted behind bushes and in boats out in the lake, all sprouting walkie-talkies. At one point, Pearson later said, "I went into the house and up the stairs. At the top, a hard-faced chap said, 'Who are you? Where are you going?'

"I replied," said Pearson, "'I live here and I'm going to the bathroom.'"

Newark ... New York ... Detroit, July, 1967 ...

In spite of the progress Johnson had made in the area of civil rights, real improvements were slow to appear and during the long, hot summer of 1967, the northern ghettos exploded. The frustration of Vietnam and its especially high black casualties, the slowness of the movement toward racial equality, and the social pressure cooker in the black areas of the big cities all combined to make 1967 one of the country's most racially violent years in history. I was struck years later by a comment of Dr. David Abrahamsen of Brandeis University, who described frustration as "the wet nurse of violence." It certainly was that year.

The riot in the Los Angeles ghetto of Watts in 1965 and the racial disturbances of 1966 were only a prelude to 1967. In Newark, New York, Detroit, and other cities in 1967 the rioters were egged on by black racist leaders, apostles of revolution who hated every bit as blindly as their white supremacist counterparts in the South. But the black leaders were smarter and in private more articulate, and this gave them an aura that attracted many white liberals to their cause. And they knew exactly how to manipulate a liberal guilty conscience.

When Stokely Carmichael, H. Rap Brown, and Eldridge Cleaver harangued crowds, it was with the slang of the streets, with atrocious grammar and angry obscenities, the word "fuck" spewing out of their mouths seemingly in every sentence. They screamed "Kill Whitey!" "Burn Baby Burn," and "It's Time to Stop Kissin' Whitey's Ass!" They called Lyndon Johnson "a mad, wild dog," charging him with murdering blacks by sending them to Vietnam. The cry of H. Rap Brown typified their belief: "Violence is as American as cherry pie."

Privately, the black rabblerousers were utterly different from their public image: intense, but speaking the language of an Oxford don. But they didn't alter their fundamental objectives: bloody revolution in the streets. Brown, who was head of the so-called Student Non-Violent Coordinating Committee (SNCC), once characterized himself to me after a New York meeting as a "black Lenin." Their call to arms was taken up by easily led followers and by simply crazy groups like the "Mau Mau" street guerilla fighters who were named after Kenyatta's Kenyan rebels.

The Newark riots erupted on July 12 and went on for five days. Twenty-six people were killed, including one dead black who was found with thirty-nine police bullets in him. As things seemed to be cooling down, I went up to that sleazy overgrown urban slum of a city to cover a meeting of relatively moderate black activists. The moderates were seeking to stop the violence, preaching Martin Luther King's non-violent approach. They were appalled by the vicious black revolutionists they felt would destroy legislative progress by frightening the Congress and the administration.

The meeting was in a Newark high school. Between two sessions, I happened to be in a classroom talking with comedian and activist Dick Gregory when "Mau Maus" crashed through the school door and began rampaging through the halls, smashing windows, and breaking moderate heads with clubs and rocks. Both Gregory and I ran to a classroom window. He pushed me out and I dropped the one story to the ground. Then I caught him as he tumbled out just moments before the screaming, swearing thugs burst into the room.

We ran to the street and, out of breath, watched others running away, some covered in blood, some crying, others going back in with their own bricks and sticks. A wan, sad smile came over Gregory's face as he said to me, "Look, I apologize. They hate me as much as you. But you know, we're not all like that. They're the fringe, madmen on our side just as the Klan is on yours."

A couple of days later I drove up to New York from Newark to cover the riots that had broken out in Spanish Harlem. I talked to the commander of the New York National Guard, who told me that if he didn't get control of the rioting, he would use hand grenades, recoilless rifles, bazookas, and other heavy equipment. The rioting did cool down, but the next day, July 24, the worst riots of all that summer broke out in Detroit.

I hopped the next plane to Detroit, and within an hour of landing I was walking in suffocating heat through the rubble-strewn streets. Forty people were killed in the Detroit riots, 2,000 injured, 5,000 homes destroyed, 5,000 arrested, and the damage ran to $350 million. "It looked like the city had been bombed," Michigan Governor George Romney said.

Whites were terrified and warned reporters not to go near the black ghettos of the city. The Detroit police called their night sticks "nigger knockers," and for looters they had orders to "shoot to maim." But if you're going to accurately report the reality of events like this, you have to feel and smell and absorb the scene. You have to be there. And so you go past the rifle-toting soldiers and National Guardsmen, past the sandbags and barricades, and into the eerie silence.

When I got to the ghetto area, most of the fires were out, but flames still crackled over some homes and out the windows of blackened apartment buildings. Few people were around and those who were, were sullen, frightened, and not in any mood to talk to a white reporter. Everywhere store windows were smashed and looters still roamed the streets. Oddly enough, there were gangs of both white and black looters, leading one official to remark bitterly that Detroit was "the first city in America to achieve integrated looting."

While I walked through the ravaged black ghetto of Detroit, National Guardsmen sprang into action to respond to a report of a black sniper in a nearby building. A tank rolled up and suddenly let loose a 50-calibre machine-gun barrage, terrifying me and a couple of other reporters nearby. No sniper was found. In another instance I was told of a

National Guard machine gunner opening fire at an apartment window behind which a black resident had lit a match for his cigarette. The bullets killed the man's four-year-old niece and hit his wife's arm, which later had to be amputated.

I got what I felt was a powerful, emotional story in the Detroit rioting that I was sure would be the number-one story on *The National* that night, as well as on CBC Radio news. Just as I was leaving my hotel in downtown Detroit to ship the film to Toronto, I glanced at a TV set in the hotel lobby. It was carrying the coverage of General De Gaulle visiting Quebec as he uttered that fateful phrase, "Vive Le Québec Libre." All the work, effort, and danger my crew and I had endured went out the window with those words. In the diplomatic explosion that followed, our stories on Detroit would up near the end of the newscast.

Throughout the United States that terrible summer, 120 different communities saw racial riots, arson, and death. About 125 people were killed, almost all of them black, and the cost of the damage, looting, and riot control was established at $2 billion. President Johnson had hoped for new civil rights legislation that year to progress beyond his 1964 and 1965 laws, but it died in the wake of the riots. And H. Rap Brown warned me 1967 was only a "dress rehearsal for revolution."

That's what the extremists wanted. "Those boys come home from Vietnam and go back to the ghettos and back to the misery of big city life," Brown told me when I talked to him once at a demonstration in a small town outside Washington. "They get mad and we welcome them because the Army has taught those boys how to shoot straight. Then we'll reverse the death figures. Then a lot of white people are going to get killed."

Dan Watts, editor of a militant black magazine, *New Liberator*, told me he envisaged hundreds of snipers and violence in cities all over the U.S. "A dozen Newarks, a dozen Detroits," he said. "You would have guerilla warfare comparable to what's going on in Vietnam right here in the U.S." Lester McKinney, the head of the SNCC office in Washington, told me in an interview, "In the minds of the people, history has proved that any meaningful social change has come through a bloody revolution."

As the summer drew to a close, I noted in a CBC-TV report for *The National*, "It seems to boil down to a race between the implementation of some sort of Marshall Plan for American cities and the running wild emotions of Negroes being stimulated by leaders who preach violence as the only way to get real equality. Unless some significant progress is made soon, the summer of 1968 – a presidential election year – may

246

make 1967 look like child's play." Even the indefatigable Martin Luther King, Jr., was discouraged: "I'll still preach non-violence with all my might, but I'm afraid it will fall on deaf ears."

Between chasing from one race riot to another that year, there were also demonstrations by rebellious young whites to cover. These mostly involved university students, following the lead of the likes of Jerry Rubin and Abbie Hoffman and listening to the glib young guru of the young, Timothy Leary, whose psychedelic message was "Tune in. Turn on. Drop out."

I covered sit-ins in Washington, pray-ins in Boston, stand-ins at the University of California in Berkeley, be-ins in New York, and all manner of other youthful demonstrations protesting not just against Vietnam, but, it seemed, against any form of organized society. In Berkeley, I ran into one new twist in our TV coverage of these events. Several times during the previous year or so, I had talked to various of the self-appointed leaders of the youth revolt, but when we sought to interview Jerry Rubin on this occasion, he wanted to be paid. This began a period when Rubin and others felt they were now well enough known to demand money whenever the cameras turned on them for exclusive interviews. As a matter of principle we wouldn't pay and didn't interview Rubin. In time, though, they stopped seeking TV money, presumably because they felt they were losing valuable public exposure.

Washington, D.C., June, 1967 ...

As the political protests against Vietnam intensified in 1967, President Johnson sought to improve his standing in the public opinion polls by conferring with foreign leaders as he had at Punta del Este. He went to Europe and he came to Canada to see Pearson. But his most eye-catching effort was a summit conference with Soviet Premier Alexei Kosygin a few weeks after his trip to Canada.

They met in June at a small state college in Glassboro, New Jersey, south of Philadelphia. As at Harrington Lake, the Secret Servicemen took over the campus, setting up command posts, installing phone lines, and putting guards everywhere. I drove up to Glassboro to cover the conference along with our Ottawa correspondent Norman DePoe. The best story we got out of the meeting was a comment we heard from the wife of the president of the college who, like Pearson, was determined not to let the Secret Servicemen totally take over her two-storey home, "Holly Bush," where Johnson and Kosygin were to meet. "They can invite Mr. Johnson and Mr. Kosygin into my house,"

247

she told reporters. "They can move my furniture about. But they are not coming into my kitchen!" The Secret Service gave up their plan to cook in the lady's kitchen and flew the President's meals up from Washington.

Johnson and Kosygin discussed the Middle East, Southeast Asia, and nuclear proliferation, not making any new deals and mostly just getting to know each other better. Like all such conferences, we saw the two men only at a couple of news conferences and at the inevitable "picture opportunity." DePoe and I then drove up to New York to do a television news special on the conference; we almost arrived after the program was to begin because of traffic jams on Manhattan's First Avenue. There had been no great agreements, but in Johnson's terms the summit worked. His Gallup Poll ratings went up.

LBJ was a man utterly obsessed by public opinion polls. I knew that from a vivid personal experience a couple of years earlier. One evening in late June of 1965, I was picking up some documents at the White House. While I was there, Johnson sent out word he wanted to see whichever reporters were present right away. There were to be no TV cameras or radio recorders. So a dozen surprised journalists, mostly American but including a Russian, a British reporter, and myself, trooped into the Oval Office wondering what big announcement was suddenly going to be made. But he had no announcement. He just wanted to talk. And talk he did, mostly about himself and about his popularity rating in polls around the world. "Look at this one from Turkey," he said, and he read some statistics. "And here, from good ol' England," and on he went.

It was an incredible scene. He pulled polls out of every pocket in his jacket, out of his pants, and even out of his shirt. Whether they were true or not, or whether he always carried them around, I never found out. But he was trying to persuade us that in spite of media criticism, he, President Johnson, was a very popular fellow with the people.

He walked up and down behind his desk, smiling, scowling, waving his arms, and scratching his behind in a mesmerizing, non-stop, obscenity-filled monologue. Never before and never after this encounter with LBJ have I heard anyone use the word "shit" so often and in so many different ways. There was "bullshit," "horseshit," "ratshit," "catshit," "chickenshit," and, on the possibility of a coup d'état in Vietnam, he said he didn't want to hear any more of "that coup shit."

As he strode about his office, glowering at his audience, he would lock eyes with one of us and concentrate the full force of his delivery on a single victim. I'd certainly heard much of "The Johnson Treatment" before, but to see it before my very eyes and to be an actual subject for "The Treatment" was intimidating to say the least. At one point he came at me, eyes boring into mine, grabbed my suit jacket lapels, and began a paralysing lecture. Here I was in the Oval Office of the White House with the President of the United States about three inches from my nose, shaking my lapels and shouting something about Vietnam. I don't know what he said because I was in a state of shock.

Later I heard a somewhat similar story from *London Times* Washington correspondent Louis Heren, who also got a very physical lecture from LBJ on Vietnam. "You can remember putting your hand on a girl's knee and sliding it up her thigh until she told you to stop?" Johnson said to Heren. In this Johnson parable the U.S. was the girl and North Vietnam was the sliding hand.

Heren later recounted the story in his book on LBJ, *No Hail, No Farewell,* and told how Johnson grabbed his leg and started moving up to his crotch. "His powerful fingers first clenched my knee and then my thigh. I cannot recall the thoughts that passed through my mind, but was immensely relieved when his fist relaxed." I knew exactly what Heren went through and after what seemed an hour, but was only a minute or so, Johnson let go of me and moved on to a reporter from the Soviet news agency Tass.

The President literally shook the Russian's shoulders and his face was so close, the two were actually rubbing noses, as Johnson alternately ranted, pleaded, and boasted. The reporter tried desperately to look away, or ease way, but there simply was no escape once you were captured. One minute the President shouted, the next he whispered. His subjects were Vietnam, how the Soviets misunderstood him, how popular he, LBJ, was with the people and with "my boys," and how hard he was working for peace. At last Johnson released the startled, exhausted, and probably terrified correspondent from Tass.

On and on Johnson went, railing against the traitorous evils of those who disagreed with him, speaking of how he "loved" his flag and his "boys" in Vietnam, and how the public loved him in spite of his critics. "We gave our word to those people in Saigon," Johnson told us, warning that if the world decided the American word couldn't be trusted, "then they'll never believe us again in NATO, the UN, or anywhere."

His sweeping generalizations and his simplistic and righteous formulations were breathtaking. Often in vivid barnyard language, he equated any and all dissent with disloyalty and desertion. "You're either for me or against me ... you're either a patriot or a traitor." With some justification, he also bitterly attacked reporters and critics who complained about American bombing of North Vietnam while largely ignoring Communist atrocities in the South. "Intellectual riffraff" and "wooden soldiers," he called them.

At one point in our Oval Office meeting, Johnson pulled out a piece of paper from his coat pocket. For some reason, I didn't immediately grasp, the President looked directly at me and, with intense ferocity, said, "I have a letter here from my man in Hanoi who's talking to those guys." As he read excerpts from the letter, he grinned sheepishly and admitted that he probably shouldn't be doing this, but it was a letter ... a report ... from a non-American official. Again and again he referred to "my man in Hanoi."

LBJ's "man" turned out to be Blair Seaborne, Canadian representative on the Vietnam International Control Commission, who had been asked by External Affairs Minister Paul Martin to pass on to Hanoi officials U.S. messages, and to report back. It was a fairly normal, if informal, diplomatic function for a friendly country. But the way LBJ boasted about it, he sounded as if he had a private pipeline into the Hanoi hierarchy.

Johnson read from the piece of paper, "This inflexibility [of the North Vietnamese] characterizes the position of this entire regime and illustrates its great measure of confidence in itself. It considers that it holds all the trump cards; that world opinion is becoming more sympathetic; that the U.S. retaliation is limited ...." Johnson smiled triumphantly, saying the report completely endorsed his policies. With this indiscreet disclosure, Johnson probably forever ruined the effectiveness of the Canadian diplomat as an informal channel to Hanoi.

Our whole session with the President lasted perhaps an hour, an extraordinary amount of presidential time. Johnson seemed reluctant to end it, but said we probably had work to do and so did he. Finally, with the broadest grin you can imagine, he waved us out of his office, saying it had been "Fun," and "you all come back, hear." This incredible display of high-level insecurity could perhaps only have happened with Lyndon Johnson and only to a president who had so escalated his country's involvement in its most unpopular foreign war in history, the Vietnam nightmare.

8 *VIETNAM*

The Pentagon, October, 1967 ...

Historians can trace the origins of the Vietnam War back to the brutal exploitation by the French starting in the 1800s, or even to those perennial invaders, the Chinese, who had been rampaging in and out of Indochina since before the time of Christ.

Some blame Roosevelt for giving the French entrée again after the Japanese were expelled at the end of World War II. Some blame Truman for his indifference. Some blame Eisenhower for acquiescing in handing over the northern half of the country to the Communists at the 1954 Geneva Conference on Vietnam, after the French regime had collapsed, only to pledge support to Saigon with Cold War rhetoric and immediately begin subverting the Geneva Agreement by authorizing CIA attempts to sabotage North Vietnam. Eisenhower and Dulles, fearful of a Communist election victory, then prevented the free elections in Vietnam that had been promised for 1956. And some blame Kennedy for continuing the Eisenhower commitment and sharply expanding the number of U.S. military advisers from just under 700 to about 15,000. But, in truth, the Vietnam War was not really launched by Kennedy or Eisenhower or Truman or Roosevelt or the French or the Chinese. It was Lyndon Johnson's War.

Johnson's emotional commitment to victory in Vietnam was emblazoned all over him whether you met him in private, listened to him in a public speech, or watched him visiting his troops. What was fascinating about Johnson's Vietnam obsession was the way he personalized it. It was "my war," "my helicopters," "my boys." He himself was wounded when he read casualty figures. Through the night, wearing pajamas and bathrobe, he prowled the White House corridors and the Situation Room in the basement, waiting for reports and giving instructions. Sometimes he personally picked or approved the day's bombing targets in North Vietnam. He sacrificed much of his Great Society program of social and economic reform in order to win his "coonskin on the wall," as he described that elusive Vietnam victory. Johnson clearly felt he had a mission in Southeast Asia and he simply could not understand anyone who disagreed with him.

I have always believed that Kennedy would never have allowed himself to be entrapped in a no-win Vietnam War. There is not a shred of evidence that JFK would have sent in combat troops and there is much evidence he opposed such a move. Kennedy had rejected a 1961 recommendation that he send in combat troops and Bob Kennedy later said, "Never. The President would never have done it. He was determined not to send troops." General James Gavin, who had been a senior U.S. military adviser and an ambassador to France, said he discussed the matter with Kennedy. "I know he was totally opposed to the introduction of combat troops in Southeast Asia."

Indeed, Kennedy wanted out. The problem was how and when to get out. In July, 1962, he instructed Defense Secretary Robert McNamara to draw up a plan for a phased U.S. withdrawal of military personnel with a target date of 1965. Prime Minister Pearson discussed getting out of Vietnam with Kennedy on a May, 1963, visit to the Kennedy Cape Cod summer home at Hyannisport. As *Washington Post* reporter Chalmers Roberts recounted the conversation, Kennedy asked Pearson what to do. "Get out," said Pearson. Kennedy replied, "That's a stupid answer. Everybody knows that. The question is, how do we get out?" Pearson didn't have an answer.

Puzzling over how to find a face-saving way to withdraw, he only half-jokingly once told his aide Kenneth O'Donnell, "Easy. Put a government in there that will ask us to leave." But he felt he had to wait until after the 1964 presidential election because he feared politically wounding attacks from Republican conservatives. He told O'Donnell in 1963, "If I tried to pull out completely now from Vietnam, we would have another Joe McCarthy Red scare on our hands. But I can do it after I'm re-elected." Similarly, Kennedy told Senator Mike Mansfield, the Senate Majority Leader, that he was going to withdraw the U.S. military force from Vietnam, "but I can't do it until after 1965 ... after I'm re-elected." Later Mansfield said, "He was going to order a gradual withdrawal. [He] had definitely and unequivocally made that decision."

It was, however, a private decision. In public he said none of this. The only hint came in September, 1963, when he said on television, "In the final analysis it is their war. They are the ones who have to win it or lose it." Two months later came Dallas.

Lyndon Johnson, with his monumental ego and Texas braggadocio, his need to prove his machismo and his love of and belief in the invincibility of the United States military, fell into a trap largely of his own making. The early months of 1964 saw Johnson consolidating his presidential power, gradually increasing U.S. aid to South Vietnam, and cocking an eye to Goldwater's warhawk rhetoric as the 1964 presidential election approached. Public support in the U.S. for aid to Vietnam was strong.

On August 2, 1964, North Vietnam patrol boats attacked the U.S. destroyer *Maddox*, which was in the Gulf of Tonkin doing some electronic eavesdropping on North Vietnam from a few miles offshore. Only one bullet hit the *Maddox* in a twenty-minute skirmish. Two days later, the *Maddox* and another destroyer, the *Turner Joy*, were again in the Gulf and reported another attack. Although they fired many rounds and took extensive zigzag action to avoid attack, there never was any hard evidence the attack actually happened – neither ship was hit by anything.

But it was too much of a national insult to the super-patriotic Johnson. He demanded retaliation. First, he got a resolution from Congress practically giving him a blank cheque to go to war, and then he used it. He went on television to tell the American people that, as he spoke, American bombs were dropping on North Vietnam in retaliation. Sixty-four sorties were flown, damaging or destroying twenty-five Communist vessels.

That was the real beginning of the Vietnam War. Johnson's popularity soared and the North Vietnamese began secretly sending thousands of troops into the South to buttress the Viet Cong they were already aiding and guiding. The Communist assassination of South Vietnamese village and provincial leaders and other government officials intensified – more than 4,000 a year were murdered – and bridges were blown up, roads mined, and villages attacked. LBJ responded with more and more military aid, more bombing, and eventually the sending of U.S. combat troops. The first Marines splashed ashore at Da Nang on March 8, 1965. By July, there was a total of eighteen American combat battalions in the country. By December, there were 200,000 American soldiers in Vietnam; by the end of 1966, 400,000; and 1967, 500,000. The war was fully "Americanized," as one Pentagon official told me, by 1965.

Undersecretary of State George Ball, who privately opposed the build-up and said so repeatedly to his boss, groaned as he looked on helplessly. I heard his friends say that Ball had become fond of quoting Ralph Waldo Emerson's line, "Events are in the saddle riding man."

As the U.S. got more deeply involved in the war and casualty reports began coming back, so domestic opposition to the war grew. At first, it was the radical far-left students and pacifists. But increasingly, anti-war support moved toward the centre. Intellectuals, students, ordinary citizens, and some prominent politicians joined the battle against LBJ as the anti-war demonstrations splashed across the headlines and dominated the TV newscasts of the country.

Following the example of Buddhist monks in Vietnam, several Americans set themselves afire in suicidal public protests. Perhaps the biggest anti-war protest came to the Pentagon in October, 1967, as more than 100,000 people, young and old, men, women, and children, surrounded the building.

It was the lead story for our CBC radio and television newscasts and in covering it I particularly noticed among the bearded hippies and young students that there were pipe-puffing professors, neatly dressed students, and housewives giving the lie to the Johnson comment that they were all "beatniks." I saw playwright Arthur Miller there and novelist Norman Mailer, whom I watched closely as he viciously provoked the authorities in what seemed to me to be a desperate attempt to get arrested. The scene later became part of his semi-fictional *Armies of the Night*.

The protesters carried huge signs with Johnson's picture and under it: "WAR CRIMINAL," and they chanted, "Hey, Hey, LBJ, How Many Kids Did You Kill Today?" I saw a sign waved by one bearded young man saying, "Where Is Oswald Now When We Need Him." Sometimes a chant of a thousand voices would go up: "Ho Ho Ho Chi Minh." Such black humour was the style of the decade; later there were songs about being "first on your block to bring your boy home in a box."

Several hundred Canadians, most of them students, had come to the Pentagon rally in special buses. One group was led by a physics professor from the University of New Brunswick. With their American counterparts they marched from the Lincoln Memorial to the Pentagon, a few miles away, and I followed them all the way to the U.S. military headquarters, which was guarded by 6,000 soldiers with unsheathed bayonets on their rifles and 5,000 policemen with nightsticks. Another 20,000 troops were being held in reserve.

When I arrived at the Pentagon a fight had broken out among the anti-war demonstrators and a group of American Nazi Party members in their uniforms and black belts, who were staging a counter-demonstration in support of the war. Tear gas calmed down the fight, but the sting and stink swept over the crowd. With tears in my eyes, I pushed my way to a Pentagon doorway where some demonstrators were trying to force their way in.

Given earlier fears of violence, however, and the size of the crowd, it was for the most part a relatively peaceful demonstration. One of the most poignant moments of the day for me was watching a pert, bright-eyed, teen-age blonde walk along a line of soldiers guarding the Pentagon smilingly popping daisies down their rifle barrels. I thought the soldiers looked at her just a bit shamefacedly.

The Pentagon demonstration, and scores of others like it, was a highly visible and vocal version of the no less intense anti-war pressures Johnson had been feeling from many columnists and an increasing number of politicians in his own Democratic Party. With increasing fervour through 1966 and into 1967, influential writers such as Walter Lippmann were openly and vigorously attacking the President. After Democratic Senator Frank Church quoted some of Lippmann's objections to the war, Johnson took Church aside at a dinner and snarled, "Frank, when you want another dam or post office in Idaho, why don't you ask Walter Lippmann."

Senate Foreign Relations Committee Chairman William Fulbright, who had supported the Gulf of Tonkin Resolution in 1964, was now haunted by that support and had become Johnson's adversary on Vietnam. So, too, had Senate Majority Leader Mike Mansfield. Their public utterances were cautiously critical, but during brief hallway conversations and a couple of off-the-record meetings in their offices, they privately exploded with indignation about, as Fulbright told me, "that madman in the White House."

At the end of 1966, when the highly respected *New York Times* correspondent Harrison Salisbury reported from Hanoi on heavy civilian casualties from American bombing, it critically damaged whatever LBJ credibility there was left, since the White House had repeatedly denied hitting civilian targets. It was a "credibility disaster," a Pentagon official admitted.

The first time I recall seeing the phrase "credibility gap" was back sometime in 1965 in an article by *Washington Post* diplomatic writer Murray Marder. A few months later "Scotty" Reston of the *New York Times* used it and the phrase was gradually picked up by all of us. It started because of the many questionable official statements and forecasts about the war. "We can see the light at the end of the tunnel" was a favoured forecast we kept hearing, to which some reporters and anti-war supporters responded, "Yes. It's the light of an oncoming train."

But it wasn't only the war that led us to talk about Johnson's credibility gap. His own exaggerations were legendary. He talked about how his great-great-grandfather had died at the Alamo when he was, in fact, a real estate agent who died in bed nowhere near the Alamo. He sometimes wouldn't admit speechwriters wrote his speeches. He wanted the public to think he drank bourbon because he thought it sounded more macho than the Cutty Sark Scotch he really preferred. He inflated the Communist threat in the Dominican Republic. His opponents cited his questionable eighty-seven-vote victory in the 1948 Senate primary. To give himself a poor-boy-makes-good aura, he told reporters he'd been born in a ramshackle Texas shack: even his mother admonished him about that, saying their home was modest but certainly no shack.

There were credibility questions, too, about how rich Johnson had become through his federally regulated radio and television empire in Austin, Texas. It all led to a joke that went the rounds among Washington reporters. A weary western traveller asked, "Where is this place Credibility Gap?" The reply was "You go due west until you smell it, then go south until you step in it."

On the other side, Johnson was under constant intense pressure from the Pentagon generals to escalate the war against the Viet Cong and North Vietnamese. "Bomb them back to the stone age," General Curtis LeMay said. Or "Nuke the Gooks," as another general told me. At first the generals demanded more bombs, more troops, and more planes. They kept saying that with just a little more, they could win quickly. Later, they talked of achieving victory more slowly by "bleeding the enemy." All this pressure was getting to him. Even as early as 1965, Press Secretary Bill Moyers quotes him as saying, "I feel like a hitch-hiker caught in a hailstorm on a Texas highway. I can't run. I can't hide. And I can't make it stop."

Camp David, April 3, 1965 ...

When domestic criticism was already becoming vocal in 1965, international criticism was also gaining in intensity. French President De Gaulle had privately been urging a U.S. withdrawal from Vietnam, and in early 1965 he urged it publicly; British and German leaders privately sought to persuade Johnson to get out. But perhaps Johnson's most painful public criticism came from, of all people, Prime Minister Pearson when he spoke in Philadelphia in April, 1965. Pearson was accepting the Temple University World Peace Award and chose that moment to publicly urge the President to "stop the bombing" of North Vietnam. His speech was carefully couched in diplomatic language, but its message was clear: stop the bombing; arrange a ceasefire on both sides; start peace negotiations.

Johnson was furious and his anger was shared by many members of his administration, who viewed the speech as an inexcusable case of a friend and ally meddling in "our own backyard." Had the speech been made in other circumstances and not on American soil, they argued, it would have been less of an affront.

"I had barely finished the last sentence of that speech," Pearson said later, "before I was invited to lunch with President Johnson the next day at Camp David." It would be a meeting totally unlike the one they had had in November, 1963, after Kennedy's funeral. "It was a warm and friendly beginning," Pearson had told me right afterwards, and quoted Johnson as saying, "I understand that Canada takes a pretty independent view of things." Pearson assured him Canada did.

At Camp David, after a less than chummy lunch, Johnson took Pearson out onto the terrace, where the Prime Minister made the mistake of asking the President what he thought of the speech. "It was bad," said Johnson. And then, for an hour, he took Pearson to the woodshed. Johnson was simply apoplectic. He bitterly denounced the Prime Minister for "shitting in my backyard," as one official told me later. Pearson got the total LBJ "treatment," complete with screaming invective and whispering pleadings, lapel-grabbing, shouts of "How could you?" and bellows of martyred outrage.

Pearson hardly got a word in as LBJ ranted on. He later said of the encounter that Johnson spoke with "great vehemence and many short and vigorous vulgarities." As he wound down, Johnson told Pearson, "It's hard to sleep these days. I'm beginning to feel like a martyr, misunderstood, misjudged by friends at home and abroad." Pearson said later, "If there had not been a kind of 'et tu, Brute' feeling about the assault ... I would have felt almost like Schuschnigg before Hitler at Berchtesgaden."

Ambassador Charles Ritchie had come up from Washington for the meeting and watched the scene in stunned fascination and increasing outrage. From some Canadian officials we later heard that LBJ had actually grabbed Pearson by the collar and lifted him up, but that wasn't quite true, according to Ambassador Ritchie. "The President," Ritchie wrote in his diary, "strode up to him and seized him by the lapel of his coat at the same time raising his other arm to the heavens. It was,'' said Ritchie, ''an expletive adjuration,'' complete with ''expostulating, upbraiding, reasoning, persuading.'' It was unquestionably the worst verbal assault any American president had ever made on a Canadian prime minister, and it forever stained their relations, though they subsequently resumed a more tranquil relationship.

If Pearson was stunned by the vituperous attack, his Canadian colleagues were outraged. As reporters, we weren't aware of the contretemps until word began leaking out from both Canadian and American officials later that night and the next day. We had been momentarily deflected on the story by Johnson's own penchant for hiding the truth. As he told reporters at Camp David, ''His visit has nothing to do whatsoever with Vietnam. That wasn't the purpose of it or anything else that you could blow up or make big and dramatic.'' The more we heard, however, the bigger and more dramatic the story became, and the angrier we got as our nationalism got the better of our professionalism. As reporters and as Canadians we felt Johnson had insulted all of us, and for a few weeks there was a snappish relationship between us and many U.S. officials.

With the coolness of hindsight, it is possible to look at the incident in a slightly different perspective. Pearson's speech was, to my mind now, an unquestionable breach of diplomatic etiquette – had an American president done something similar on Canadian soil there would have been a huge furore. When President De Gaulle made his unfortunate remarks in Montreal a couple of years later, Pearson denounced him in such terms that De Gaulle cut short his visit. But if anyone knew the diplomatic niceties, it was Mike Pearson; he simply decided that speaking out on Vietnam was more important than sticking to the rules.

At the same time, any Canadian prime minister criticizing U.S. conduct in Vietnam was guilty of more than a little hypocrisy. Throughout the war, Canadian business was raking in hundreds of millions of dollars selling to the U.S. war machine. We sold everything from planes, guns, and bullets to nickel, iron ore, lead, and zinc. Most of the nickel used in U.S. planes, missiles, and military vehicles came from Canada; the steel used came from our iron-ore mines; military barracks were built with our lumber. A lot of Viet Cong and North Vietnamese were killed with the help of Canadian material. Indeed, a large part of the American stockpile of nuclear bombs and warheads up to this point had been produced from uranium sold to the U.S. by Canada. The incongruity of our preaching peace while we profited from Vietnam was not lost on our American allies. With some justice, some officials in Congress and the administration viewed us as two-faced.

About a month after the Pearson speech another unpleasantness developed over Vietnam; this time the culprit was the CBC's highly popular and controversial program *This Hour Has Seven Days*. It had run an interview about the war with White House foreign policy adviser McGeorge Bundy. In editing the interview, the *Seven Days* producers made Bundy sound even more of a "warhawk" than he actually was. It was, I thought, an unprofessional edit.

While both Don Minifie and I were personally opposed to the war – Don particularly so – we were careful not to let our personal bias affect our reportage of the Vietnam story. We sought to report as accurately as we could the statements and attitudes of the Johnson administration as well as the progress of the anti-war movement. Radio and television reporters and editors have a special responsibility to be careful because the juxtaposition of previously unrelated sentences in editing a tape or leaving out qualifying statements can distort and do damage to the truth. With TV and radio the damage is deepest because the official is seen and heard saying the words. And, since television has by far the greatest emotional impact of any of the media and has become the chief source of news for most people, it has an enormous effect on the attitudes formed by the public.

When we read the *Seven Days* transcript, Don and I felt the edited interview had somewhat distorted Bundy's position. But if Don Minifie and I were offended as journalists, Bundy, the White House, and the State Department were absolutely infuriated. The program, the CBC, and Minifie and I, as the CBC's Washington correspondents, were denounced publicly and privately. The CBC was accused not just of a biased edit, but of deliberate distortion and "helping the enemy." The outpouring of contempt and vitriol against us was both astonishing and painful, especially since Minifie and I had had absolutely nothing to do with the interview and hadn't even known it was being done.

At news briefings our questions were ignored, and sources didn't return our calls. Then, within a few days, we were barred from background briefings at the State Department and White House, and we no longer were informed of off-the-record sessions. We protested to the State Department and White House press offices and to our other contacts, but while a few U.S. officials sympathized with our predicament, the isolation continued for weeks. At one point, we even asked Ambassador Ritchie to intervene on our behalf. I don't know whether he did or not, but little by little our "Coventry" of isolation relaxed, and eventually we were invited back to briefings and our phone calls were returned. But our punishment for the *Seven Days* interview certainly damaged our ability to properly cover Washington news for a couple of months and illustrated the depth of sensitivity within the administration about Vietnam.

With media criticism, protests in Congress, and demonstrations in the streets, Johnson was feeling the pressure but was still defiant: "Why should I listen to all those student peaceniks marching up and down the streets?" Even within his administration some of his own officials were turning against the war, especially in the middle and lower levels, some for philosophical reasons and some for the practical reason that the cost of the war was cutting into social programs and undermining public support for them. The U.S. was spending $12 billion on the war in 1966; $22 billion in 1967; and the cost was heading for $30 billion a year.

The time-consuming complexity of covering the Vietnam story is illustrated by my own activities in a typical week in March of 1966, when I was chasing background information and reaction to a speech by Senator Robert Kennedy, who urged a halt in American bombing of North Vietnam. According to my notes, the following was my schedule for contacts on that story, one of a couple of dozen stories I was following that week. On Monday, an off-the-record discussion in his office with Senator William Fulbright, Chairman of the Senate Foreign Relations Committee, who supported Kennedy. On Tuesday, I attended a "deep background" meeting for half a dozen other foreign correspondents with Secretary of State Dean Rusk, who opposed Kennedy. On Wednesday, I had lunch with a senior official of the Soviet Embassy who, of course, argued the bombing should stop. On Thursday, I went to a presidential news conference and later that day met privately with a White House official to get some off-the-record expansion on what Johnson had said. On Friday, at dinner with a senior official of the U.S. Information Agency I sought further explanation of the implications of Johnson's comments.

When it was all over, I hoped I had something close to the right story. Then I'd check it with contacts in the Canadian Embassy and with the State Department. But always I had to remember that every contact was trying to put his own "spin" on the story and I had to make allowances for that.

Undersecretary of State George Ball persisted in his criticism of the war, but he kept it out of the public light. Surprisingly, Johnson didn't fire him because of his attitude, and sometimes almost proudly referred to Ball as "my Abominable 'No Man.' " He was less charitable with others, however. In February, 1965, Vice-President Humphrey had expressed some mild reservations about Vietnam at a White House meeting and LBJ froze him out of all White House Vietnam meetings for a year. Humphrey promised not to dissent again and Johnson let him back in. Humphrey never did speak out against Vietnam until Johnson announced his retirement and Humphrey was a candidate to succeed him. Even then, he was extraordinarily circumspect in his public comments. Only at the end of September, 1968, did he publicly edge slightly away from Johnson.

Bundy, in time, began to feel uncomfortable with some of the Vietnam policies and happily took the job as president of the Ford Foundation when it was offered in 1966. Press Secretary Bill Moyers was uneasy, too, about Vietnam and other matters and left the White House in 1966. Worse still for Johnson, Defense Secretary Robert McNamara was being eaten by doubts. He was still in touch with Bob Kennedy, a fact Johnson resented deeply, and privately agonized over the trap he felt the U.S. was in. Eventually, Johnson made him president of the World Bank; his replacement was Clark Clifford.

Washington, D.C., December, 1966 ...

Johnson, however, could always rely on Secretary of State Dean Rusk, who loyally followed every Johnsonian twist and turn on Vietnam. As reporters, we met Rusk at his news conferences and occasionally at off-the-record sessions and we listened to him in public speeches and congressional testimony. He preferred to let Johnson make the major statements and overtures on the war, but he took one major initiative on his own, which was to the CBC's journalistic benefit and clearly showed we'd finally been forgiven for the Bundy interview by *Seven Days*.

Minifie and I had been seeking an interview with Rusk as part of our annual CBC correspondents year-end TV program. Rusk was known to reporters and State Department officials as "The Buddha" both for the way he looked and for his inscrutibility, so we didn't expect he'd agree. To our surprise and delight, he did.

In the interview, Rusk gave us what became known as his "14 Points." He said the U.S. was prepared to undertake "negotiations without precondition" and he talked of a bombing pause. I learned later this had grown out of White House meetings a few days before when Johnson, pressed by generals on one side and conscious of the anti-war pressures on the other, said he'd "take a gamble" and make a peace proposal. It wasn't much of a gamble, however, because the U.S. continued trying to bomb Hanoi to the negotiating table even though there was a brief Christmas bombing pause shortly after our interview. In any event, Hanoi ignored the overture.

While taken aback at our journalistic good luck in the Rusk interview, Minifie and I were further surprised that, shortly after we did it, the State Department reproduced and circulated to other reporters the entire interview, had the text broadcast on Voice of America, and sent it around the world. Clearly, the Secretary of State had used Minifie and me to transmit an "open" message to Hanoi, a message artfully contrived to appear to be a spontaneous response to media questions. The "14 Points" were thereafter trotted out by Rusk from time to time as indicative of how hard the U.S. had tried for peace and failed. They were used later, though, as the basis for subsequent American negotiations with Hanoi that eventually led to more informal talks which, two and a half years later, led both sides to a peace conference negotiating table in Paris.

Through 1967 the anti-war clamour mounted and Johnson's beloved public opinion polls told him an increasingly sad story. In October, 1967, at the time of the Pentagon demonstration, the polls reported that more people opposed his war than supported it. Increasingly, he felt cornered as he pursued what he claimed was a "middle course" between his generals and an increasing number of "dovish" advisers.

A voracious reader, Johnson gobbled up thousands of pages of documents from the Pentagon, the State Department, and his White House advisers, taking eighty or a hundred memos, reports, and position papers to bed with him at night. Johnson took to calling Vietnam "that damn little pissant country." More frequently now, he couldn't sleep and would often go down at three or four in the morning to talk to the five or six young officers on duty in the Situation Room, which was connected to every U.S. military headquarters in the world, to every embassy, to the silos of the Minutemen ICBMs, and to the Polaris submarines. It was also where the hot line to Moscow was located. He would examine the huge map on the wall and read the bombing reports as they came in from Vietnam 10,000 miles away. "I felt that I was being chased on all sides by a giant stampede coming at me from all directions," he told biographer Doris Kearns. He simply couldn't understand how those "little people in black pajamas," as one aide told me Johnson called the Communists, could frustrate the mighty U.S. Army.

By November, 1967, the relentless night-after-night "bang-bang" of Vietnam television coverage, along with repeated revelations of official lying about what was really happening, created a credibility gap of unbridgeable proportions.

Saigon, November, 1967 ...

For years I'd been covering the Vietnam War from a distance. Now I wanted to go to Saigon to see it first hand. My editors agreed with a proposal I made for a half-hour *Newsmagazine* program, but, because we were in one of our regular budget crunches at the CBC, I had to go over without a camera crew, picking one up from the Visnews bureau in Saigon as I needed it. Visnews is a worldwide news film and tape agency with headquarters in London that acts as a visual counterpart of a print news agency. The CBC had helped set it up a decade or so earlier in participation with the BBC and other Commonwealth broadcasters who didn't want to be so dependent on American visual news services.

At four o'clock on November 20, 1967, I got aboard the Pan American flight from Washington to Saigon. It took forever to get there – about twenty hours of flying via San Francisco, Honolulu, Wake Island, and Guam. The flight was jammed with soldiers returning from leave and I spent the trip squashed in a middle seat. When we finally touched down at Saigon's Ton Son Nhut Airport, in more ways than one I had travelled a long way from Washington.

In an antiseptic Pentagon boardroom or State Department office, I had heard carefully articulated intellectual discussions about the war. In the corridors, bureaucratic backrooms, and congressional committee hearing rooms I had heard the bloodless debates on the rationalization of the war. To paraphrase Walter Lippmann, I had heard the old men talk and plan a war for young men to fight and die in. Now I would be face to face with the flesh-and-blood reality.

I got off the plane into a steamy, blindingly bright Saigon day and into the usual confusion of airport arrivals made worse by the security and the military lineups for everything from changing money to getting a bus to town. You were supposed to change all your American money at the official rate on arrival, but, like most others, I didn't, changing only $100 and keeping the rest of my dollars to exchange at almost double the official rate on the black market. Lugging my bag and typewriter, I grabbed a green U.S. Army bus into town. I was made immediately aware of the war by the bus's wire-mesh window screens designed to keep hand grenades from being thrown in the windows. In downtown Saigon, I was let out at the sandbagged U.S. military headquarters building and walked the couple of blocks to my hotel, the Caravelle. It was reputed to be the safest hotel in Saigon because the owners reportedly contributed money to the Viet Cong. After checking in, I went over to the Visnews bureau and met my cameraman,

Neil Davis, an Australian, and my soundman, Sung Chan Hong, a Korean. They directed me to an Indian moneychanger down the hall from their office and I was ready for business.

Saigon was still called "The Paris of the Orient," but by 1967 remaining French traces were few except for the language and a couple of decent French restaurants. More than two million people were squashed into the city, making it the most densely populated in the world for its size. And it was as if the Saigonese knew their time was limited as they frantically chased the American dollar. Black marketeers were everywhere, their makeshift stands lining the main streets and their big marketplaces down the side streets. They sold everything from American Army C rations to army clothing, guns, cigarettes, radios, TV sets, drugs, and condoms.

With money in my pocket, I ignored these black marketeers and went out to the main U.S. military PX in the suburb of Cholon. It was like an Eaton's department store selling everything you needed at bargain prices. A special pass was required to shop there, but reporters were given these and I outfitted myself in fighting clothes, buying big heavy black boots, three green Army shirts, pants, four pairs of socks, and a jacket. I also had to buy a new watch since mine had been stolen during my first walk through Saigon streets. I had been strolling along on the way back to my hotel when a gang of street urchins ran past, one of them grabbing my expandable metal watch band and flicking the watch off my wrist. I chased him a couple of blocks to the river but he ran out on a wharf and leaped into the water, holding the watch above his head. I figured if he wanted it that badly, he could have it.

Saigon was the most corrupt city I'd ever seen. It was hard to believe that a few miles away men were killing and being killed. There was a saying in Saigon that "You can't buy love, but you can rent it for a while at any bar in town." My colleagues and I counted 400 different bars and forty nightclubs in the city centre alone. We didn't try to count the drug dens and massage parlours that were really brothels. The giggling, chattering bar girls of Tu Do Street in downtown Saigon were undoubtedly among the most beautiful women in the world. They hovered outside the bars and inside behind beaded curtains, waiting to pluck the American soldiers clean. In the bars you paid as much as seven U.S. dollars for a Scotch and soda and four dollars for a Coke. And you paid for the girls' drinks at the same prices although they drank only a weak tea. Front-line soldiers on leave with a month's pay in their pockets were ripe pickings for these prostitutes and their pimps.

With Washington pouring billions into Saigon, a lot of South

Vietnamese and a few American racketeers became millionaires through graft, theft, corruption, and black marketeering. The Americans tried to pressure South Vietnam government officials to stop the blatant corruption, but with most officials tired, underpaid, uninspired, and likely on the take themselves, little was done. Before going out into the field, I talked to American and Saigon officials, and to Canadian diplomats working for the International Control Commission, the group established by the 1954 Geneva Conference to monitor the armistice that never was. The Canadians who flew back and forth between Saigon and Hanoi as part of their job told me South Vietnam needed thousands of dedicated, committed leaders but most who had those qualities were working for the Communists, not for the Saigon generals.

A reporter's life in Saigon was pretty easy. Many correspondents went out on one-day excursions to fighting areas, and some just went to the U.S. military headquarters and the U.S. Embassy for briefings or to lunch and dinner with American and other diplomats and with military officials. At night we sometimes would go to the rooftop bar of the Majestic Hotel or the Caravelle to watch flares over the rice fields across the river and to listen to the gentle-sounding thump of artillery in the distance.

A favourite watering hole for reporters was the terrace bar of the Continental Palace Hotel in the city centre. The bar was straight out of Somerset Maugham, with tile floor and slowly revolving ceiling fans, barefoot, ragged kids darting in from the street to beg, men in safari suits and beards, con men, prostitutes, and sleek, exotic women in slit skirts. It was here, at a corner table, that Graham Greene scribbled the first draft of *The Quiet American*.

The bar was open to the street, so you could watch Saigon's passing parade of motorbikes, bicycles, military trucks, rickshaws, beggars, soldiers, and jeeps honking by. I was told that once in a while a Viet Cong would cycle by and throw a small bomb into the bar. This would discourage reporters and others from frequenting the place for a few days, but gradually, after the cleanup, the crowds would gather again. The bar was simply so comfortable and so convenient for meeting contacts.

If the city seemed unreal, even more so were the briefings by U.S. military public relations officers in Saigon. The military head-quarters – MACV, Military Assistance Command Vietnam – was a five-minute walk from the Continental Palace bar. But when you walked through the sandbagged entrance, you were in another world. This was Pentagon East. Here at MACV the generals planned. They talked of the war in terms of dry bookkeeping statistics, of KIAS (killed in action), of "killing grounds" and "kill ratios," and of "bleeding the enemy." This quickly took on an absurd reality. At one briefing a colonel told reporters of one village that had to be totally destroyed in order, he said, to save it from the Communists. The public relations people simply overflowed with optimistic talk of "real estate gains" and of "victoriously phasing down" the war.

That November the U.S. Commander, General William Westmoreland, a tall, erect West Pointer, was also exuding optimism about lights at the end of tunnels. And in fact, he had some reason to be pleased. Without the American fighting men, South Vietnam would certainly have fallen to the Viet Cong and North Vietnamese two years earlier. There now were half a million U.S. troops in South Vietnam, General Nguyen Van Thieu had just been elected President, and Air Force Vice Marshall Nguyen Cao Ky was Vice-President.

In spite of their optimism at the U.S. military headquarters, they also lied. I didn't realize how blatantly they lied until I'd been out in the field, although other reporters clearly agreed with Aeschylus that "In war, truth is the first casualty." Here at Pentagon East defeats became victories, lost villages became won villages, enemy casualties were always heavy while American and South Vietnamese losses were negligible. If an area was described as "ours" it was probably fairly safe. If an area was "secure," it meant it was safe for a few hours a day. And if an area was "contested," it belonged to the Communists. If there was increased bombing in some area, it was described as "accelerated pacification."

At one briefing an officer boasted about the dollar cost of the war with a history lesson in the price of killing. It cost, he told us, seventy-five cents to kill each enemy soldier during Caesar's day; $25,000 to kill a man in World War I; $50,000 each in World War II; and $332,000 for every enemy killed in Vietnam. Another officer graphically characterized the American military strategy and the effort to bring about democracy to the country by embroidering on a then-popular U.S. slogan. He told reporters, "You grab 'em by the balls, and their hearts and minds will follow."

Vietnamese officials held a daily briefing at 4:15 p.m. and after attending that I would go over to the formal American briefing at the MACV auditorium at 5:00 p.m. The latter became known as "The Five O'Clock Follies" and a lot of correspondents didn't bother going at all because it was such a propaganda exercise. At one briefing when I first arrived in Saigon, I was taken aback at the hoots of derisive laughter that greeted some of the claims being put forth as fact by the public relations officers. Guffaws or smiles accompanied much of what was said. There was a particularly large outburst of laughter when someone quoted General Westmoreland talking about "phasing down" the war into victory within two years. (Seven years later, the Americans would leave Saigon in shame and disgrace.) Similar reactions greeted comments that "our boys" would be home by Christmas, as I heard at one briefing.

Official visitors to Saigon – congressmen, White House advisers, State Department and Pentagon officials – were given the same sanitized statistics and overly optimistic forecasts. And usually their visits were so brief they never had a chance to compare official pronouncements with battlefield reality. No wonder LBJ was bamboozled by visions of triumph. No wonder official Washington was so out of touch with reality. No wonder the public contradiction between the official "line" and what you saw on television.

Having got my fill of Saigon statistics, I went out to see the soldiers in action. It was fairly easy to do; you just told the military public relations people where you wanted to go and you got on the next plane from Ton Son Nhut Airport that was going to your destination. Once out in the field, you simply hitchhiked from place to place on planes, helicopters, trucks, and jeeps. You'd arrive at a base, see the commanding officer or one of his aides, tell him what you wanted to do, and it would be arranged. "You want to go on a mission?" one officer asked me. "No problem. Just be here at 5:00 a.m. tomorrow." You could wander freely about talking to the Marines or go over to talk with the South Vietnam officers who were attached to the U.S. groups. Some of them spoke English and if not, the U.S. military supplied an interpreter.

Mostly I travelled about Vietnam on my own because Neil Davis, my cameraman, had other assignments and I really didn't need him all the time. When we were together, however, Davis was a wonder. Baby-faced, tall, thin, and blond, he had covered the war from the beginning and had been everywhere and seen everything. He escaped without serious wound even though he had been in many heavy small-arms battles, known as fire fights. He stayed on in Saigon for a while after the Communists took over and then went on to cover other wars, still leading his charmed life. Along with a gentle nature and quiet confidence, he was the best cameraman I ever worked with in a war situation because, not only was he good with a camera and a fine raconteur, even more important he knew precisely the difference between incoming and outgoing fire, what areas looked suspicious, and how to hitchhike to any part of the war.

On my first trip I flew from Saigon to Pleiku in the Central Highlands.

The town was filled with tribesmen from the surrounding mountains and was a key base for directing attacks against North Vietnamese coming down from Laos and Cambodia along the Ho Chi Minh Trail – the infiltration route into the country from North Vietnam.

It was night by the time I found my barracks-room bed in a Quonset hut and had organized my next few days. I had dinner in the officers' mess, took a brief walk in the star-lit, chilly night air, and went to bed about 10:00 p.m. so I could get an early start in the morning. At breakfast and later the next day, I talked to scores of "grunts," the footslogging U.S. Marines who did the fighting and the dying.

They were defiantly proud of doing what they felt was maybe an unappreciated but a necessary and dirty job. They believed in Lyndon Johnson, in General Westmoreland, and in the rightness of the war. They had to, really. It was emotionally unendurable to believe anything else. "We're doing a good job here," one soldier told me at his forward gun position. "We're stoppin' communism from spreadin' and we're really helping them," said another. "I don't want my children to go to school under communism," said an M.P.

Talk was not something you did during a fire fight except for muttering the occasional obscenity. Just before one fight began, I injudiciously helicoptered into a small mountaintop forward fire base called by a number which was either "Hill 1001," "Hill 875," or "Hill 876" – I'm no longer sure and my notes are now not clear. (Most such bases were called by numbers not names.) The base was near Dak To, a few miles up from Pleiku. The Viet Cong and North Vietnamese wanted to take the high ground on which the base was located.

The fight started slowly with the "caarumph" of mortar shelling, then suddenly exploded with the staccato of machine guns, the popping of rifle fire, and the whooshing of mortar splinters slashing through the air. Then the enemy – "Gooks" or "Slopes" in Marine jargon – broke through the outer perimeter around the base. As I hunkered down into my little trench and someone tossed me a helmet, a strange sense of detachment came over me. It was as if I were watching a movie or a documentary. Then suddenly the trench would bounce and dirt would fly into my face or a shell would hit one of the dirty brown tents nearby, sending fragments in my direction. Off a few hundred yards, I could see men firing their M-16s at the attackers, but I never did actually see any of the enemy myself, except dead ones later. Some of our soldiers fell, flailing their arms, tumbling head over heels, and clutching a stomach, head, or leg. Others just quietly folded up.

In spite of the ear-splitting noise and the dirt on my glasses, in my eyes, and in my mouth, my sense of detached voyeurism continued.

It was like looking at a photograph of World War I trench warfare. The fight seemed to last a lifetime and yet, in truth, it took no more than twenty or thirty minutes. Slapping the air above us, helicopter gunships came in from Pleiku and other centres to beat the enemy back and chase them down the hill until they finally disappeared into the trees.

When the fight was over, one of the helicopter pilots landed beside us and came out grinning, smoking a cigar, and wearing a helmet which, for some whimsical reason, had emblazoned on it, "Mao is a minor poet."

With several officers and non-coms, I went out on a tour to the perimeter and a bit beyond. Trees and stumps were still smoking and sandbag bunkers smouldered. Men gathered in groups, most of them silent, looking as we were, at the bodies. Dead and wounded GIS were being carried away, and to my surprise there were far fewer casualties than I'd thought. But there were many more dead Viet Cong and North Vietnamese. I started counting the bodies but couldn't continue. A South Vietnamese colonel named Luat proudly told me he and his men had killed twenty-three and captured two Russian rifles.

We came across hands and legs sticking up out of the ground, appendages blown off and lying about. I was told the military counted the arms and legs, calculating one body for every two arms and one leg, or two legs and one arm. There were bodies hanging upside down in the trees and on the ground. I turned over the body of a young North Vietnamese soldier and, reaching inside his shirt pocket, found a photograph of him, his wife, and two children. On another piece of paper he had written a note which a South Vietnamese translated for me: "Member Communist Party. First entered South Vietnam April, 1967." He had lasted seven months.

Some South Vietnamese and American soldiers poked through the bodies looking for souvenirs. The Americans took hats, insignia, and weapons while the South Vietnamese took watches, money, and shoes. I saw enemy bodies with the ears chopped off by vengeful South Vietnamese soldiers. For some reason, the left ear was particularly prized. Heads were also valued as battle trophies. Although I never saw them, in some South Vietnamese forward bases Communist heads were perched on poles and ears displayed on boards as signs of victory. The South Vietnamese officers tried to discourage this savagery, but one officer told me it was at least partially tolerated as revenge for a recent Communist flame-throwing massacre in a nearby village.

Big battles and little skirmishes continued in and around Dak To for twenty-two days, the most intensive fighting of the entire war up until then. The Communist bases in the dense jungles of the area were blasted by B-52s, the trees denuded by U.S. chemical defoliants, and back in Saigon, General Westmoreland said, "the enemy's hopes are bankrupt."

After a couple of hours I helicoptered back to Pleiku and spent the next few days around the base, visiting the nearby town of Kontum. I went back briefly to Dak To to watch the commander in the area, General Ray Peers, a cigar clenched in his teeth, hand out medals to the young soldiers. Then I flew up to the big U.S. base at Da Nang, many times the size of Pleiku.

Da Nang was the centre of U.S. operations in the part of South Vietnam south of the misnamed "Demilitarized Zone" that separated North and South Vietnam. The DMZ had been established at the Geneva Conference in 1954 as a buffer area in which no military activity would take place. By now, though, a lot of fighting was taking place in and around the DMZ. (I kept referring to the zone in my Canadian way as the "Dee-Em-Zed," to the perplexity of American officers. Eventually I realized I should pronounce it "Dee-Em-Zee.")

At 4:30 the morning after my arrival at Da Nang, I boarded a jeep to drive through town and join U.S. Marines heading out from their camp a few miles north. Officers at Da Nang had told me this was a relatively safe and secure area. When I joined the patrol, I mentioned this to a lieutenant who laughed, saying, "Yeah, this is secure all right. It's ours in the daytime and theirs at night."

About 100 of us tramped alongside the road up and down hills with empty fields on either side of us and with mud smeared on our faces and arms as a rough camouflage. We chewed salt tablets and sweated under flak vests in spite of the soft wind blowing. On everybody's mind – mine, too – was the ever-present possibility of stepping on land mines or into booby traps. Everyone had seen friends blown up and killed or maimed. The members of the patrol were all young kids, and mostly white, surprising in view of the very large number of black soldiers in Vietnam.

I walked along with a kid from Kansas, no more than nineteen. He carried a fifty-pound pack, a belt of machine-gun ammunition was slung around his neck, and he was scared to death. His buddy had been killed a few days earlier and he just knew it was his turn next.

As we tramped along beside the road and then through open fields, he talked endlessly of his loneliness, of growing up on a Kansas farm, of his school chums and their dreams, of his longing for a hamburger and fries and to see his girl friend. He gave me a letter to mail to her when I got back to the U.S. He told me how he deeply believed in the rightness of the war and that he couldn't understand what he considered to be the treachery of young people back in the States. He had no overview of the conflict. He just knew he was there, that his President and his officers told him he was fighting a righteous war to prevent Communists from taking over, and that it was the right thing to do. He didn't have much time or desire to question all this. His prime objective was to do his tour of duty, stay alive, and get back home.

As we walked and talked, he perspired from heat and fear. A couple of times, when small-arms fire cracked near us, he stopped to vomit. His fear was palpable, but he wasn't a coward. Heroes were a dime a dozen in that particular area and he was one of them: his friends all told me of his bravery under fire.

When you're being shot at and your friends are dying beside you, you're not inclined to philosophize too much. It's simply kill or be killed. So he killed, and tried to stay alive. His only objective, as it was for all the grunts, was to get home, at worst with what they called "an easy wound," at the end of his year-long stint in Vietnam.

At dusk we stopped in an open field, set out a perimeter guard, dug fox holes, and put up little poncho tents over them. My Kansas friend and I shared cold C rations and tried to get some sleep. But he wanted to talk and so we did, late into the night. Whether he got back to Kansas to raise corn and grow old, I don't know. He was one of the many fleeting intimacies of war: I even lost the note I made of his name.

After a couple of days on patrol, I hitchhiked a jeep ride back to Da Nang, feeling guilty at abandoning my Kansas friend and the other grunts, but nevertheless grateful to be going back to a bath, a bed, and hot food. On this mission, I talked with a lot of ordinary soldiers, and with variations they all had the same story, the same fears, the same hopes.

Back at Da Nang I felt even more guilty about leaving the patrol as I showered the dust out of my body and then went to the officers' mess where I had several rum and Cokes and unexpectedly ran into CBC producer Beryl Fox, who was filming a documentary. We talked of our experiences and of the possibility of going home via the ancient ruins of Angkor Wat in Cambodia, something which, in the end, I didn't have time to do. It seemed incredible to be sitting there sipping a drink and chatting with Beryl, before going into the dining room for a shrimp cocktail and a charcoal-broiled Kansas City steak dinner with baked Idaho potatoes. I finished the evening watching *Perry Mason* on the Armed Forces television network.

After a couple of days prowling about the city of Da Nang, talking with officers and soldiers, I arranged to take a small plane to Khesanh, a key U.S. base up near the DMZ and just a few miles from the Laotian border. It had been rapidly expanded during the summer by General Westmoreland, who wanted to use it as the central point of a thrust against Communist bases in Laos.

Along with some Marine replacements for those who had been killed or wounded or lucky enough to be going home at the end of their tours of duty, I flew in over the heads of 40,000 North Vietnamese infantry who were besieging Khesanh. It had been only a small outpost in the summer, but now Westmoreland had poured in 6,000 American Marines and South Vietnamese troops. He had even considered using tactical nuclear weapons for defensive purposes until the Pentagon told him to dismiss any such notion.

We landed on Khesanh's bumpy, primitive airstrip and, as you did all across that part of Vietnam, we ran like hell as soon as we got out in case of enemy fire. I had arrived at the very beginning of what was to be a major confrontation and one that took on unusual importance. President Johnson became obsessed with Khesanh, even having a sand-table model of the area erected in the White House Situation Room. Keenly sensitive to criticism that his defence of Khesanh might lead to a crucial defeat similar to that suffered by the French at Dienbienphu, Johnson told General Earle Wheeler, Chairman of the U.S. Joint Chiefs of Staff, "I don't want any damn 'Din-Bin-Foo.' " In Saigon, General Westmoreland told his staff, "We are not, repeat not, going to be defeated at Khesanh."

When I arrived the atmosphere was incredibly tense. Despite the big military buildup, there were fears that this surrounded American outpost would be overrun. There was much argument among the junior officers I talked to as to whether the Communists really wanted to capture the base or simply were trying to draw U.S. forces away from the populated areas, leaving them more vulnerable to Communist infiltration.

In the end, the struggle for Khesanh cost 10,000 Communist lives and only 500 U.S. Marines. The much lower U.S. death rate was probably attributable to the immense U.S. firepower brought to bear, including not only the big and little guns of the base itself and its helicopter gunships, but also the saturation bombing of B-52s. The enemy, however, was made up of no untrained guerilla groups. I talked to one Marine officer in his makeshift, disarranged office. He told me, "Make no mistake about it. These guys are from the North and they're professionals. There's no ragtag army in black pajamas out there."

As I walked about the base in the heat of early December, the dust flying into my eyes, teeth, and mouth, I looked at the dirty brown tents, the machine-gun emplacements, and the howitzers and mortars. Artillery boomed several times a day and small-arms fire crackled regularly along the perimeter. I saw huge rats scurrying into the trenches and wooden sheds, and I think they frightened me more than anything else. The men seemed not to even notice them, preoccupied as they were with the mundane problems of getting rid of the dust or the red mud that covered everything when it rained.

I spent the morning wandering around with plugs stuck in my ears to lessen the shelling noise and talking to the Marines. For most, it was four hours on duty and four hours off, and they alternated between terror and boredom. On duty they patrolled, shelled, waited, and trained. Off duty in their tents, bunkers, and barracks they ate, slept, and read. I saw far more pocketbooks than girlie books.

That afternoon I went on a helicopter patrol. There were four of us – the pilot, a machine gunner at each of the open side doors, and me in between them. As I boarded, a sergeant handed me a large steel dish, which he explained I had to sit on "to avoid getting shot in the ass by ground fire." We lifted off along with five other helicopters on a routine mission to observe what was happening in the Communist-controlled area surrounding the base and to shoot up any "targets of opportunity." We choppered over the base and then swung out beyond the perimeter. Small-arms fire leapt up at us and our two machine guns blasted away at a village and suspected enemy areas.

In one swing our six choppers fluttered over a hamlet in a co-ordinated attack. As the machine guns roared and the helicopter shook and swayed over the village square, my ear plugs almost popped out. I could see flashes from the ground, but nothing hit us. Vietnamese villagers ran wildly into shacks or into the nearby trees. Some were caught by our bullets; others were trapped inside their flaming hovels. We were back at the Khesanh base within half an hour with no losses and no damage.

The helicopter pilots and gunners lived a more antiseptic life than the grunts on the ground. But they likewise faced death every day. I wondered how these men survived emotionally, and I understood their susceptibility to the easily available drugs.

But I learned, as the soldiers had to learn, to live in mental compartments, only rarely letting my mind be possessed by the fright of battle once I was back in relative safety. The soldiers who let the horror leak through often suffered mental breakdowns. Even reporters, with our much more limited exposure, occasionally got too much, but we at least could escape into area headquarters or back to Saigon and the Continental Palace terrace bar. I saw some of these emotional cripples in the streets of Saigon: soldiers on leave wrecking bars on Tu Do Street, punching out bar girls, overdosing on drugs and booze, and boasting of their "Gook" slaughter ... some not entirely clear or caring whether it was the Communist enemy or innocent villagers they had killed.

After a couple of days at Khesanh, I happily ran out to the airstrip and jumped into a plane (they never stopped the engine in case there was an attack and had to take off immediately), slapped my steel dish under me, and took off for Da Nang. I spent the next day trying to hitchhike a flight back to Saigon. In the late afternoon I finally got on a cargo plane jammed with a couple hundred American soldiers and Vietnamese civilians. There were no seats, so we stood all the way to Saigon, making room for a few mothers and children to sit on the floor of the plane.

A few weeks in Vietnam did not give me any great wisdom on that wretched war, but I did come away with a deep affection and admiration for the average American front-line soldier, probably not a fashionable attitude. There were some thugs, madmen, and even murderers among the soldiers – war lovers who were turned on by torturing and killing – and they got a lot of attention. But in my experience, they were certainly not representative of the average GI, who was just a scared kid trying to stay alive.

By contrast, I developed contempt for most of the Saigon warriors, the desk-bound nine-to-fivers whose greatest risk was "Ho Chi Minh's Revenge," the virulent Vietnamese version of venereal disease.

I flew out of Saigon in mid-December to Washington, briefly, and then up to Toronto to edit and script our TV documentary in which I contrasted the war in Vietnam and the anti-war battles within the U.S. "The United States is bitterly divided, deeply confused, and susceptible to glib purveyors of easy solutions," my script said. Johnson, I speculated, was in deep trouble for his re-election and I even hinted he might not run again, although I tended to dismiss that suggestion. It was clear to me that the Americans were slowly winning the war in Vietnam, but they were hitting hornets with sledgehammers and there seemed to be an ever-multiplying number of hornets. On the program and later in a full-page article for the *Financial Post*, I speculated that the Americans could "win" the war by 1983, but "the cost will be more than $450 billion, tens of thousands of lives, possibly a devalued U.S. dollar and chaotic U.S. bitterness and strife. The result in Vietnam will be a society in the South like South Korea's. There will have to be more than 100,000 U.S. troops stationed there permanently.'' It didn't come to that, but before the Americans got out the damage to the U.S. was close to what I'd forecast in all but dollar cost.

Looking ahead, I speculated also that ''if the Americans did withdraw there is no question the country would fall to the Viet Cong and the domination of Hanoi,'' and I noted from what I'd heard in Vietnam that, while the American bombing of North Vietnam made the war more expensive for Hanoi, it had little effect in curtailing shipments of men and supplies south. These were not unique insights, but my trip to Vietnam gave me a perspective I hadn't had before. It also caused me to reflect on the way the media was influencing the conduct of the war.

The most important effect on the practice of journalism was that reporters were never again as trustful of their government sources on and off the record. When an official tells you something that you personally know to be a lie, it erodes the relationship with that official, and when a lot of officials lie, you begin to suspect all officials. Authorities in a democracy cannot tell lies and get away with it for very long if the media are doing their job – as President Nixon found out with Watergate. They may for a while, but presuming reporters are doing their work diligently and professionally, liars will be exposed and governmental credibility diminished.

In reflective moments during Vietnam some American officials admitted to ''embroidering'' reality as a weapon of war. One told me he endorsed Arthur Koestler's comment in *The Yogi and the Commissar*: ''In this war we are fighting against a total lie in the name of a half truth.'' I felt then and feel now that such thinking is dangerous rationalization in a democratic society. Unquestionably it backfired in Vietnam because it was Vietnam, not Watergate, where official lying first destroyed a government and a president.

Officials often denounced reporters in Vietnam for bias but, while this was true in some cases, it was not true as a generality. The work of Peter Arnett of AP, of David Halberstam of the *New York Times*, and of Canadian and ex-CBC correspondent Morley Safer of CBS was simply outstanding. Johnson harboured a particular resentment against Safer, who reported more effectively and more compassionately on the war than anyone else in television. Johnson said Safer was a Communist and demanded that CBS fire him. CBS refused and when Johnson was told repeatedly that Safer was a Canadian, not a Communist, he reportedly replied, ''Well, anyway, I knew something was wrong with him.'' Safer's fellow journalists were outraged at LBJ's efforts to get him fired, but relieved that CBS did not knuckle under.

Generally, reporters provided a far more realistic portrayal of what was happening in Vietnam than did the official public statements. But the media cannot entirely escape criticism for their coverage of Vietnam. The constant demand from network head offices in New York for "more bang-bang" meant people at home were primarily watching individual fire fights, the wounding and killing, the capture of villages, and bombing attacks. They were watching a whole series of isolated events and too seldom were shown any broad perspective on the war.

The NBC, CBS, and ABC news bureaus mostly gave up trying to "sell New York" on political, social, or economic stories that provided the background, implications, and nuances of the war. So the American viewers were denied stories they needed to understand the whole picture. This lack of textured coverage in network day-to-day reporting, I believe, accelerated the American public's disenchantment with the war and continues today to frustrate Americans trying to come to terms with their defeat in Vietnam. Why? Why did we get into this? they want to know. We in the media failed to tell them why at the time, and it's too late now.

There were exceptions, of course. British, French, Dutch, and Canadian television networks, among others, provided a less battle-intensive and more issue-related coverage. Sometimes American documentaries provided perspective, as did Walter Cronkite on his early 1968 visit to Vietnam. The print media, in general, did a much better job of providing texture than their electronic brothers.

The year 1968 began with Johnson still determined and confident of victory, at least in public. But at the end of January that determination and confidence was profoundly shaken. On January 31 throughout South Vietnam, the Communists broke their promise to observe a ceasefire during the Vietnam Lunar New Year holiday Tet and launched the devastating Tet offensive. Seventy thousand Communist soldiers surged into more than 100 cities and towns, including an attack on the U.S. Embassy itself in Saigon. As much as anything, it was the dramatic television news pictures of the embattled Marines defending the embassy and the dead bodies on the embassy grounds that got to the American people. Official Washington was also in a state of shock. "How could this happen?" one mid-level State Department official asked me when I called him the next day. "I thought we were winning."

So did the American public, and the Tet offensive exposed even more the LBJ credibility gap. It didn't matter that, in fact, Tet turned out to be a military defeat for the Communists because it cost them so much in blood (a final estimate of up to 27,000 killed) and that eventually they lost most of the territory they had taken. It was a massive psychological triumph for them and the real beginning of the end for the Americans in Vietnam and for LBJ in the White House.

A month after Tet, another blow to Johnson came when CBS anchorman Walter Cronkite came back from his Vietnam trip. On February 27 he broadcast a gloomy report on the war and the failure of U.S. policy. He said he was "more certain than ever that the bloody experience of Vietnam is to end in a stalemate." When he saw Cronkite that night, LBJ knew he was beaten. "When we lost Cronkite, we lost the war," one official at the White House told me later, echoing Johnson's own comment that losing Cronkite meant losing "Mr. Average Citizen." Cronkite's assessment did profoundly affect the American middle class. If good old honest Uncle Walter felt it was time to get out of Vietnam then, by golly, it was time to get out. He helped make the anti-war attitude respectable and his reluctant conclusion that the war was wrong was one of the last straws for LBJ, spurring his decision not to run again.

Clark Clifford, Johnson's new Secretary of Defence, was an old-time Democratic presidential adviser who had worked for Truman in the White House and later became a millionaire Washington lawyer and lobbyist. A tall, patrician, soft-drawling, sharp-minded Kansan, Clifford knew politics like few people in Washington. And he knew Johnson. He had been a key Johnson adviser on Vietnam, a hawk who had urged the President to reject recent dovish recommendations coming from McNamara. Now, he was Secretary of Defense, utterly trusted by Johnson. He called in his generals to get their assessment of Vietnam.

As he recounted those days years later to reporter Stanley Karnow for a PBS television series, Clifford asked his generals: "How long would it take to succeed in Vietnam?" They didn't know. "How many more troops would it take?" They couldn't say. "Were 200,000 the answer?" They weren't sure. "Might they need more?" Yes, they might need more. "Could the enemy build up in exchange?" Probably. "So what was the plan to win the war?" Well, the only plan was that attrition would wear out the Communists and they would have had enough. "Was there any indication that we've reached that point?" No, there wasn't.

Clifford was shattered. Then and there he turned against the war and began the delicate process of trying to turn Johnson. He wanted a gradual slowdown in U.S. involvement and then gradual withdrawal. His first of a series of recommendations went to Johnson four days after he'd been in office. They were a modest beginning of what he knew would be a complex, subtle, and extraordinarily difficult job. He was helped by the New Hampshire Democratic presidential primary election.

That winter of 1968 I remember tramping through the snow of New Hampshire with Senator Eugene McCarthy, who had seemed an impossible longshot when he first declared his anti-war presidential candidacy. In the aftermath of Tet, however, you could see he was having an impact on the rock-ribbed conservative citizens of the state. If New Hampshire was listening to his arguments against the war, then the country as a whole was, too.

The White House poured in money and talent to undermine McCarthy. One sign I saw read, "A vote for McCarthy is a vote for Ho Chi Minh." A billboard I saw several times as I criss-crossed the state proclaimed, "The Communists in Vietnam are Watching the New Hampshire Primary."

If they were, they, as well as Johnson, got a surprising message. On Tuesday, March 12, "Clean Gene" McCarthy, as his supporters dubbed him, got 42.2 per cent of the total vote – only about 250 votes less than Johnson. Because of the peculiarities of the New Hampshire delegate-selection system, McCarthy won twenty of the state's twenty-four delegates to the Democratic Convention to be held in Chicago the following August. It was a crushing defeat for an incumbent President.

A few days later, whatever his growing doubts, Johnson continued publicly to speak of "victory" in Vietnam. By March 20, however, he was in fact turning. He asked Clifford that day to prepare a "peace proposal." Clifford called an emergency meeting of "wise men" including that tough old Cold Warrior, Dean Acheson, as well as George Ball, McGeorge Bundy, several generals, and other Johnson friends and advisers. On March 25, the wise men met Johnson at the White House and LBJ was astounded when most of them urged disengagement. In his memoirs, Johnson recounted the moment: "If they had been so deeply influenced by the reports of the Tet offensive, what must the average citizen in the country be thinking."

Several weeks earlier, Johnson had scheduled a major television speech as a report to the nation on Vietnam and it was now set for March 31. His speechwriters had started out working on a war speech and in the last week were suddenly switched to working on a peace speech. It would announce a partial U.S. bombing halt, make a plea for negotiation, and, as Johnson told an aide, "I may have a little ending of my own."

Knowing the speech would be important but not knowing the "little ending," I came up to Toronto to do what was called a "Gulch

Special.'' If a program was slotted in ''The Gulch,'' it meant the program-scheduling decision-makers felt the news was moderately important but not important enough to interrupt regular evening fare.

In the videotape recording offices of the CBC in Toronto at nine o'clock that Sunday night I was sitting watching a battery of TV monitors as LBJ spoke. From his phrasing and mannerisms, I began to get the feeling he was working up to something very important. ''Hell,'' I exclaimed, ''he's going to quit!'' When he began his last half dozen paragraphs, I was sure. He paused, lifted his right hand slightly, and spoke the words that have become so famous: ''Accordingly, I shall not seek and I will not accept the nomination of my party for another term as your President.''

I rushed into a studio and did a quick bulletin on the air a few minutes after he spoke. Then, after consultation with producer Ross McLean, I quickly prepared a short report to be inserted in McLean's program, *The Way It Is*, the CBC's prestige public affairs program at the time. Next, I and my news colleagues scrambled for tape, background material, and comment for *The National* at 11:00 and for the ''Gulch Special'' at 11:30.

It was an exhilarating moment – a profound change in American policy combined with the quitting of the President in the middle of a war. Our adrenalin was pumping with the excitement of the story and the panic of getting a program together on such short notice. On camera during live television programs with these kinds of breaking stories, you're out there on your own high wire with no net. At the same time, you're utterly dependent on so many other people, from producers and directors to sound technicians and cameramen, to feed you information and to get the signal out. I can't think of another business, in which seconds are critical, that is so dependent on so many people all at the same time.

Paris, May, 1968 ...

With Johnson's speech, most American bombing of North Vietnam stopped and Communist troops pulled back from besieged Khesanh as a reciprocal message of de-escalation. With the help of the United Nations and diplomats in world capitals, Washington and Hanoi began a complex diplomatic dance, each seeking advantages in the formal meeting they had now agreed to. From my Washington base, I followed the story as arguments arose over where to hold the meeting: Rangoon, Geneva, Phnom Penh. Ten different cities were considered but Paris was the back-pocket favourite of both sides and Paris it was. Then there were arguments about what to call these Paris meetings. It was agreed the preliminary informal conversations before the meeting would be characterized as "contacts." The Washington-Hanoi talks themselves would be called "talks." And then, if successful, the "contacts" that became "talks" would become "negotiations."

Now there were more arguments about who would sit where. It was decided the Americans would sit on the left side of the room and the North Vietnamese on the right. It was another eight months before Saigon itself was willing to sit down with Washington and Hanoi and then only after endless silly arguments about the shape of the table. Should it be round, square, oblong, horseshoe, or no table at all? Finally, they all agreed on a gigantic round table.

But in May, Hanoi and Washington at last were ready to sit down and I flew to Paris to cover the opening round of the first official meeting.

The Majestic Hotel where all this was taking place was just a stone's throw from the Arc de Triomphe, a dozen blocks from the CBC Paris office and, oddly enough, had been a Gestapo headquarters in Paris during World War II. Along with other reporters, I went into the meeting room before the conference started to get a sense of the atmosphere. Workers were tacking down red carpet, florists were putting bouquets on the table, and technicians were testing the microphones. Dominating the room was a Louis XIV tapestry which, upon examination, turned out to have about an equal number of hawks and doves flying around, along with all kinds of pigeons, ostriches, peacocks, swallows, bats, and angels.

As the talks were about to begin, two French Air Force jets streaked overhead in salute. The North Vietnamese arrived first in their black Citroëns, led by the Vietnamese poet-revolutionary Xuan Thuy. They were followed seconds later by the Americans, led by that multi-millionaire with a keen social conscience, Averell Harriman, nick-named by his colleagues "The Crocodile." We watched with a mixture of excitement and disbelief – the war in Vietnam had finally shifted from the Mekong rice paddies and Central Highlands to the conference table in Paris. In they went to sit in black plastic chairs around the table and begin what was called the "salami approach" to peace – trying for a lot of little agreements and building up to big ones later. My estimate of how long it would take was woefully wrong. In a Paris article for the *Financial Post* I wrote, "All of this will take at least a year or two." In fact, the process lasted for five years and, before an agreement was ultimately reached, more Americans were killed in

Vietnam than had died up to that point – a total, when it was all over, of 57,939 dead.

After a week or so, these first Paris talks rapidly deteriorated into the typical and relatively boring routine of all international conferences. I would take in the American briefings at the U.S. Embassy, sit in on whatever North Vietnam briefings there were, and watch every day as the delegates went into the Majestic in the morning and came out at night. I would even watch the delegates leave their hotels: the posh Crillon where the Americans stayed, the Left Bank Letitia – a favourite of French travelling salesmen – for the North Vietnamese. But the conference soon became a parched desert of information.

I stayed on in Paris for a week or so after the Vietnam conference was underway, not so much to pursue that story but to follow the student riots in the French capital. Every day there were marches and demonstrations up the Champs Elysées or over on the Left Bank. The stifling rigidities of the De Gaulle regime were breaking down as students, liberals, and labour leaders demanded a more open society. French television newscasts, for instance, simply reflected the De Gaulle line. The opposition was given little attention. French TV was essentially an instrument of the state to promote the interests of the government. The left demanded change, and so did many of those working in broadcasting. Their demands and the resulting riots hastened the resignation a year later of General De Gaulle.

I recall going over to the Left Bank one day to cover a riot by several thousand students along with NBC correspondent John Chancellor. We went over to the students' side of a line and as we were chatting with them, cannisters of tear gas came lobbing over from the police. A couple landed on the street a few feet away, rolled toward us, and spread their clouds. Instantly we were in bitingly painful tears. We all ran, and Chancellor and I took early refuge in the first open bar we could find to dry our eyes and gain strength.

A few days later I flew back to Washington.

Washington, D.C., January 20, 1969 ...

During his final six months in office, as others vied for the Democratic presidential nomination, Johnson was increasingly a sad and isolated man. He fought with Saigon for delaying and frustrating his peace efforts. He fought with fellow Democrats, many of whom wanted a much stronger and broader peace plank in the Democratic Party platform than he was prepared to accept. He sensed betrayal on all sides.

In an extraordinarily revealing conversation with biographer Doris Kearns, Johnson later said, "I knew from the start that I was bound to be crucified either way I moved. If I left the woman I loved – the Great Society – in order to get involved with that bitch of a war on the other side of the world, then I would lose everything at home. All my programs. All my hopes to feed the hungry and shelter the homeless. All my dreams to provide education and medical care to the browns and blacks and the lame and the poor.

"But if I left that war and let the Communists take over South Vietnam, then I would be seen as a coward and my nation would be seen as an appeaser and we would both find it impossible to accomplish anything for anybody anywhere in the entire globe.

"... there would be Robert Kennedy out in front leading the fight against me telling everyone that I betrayed John Kennedy's commitment to South Vietnam ... that I was a coward. An unmanly man. A man without a spine.

"Oh, I could see it coming all right. Every night when I fell asleep I would see myself tied to the ground in the middle of a long open space. In the distance I could hear the voices of thousands of people. They were all shouting at me and running toward me. 'Coward! Traitor! Weakling!' They kept coming closer. They began throwing stones. At exactly that moment, I would generally wake up ... terribly shaken."

Lyndon Baines Johnson was the most fascinating, though certainly not the most attractive, public figure I covered in my years as a Washington correspondent. He was, as Hubert Humphrey told a group of us one night during the 1968 campaign, "a tidal wave." His aide Jack Valenti once explained it by saying Johnson had "extra glands." He was, in fact, a goddamn wild man. But, in spite of the many repulsive aspects of his personality, I disagree with those, most recently his biographer Robert Caro, who ascribe to him only the meanest of motives: power at any price. They say he was a man without principle or idealism, but I think the public record argues differently. Johnson's passionate and successful efforts to pass landmark social welfare legislation, the Civil Rights Bill of 1964 and the Voting Rights Act of 1965, his education and housing measures – all showed a soul deeply committed to helping his fellow man. Repeatedly he would reflect on the satisfaction and inspiration he had gotten teaching dirt-poor Mexican kids in a Texas school in the 1920s. His "tidal wave" personality got things done, but he wasn't a "nice" man and his crude, bullying style offended the sophisticates who, to Johnson's pain, are the country's leading communicators and historians.

In the end, it was Vietnam that drove him from the presidency, not his crudeness, and it is Vietnam that marks him in history as a failure. His old "Abominable 'No Man' " on Vietnam, George Ball, has since said the war was "probably the greatest single error made by America in its history."

His own mournful words as he headed back to the LBJ Ranch on the Pedernales in the Texas Hill Country form a suitable epitaph for his presidency: "So little have I done ... so much I have yet to do."

9 THAT SLUM OF A YEAR

Washington, D.C., January, 1968 ...

The writer John Updike called the 1960s "a slum of a decade." I don't think it was; there were the bracing sense of hope and confident elegance of the Kennedy New Frontier with its Peace Corps and Alliance for Progress; Johnson's achievements on civil rights and social reform; and the first Americans in space. But 1968 was indeed a slum of a year. Everything seemed to go wrong. People began quoting W.B. Yeats: "Things fall apart; the centre cannot hold. Mere anarchy is loosed upon the world."

As the year began, the White House was under siege by the antiwar movement, the nation was still in a state of shock after the racial chaos of the previous summer, and nasty political infighting had broken out as Democrats looked to the November presidential election. In the centre of it all was Robert Kennedy. For months, he had been pressured to defy tradition and try to snatch the Democratic nomination from a sitting president. And Johnson was terrified Kennedy might try.

The first time I saw any evidence of Kennedy's presidential possibilities was during the congressional election campaign in the fall of 1966. He campaigned for his friends in the South, North, Midwest, and West. Before that there had been gossip and jokes about the possibility of another Kennedy in the White House but there had been no concrete demonstration of his national appeal.

That October, I flew with him to Iowa. There, Kennedy was as astonished as we were at the crowd exuberance that exploded all around him. "Kiss me Bobby!" young girls screamed; "RFK in '72" a sign

284

said; "It's magic," said a local politician. For the first time people were talking seriously of him as a presidential candidate, but they were talking of 1972, after Johnson's second term. Some of the crowd enthusiasm came from memories of John Kennedy, and Bob made several references to him; some of it came from his increasingly loud opposition to the Vietnam War, which appealed especially to the young; and some simply came from his own newly discovered political charisma.

I wanted to see how he reacted to all the talk of being a "future President" so I'd tag right behind him to listen as he shook hands at airports, on streets, and at receptions. He'd only smile a bit shyly at such talk and say, "Well, thank you," or "Gee, that's nice of you." Later, in Sacramento, when asked about the presidency, he said, "Oh well, I just quite frankly don't know what the future brings." He seemed fatalistic about his own future. But Adam Walinsky, a key, young Kennedy aide, took one look at the enthusiasm of the Iowa crowds and decided then and there he would do everything he could to persuade Kennedy to run in 1968, partly because Walinsky was so opposed to the war.

In a conversation I had with Kennedy on that trip to Iowa, he sought to soften his differences with Johnson. He said he wanted to enrich the Johnson War on Poverty and if the bombing of North Vietnam were stopped and U.S. aid reduced, it would free up more money for the LBJ Great Society.

By the spring of 1967, the pressure on Kennedy intensified. A "Citizens for Kennedy-Fulbright" committee was formed in New York. In the summer, the Gallup Poll put him only six percentage points behind Johnson in national popularity. In the fall, the clamour for him to run on an anti-war platform against Johnson reached a new peak and he began to think about it seriously. The greatest pressure was coming from an angry group of anti-Johnson Democrats led by Allard Lowenstein, a young activist New York lawyer and Kennedy ally in New York politics who thought Kennedy was the ideal anti-war candidate. (Lowenstein, a man who proved that one individual can make a difference, was murdered in 1980 by a former protégé.) Kennedy was reluctant, but Lowenstein persisted, pointing to the October Harris Poll which reported 52 per cent support for Kennedy for President and only 32 per cent for Johnson.

His advisers were sharply divided – the old John Kennedy staff members, such as Ted Sorensen and Kenneth O'Donnell, were against running, while his newer, younger Senate staff, such as the energetic, aggressive Walinsky and researcher Peter Edelman, were gung ho to go. His brother Ted said "No"; his wife Ethel said "Yes." He discussed what he should do endlessly with friends, advisers, reporters, and such key politicians as Mayor Daley of Chicago, who also was worried about Vietnam. I went along with Don Minifie when he was doing an interview with Kennedy in late November and he told us, "I don't plan to run, but all my friends are pushing me." All who talked with him reported an anguished and indecisive man. His heart told him to go for it, but his head told him no. Finally, Kennedy told Lowenstein, "I just can't do it." It would be viewed, he said, as a personal vendetta against Johnson; it might irreparably split the Democratic Party; and besides, there wasn't a chance of beating an incumbent president for the nomination.

Instead, Kennedy suggested to Lowenstein that he approach General James Gavin, who opposed the war, but Gavin said he was a Republican. Economist and former JFK ambassador to India John Kenneth Galbraith was another Kennedy suggestion, but he couldn't do it because he had been born in Canada and therefore was constitutionally barred from running. Senator George McGovern was reluctant, but one man Kennedy suggested was not: Senator Eugene McCarthy of Minnesota. On November 30, McCarthy, the quixotic, poetry-loving liberal dilettante, announced he was running. But as December rolled by, McCarthy wasn't having much impact and Kennedy was still listening to his inner urgings to run in spite of his earlier decision.

On the CBC's year-end correspondents' program I forecast that 1968 would be one of the most explosive political years in American history. It was at least one prediction that came totally true. It would also be a whirlwind of activity that would climax my career as a correspondent.

In early January I plunged into a work pattern that continued all through the year whenever I was in Washington. Most days I'd get up at 6:00 a.m. to do a radio report for the CBC's *World at Eight*. Usually I did two daily television reports, for the early evening news and *The National*, a weekly report or interview for *Newsmagazine*, and a piece for *Sunday Report* on radio. On Saturdays and Sundays I'd find time to write my weekly articles for the *Financial Post* along with sporadic writing for other Canadian magazines. And I was still editing the monthly newsletter for IFAP. As the political year heated up, I seemed to go to more lunches, dinners, and cocktail parties than ever before. And, of course, there were the usual rounds to be made at the Congress, White House, State Department, and Pentagon, plus the Canadian Embassy. The ambassador now was Edgar A. Ritchie, to my mind the best-informed, most effective ambassador we've ever had in Washington; he was an invaluable source of background information. All the work was doubly hard because Don Minifie, my friend, colleague, and mentor, had suffered a stroke in December and was out of action.

In my date book for that year is a notation for Sunday, February 11, which says, "Nuthin!" and in the whole book the only free days were that one and Thursday November 14, nine days after the election. For that day, my date book entry reads: "Nuthin! Bogart double feature and Monopoly."

On January 30, Bob Kennedy had breakfast with a half dozen reporters at the National Press Club and I heard from a couple of those who attended that he had remained sceptical of McCarthy's efforts, but as to whether he might run, he had said, "No. I can't conceive of any circumstance that would lead to my running." A circumstance that he couldn't conceive occurred the next day with the Tet offensive. This changed everything, and once again he was reconsidering whether to run. Meanwhile Senator McCarthy was doing better and warned Kennedy on February 6, "He will have a fight on his hands to see who has the most strength. I will not step aside voluntarily."

On Valentine's Day, February 14, I made my first trip to New Hampshire. I've had a love affair with politics and politicians since before I got my first pair of long pants and this was to be a political year I'd never forget. As I gossiped and drank with fellow reporters in the Holiday Inn in Manchester, N.H., the stories inevitably got around to a Democratic Senate primary eighteen years before in Florida. In those days in Florida, winning the Democratic nomination was tantamount to winning the election.

On this occasion, New Deal Senator Claude Pepper was being challenged by conservative Democrat George Smathers, a friend of John Kennedy. Smathers conducted a "Red scare" campaign attacking Pepper for being left and lewd. Calling the Senator "Red Pepper," Smathers travelled through the small towns and farms of Florida with a barrage of double talk designed to alarm voters about Pepper's character. "Are you aware," *Time* magazine quoted Smathers as saying, "that Claude Pepper is known all over Washington as a shameless extrovert? Not only that, but this man is reliably reported to practice nepotism with his sister-in-law, and he has a sister who was a thespian in wicked New York. Worst of all, it is an established fact that Mr. Pepper, before his marriage, habitually practiced celibacy."

The good Floridians certainly didn't want anybody to represent them in Washington who was involved in such things as celibacy and nepotism, and they threw him out of his senatorship. Smathers later claimed he never said exactly those words. In any event, it was a legendary campaign.

So, too, was the 1968 New Hampshire primary to be a legendary campaign. McCarthy trumpeted his anti-Vietnam politics ten and twenty times a day at factory gates, coffee parties, schools and churches, on the streets, and on the air. In an interview, he told me, "in the name of God, the killing must end."

He was an awkward campaigner. He felt and looked embarrassed every time he stuck out his hand to say to a stranger, "Hi, I'm Gene McCarthy." "I really don't like doing that," he told me, "but I guess I have to." At one point he went into the wrong factory and the owner ordered him out. At other factories he'd wander up and down aisles, smiling hesitantly and diffidently saying hello to workers bending over their machines. In one plant where I walked with him, he almost clutched me in gratitude at having someone with him whom he had seen before. He seemed so alone and unsure as he moved along, hesitatingly looking for which way to go, and breathing a sigh of relief when it was all over. It was agony for him.

As a former sociology professor, what he liked best of all was speaking to students, whether on a platform or at an informal gathering. He was energized by his encounters with the young and would charge out again into the streets and homes of New Hampshire to meet the people in his low-key, high-brow campaign.

One revolution McCarthy started in New Hampshire was the involvement of youth in the political process. They were amateurs, but then so was McCarthy an amateur in the business of running for President. By the thousands they poured into New Hampshire and later into Wisconsin, Indiana, Oregon, and California. Known as "The Children's Crusade," they rang doorbells, stuffed envelopes, and made phone calls. At first they were undisciplined, sloppily dressed, loud, and boisterous, but as McCarthy became a serious presidential candidate, the game-playing ended and beards had to be shaved off, hair cut, and mini-skirts abandoned.

I ran into them all over the primary states as they joined McCarthy to, as one told me, "give the system one last chance." That was crucial in 1968 because that was a year of "hippies" and "yippies" who had given up working within the political system and had taken to the streets in anarchy. Some of the dedicated, hard-working youngsters moved over to Bob Kennedy later, but most stayed loyal to McCarthy through the Chicago convention.

As much as he was recharged by his youthful loyalists, I always felt McCarthy never really understood them. He kept himself apart from and above them. He accepted them, used them, and felt good about them. But he never gave himself to them as, say, Bob Kennedy did to his young supporters. With this behaviour and a less than forceful effort in Chicago, in the end, I felt McCarthy betrayed the young.

In early March, however, McCarthy's anti-Vietnam War arguments were sinking in on the New Hampshire voters in a way no one had ever dreamed with the possible exception of Allard Lowenstein. Meanwhile, Kennedy was edging closer to running, as his rhetoric indicated. He told a Chicago audience, "Our enemy, savagely striking at will across all of South Vietnam, has finally shattered the mask of official illusion with which we have concealed our true circumstances even from ourselves.... It is time," he said, "for the truth.... we must actively seek a peace settlement ... give the Viet Cong a chance to participate in the political life of the country – not because we want them, but because that is the only way in which this struggle can be settled." Johnson privately told reporters that such comments were killing American soldiers in Vietnam. Richard Nixon, campaigning for the Republican nomination, said Kennedy's speeches were "prolonging the war by encouraging the enemy."

On March 9, Kennedy flew off to Iowa for dinner with Governor Harold Hughes and other political friends and the next day he went to California where, among others, he talked to his friend Cesar Chavez, the leader of Mexican-American migratory grape pickers. Vietnam preoccupied everyone he saw and he sensed their support if he ran. Coming back from that trip he had decided to take the plunge. For the next day or two the debate was when to announce his candidacy.

He told his friends he didn't want to announce before the New Hampshire primary because that might unfairly undercut McCarthy who, he hoped, would later join forces with him against Johnson. Then, when McCarthy scored his stunning triumph in New Hampshire, Kennedy knew he'd be accused of being a cowardly latecomer, trying to ride in on McCarthy's coattails. The Friday night before announcing, he sent his brother Ted to tell McCarthy, who was campaigning in Wisconsin. That same Friday, Kennedy flew to New York City for a series of political rallies and meetings. At one of these, he sat beside Leonard Hall, a former Republican Party chairman and campaign manager for Eisenhower. There was a microphone on the table to carry the speeches, but it was accidentally turned on early and picked up and broadcast over a New York station the following conversation between Kennedy and Hall.

Kennedy: "Do you think I'm crazy?"
Hall: "What will McCarthy do?"

Kennedy: "He'll stay in. So it's going to make it tough. It will
          make it much tougher."
Hall: "Are you going the primary route?"
Kennedy: "Yeah."

I was in Washington but was told of the conversation that night. Now there was no doubt that Kennedy was going to run.

The next day, Saturday, March 16, at ten in the morning, I and a couple hundred other reporters jammed into the Senate Caucus Room to hear his formal announcement. A bright-eyed Ethel Kennedy in white gloves and white net stockings was there with nine of the ten Kennedy children, and so were a dozen or so Kennedy clan members. It was the same room where Bob Kennedy had first come to public attention in the Senate Labor Rackets Committee hearings, and the same room where his brother had announced his candidacy for the presidency.

With his unruly hair neatly combed and wearing a conservative blue suit and red-and-blue tie with a PT-109 tie clasp, he told us, "I don't run for the presidency merely to oppose any man, but to propose new policies." It was not only because of Vietnam he was running, he said, but because "The crisis in gold, the crisis in our cities, the crisis on our farms and in our ghettos all have been met with too little and too late." Trying to defuse the accusation of a personal vendetta against Johnson, he told us, "My decision reflects no personal animosity or disrespect toward President Johnson. He served President Kennedy with utmost loyalty ... I have often commended his efforts in health, education, and many other areas and I have deep sympathy for the burdens he carries today. But the issue is not personal, it is our profound differences over where we are heading."

When he finished, we began questioning him. After New Hampshire, was he not being opportunistic? No, he said. Was he being divisive? No, he said. Was he being ruthless? No, he said. His supporters applauded as reporters scribbled, slightly annoyed at the Kennedy claque's presence at a news conference. When it was over, he, Ethel, and the children pushed their way through the crowd and almost danced down the wide, winding marble staircase outside the Caucus Room to a waiting car. He went straight to the airport to fly to New York to march in the St. Patrick's Day Parade being held that first day of his campaign for the presidency.

Seventeen years before, he had come to Washington fresh from graduating from the University of Virginia Law School to work in the Internal Security Division of the Justice Department. He took time out to run his brother's successful Senate campaign in 1952, and in 1953 he was hired as one of fifteen assistant counsels on Senator Joseph McCarthy's Senate Permanent Subcommittee on Investigations – a job he got because his father was a McCarthy friend and contributor. Kennedy's responsibility was to study trade between allied nations and Communist countries. He quit after six months, liking McCarthy personally but complaining bitterly about his tactics. He later rejoined the subcommittee as the Democratic Minority Counsel, eventually becoming Chief Counsel and Staff Director under a new chairman, Senator John McLellan, in 1955. In 1957 McLellan named him Chief Counsel of what was called the Senate Select Committee on Improper Activities in the Labor and Management Field but which rapidly became known as the Senate Labor Rackets Committee. I had followed his career since then.

Of all the public figures I covered during my years as a Washington correspondent, it was Robert Kennedy I got to know the best. Although we never were friends in the normal sense, I had seen a lot of him going back to the late 1950s and later when he was running his brother's 1960 presidential campaign. Like his brother, he enjoyed talking to reporters and knew their political usefulness. When he was Attorney General I saw him little as he became his brother's principal adviser and led the civil rights battle. I'd see him at news conferences from time to time and I recall one visit to his office at the Justice Department with half a dozen other journalists, led by a reporter from the *New Orleans Times-Picayune* named Edgar Allen Poe. It was an informal meeting at which we invited him to attend a White House Correspondents Association party.

His office, the one traditionally used by the U.S. Attorney General, was the biggest I have ever seen, a vast, somber, walnut-panelled room with an arched ceiling and a fireplace. Sofas, chairs, and tables were scattered around but the room was dominated by a huge desk at one end of the room and the big black leather judge's chair behind it. Trays on his desk were stacked high with reports, letters, and memos and he had two phones, one a direct line to his brother a dozen blocks away at the White House. I think he enjoyed the sense of power it all conveyed; it was, in fact, a much more elaborate setting than his brother's. But unlike JFK, Bob added many informal family touches. Scotch-taped to the walls was art work done by his children – scrawled drawings of horses and dogs, houses and cars, men and women. Photographs of his family were scattered all over his desk and on tables around the room. I knew that on weekends, his youngsters often would come to the office with "Daddy" and sometimes his huge, black, ferocious-looking Newfoundland dog Brumus romped around the office, the evidence of which was clear from the splotches on the rug.

When he chatted, Kennedy usually had his jacket off, his tie askew, and his shirt sleeves rolled up. In this case he sat in his big armchair behind his desk with a foot propped up on an open desk drawer. When one of us was talking, he'd clasp and unclasp his hands and stare at him with his ice-blue eyes. Then he'd start to question the reporter, a role reversal that happened all the time.

Bob Kennedy was always asking questions, whether in his office, campaigning, or at his home. A couple of years later, after he'd been elected to the Senate, I was invited out a couple of times to Hickory Hill, his big white house in the rolling Virginia countryside just outside Washington that had at one point been the Union Army Headquarters in the Civil War. One occasion was a party for two dozen or so reporters. While treading water and chatting in the swimming pool behind the house, I mentioned to him that I'd spent the better part of a day with Ché Guevara. Kennedy was intrigued and for ten minutes or so he cross-examined me as though I were a witness, trying to get a better picture of the character, style, and personality of the Argentine revolutionary. Although he disagreed with Guevara profoundly, Kennedy nevertheless recognized the impact he had had, not only on the youth of Cuba but on those of the world. "A revolutionary hero," he said. During his presidential campaign, he sometimes would refer to Guevara and his writings.

Hickory Hill was always filled with friends, dogs, ponies, pets of all kinds, and a horde of children, his own and the neighbours'. I observed his special fondness for children on many private and public occasions even during the most trying period of his life. A month after his brother's assassination, at a Christmas party for children of the Justice Department employees, one tyke said to him with a worried look, "Your brother is dead." Those who heard this gasped, fearing Bob might break down. Instead, his face softened, he picked up the child, and said gently, "Don't worry, I have another."

He had been at his Hickory Hill home when J. Edgar Hoover phoned him with news of his brother's assassination. It blew apart the centre of his universe. For months he endured an intense private agony. He lost weight, seemed listless, and saw few people. When I did get a glimpse of him on some official occasion, he looked like the loneliest man on earth.

He was clearly unhappy as Lyndon Johnson's Attorney General and, after a few months, their relationship had worsened. There was more gossip than ever about their dislike for each other. Aside from their policy differences, Kennedy found Johnson crude, insensitive, paranoid, and a braggart and a bully. Besides, as Bob told Arthur Schlesinger, "he lies all the time." Even so, tantalized by the possibility of continuing his brother's presidential objectives, he flirted with the idea of being Johnson's vice-presidential running mate in the 1964 election and becoming the presidential heir apparent in 1968 or 1972. There was a good deal of support for this idea. In January, as the 1964 presidential election year began, the Democratic Party organization in Buffalo had endorsed Kennedy for Vice-President. In March, in the New Hampshire primary, he received 25,000 write-in votes for Vice-President, only 3,000 fewer than Johnson got for President. And in April, a Gallup Poll on the favourite choice for LBJ's Vice-President gave Kennedy 47 per cent, Humphrey 10 per cent.

I had heard that Ethel, who was always pushing him into action, was urging him to seek the vice-presidency, but I had also heard that most of his friends and advisers were against it. While attracted to the idea initially, he knew that with his own fiercely independent nature and his personal distaste for Johnson, he could never be the kind of sycophantic Vice-President that Johnson demanded. Congressman Emmanuel Celler once told reporters, "I heard Johnson say one time that he wanted men around him who were loyal enough to kiss his ass in Macy's window and say it smelled like a rose." That was hardly Bob Kennedy's style. In any event, Johnson would never have had Kennedy, and told him so.

By mid-1964, Kennedy wanted out of the LBJ administration. He wanted to assert his own leadership and in August he resigned as Attorney General to run for the Senate from New York, where he was accused by his Republican opponent, Senator Kenneth Keating, of being a "carpetbagger" since his homes were in Washington and Massachusetts. He took an apartment next door to the United Nations in the UN Plaza and, on his own for the first time, campaigning for himself instead of his brother, Bob Kennedy won easily.

Now a new and different Bob Kennedy began to emerge. He no longer sought to submerge his personality within somebody else's administration. He never did recover from his brother's death, but he seemed to come to terms with it. He began to meet with reporters more often, resuming his old questioning ways. He made speeches more frequently and increasingly moved to the political left of Johnson.

He was no ordinary senator. There was an old saying in Congress that I'd heard several times from Sam Rayburn of Texas, the revered, long-time Speaker of the House of Representatives and Lyndon Johnson's mentor: "The way to get along is to go along." Kennedy wouldn't do that, carving out his own independent course. Like his brother before him, he never became a "member of the club."

In his first year as senator he sponsored major amendments to bills on school aid, the anti-poverty drive, voting rights, and foreign aid, each time expanding on the Johnson administration's original intentions. By the end of that first year he was also attacking Johnson's Vietnam policy. In early 1966 he was urging an end to American bombing of North Vietnam and recommending that the Viet Cong become part of a coalition government in Saigon. Vice-President Hubert Humphrey scoffed at the idea, saying it was like inviting "the fox into the chicken coop." At the time, Kennedy's proposal was considered to be a political mistake by most of us in Washington since Johnson's popularity was still high.

Kennedy also urged closer American relations with China, another politically daring suggestion for the time, and he demanded more speed in U.S. negotiations with the Soviet Union for a treaty against nuclear arms proliferation. He travelled to Latin America in 1964 and 1965 and came back pleading with the White House for a revitalization of the Alliance for Progress. He flew to South Africa in 1966, where he spoke to a meeting of young people and gave one of the best speeches of his life. It captured the philosophy that formed his campaign for the presidency two years later. He said:

There is discrimination in this world, and slavery and slaughter and starvation. Governments repress their people. Millions are trapped in poverty while the nation grows rich and wealth is lavished on armaments everywhere.

These are differing evils, but they are the common works of man. They reflect the imperfection of human justice, the inadequacy of human compassion, our lack of sensibility towards the suffering of our fellows....

The answer is to rely on youth, not a time of life but a state of mind, a temper of the will, a quality of imagination, a predominance of courage over timidity, of the appetite for adventure over the love of ease. The cruelties and obstacles of this swiftly changing planet will not yield to the obsolete dogmas and outworn slogans; they cannot be moved by those who cling to a present that is already dying, who prefer the illusions of security to the excitement and danger that come with even the most peaceful progress....

Each time a man stands for an ideal, or acts to improve the lot of others, or strikes out against injustice, he sends forth a tiny ripple of hope. And crossing each other from a million different centres of energy and daring, those ripples build a current that can sweep down the mightiest walls of oppression and resistance. Few are willing to brave the disapproval of their fellows, the censure of their colleagues, the wrath of their society. Moral courage is a rarer commodity than bravery in battle or great intelligence. Yet it is the one essential vital quality for those who seek to change a world that yields most painfully to change.

And I believe that in this generation those with the courage to enter the moral conflict will find themselves with companions in every corner of the globe.

At the start of his 1968 campaign he carried with him two burdens from his past: lingering suspicions about the genuineness of his liberalism and a reputation for ruthlessness. His liberal credentials were questioned by those who recalled his early involvement with Senator Joseph McCarthy. His reputation for ruthlessness essentially began with the single-minded intensity of his assault on Dave Beck, Jimmy Hoffa, and the Teamsters Union during the Labor Rackets Committee investigations. His unremitting demands and day-and-night work won his brother the nomination for President in 1960 but won him some enemies among those he ran over. "I don't try to antagonize people but somebody has to say 'no,' " he said. A joke I heard going the rounds of the National Press Club at the time of his 1968 announcement to run was that the nomination race between Johnson, McCarthy, and Kennedy was a race between a hawk, a dove, and a vulture.

He was the smallest and thinnest in the Kennedy family and once said, "I was the seventh of nine children, and when you come from that far down you have to struggle to survive."

His reputation for ruthlessness mystified him, but he was able to joke about it. At one point in the campaign for the nomination he was speaking in Seattle in a jammed gymnasium at the University of Washington. We in the media were standing up in front of him, taking pictures and straining to catch his words and he told us, "Those of you in front who really don't have to stand, sit down." He paused, smiled, and added, "There I go being ruthless again."

A couple of days earlier, as we flew to Oregon with him, CBC cameraman Eddie Higginson, who had been lugging around heavy camera equipment during several gruelling campaign stops, flopped sweating and exhausted into his seat on the plane, his shirt hanging outside his pants and a heaving belly in plain view. Kennedy, a bit of a stickler for propriety, looked over at me and Higginson, smiled wanly, and said, "If you don't think I'm being too ruthless, would you mind putting your shirt into your pants. It's getting me all excited."

In my judgement his so-called ruthlessness was primarily directed at himself. And like many men who demand much of themselves, he demanded a great deal of those around him. His theme was always "That's just not good enough. We can do better." It was this drive that motivated him throughout his career – and never more than in his campaign for the presidency.

His very intensity, I suppose, frightened some people. In some ways he was a bit of a Katzenjammer Kid. Certainly he was no choir boy, and he could be devastatingly cutting when angry. He seldom swore, but he could be brutally direct when trying to get things done. It was his impatience to improve the way the world worked that brought resentment among those content with the status quo. But I never saw evidence that he hated anyone, except Jimmy Hoffa.

What I saw through the long, exhausting days of the primary campaign was a man who had emerged from political battles and personal tragedy with his ideals intact and a growing understanding and sensitivity, someone whose seriousness was tempered by a playful, impish spirit and the ability to laugh at himself.

To formulate policies and organize his campaign, Kennedy called on many of his brother's experts and advisers, including Sorensen, Schlesinger, and Pierre Salinger, but he added his own who were to the political left of the older "Camelot" colleagues and whom we reporters sometimes called "The Kiddie Corps." Above all, he campaigned for an end to the Vietnam War, wanting to shift government priorities and spending from guns, bullets, and planes to schools, hospitals, and food.

In fact, Bob Kennedy was now to the left of his brother Jack in his political philosophy. John Kennedy had been intellectually concerned about the blacks, the Hispanics, the downtrodden, the hopeless, and the frail, but Bob Kennedy seemed to feel his concern in his guts as well as his head. He didn't just identify with society's wounded he became wounded himself.

He once met a young girl in a New York slum whose face had been disfigured by rats that had gnawed at her while she slept. That memory stayed with him. During his primary campaign he told reporters that in 1967 Congress had rejected a proposed rat-control program for big cities and now there were more rats in New York than people. Several reporters snickered and his face froze as he said, "Don't laugh!"

Kennedy had decided he must go "the primary route" because, like his brother eight years before, he had to show the political establishment he had voter clout. "I have to win through the people," he said. He had to win the primaries to win the big-city bosses who generally favoured good old Hubert Humphrey as a safe and relatively conservative candidate. Most of all, Kennedy wanted to win over Chicago Mayor Richard Daley, whose support was so critical in his brother's triumph. "Daley means the ballgame," he told me. If he could win Daley, he would win most of the other political bosses in the country and thereby win the nomination.

I talked with him as he flew off on his first campaign swing to the Midwest. He wasn't sure what kind of a reception he would get, especially in an area that had never been "Kennedy country." "We'll see," he grinned. What he saw was astounding.

In rock-ribbed Republican Kansas, 2,500 screaming, leaping supporters jammed the airport at Topeka where only a handful had been expected. They had been waiting two hours for him. When he got to Manhattan, where Kansas State University is located, 14,000 people were in and all around the university fieldhouse. A couple of hours and eighty miles away at Lawrence, a brass band led 20,000 in thundering their support for him at the University of Kansas. "Kiss me, Bobby" ... "Sock it to 'em, Bobby" ... "Give 'em hell, Bobby" ... "I Love You, Bobby" ...

In his speeches, he talked about Vietnam and about social programs, youth, the unemployed, and the hungry. "Our country is in danger," he said, "not just from foreign enemies, but above all from our own misguided policies." He admitted his own early support for the Vietnam War, but quoted Tacitus: "Past error is no excuse for perpetuation." Almost anything he said set off wild cheers. It took him an hour to deliver a fifteen-minute speech. The hunger for a fresh start among the young, the thirst for a hero, his ideas, and the aura of the "New Frontier" all combined in this outpouring of affection and support.

When I talked with him later he admitted that Kansas both startled and pleased him. He knew the television pictures would magnify what was a magnificent start to his campaign for the presidency. "Three minutes on the six o'clock news," one of his aides remarked, "is worth all the rest of the publicity you can get." (Ironically, the same thought had been expressed to me by an old friend and aide to John Diefenbaker, Gowan Guest, who during an evening of tequilas in Mexico City on a prime ministerial visit there, had commented, "Give us control of *The National* at eleven and give everything else to the Liberals and we'll keep Dief in power forever!") Within a couple of weeks of his declaration as a presidential candidate, Kennedy had visited sixteen states and met much the same frenzy everywhere.

The early days of the campaign, however, were disorganized as the Kennedy machine sputtered into action. Reporters' phone calls wouldn't be returned or were left dangling, schedules were mixed up, people were double-booked on the campaign plane, and copies of his speeches were slow to reach us. But within a week, the vaunted machine was running smoothly.

Following Bob Kennedy on his campaign for the presidency was like following no other politician I've ever covered. Not even the early Pierre Trudeau generated anything like the excitement Kennedy did.

He was forty-two years old and much thinner in person than he seemed in his pictures. In fact, at 5'10'' and less than 150 pounds, he was downright skinny. Even though he'd cut his shaggy, sand brown hair (now flecked with grey), it still flopped over the side of his face. He was forever brushing it back with his hand.

He particularly appealed to the young and struck a chord every time he told an audience of an inscription he said he'd seen on an Egyptian pyramid: "No one was angry enough to speak out." To a degree, what made him exciting to the young made him disturbing to the old. He also appealed to the working class, capturing their votes as he did those of the blacks, the Mexican-Americans, the Puerto Ricans, most immigrant groups, and many of the Liberals and intellectuals. He quite simply was the most electrifying politician of the age and was forging the kind of coalition that hadn't been seen since the early days of Franklin Roosevelt.

I travelled with him much of the way in his eighty-five-day campaign, from French Lick to Floyd's Knobs in Indiana, from Fresno to Modesto in California, to villages, towns, and cities all across the United States, to universities, high schools, ghettos, old folks' homes, factory gates, and farms. It was the most rewarding political campaign I ever covered, largely because of the man himself. Kennedy had that rare talent among politicians to grow and learn as he campaigned. He would question labourers, farmers, businessmen, and teachers in a way that showed he really did want their answers. Sometimes he'd run across students loyal to Gene McCarthy, and he'd talk to them late into the night, not so much trying to win their support, but trying to understand their motivation and their concerns. He had an unquenchable curiosity.

On planes or in hotel rooms, he would sometimes chat with us about his strategy and his tactics, thirsty for opinions on how he was doing. He wanted cold, hard appraisals and would quickly turn away from anyone offering ingratiating flattery. But now as always he found it awkward to talk introspectively about himself. He said he couldn't deal with "couch questions," and if somebody asked him one, inevitably there would be a long silence before he dodged the question.

Occasionally, we would point out to him the risks he was taking every day. "Life is a risk," he told me on one trip. "So many people hate me," he told another reporter, "that I've got to give the people who love me a chance to get at me." He recognized the reality that someone some day might try to kill him. But it was something he said he just had to live with. He didn't think it would be for political reasons, he once told Pierre Salinger, but for "plain nuttiness, that's all."

In these quiet, private conversations, I heard more of the Kennedy maxims I'd learned from JFK, such as "Kennedys never say can't" and "Kennedys don't cry." He came across as a contemporary man, but a fairly strict family man, slightly prudish, who swore little and did not like dirty jokes. Years later, there were stories of him having a love affair with Marilyn Monroe, but I've always dismissed that as nonsense gossip, something that simply was not in his character.

As the campaign weeks went by he increasingly displayed his mischievous self-mockery. In an Indiana hotel one night, he was called to the phone while having a shower. A reporter who was one of several present told me that, with a towel wrapped around his dripping body, he pranced out of the bathroom and across the sitting room, shouting "Make way for the future leader of the free world." His wife Ethel would sometimes say to him "Hail Caesar" and often would kid him in front of us about his toothy grin. He once came up to her outside a hotel room saying, "Let's go, Ethel. Here comes Bugs Bunny."

He began to tease his audiences, too. More than any politician I've seen, he could turn a speech into a conversation, especially at small gatherings. "I've got to go now," I heard him tell one group. "I have lots of fans waiting ... I hope."

"You'll remember to vote for me?" he asked another group. "Promise? Promise? Think of my children. Think if I lost, think of all the little tears that will run down their cheeks." In Oregon I heard him offer a variation of that, telling an audience, "Can you imagine the conversation with my children at home? They'll say, 'Daddy, you did well in Indiana and Nebraska, but how did it go in Oregon?' If I have to tell them I lost, can't you see the tears coming to their eyes and running down their little cheeks? You wouldn't want that, would you?"

He joked about his reputation for ruthlessness and told one crowd of a Senate resolution wishing him well after an illness. "I was sick last year," he said, "and I received a message from the Senate. It said: 'We hope you recover.' It passed 42 to 40." To an Indiana audience, sensitive to complaints that he was being careless in his Vietnam criticism, he said, "Make like not war. See how careful I am?"

He campaigned far harder than his opponents, visiting many more communities than they did. "What?" he'd exclaim in mock indignation. "Humphrey didn't come here? McCarthy didn't come? Well, you wouldn't vote for someone who didn't care, would you?" He told another audience that he knew some people disliked his candidacy and said even his own family was unsure. "I took a vote among my family ... three are for me ... two for McCarthy ... two leaning to Humphrey ... two undecided ... and one for Dr. Spock."

But he was serious, too, harping on his anti-Vietnam War theme (although he never advocated unilateral U.S. withdrawal), demanding action to fight poverty and racial inequality – he often mentioned to his audiences that he understood the problem because his family had faced discrimination in their early days as Irish immigrants in Boston.

He said the U.S. should take the lead in seeking to alleviate suffering, quoting Albert Camus: "Perhaps we cannot prevent this world from being a world in which children are tortured. But we can reduce the numbers of tortured children." To an Indiana audience in a speech that would be as timely today, he worried about the U.S. trying to be a policeman to the world. "The worst thing we could do would be to take as our mission the suppression of disorder and internal upheaval everywhere it occurs."

Following any political candidate, I like to wander away from the platform to talk to members of the audience and local officials. If you wander too far, it can be dangerous because you might miss the campaign bus, since it usually takes off the second the applause dies down. The reporters with Kennedy had a secret way of avoiding being left behind. Bob loved to quote everybody from Sartre to Shakespeare, from Camus to Ché Guevara, ending almost all his speeches with a ringing quotation. His favourite was George Bernard Shaw. "As George Bernard Shaw said, some men see things as they are and say why. I dream of things that never were and say why not?" No matter where I was in the crowd, as soon as I heard the words, "As George Bernard Shaw said," I ran for the bus, as did all of my colleagues.

Once in a while, Kennedy would end his speech by quoting somebody else, and some reporters would be left waiting to hear from George Bernard Shaw. A few times, Kennedy mischievously ended a speech by saying, "As George Bernard Shaw said, let's run for the bus." It left an utterly mystified crowd trying to think what on earth

Shaw could have meant. At a hotel suite party one night, everybody was toasting everyone else, and Ethel Kennedy shouted, "Let's drink up for George Bernard Shaw."

Honolulu, April 4, 1968 ...

In the last few days of March I broke away from the Kennedy campaign to follow Richard Nixon in his drive to win the Republican presidential nomination and then I flew up to Toronto to anchor the Gulch Special on what turned out to be Johnson's retirement speech. All of a sudden, Kennedy was no longer such a longshot.

Four days later, I flew to Honolulu to do advance radio and television reports on the meeting between LBJ and President Thieu scheduled for the next day. While I was in mid-air Martin Luther King, Jr., was shot and killed in Memphis, Tennessee, and the meeting was cancelled. So on arrival in Honolulu I turned around and caught the same plane back, going immediately to Toronto to anchor CBC television coverage of the ensuing riots (these were occurring as the Liberal Party met in Ottawa to choose Pierre Trudeau as its new leader).

The murder of Martin Luther King, Jr., set loose a violent reaction reminiscent of that which had followed the assassination of his idol, Mohandas Gandhi, thirty years before. The Detroit riots of the previous summer had only hinted at this explosion. The United States seemed to be in flames. Lootings, fires, and riots broke out in 125 cities in twenty-five states. Forty-five people were murdered (all but five of them black) and the wonder is that hundreds weren't slain. A total of 28,000 people were jailed across the U.S.

As I watched our news feeds come in from Los Angeles, Detroit, Chicago, Cleveland, New York, and Washington, the U.S. looked like a nation under occupation after a war. But it wasn't until I flew back to Washington three days later that I really felt the terror. As the taxi approached my southwest Washington home I saw a sandbagged machine-gun post set up on the corner of my street, broken Molotov cocktail bottles scattered on the road, and armed military patrols. That brought home to me, more than all the statistics and all the film of riots, just how close to the edge of anarchy the United States was at that moment.

I wondered if American society might be torn apart by the twin tragedies of the race riots and Vietnam. I wondered if the American democracy could withstand the bloody, apocalyptic crises engulfing it. Not since the Civil War had the U.S. been so bitterly, deeply, and seemingly irreparably divided.

Kennedy was campaigning for the Indiana primary when he heard of King's murder. He arrived at a rally in Indianapolis where 70 per cent of the audience was black and most had not heard of the assassination. He told them:

I have bad news for you, for all our fellow citizens and the people who love peace all over the world, and that is that Martin Luther King was shot and killed tonight.

For those of you who are black and are tempted to be filled with hatred and distrust at the injustice of such an act, against all white people, I can only say that I feel in my own heart the same kind of feeling. I had a member of my family killed but he was killed by a white man. But we have to make an effort in the United States, we have to make an effort to understand, to go beyond these rather difficult times.

My favourite poet was Aeschylus. He wrote: "In our sleep, pain which cannot forget falls drop by drop upon the heart until, in our own despair, against our will, comes wisdom through the awful grace of God."

What we need in the United States is not division; what we need in the United States is not hatred; what we need in the United States is not violence or lawlessness, but love and wisdom and compassion toward one another, and a feeling of justice toward those who still suffer within our country, whether they be white or they be black.

The next day he was in Cleveland where, almost overcome with emotion over the death of King and with agonizing memories of his brother's assassination, he gave one of the most eloquent speeches of his life to the City Club. He said:

Violence breeds violence, repression brings retaliation, and only a cleansing of our whole society can remove this sickness from our soul. For there is another kind of violence, slower but just as deadly, destructive as the shot or the bomb in the night. This is the violence of institutions: indifference and inaction and slow decay. This is the violence that afflicts the poor, that poisons relations between men because their skin has different colours. This is a slow destruction of a child by hunger, and schools without books and homes without heat in the winter....

We must recognize that this short life can neither be ennobled nor enriched by hatred or revenge. Our lives on this planet are too short and the work to be done too great to let this spirit flourish any longer in our land.

302

Kennedy's words and his candidacy didn't win over his adversaries, such as the FBI's J. Edgar Hoover, whose closest friend and aide, Clyde Tolson, said later that spring, "I hope someone shoots and kills the son of a bitch."

After King's assassination, I stayed in Washington for the next couple of weeks and then at the end of April flew up to Toronto for a speech to the Association of Canadian Advertisers and another in Owen Sound to a joint Kiwanis-Rotary Club meeting. From there, I went back to covering the Kennedy campaign in Indiana where, on May 7, he walloped McCarthy, getting 42 per cent of the vote to McCarthy's 27 per cent.

A few days before the Indiana vote, I had flown to Paris to cover the beginning of the Vietnam peace talks. Two weeks later I returned to Washington for a few days and then flew to Toronto to do a report on the Nebraska primary on April 14. Kennedy beat McCarthy 51 per cent to 31 per cent.

With Indiana and Nebraska under his belt, Kennedy had McCarthy on the run. Then came Oregon. His organization was poor in Oregon, a state with few from his natural constituencies. There was failure in Oregon even among his advance men, those anonymous political warriors who go into cities and towns just ahead of the candidate to organize the "spontaneous" welcomes.

Jerry Bruno, who advanced for both Jack and Bob Kennedy, once told me that the cardinal rule in booking a place to speak was always to get a place just a bit too small so the crowd would overflow and the public and the media would be impressed with the candidate's drawing power. In Oregon, however, there were many empty seats for Kennedy.

While Kennedy struggled in Oregon, McCarthy took off. When a campaign is going well, you can smell it in the attitudes and the feel of those around the candidate. I switched over to McCarthy for a couple of days and saw a much-revived candidate. It was the McCarthy of New Hampshire, not the lacklustre McCarthy of Indiana and Nebraska.

As the day of the Oregon primary neared, at Kennedy headquarters in Portland defeat was considered "possible," something frighteningly new for his young, exuberant campaign workers. On May 28 Kennedy lost, 39 per cent to McCarthy's 45 per cent. It was the first time a Kennedy had ever been defeated at the polls.

Los Angeles, May 29, 1968 ...

California was next and I flew down to Los Angeles to cover the final days of his campaign there. It was a much quieter, more somber Bob Kennedy I saw get off the plane from Oregon the morning after his defeat. His eyes were bloodshot, and his voice weak. "Coming second is not good enough," he told us. Asked how he felt, he shook his slender shoulders, looked down at his feet, and replied, "I feel like the man Abraham Lincoln described who was run out of town on a steel rail and said, 'If it weren't for the honour of it, I'd rather have walked.' " As he spoke, I was reminded of something he had said a couple of years earlier that typified his attitude. "Good luck," he had told me, "is something you make. Bad luck is something you endure."

He previously had refused to have a TV debate in California with McCarthy, but now he was willing. Asked why he had changed his mind, he told us, "Well, that was before Oregon ... anyway, I'm not the same candidate I was before Oregon."

He seemed to perk up a bit as the airport news conference ended and he got ready to campaign through downtown Los Angeles. We ran off to our car to follow him, swinging in just one car away from his and right behind the still photographers' car. We sped in from the airport with only a few waves from the sidewalks, and then we turned off the freeway into downtown.

I had seen a lot of political crowds before, but nothing quite like this one. It was simply apocalyptic. Mayor Sam Yorty of Los Angeles was no friend of Kennedy's and so had provided minimum police escort. But rather than damaging him, it made the Kennedy caravan seem even bigger and more astonishingly exuberant. The sidewalks were jammed to the building walls, with people spilling out into the street and blocking his car as it honked and crept along. Tons of confetti tumbled out of the buildings, splashing into Kennedy's hair and filling his car ankle deep. Hundreds of people shouted, cried, and ran up to his car to touch him. He was moving so slowly through the mass of people, I got out of our car and ran up to walk beside Kennedy's.

He took off his jacket, tucked his loosened tie between his shirt buttons, and stood in the back of his convertible in his shirt sleeves, shaking hands with both hands, waving, laughing, smiling. The hot midday sun poured down and he kept wiping away perspiration on his forehead as well as his damp, tousled forelock. His shirt was soaking wet. Somehow he lost his shoes and he told me later he also lost both of his cufflinks. He would have had his tie taken, too, if he hadn't tucked it into his shirt. His hands were raw red from so much hand-shaking. Pieces of paper and autograph books were thrust at him to sign, which he did in his cramped, indecipherable scrawl made even worse by the jerking car. Some women galloped up to the car to kiss him, much to his embarrassment.

He seemed a bit nervous, too, at being the object of all the adulation.

304

In the car beside him and sometimes walking beside the car were two of his friends and bodyguards, Rafer Johnson, the Olympic decathlon champion, and Roosevelt Grier, the Los Angeles Rams football star. They both seemed overwhelmed by the orgy of enthusiasm all around them, as they tried to protect Kennedy from bodily harm and also tried to clear the way for his car. He didn't say much, and he couldn't be heard very far anyway. I heard him mutter over and over, "Thank you ... thank you very much ... Gee, this is incredible ... thank you ... look out, don't get hurt."

He clearly drew strength from those few blocks of downtown Los Angeles, and when we finally arrived at his hotel, he was utterly exhausted. In wonderment and excitement, he told us, "If I died in Oregon, Los Angeles is resurrection city."

The same astonishing reception continued over the next week as he toured Los Angeles and environs. It continued, too, after he left Los Angeles. He visited a black ghetto in Oakland across the bay from San Francisco, talked with Mexican "stoop labour" – the men and women who pick tomatoes, beans, grapes, and cherries on southern California's farms – and he spoke in town squares between Los Angeles and San Francisco. Everywhere the reaction was the same.

Driving away from one rally our caravan stopped on a highway and Kennedy got out. Some of us started to go after him, but "Rosy" Grier said, "No ... let him alone for a couple of minutes." As much as he loved arguing, kidding, and talking to friends and reporters and knew the value of the adulation he elicited, he also needed to be alone. I watched him walk away from his convertible through the fields off the highway, pick up a piece of grass and chew it, and stop and fold his arms and just stare out across the empty fields. At that moment he seemed so alone and vulnerable. Then, after four or five minutes, he turned, smiled, waved at us, jogged back to the car, and we were off again.

California was critical to him. After Oregon, he had to win here. With Johnson quitting and Humphrey the heir apparent, Kennedy had to knock off McCarthy in California to prove to the Mayor Daleys of the Democratic Party that he was the people's choice and that only he could win against Nixon. California was basically the end of the primary route and from then on he would be concentrating on more direct persuasion of the power brokers in his battle with Humphrey for the nomination. So as the final days of the California primary went by, he drove himself as if there were no tomorrow.

His final campaign swing was a whistle-stop train ride through California's Central Valley from Fresno to Sacramento, talking from the back of his train to farm labourers and small-town Americans. With a CBC camera crew, I went along to watch the campaign conclusion and to do a final interview with him. The media car was in the middle of the train, but I spent much of the trip in Kennedy's car, the last one. It was crowded with politicians, aides, and friends, but most of the time I was the only reporter.

You could talk intensively and even intimately with Kennedy before and after an interview, but when the camera was rolling he often stiffened and was awkward and always called me "Mr. Nash" instead of the customary "Knowlton." He was optimistic that he would win California and his mind was now on Chicago and Hubert Humphrey, whom he always felt was his prime adversary. But he was reluctant to talk much about the future. "I can't ... I don't plan very much ahead. I just can't, you know. Fate is fickle."

He was critical of McCarthy for not going into the ghettos to campaign. "He just likes to take it easier than I'm prepared to do," he said. On Vietnam, he told me, "We just can't continue to support a government in Saigon that doesn't have the support of its own people." He urged a coalition government be formed. He told me Canada (pronouncing it like his brother as "Canader") should be more independent of Washington in its foreign policies. With that, the interview ended, he took off his jacket, and it was back to "Knowlton." As it turned out, it was one of the last television interviews he ever gave.

As the train clacked by Madera, Merced, Turlock, Modesto – one small town after another – it was fascinating to watch Kennedy greet the local politicians. They would get aboard at a stop or two ahead of their area to have their pictures taken with the candidate while he quizzed them about their communities. From my seat at the far end of his car, I watched him give each one a quick handshake, a little nod, and then get right down to his questioning with little or no chatter beforehand.

Then, at each stop, he would get up and go out on the platform of the car with the appropriate local politician and greet 500 or 1,000 or 2,000 supporters shuffling over the tracks behind his railway car. He'd give his standard campaign rhetoric: "Only those who dare to fail greatly can ever achieve greatly" ... "the hottest place in hell is reserved for those who keep quiet in time of moral crisis" ... After sketching his policies, he would say, "Will you help me? ... I've come to ask for your help. Give me your help. Please give me your help." He denounced U.S. "Big Stick" policies, saying, "It doesn't make any sense for us to be policemen to the world."

He'd stand slightly slouched, nod, smile shyly, wave to the crowd.

And at every stop he would tease them and bring in his newly acquired local knowledge. "When I was thinking of running for the presidency, Ethel told me I'd have to come to Turlock because it's the turkey capital of the world. And that's why I'm running today." In a tomato-growing community he pleaded for their votes by noting his ten children and saying, "My family eats more tomatoes than any family I know." He'd hold up a basket of cherries grown in another area and say, "We've been eating these all day."

After the whistle-stop tour with him, I flew back to Toronto to work on a *Newsmagazine* program on the campaign, which was to be aired Tuesday, June 4, the night of the vote. And that night, Kennedy was triumphant. He not only won California, but South Dakota, too, where he beat Humphrey as well as McCarthy. (He'd beaten Humphrey a few weeks earlier in the District of Columbia primary.) Now, McCarthy seemed to be finished and Humphrey was the next target. From our control room at CBC Toronto, I watched on television as Kennedy entered the Ambassador Hotel in Los Angeles and spoke to his cheering supporters. His hands trembled slightly and his deep, hollow eyes suggested a man who was utterly exhausted. With him on the platform were Ethel, Cesar Chavez, a dozen other supporters and friends, and, in fact, almost everybody except his dog Freckles, who also had been along during the campaign and had gotten a lot of publicity. "I want to express my thanks to my dog Freckles. I'm not doing this in the order of importance. I also want to thank my wife Ethel."

Perspiring under the television lights on a hot June night and with the crush of people, he smiled, "Everybody must be dying from the heat." And he added, "We are a great country, an unselfish country, and a compassionate country. I intend to make that the basis for running." Then he looked out over the cheering faces and said in a final salute, "My thanks to all of you and on to Chicago and let's win there."

With Ethel at his side, he ducked out a side entrance, went through the hotel kitchen, and met the .22 calibre bullets of Sirhan Sirhan.

Bob Kennedy's last words – as heard by Paul Grieco, a twenty-one-year-old student and part-time bookkeeper who was an onlooker as Kennedy lay bloodied on the kitchen floor – were: "Is everybody okay?" He died a day later.

"Is everybody okay?" Those, I think, were quintessential Bob Kennedy words: his first concern was always for others.

To me, it was stupefying. First John Kennedy, then Martin Luther King, Jr., and now this. If ever the world seemed to be falling apart, this, I thought, was it. I was personally shaken partly by this accumulation of tragedy, and even more because I had admired him so much. Remembering he was just two years older than I was, I questioned what I had done with my own life, contrasted to the contribution to society he had made. But that night I had to shake off my melancholy as we quickly organized special news programs on the shooting. The next day I flew to New York where the funeral was to take place.

When I met my colleagues, the heartiness and camaraderie of the Kennedy campaign were gone. For many of us, as for many around the world, it was tragic history repeating itself, the same trauma we had gone through four and a half years before. In an almost trancelike state, we reporters went through the motions of checking the size of the crowds, getting details of the mass and burial, and finding out who would be there.

The day before the Saturday funeral New York steamed and stank in ninety-degree heat, but tens of thousands sweated in line for as much as seven hours waiting to pass by his coffin lying in state inside St. Patrick's Cathedral. Pushcart salesmen sold gallons of orange juice, grapefruit juice, and soft drinks. The Red Cross distributed water for free.

By Friday night, an estimated 150,000 had passed by, some touching the purple-draped casket, most crying, some fainting, most in pain, and all wondering, "Why? Why?" I walked up and down the lines, mostly just looking, but sometimes stopping to chat softly. "Such a good man" … "He cared" … "I came because he cared for me" … "Why did it happen?" "Why?" "Why?" "What's wrong with us?"

At noon on Friday I was standing outside the great bronze front doors of the Cathedral when Ethel Kennedy, pregnant with their eleventh child, arrived. The crowd's quiet murmuring stopped as Ethel came up the steps. She was drawn, pale, and seemed somehow thinner and smaller than I remembered her. She came again late Friday night. At 5:00 a.m. Saturday, they closed the Cathedral doors, and still there were thousands waiting.

Later that day I stood outside the Cathedral watching the arrival of the 2,300 guests including President and Mrs. Johnson, all of Kennedy's political rivals from Nixon to Humphrey, six cardinals, six archbishops, the prime ministers of Ireland, Jamaica, and Guayana, and other diplomatic representatives, Hollywood stars, writers, poets, politicians, and the Kennedy family.

Many of the mourners had made a similar trip four and a half years earlier. Once again, Cardinal Cushing, now seventy-two, was there. And again, a flag-draped coffin. And again, the painful eulogy.

The voice of the last Kennedy brother, Ted, broke as he read his text. Off to the side, I noticed the one man Bob Kennedy sought to impress more than any other with his vote-getting appeal, the man he had said was "the ballgame" in the battle for the nomination, Chicago Mayor Richard Daley. Tears poured down his mournful old Irish face.

That afternoon a funeral train took Kennedy's body to Washington, where he was buried near his brother in Arlington National Cemetery in a grave marked by a simple white cross.

Miami Beach, July 29, 1968 ...

By mid-June, the American presidential primary season was over and backroom jockeying began for the two conventions. With Kennedy dead and McCarthy a spent force, Humphrey seemed a cinch for the Democrats. Nixon was far ahead of his Republican rivals. The Republican Party convention of 1968 marked one of the most remarkable political comebacks in American history. By the time Richard Nixon reached Miami his nomination was a sure thing.

Back in November, 1962, few commentators, myself included, would have thought it possible. His 1962 campaign for the governorship of California was his most humiliating defeat before Watergate. It was during that campaign that I clearly saw the worst side of the man. A painful vignette comes to mind.

A motel room just outside Los Angeles: Nixon's news aide, Herb Klein, had arranged an interview for me, and my camera crew and I were waiting for Nixon to return from a campaign rally. Our cameras were ready and lights set up when we heard cheers outside, horns honking, and brakes squealing as Nixon arrived. I watched him from the window, smiling, waving, shaking hands, and smiling some more as he moved toward the motel room.

In he came, the cheers ringing in his ears, and suddenly the smile fell off his face. Not a word was said. He looked to the floor and not at any of us. Finally Klein said we were from the CBC and were going to do an interview with him as they had discussed earlier. His small dark eyes flashed fire, his mouth tightened, and his face flushed. "Shit," he shouted. "I told you ... no interviews! Goddamned idiot. No interviews. How stupid can you be?" I could still hear people cheering outside.

Klein, a gentle, veteran San Diego newsman and long-time, long-suffering Nixon associate, quietly said, "You did agree earlier, and now they're here."

"Shit!" said Nixon, "I never did!" Then, turning to me, Nixon said, "Well, let's get it over with."

I quickly got out my notes, the lights went on, the cameras rolled, and as I asked my first question, suddenly the smile was back and he purred, "Well, Knowlton, you've been covering us for some time for my good Canadian friends, and you know ...." It was the oily smile of a snake charmer. And during the interview he'd look at me as I asked a question and then turn away and give his answer to the camera lens. When he finished, he'd turn back to me for the next question.

On we went for five or ten minutes. I said thanks, the lights went out, and so did the Nixon smile. He shook hands limply, told Klein, "Come in here!" as he went into an adjoining room, and we got the hell out of there before what we figured would be another embarrassing verbal tongue-lashing. What appalled me was not that Nixon blew his stack, but the sadistic way he bawled out his own deputy in front of us.

After the 1960 presidential election defeat, to most of us Nixon seemed politically dead. But he brooded only briefly before planning his resurrection. He had no particular desire to be Governor of California and state politics bored him, but he thought the governorship would be a good launching platform for another presidential try in 1964 or 1968. So he built a team, including those who would be with him to Watergate: Haldeman, Ehrlichman, and Ziegler.

It was, however, an almost suicidal, kamikaze campaign. I followed part of it and he was dogged every step of the way by his defeat by Kennedy, by his naked presidential ambitions, and by his preoccupation with international and national issues instead of state concerns.

He was dogged also by an old scandal involving a highly questionable $200,000 loan made to his brother by Howard Hughes. I remember one rally in San Francisco's Chinatown where Nixon was greeted by Chinese music, elaborately costumed dancers, firecrackers, and huge banners across the street carried by young people. The banners were in Chinese and I noticed a number of people snickering as they saw them. Rather than hailing Nixon, the banners said, "What about the Hughes loan?" and "No to Nixon." I learned later that some Democratic "dirty trick" prankster had supplied the banners and signs to unsuspecting, non-Chinese-speaking Nixon supporters who, of course, didn't have a clue as to what they actually said.

By the way he acted, you sensed Nixon knew he was going to be beaten. It infuriated him because it was one thing to narrowly lose the presidency to the charismatic magic of John Kennedy, quite another to lose the California governorship to an amiable but bumbling Pat Brown. But lose he did. He tried to hide his hurt, saying "It's like being bitten by a mosquito after being bitten by a rattlesnake."

310

His bitterness and remorse burst through, however, when he held his "last press conference" the day after the election. It was one more showdown in his three-decade running battle with the media, a battle that had begun with his dirty congressional campaign of 1946 and would end only with Watergate.

I watched the conference on television from New York where, the night before, Don Minifie and I had reported his loss in a CBC news special on the U.S. mid-term elections. Now, unshaven and haggard, he faced the cameras and the reporters: "As I leave you, I want you to think just how much you're going to be missing. You won't have Nixon to kick around any more because, gentlemen, this is my last press conference." He snarled out the words in an astonishing display of bad temper.

A couple of years later in a speech at the annual Gridiron Club Dinner with Washington correspondents, he began by saying, "My friends in the press ... if I have any ...." He meant it as a joke, but it wasn't really funny. We knew he despised us but the extent of that loathing wasn't publicly revealed until we listened to the Watergate tapes.

After California, he really did seem to be through with politics. *Time* magazine said, "Barring a miracle, Nixon's public career has ended." With his remarkable resilience, however, he began working on that miracle. He moved to New York, "the fast track" as he called it, and became a big-time Manhattan lawyer. He travelled the world, ostensibly on behalf of his principal client, Pepsi-Cola, but always finding time for well-publicized meetings with presidents, prime ministers, chancellors, and kings. Back home, he criss-crossed the United States, addressing hundreds of Republican fund-raising meetings and collecting political IOUs for future use.

He wrote articles, gave lectures, and wrote his book, *Six Crises*. He flirted with trying for the Republican presidential nomination in 1964. But it was too soon after his defeats and the mood of the party was too conservative even for Nixon. But he carefully positioned himself as a middleman between the extreme conservatism of Goldwater and the liberal conservatism of Rockefeller. Then he worked hard in the 1964 campaign, visiting thirty-five states and making hundreds of speeches.

He emerged from the Goldwater defeat unscathed and having rebuilt much of his support. And he had now staked out new ground as a peacemaker and healer within the party. In just over four years he had finally come back to being recognized by Republican leaders across the country as the national leader of the party. So he looked to 1968.

Ronald Reagan and Nelson Rockefeller were also looking to 1968. And that was ideal for Nixon. It put him exactly where he wanted to be: right in the middle of the party between Reagan's conservatism and Rockefeller's liberalism. Neither of them really had a chance. Nor did Michigan Governor George Romney and a few others who also had presidential ambitions.

Romney was victimized by his own foot-in-mouth predilections when he admitted he was "brainwashed" by the U.S. Army about Vietnam. I once interviewed him while we went jogging together one cold spring morning in Michigan. My cameraman sat in the back of a panel truck, his feet dangling over the edge of the gate just in front of us as Romney and I puffed along city streets for a couple of miles. He was a nice man, scrupulously honest, didn't drink anything stronger than cocoa, was well-intentioned, and looked good. But he never had a chance against Nixon. He knew it and withdrew before the New Hampshire primary vote.

In New Hampshire, Nixon had the field pretty much to himself. One man did pop up to oppose Nixon in New Hampshire, though, and that was Harold Stassen, who chased the presidency first in 1948 and subsequently with determined but boring regularity. In his later years he started wearing a wig so badly shaped it looked like a cat up there ready to leap. I watched him scamper about New Hampshire in 1968 in his perennial but hopeless quest. The one-time "boy governor" of Minnesota gave new meaning to the word "dull."

In the 1950s, Stassen had been a mid-level Republican mover and shaker, a liberal gadfly who once sought to dump Nixon as Eisenhower's vice-president. He had an unquenchable ambition to be president, an overwhelming self-confidence that he could do the job, and absolutely no support whatever among the voters or the party. Undeterred, unfinanced, and uninvited, he nevertheless came into New Hampshire for his lonely destiny in 1968. He was excessively grateful when any reporter spent a day with him. When I did, it was the longest day of my life. Main-streeting with Stassen was agonizing.

People were suspicious of this sombre, tall, grey-coated and grey-hatted, moon-faced soul who wanted to talk to them. Mostly he spoke to single individuals because people didn't turn up at meetings. He was left of centre in the Republican Party, a man filled with desire to do good and a woeful arrogance that he was the best man to be president. He kept on trying and in 1980 I got from him a poster saying, "Stassen Can Beat Carter." He even announced he was a candidate in 1984.

I was in New Hampshire primarily to follow McCarthy, but I peeled off for a few days to cover Nixon, too. At his campaign kickoff in a hotel meeting room he joked with reporters, standing on a wobbly chair, looking around and smiling broadly, saying, "Gentlemen, this is not my last press conference."

New Hampshire was the first time we glimpsed the "New Nixon." He no longer seemed to be the "rocking, socking" campaigner who slashed his way through the opposition. He was witty and relaxed as he took the unfamiliar high road. But the new facade couldn't hide the man. Backstage at a night rally I saw him abusing a campaign worker for something that had gone wrong. Later, in Wisconsin, I watched him tear into a local worker because the band had played the wrong entrance music for him. But for the most part, until nearly the end of the 1968 election campaign, the facade remained in place. He was different, and his campaign was different. It was the most controlled campaign I've ever seen. That Teutonic overlord of organization, Bob Haldeman, ran the tight Nixon ship. He exposed the candidate to the media as little as possible. Few news conferences, no mainstreeting, and controlled meetings and television – that was the Haldeman-Nixon ticket for success. Occasionally, he would call a quick news conference and once in a while grant a brief interview.

And it worked. By isolating himself from inquiring reporters, Nixon avoided mistakes, troublesome off-the-cuff remarks, and provocative comments. He swept through New Hampshire in triumph, and then Wisconsin and every single primary he entered.

During the primaries he would not do a televised interview for us but was willing to talk off the record. I spoke to him once in a Holiday Inn motel room in Manchester, N.H., and once on a plane flying to Wisconsin. Conversation with Nixon always began awkwardly. He was a shy person with anyone other than an intimate. After shaking hands, there would usually be silence for a moment or two, a forced smile, and then he'd say something about the weather or a football game, or baseball. He had little social grace and was clearly uncomfortable in getting a conversation going. He would jump from weather to sports to "nice" Canadians he'd known and back to weather again. Only after I finally put a substantial question about politics or foreign policy would the awkward tension disappear and he would seem at ease.

Ironically, given their political and personal polarity, Richard Nixon and Robert Kennedy had the same problem in starting a conversation with a relative stranger. Both were basically shy, introverted men in a business of loquacious extroverts. Kennedy was, in a way, even worse because he had little or no small talk at all and wouldn't talk about the weather or other such inconsequential things. At the beginning of a conversation he would stare at his feet in silence. Nixon, on the other hand, would talk nervously and wildly about almost any trivial thing to avoid a silence while Kennedy just kept quiet, leaving it to you to get things going. I wondered more than once what the first moments of a conversation between Nixon and Robert Kennedy would be like, one nervously chattering about the weather and football and the other staring at his feet.

In private conversation, Nixon constantly referred back to the lessons he had learned in defeat and in triumph, reliving the highs and lows of his life. "I'm a very pragmatic person in politics," he told me on the flight to Wisconsin. "I'm really a fatalist." He said to me that when he was a boy his mother had wanted him to be a Quaker missionary in Central America – as improbable a career as I could imagine for Nixon.

Even these private conversations were no more specific than his public vagueness, except when he started reminiscing about old campaigns. He often spoke of how "tough" you have to be as a political leader. Indirectly saying how tough he was, he admiringly quoted Harry Truman's maxim: "If you can't stand the heat, get out of the kitchen."

He had an encyclopedic knowledge of American politics. And he was insatiably curious about how other politicians did things. He was especially curious about our parliamentary system. He felt the leader had more power in the parliamentary system, particularly if the party in power had a big majority. But he felt the American system of choosing a leader was more democratic. And he said he preferred also the so-called checks and balances provided by the three independent branches of government in the U.S. – the Executive, the Legislative, and the Judicial.

After the primaries, he appeared on podiums, in parades, and on television, but most of us never again were alone with him. The logistics made it difficult for it to be otherwise and, in any event, that's the way he preferred it. By the time of the Republican Convention in Miami Beach not only Haldeman was "controlling" Nixon, but so too was that one-time Disneyland tour guide and Mickey Mouse flack who now served as Nixon's news aide, Ron Ziegler. Ziegler was capable and, above all, loyal. With reporters he was usually evasive, defensive, and protective of Nixon. Unlike Herb Klein, he was no barstool buddy of journalists. Altogether, Ziegler suited Nixon just fine.

314

Rockefeller played Hamlet in 1968, dilly-dallying through the spring about whether to be or not to be a candidate and finally deciding to be one only at the end of April when it was too late. He hoped for a win at the convention even if he didn't enter the primaries, a forlorn hope as the Nixon steamroller flattened all opposition. By late spring, Reagan, too, was making presidential noises, first coyly denying he was interested as he criss-crossed the country making speeches and holding rallies. He didn't formally declare himself until the last minute. Although he had a lot of southern and conservative support, it was just too late, the primaries were over, and Nixon was an easy winner.

During late June and early July I had spent most of my time in Washington with quick side trips to assignments in the Bahamas, New York, and Toronto, and to Montreal for a speech. In mid-July, I was in Honolulu for the Johnson-Thieu meeting postponed from April, and then back to Toronto for several news programs. Now, at the end of July, I was in a hot and steamy Miami Beach for the Republican Convention.

Never before had I seen a convention run so slickly, smoothly, and successfully. There always is more decorum in Republican Conventions than at the rowdy, raucous Democratic get-togethers, but Miami Beach was a textbook case of organizational efficiency. I spent half my time covering the convention itself. The other half, I spent covering the race riots that broke out six miles away in the black section of Miami and Vietnam protesters marching up and down outside the convention hall. They were only a foretaste of what would happen at the Democratic Convention in late August.

The black riots – in which three blacks were shot dead, snipers fired from rooftops, and hundreds of fires were set – seemed to bother Nixon not a whit. At the end of the convention, as he and Spiro Agnew stood triumphant on the platform looking into a sea of jubilantly confident Republican faces, I recall being saddened as I watched the flag-waving, cheering delegates from my vantage point high in the rafters of the auditorium. The "New Nixon," it seemed to me, was the "Old Nixon" in a different package. And unsavoury stories about Agnew were already circulating among reporters. The "New Nixon" was still a man of situational ethics and cutthroat tactics, a brilliant but ruthless opportunist. I was drawn from these thoughts by the political cacophony before me and the sudden eruption of "Buckle Down Winsocki," the Nixon campaign tune I'd come to loathe after hearing it at every one of his primary campaign stops.

His acceptance speech was a flag-draped compilation of what he had been saying to "the folks" in the primaries and which we had come to call "The Speech." For the convention, he added a touch of Lincoln, invoked his Quaker mother who, he said, wept when he went off to war, and noted that Eisenhower was hospitalized with a heart attack. He closed by saying, "Let's win this one for Ike!"

At that point, I felt Hubert Humphrey would win the presidency, provided he had a united Democratic Party behind him at Chicago.

Chicago, August 23, 1968 ...

I flew back to Washington on August 12 and then up to Toronto the next day to discuss our coverage of the upcoming Democratic Convention, then on to New York. At the end of the week I was back in Washington on what my date book calls an "Ike watch," as former President Eisenhower lay near death at the Walter Reed Army Hospital in Washington. He survived, however, to see Nixon elected and sworn into office. (He died in March of 1969.) In the midst of the "Ike watch," the Russians invaded Czechoslovakia and that meant a tornado of work reporting on the American reactions. A few days later I was off to Chicago.

Just about every crackpot in the country came to Chicago that August, along with thousands of deeply concerned citizens. There were rallies of up to 100,000 Vietnam protesters, black-power street marches, and even a plan by what was billed as the "Bare Breast for Peace Brigade" for a thousand women to march topless through downtown Chicago streets. The march was subsequently cancelled. Scores of bombing threats and riot plans were uncovered. Most were pipe dreams of the fanatics or products of overactive police imagination.

There were 6,000 police on duty, 5,000 National Guardsmen, 6,000 regular Army soldiers, 200 firemen, including bomb disposal experts, and thousands of Secret Service, FBI, and other security men. Altogether, about 25,000 men were on patrol and on guard, and they were itching for a fight. Preparations were made to handle mobs, marches, riots, snipers, fires, and bombs. The convention hall was an armed camp. A high fence was thrown up around it, topped by barbed wire. Police sharpshooters were stationed on the roof. Tanks were parked menacingly nearby. For blocks from the site, manhole covers were sealed. Helicopters constantly circled overhead.

For reporters, it was war coverage, not political coverage. My colleagues and I took hard hats and gas masks, as well as our typewriters. As I travelled from one demonstration to another, I pretty soon began to hate the Chicago cops, a sentiment shared by most of the reporters. While there was some violence, most of the protesters were peaceful, though loud. Nevertheless, the cops, flailing big black riot sticks, repeatedly cracked heads and smashed arms and shoulders. The police attacked us, too. Photographers had cameras smashed. Reporters were shoved, punched, and beaten.

There were killings and beatings, bombings and fires. The police did the former, the mob the latter. The worst police riot I saw – and that's what it was, an authorized police riot – was in a park not far from the convention headquarters hotel, the Conrad Hilton. I watched as sky-blue helmeted, shield-carrying cops charged into a peaceful march of several thousand anti-Vietnam War protesters. "Kill the Commies ... get the bastards," the policemen screamed as they charged, crashing their black sticks into young heads; some of them giggled as blood ran down the youngsters' faces. They smacked men in the testicles and women on the breasts. Jeeps with barbed wire attached to the front end were used as a crowd-control device and half a dozen of them would drive in close formation pressing slowly into the crowd and cutting into people as they went. It was Berlin, 1936, not Chicago, 1968.

I heard one youngster cry out, "For God's sake, stop!" and ran to where he had fallen. Suddenly something crashed into my head and I fell beside the kid. I was momentarily stunned and then I felt a sticky oozing on my head. When I gingerly touched the spot, my hand came away bloody and I staggered off and sat down a couple of blocks away. Somebody passed by and said, "You'd better get that looked at."

I was embarrassed at what had happened and was reluctant to go to the hospital. But blood kept oozing and my dizziness continued, so I flagged a cab and went to the nearest emergency ward. It wasn't bad and needed only a few stitches. But, rightly or wrongly, I felt it had been unprofessional of me to get personally involved in the riot and I sneaked back to my hotel room, not saying a word to my colleagues. I never knew who hit me, but the police were the only ones I saw with clubs. Nor was I the only reporter injured in the outbreaks. Altogether, sixty-three of my fellow workers were reported physically attacked by Chicago's finest.

The stench and sting of police tear gas hung over downtown Chicago and in the Conrad Hilton Hotel the foul smell of protesters' stink bombs permeated the lobbies and corridors. And yet, I went out again the next night and this time found a "good cop." I thought it prudent to follow closely as this captain walked along directing his men and talking with the protesters. After my experience the previous night, it was remarkable to hear him say over and over, "Now take it easy, boys. Be careful. Be careful. No rough stuff. They've got rights, too,

317

you know. Take it easy. Take it easy.'' Too bad there weren't more like him.

The McCarthy headquarters was at the Hilton and the cops claimed the young McCarthy supporters were helping the rioters and throwing things out the window at the police. Most of the McCarthy youngsters sympathized with the protesters in the streets and some joined them, but I never saw anything being thrown from the windows. One night, with the convention nearly over, a hundred or more police broke into the hotel lobby, scrambled up to the McCarthy floor, and went from room to room smashing heads. McCarthy later came to see his bleeding and bruised supporters, many of whom were wrapped in ripped bedsheets being used as bandages. He was in tears, one of the rare times he displayed his emotions instead of his intellect.

The scene inside the convention hall was almost as bad as the one outside. Arthur Schlesinger has labelled the convention as ''the politics of frustration.'' Many of the delegates certainly were frustrated.

We called the building ''Fort Daley.'' To get in you had to go through lines of police and soldiers, past the sharpshooters, the barbed wire, and the jeeps. Accreditation was checked four times and you were searched. Inside, you were constantly asked to show your credentials. The security guards pushed and shoved media and delegates, and fistfights occasionally broke out. Some delegates, including prominent ones such as New York Congressman Paul O'Dwyer, were taken into custody on the convention floor for not ''moving along'' fast enough. Reporters were harrassed. CBS reporter Mike Wallace was socked in the jaw by one cop, and Dan Rather was punched in the stomach by another. At one point Walter Cronkite looked on aghast and told his audience, ''We've got a bunch of thugs here.''

The evil mood of the convention was illustrated best when Senator Abraham Ribicoff denounced the ''Gestapo'' tactics of the Chicago police. In one of the most memorable images from the convention, a red-faced, spittle-dribbling Mayor Daley leapt up to scream ''Fuck off!'' in response. His shout was taken up by Illinois delegates and then by the gallery, packed with Daley supporters. Other delegates screamed back, especially those from California, and Ribicoff looked down at Daley twenty feet in front of him, saying, ''He can't take it. He can't take it.''

I happened to be on the convention floor when the outburst occurred, and ran over to where the Illinois delegates were sitting. Daley cupped his hands to his mouth, screaming the expletive over and over again. He and his supporters were laughing one minute and contorted in anger the next. Signs went up in the galleries proclaiming, ''We love Mayor

Daley." Later, I found out they were hoisted by Chicago policemen in plain clothes. Then the band struck up and eventually the turmoil subsided. But no amount of sweet music could take away the sour taste of the convention. At one point I shook my head in wondering amusement as the band played "Chicago, Chicago, That Toddlin' Town" and "Happy Days Are Here Again." It wasn't, and they weren't.

Away from all the chaos, my old acquaintanceship with Pierre Salinger came in handy at this convention. Thanks to him and to the persuasiveness of Don Cameron, who had come from Toronto to produce our TV coverage of the convention, we actually got inside Senator George McGovern's campaign, which Salinger was masterminding. We were able to film McGovern's backers' secret meetings and strategy sessions.

Ironically, McGovern's planning all took place in the original "smoke-filled room" at the Blackstone Hotel where the phrase was coined in 1920. In that year Warren Harding came out of the same room as a presidential candidate.

This first run at the presidency by McGovern was an eye opener for me. The South Dakota senator was. a liberal and a vigorous anti-Vietnam dove. I had spent some time with him years before at the start of the Kennedy administration when he was head of Kennedy's Food For Peace organization and found him dedicated but not especially assertive. This was particularly true now that he suddenly and unexpectedly found himself in presidential politics. His backers were basically the Kennedy people like Salinger and Ted Sorensen, and some thought McGovern was a stalking horse for Senator Ted Kennedy but others genuinely wanted McGovern.

Late one afternoon I was sitting talking with Sorensen, who was writing a speech for the candidate. The senator came into the room, and after we chatted briefly I moved off to the corner. McGovern took off his jacket and stood as Sorensen lectured him on what he should and should not do as a candidate. The senator nodded vigorously and continually, lapping up his instructions with "Uh ... uh ... huh, uh-huh." Occasionally he would say, "Couldn't I ..." but Sorensen would cut him off, saying, "No ... let me lay it out." There was no doubt who was puppet and who was puppeteer.

With our cameras, we would go in and out of meetings, and sometimes I would be there by myself just watching and taking notes. The rooms were not only smoke-filled, but liquid-filled, too, with Scotch, bourbon, gin, and vodka, along with buckets of melting ice. In one the organizers of the McGovern campaign were working in shirt sleeves,

319

puffing cigars and cigarettes, sometimes shouting, sometimes laughing, and always arguing.

Another room was usually empty except when a delegate was being wooed. It was neat and quiet. The corridors were filled with messenger boys, hangers-on, and bellhops passing by with ice buckets, club sandwiches, coffee, and soft drinks.

For Salinger, it was a week of two or three hours' sleep a night, and the rest of the time drinking, eating, and breathing politics. It was days of hamburgers, sandwiches, a few beers, late night Scotches, and talk, talk, talk. His objective was to get a liberal platform, especially a dove approach on Vietnam. He wanted also to make as strong an effort as possible for the nomination, realizing it would be a miracle if it went to McGovern.

Salinger, Sorensen, and other Kennedyites, with the support of the McCarthy people, were successful in moderating the platform on Vietnam, although they didn't get as much as they wanted. Their problem was Lyndon Johnson, who was blazing mad at anything he perceived as a desertion from total loyalty to his policies. He never came to Chicago, but Johnsonian rockets aimed at thwarting the doves were fired endlessly from the White House to the convention. There was less success with the McGovern presidential gambit. They had picked up much of the Bob Kennedy strength in California and a few other states, but the Humphrey people were just too powerful.

And the Humphrey organization played tough. At the McGovern suite I chatted with one Washington state delegate who was totally committed to McGovern. But he couldn't vote for him. He told me why while he was waiting to explain his dilemma to Senator Ribicoff, a McGovern official.

"They threatened me," he said. "They'll publicly embarrass me. And they'll get me fired."

"Who will?" I asked.

"Humphrey's people," he said, as tears brimmed in his eyes. "I want to go to McGovern but I just can't. I'm a traitor to my conscience but I've got to keep my job for my wife and kids." So, the Humphrey steamroller flattened everything and everybody.

There was one moment of dignity during the Chicago debacle that stands out for me in stark contrast to the madness that seemed to be everywhere. It came on the final night of the convention when the delegates united to pay tribute to Bob Kennedy by showing a thirty-two-minute film on his life. Four years before, his brother had been similarly honoured and now, as then, there were cheers and tears as the film ended and the lights came up.

But then, suddenly, something wonderful happened. The cheers and the tears turned into singing, and from thousands of throats came the words of the "Battle Hymn of the Republic." With each line the singing became louder and louder. Magically, the fractious delegates had united in tribute.

I was standing just outside the entrance to the convention floor, listening and remembering. I felt I simply had to get onto the convention floor to share that moment, but I had left my floor pass back at the bureau. Nonetheless, I walked by a guard who barked, "You've got no pass!" Tears were brimming in my eyes and I looked at him with such ferocity that, without my saying a word, he said, "Oh ... okay," and let me walk out onto the floor.

All around me the delegates and observers were on an emotional binge, singing with more pride than I'd ever heard before. It wasn't mournful, but rather a chilling, defiant, last hurrah for the Kennedys. Or maybe it was a kind of Irish wake. As I stood there, I couldn't help thinking of a telegram the Ted Kennedy headquarters had received a couple of days before from someone in Atlanta, Georgia. "Roses are red, violets are blue," it said, "we got two Kennedys, and we'll get you." And I wondered why anyone would go into politics with all its dangers, heartbreaks, and demands. As I stood there on the convention floor bathed in the singing and cheering, my mind reeled back to the Bob Kennedy I had seen and come to know slightly over the previous dozen years. But I was sharply brought back to the present by the sight of Mayor Daley.

Instead of the tear-stained man in agony whom I'd seen at St. Patrick's Cathedral, there was a red-faced, shouting, fist-waving hooligan trying to stop the singing and cheering for Kennedy. Daley had thrown his support to Humphrey and perhaps saw this emotional outpouring for Bob Kennedy as a threat to his control of the convention. My own tears stopped and anger, even hatred, swept over me as I watched Daley.

I must have reached some kind of emotional overload; I had to get out of that hall. I pushed my way through the crowded floor, glowered at the guard who had let me onto the floor, and went for a walk outside. As the intensity of feelings subsided I began feeling guilty at having let my emotions override my professionalism – the distance a reporter is supposed to put between himself and his story. I worried about it for a while, walked a bit more, and then said to myself, "To hell with it!" In this case, I didn't give a damn about my failure.

Washington, D.C., November 5, 1968 ...

In the end it came down to the wire, but in the aftermath of the Chicago convention, Richard Nixon's election appeared to be a certainty. Hubert Horatio Humphrey, the "Happy Warrior," had won his lifelong ambition to be the Democratic presidential nominee. But this apostle of "the politics of joy" had won only the remains of the party that had committed suicide that August in Chicago. He came out of the convention fifteen points behind Nixon in the opinion polls with the blacks and the liberals against him and a party organization split asunder. With the deaths of Martin Luther King, Jr., and Robert Kennedy, many blacks simply gave up on the system and either stayed home or actively fought against it.

Humphrey was once a liberal "young Turk" but had become Lyndon Johnson's "Little Sir Echo," and he was paying for it among the blacks, the young, and the liberals. Before getting the presidential nomination, he had told reporters, "You remember that old song, 'Everything I am I owe to my mother'? Well, I've changed that to 'Everything I am I owe to my President.' "

After the convention, I flew back to Washington and one day later flew up to New York to cover Humphrey's first days of campaigning. "I'm going to march up Fifth Avenue and right into the White House," he told a New York rally at the start of the campaign against Nixon. But it was going to be a long march. I watched him do all the right things at the New York rally ... holding babies, kissing beauty queens, slapping backs, and smiling non-stop. Nothing worked. Nothing worked then, or for weeks.

It was sad to see the ebullient, talkative, and friendly Humphrey so hurt by the pallid public response, doubly so because he was well-liked by reporters. The previous March at the Radio-Television Correspondents Annual Dinner in Washington, I had taken along my boss from Toronto, Marce Munro, who was head of news and public affairs for the CBC. After the dinner we went upstairs in the hotel to visit the various rooms where different news organizations held parties long into the night. At the NBC suite we chatted with network reporters and executives and Vice-President Humphrey came in. I walked over to him, said "Hello, Mr. Vice-President," and I introduced my boss. Knowing a good chance to do a correspondent a favour, he immediately smiled broadly and shook my boss's hand, saying, "You know, Knowlton is one of the best ..." and on he went for a couple of minutes of exaggerated and wonderfully satisfying flattery.

Another indication of Humphrey's thoughtfulness to reporters was

322

his habit of sending a thank-you note to reporters after a campaign swing – with a carbon copy to our editors. He wrote to me near the end of the 1966 congressional election campaign and said, "As I start out on my last campaign swing of 1966, I thought I would let you know how much I appreciated having you on our recent trips. I hope we can travel again together in the future but under less hectic circumstances. Very best wishes, Hubert H."

He was also wonderful to interview for radio or television in that he would give you just what you wanted in terms of the length of his answer. I'd interviewed him as a senator and a few times as Vice-President. Each time, he'd say, "Look, do you want a thirty-second comment, forty-five seconds, a minute or what? Just tell me and I'll do it." And he would, neatly packaging his answer into the desired length. That way he knew you would use every word and so he was able to largely control what was used on air.

But on the campaign trail of 1968, nothing seemed to be working for him. The crowds were thin and enthusiasm thinner still. He faced not only the united Republicans, but deserting fellow Democrats who picketed his rallies, denounced his support of LBJ on Vietnam, and carried signs, "Dump the Hump." Worse still, racist George Wallace was getting 21 per cent in the public opinion polls and Humphrey was close to being third behind Nixon and Wallace.

The Alabama governor was a shifty-eyed, slick-haired, street-smart demagogue who parlayed his white supremacist hatred into national support. Over the years, I talked with Wallace perhaps a dozen times, both when he was governor and when he was running for president.

During his primary campaign for the 1964 Democratic Party presidential nomination, he told me, "Ah'm gonna shake 'em up all over this country." He withdrew from the primaries before the convention but in 1968 he went all the way as a third-party candidate.

He gained surprising support not only among many white southerners, but among northerners, too, mostly the "hard hat" constituency (many of whom, oddly enough, had supported Bob Kennedy earlier). They were worried about blacks taking their jobs, suspicious of authority, and hated all intellectuals. Wallace understood the fears and prejudices of his constituency and played on them with grotesque oversimplications.

Over and over again at rallies, whether in Madison Square Garden in New York, in Dallas, or in Baltimore, I heard him offer the same message. He attacked "pointy-headed professuhs" and the "uppidy nigras" who were taking over the country, the Commies, Reds, and liberals who he said ran the government, and those who he said would "mongrelize" the races through integration. He once called a judge who sought to uphold the law "a low-down, carpetbaggin', scalla-waggin', race-mixin' liar." With each salvo of invective, roars of approval would echo through the meeting halls and auditoriums. His supporters idolized him and, agreeing with his own characterization, saw him as the last champion of Anglo-Saxon Christianity. For them and for him, the campaign was a crusade – a crusade of hate.

I remember chatting with Wallace in his motel room at the end of a rally just outside Baltimore. Off the platform, he claimed he wasn't really anti-black and said some of his best friends were Negroes. "Even," he smiled, "even I like reporters sometimes, too." He told me the Ku Klux Klan consisted mainly of "poor boys who couldn't get into the country club." But what I most remember is my impression of the man – a pint-sized character full of hostility, his crafty, small eyes darting back and forth. As I left, he smiled in an oily way and said, "Now, y'all come back, heah! And just see for yo'self how these northern people love me just as much as my southern folks do."

Wallace in 1968 chose General Curtis LeMay as his vice-presidential running mate, a World War II hero who had successfully run the Berlin blockade airlift and had been Chief of Staff of the U.S. Air Force. He was also a nut on the subject of communism. His nickname was "Old Iron Pants" and he was the "hawk of all hawks," advocating preventive war and the use of nuclear weapons.

At his first news conference the meaty, cigar-chomping general told us, "I think there are many times when it would be most efficient to use nuclear weapons." He later expanded on this, telling us, "I don't believe the world would end if we exploded a nuclear weapon." Why, he said, he'd seen a film of the island of Bikini where there had been twenty nuclear weapons tests. "The fish are all back in the lagoons." As we scribbled incredulously, he continued: "The coconut trees are growing coconuts ... the birds are back. As a matter of fact, everything is about the same except the land crabs ... there's a question about whether you should eat a land crab or not." He added a final comment about rats. "They're bigger, fatter, and healthier than they ever were before." Then he told us he was worried about being misquoted. "I'll be damned lucky," he said, "if I don't appear as a drooling idiot."

Even Wallace was appalled. I was told by a Wallace aide later over a drink that Wallace had told LeMay, "Keep your bowels open and your mouth shut." LeMay did for most of the time after his first news conference.

At one point during the 1968 campaign, politicians and political observers feared Wallace might get as many as 15 million votes running on his third-party ticket and be powerful enough to deeply influence, if not dominate, the man elected president as Joseph McCarthy had influenced Eisenhower after 1952. In the end, Wallace got about nine million votes, still frighteningly large but not large enough to give him the power he sought. Certainly he scared a lot of Democrats and Republicans. During the campaign some politicians skewed their own rhetoric to try to appeal to the Wallace supporters.

While Wallace sucked away Humphrey's white votes, black votes were being lost, too, to fringe candidates such as Eldridge Cleaver, a leader of the Black Panthers and a presidential candidate for the Peace and Freedom Party. Cleaver was surely the most publicly profane presidential candidate in American history. At one meeting in New York City I covered, he attracted 1,500 people who roared with approval at his profane blasts at the "establishment." He used every conceivable swear word and some inconceivable ones. In my report on Cleaver I had an extraordinarily difficult time trying to find one sentence of his with less than three or four "fucks" in it. When I talked to him after one rally in New York, I told him of these language problems. He laughed and said, "Fuck, man, the dirtiest word in the English language is not *fuck*, it's *napalm*."

While Humphrey struggled, Nixon had been rolling ahead with his "zero mistake" campaign, a dull, boring, efficient tour of the country. He was on time everywhere, his appearances were well-controlled, and his organization was perfect. He lived a spartan existence when campaigning, and shaved twice and sometimes three times a day. It didn't matter, for even after a shave he still had a five o'clock shadow. He drank little – nursing a Scotch and soda or two but no more – in sharp contrast to later Watergate-era stories about his heavy drinking.

It was the same story whenever I followed him. His organization made sure by careful scheduling and co-operative police that demonstrations were minimal. Even in Chicago, there was only a handful of anti-war protesters, and no hippies or yippies. The rallies consisted of well-dressed, mostly older people with bands blaring, balloons floating, a couple of warm-up speakers, and then the ten or fifteen minutes of Nixon platitudes. Occasionally Nixon's daughter Tricia would speak briefly, as she did at Chicago, ending her comments with, "So, please elect my daddy."

In his campaigning, he was forever telling audiences about his mother's apple pie, how he was a grocer's son, how he'd had to wear his brother's shoes, how he'd worked after school, how he admired his old football coach, his teacher, his minister, and his "courageous, loyal wife," Pat. He would speak of his childhood dreams of "far away places.'' It was calculated cornball politics for ''the folks,'' delivered with unctuous solemnity. Even when he spoke on public issues, he was simplistic, patronizing, and vague. He hinted at a ''secret plan'' he had to end the Vietnam War, but he deflected all questions about it, and in conversation with him you sensed he had no specific plan at all. Nixon seemed to be all sail and no boat.

And yet, in quiet, reflective moments he could be impressively articulate in setting out his ideas. Flying over the Midwest during the campaign, I sat with him once at the front of the plane, spellbound as he spoke of the complexities of current world problems. He knew the leaders and the issues, the details and the nuances. It was a fascinating twenty minutes of geopolitical brilliance, and a rare glimpse of the best qualities of the man behind the mask.

Inevitably, reporters following a presidential campaign hear the same words, the same phrases, and the same jokes over and over and over again. And this was especially true of the ''zero mistake'' Nixon campaign. He would always enter to the tune of ''Buckle Down Winsocki'' and his basic message was the same: he was against crime, communism, and corruption. He was for a strong America, old-fashioned values, and clean government. Repeatedly, often in the same speech, he'd say '' ... now, let me make it perfectly clear,'' or ''to be perfectly honest,'' or ''candidly speaking,'' or ''speaking quite frankly ....'' And he would proceed to say something that was not at all clear or candid or frank. It was all part of his and Haldeman's determination to run a perfect campaign of controlled exposure and safe generalities.

Often he would say to a group, ''Now, I've got some appointments and other people waiting for me, but I'm enjoying myself so much with you folks, I'm going to stay a bit longer and let the other things wait.'' Cheers of appreciation would go up from the audience, red-and-white signs emblazoned ''Nixon's The One'' would wave, and reporters would groan, as we knew his schedule showed no appointments at all for hours ahead. We would often chuckle also at how many quite obviously pregnant women used to vigorously wave those ''Nixon's The One'' signs, suggesting the improbable if not the impossible.

On the campaign trail he kept his dislike of reporters in check, but his relationship with ''the boys on the bus'' was never comradely even when he was winning. Occasionally, he would try to be ''one of the boys,'' but it just wasn't in his nature. ''They're all against me,'' he would often warn aides and supporters. And I think he believed we were. In his heart, he hated us, perhaps because he couldn't control us. He mouthed all the right words about freedom of the press, and in the abstract I'm sure he believed them. But in the specific case of Richard Milhous Nixon, he demanded the media reflect only his own self-image. When that didn't happen, he felt betrayed, abused, and misunderstood.

His distrust of the media was often mirrored by those around him. At a Pennsylvania campaign stop, I watched outside a school auditorium where Nixon was addressing a small group. A pleasant, middle-aged, grey-haired lady came rushing up to one Nixon aide, beside whom I was standing, and shrieked, "There are reporters in there taking notes and writing down everything Mr. Nixon is saying." Clearly, she felt this was a terrible thing, and she, too, knew we were all "against him."

Despite all the precautions, mistakes began to be made. Agnew made them first, bumbling about the country early in the campaign with his characteristic racial slurs, calling a Japanese-American reporter a "fat Jap," talking of "Polacks," and telling one meeting that "some of my best friends are Jewish." It was astonishingly inept, and Nixon forced him to apologize.

Nixon made some verbal slips, too. Whistle-stopping with him up through Pennsylvania, I saw him stand at the back of the train with his wife Pat at his side and demand economic progress, saying thunderously at the close of his speech: "We simply can't stand pat." He grinned sheepishly at his wife, waved, and the train moved out. In fact, he did it several times at various stops, to the increasing annoyance of his wife. She didn't like politics anyway, disliked campaigning, and was hurt deeply by attacks on her husband. She would nod tight-lipped to reporters but seldom spoke to us; she never was "one of the boys" as Ethel Kennedy was, or "Happy" Rockefeller or Muriel Humphrey.

Nixon's biggest problem in 1968 was over-confidence among his troops. No matter how far ahead in the polls he was, Nixon knew he still could lose. He well remembered Thomas Dewey's 1948 loss to Truman and his own loss to Kennedy in 1960. And he worried about some last-minute trick by the Democrats. But throughout most of the campaign he stuck to his "country-club" approach. In the end, as Humphrey finally began to move up in the polls, the old Nixon had to come out of hiding. The contrast was not lost on the electorate.

Throughout September I had trekked after the candidate through New York, Los Angeles, San Francisco, Chicago, San Diego, Miami, Atlanta, and scores of other cities and towns, sometimes hitting half a dozen a day. In between I made speeches in Hamilton and Vancouver and, for variety, covered the World Bank and International Monetary Fund meetings in Washington at the end of the month. Aside from a quick trip to Vancouver and Victoria, I stayed in Washington the first couple of weeks of October. Traditionally, the U.S. presidential election race doesn't really get serious until after the World Series, and in 1968 it not only got serious, it got tense and often dirty.

The Kennedy and McCarthy people started working hard for Humphrey when they finally faced the probability of a Nixon victory. Even more important, so did Lyndon Johnson. He desperately sought to accelerate the Vietnam peace talks and he was making progress. His message to Hanoi was to co-operate with him because if the Democrats lost the presidency, they'd have a much nastier time with Richard Nixon in the White House. He announced a total bombing halt and suddenly things were looking better for Humphrey.

Nixon's people sought to offset the LBJ offensive by secretly encouraging the South Vietnamese to refuse to go along with Johnson's peace drive on the grounds that Saigon would be better off with Nixon as President. It was an extraordinary diplomatic spectacle: Johnson trying to make Hanoi be reasonable; Nixon trying to make Saigon be unreasonable. As was his style, Nixon didn't do things himself. Intermediaries dealt with Saigon, notably Mrs. Claire Chennault, the far-right-wing Chinese widow of an American general and World War II hero with close contacts among the Saigon leadership and who was vice-chairman of the Republican Finance Committee. She was effective in stirring up enough trouble to blunt much of the LBJ peace offensive, but according to the polls, the women's vote began to move to Humphrey. Miraculously, he was catching up.

At first, Nixon didn't turn totally back to his old style. He tried to have it both ways. He would note some vile accusation that had been made against Humphrey and then add, "Now, no, I don't make that charge. But some people do ... some people I respect ... and some of my supporters share that view. But I don't make the charge myself." In that way, he would publicize the accusation but escape being called an accuser.

A week before the vote, Humphrey was only three percentage points behind Nixon in the polls, and the old "rocking, socking" Nixon and Agnew slashed across the country lambasting Hubert for being "squishy soft" on Communists, crime, and corruption. Both presidential candidates lost their cool, in those final days, especially Nixon. He said Humphrey had "the fastest, loosest tongue" in the country and attacked Johnson as well, saying "When you fire the ventriloquist, why hire the dummy." Humphrey responded by saying the Nixon cry was,

"Throw the rascals in." By November 5, the polls showed them almost even.

If the campaign had gone on another few days, Humphrey would have won. If Johnson's peace offensive had started sooner, Humphrey might have won. If the Kennedy and McCarthy people had started sooner ... if there hadn't been Chicago ... if ... if ... if. And by the skin of his teeth on that first Tuesday in November of 1968, Nixon won the presidency. He won with 43.4 per cent of the vote against Humphrey's 42.7 per cent, with most of the rest going to the racist George Wallace. So Nixon, the two-time loser, the man who had been utterly written off six years before, had clawed his way back to the top.

Looking back with the benefit of more than a decade and a half of hindsight, I think Bob Kennedy would have won over Hubert Humphrey and become the Democratic Party nominee for the presidency. I think, too, he would have beaten Richard Nixon. And finally, I think he had the potential to be not just a good president, as his brother was, but a great president, as Franklin Roosevelt was.

It is hard to imagine the hatred Bob Kennedy stirred up in his brief lifetime. He stimulated venomous passions within not only such people as Jimmy Hoffa, but also Lyndon Johnson, Republicans, conservatives, and even among some liberals. "A little Torquemada," Gore Vidal called him. "An emotional juvenile," said Hubert Humphrey. He was that "little son of a bitch" according to Lyndon Johnson. Others called him "the ruthless brat," "the bully," "the savage," or "the liberal fascist."

It was, I think, his very intensity, as well as his many contradictions, that stimulated these attacks. But I believe Ted Kennedy's moving eulogy at his brother's funeral was the closest to the truth: "He should be remembered simply as a good and decent man who saw wrong and tried to right it, saw suffering and tried to heal it, saw war and tried to stop it." From the time I first saw him as chief counsel at the Senate Labor Rackets Committee hearings, through his stint as Attorney General and U.S. Senator, to his brief but inspiring run for the presidency, I saw a passionate, intelligent, and compassionate man who truly wanted to make things better. Of all the tragedies of that slum of a year, 1968, his death seems to me to have been the greatest.

10 *BACK HOME AGAIN*

Washington, D.C., January, 1969 ...

I didn't see much of Richard Nixon after the 1968 election. I watched as he was sworn in to begin his furtive presidency, and I went to his inaugural ball. But several years later, at the height of the Watergate crisis, I did have one other glimpse.

On April 14, 1973, I flew down to Washington to attend the annual White House Correspondents Association Dinner. A thousand editors, reporters, White House officials, judges, cabinet secretaries, senators, congressmen, admirals, and generals packed the banquet hall at the Washington Hilton for what promised to be a dramatic evening. The dinner is traditionally addressed by the President, and Nixon had agreed to come. But this particular dinner was also honouring *Washington Post* reporters Bob Woodward and Carl Bernstein with a $1,000 award for their investigative reporting of Watergate.

The expected confrontation between the President and his journalistic nemeses was the only topic of conversation as we sliced through our steaks and waited. But Nixon fooled us. He didn't show up until a few minutes after the award was made.

The President entered the room to polite applause and the presidential salute of ''Ruffles and Flourishes,'' an ovation considerably less enthusiastic than the one that had greeted Woodward and Bernstein a few minutes before. Nixon looked pale and drawn as he moved to his place at the head table, smiling wanly and not stopping to shake hands. After he sat down, I watched a forced smile occasionally crease his features as he went through the motions of chatting with those on either side of him. He didn't eat. Then he rose, spoke for ten minutes about peace and statesmanship, and, about an hour after having arrived, departed, leaving the audience still crackling with suspense and speculation about Watergate. Normally, the President would stay at these dinners for a couple of hours and afterwards visit some of the hospitality rooms. But not this time. It was all "terribly painful," he said later.

It was a lot more painful than any of us imagined. That very day was one of the most frantic of all of the Watergate coverup days. The Watergate burglars were threatening to spill their story in public and Nixon was seriously considering for the first time that he might have to get rid of his palace guard of Bob Haldeman and John Ehrlichman, as well as White House Counsel John Dean. The whole carefully contrived deception was disintegrating and Nixon had been meeting with Haldeman, Ehrlichman, and others right up to the moment he left the White House for the dinner. He went back to more desperate coverup discussions that lasted into the early hours of the morning as he and his henchmen sought to forestall their inevitable disgrace.

But, in January, 1969, Watergate was off in the future as Nixon settled into the job he had coveted for so long and I packed for Toronto. Just after the election, I had received two tempting job offers in Canada. One was the editorship of *Maclean's* magazine and the other was to be head of all journalistic programming on the CBC English network.

In the mid-1960s, I'd been asked by producer Bill Cunningham to audition as anchor for *The National*. I did, but I wasn't anxious then to leave Washington, and Stanley Burke got the job, making him the first journalist to anchor *The National*. Up until then the anchorman was always an announcer with no journalistic background. A few years later, CTV asked me to be head of their fledgling network news and current affairs programming. I was tempted, but after much thought I rejected the idea. My colleague Peter Reilly then took on the job briefly, followed by Charles Templeton.

I had loved living in Washington and thoroughly enjoyed my American (and worldwide) journalistic beat, but increasingly in the late sixties I thought of coming home. My personal life had changed, too: my Mexican marriage had ended after nearly a decade. Later, when I had remarried, it was to a Canadian from Vancouver who, although we both enjoyed Washington, encouraged my growing sense of Canadian nationalism. The two job offers were therefore awfully tempting for personal as well as professional reasons.

The *Maclean's* proposition was considerably more attractive than the one a few years earlier when then-editor Ralph Allen came down to Washington to persuade me to become their full-time Washington correspondent. I declined then because I had wanted to stay in broadcasting and continue my freelance work. But in recent years, with the increasing demands of television, I had been working less and less as a print journalist and I missed that world. After all, it was where I'd got my start. To be offered the editorship of Canada's most prominent magazine I found enormously gratifying.

The harder job for much less money and much longer hours was with CBC in Toronto. But through the Correspondents Association and at other meetings for several years, I had been sounding off about the changes needed in the way the CBC handled the news and I was under a lot of pressure from my colleagues to take the job. The correspondents, news producers, and others in the CBC News Service had been through many bureaucratic wars together since the spring of 1966 when the CBC had nearly self-destructed over the so-called *Seven Days* affair. CBC brass cancelled the highly popular and controversial Sunday night TV current affairs program to the consternation of the viewers and the apoplexy of the producers. Major internal and external battles ensued which, ultimately, led to profound organizational changes at the network as well as the departure of most of the program's leading lights.

The *Seven Days* explosion came in the middle of a battle by the news service for greater resources. We wanted more people, more money, more facilities, more clout within the organization. First as vice-president and then president of the CBC Correspondents Association, I became involved in arguing, memo-writing, and phoning, often in the midst of news assignments. The correspondents were part of a group of TV news producers and editors who held meetings with CBC President Alphonse Ouimet and countless informal sessions with vice-presidents and other officials. Finally, we achieved some of our objectives, but not all. So we continued over the next couple of years to argue forcefully for a fundamental reorganization of all information programming. Now I was being given the opportunity to argue from a position of strength and a chance to actually make some of the changes I believed in. In effect, CBC was telling me to put up or shut up.

It was an agonizing choice: stay in Washington, go to *Maclean's*, or go to CBC in Toronto. But the challenge of reshaping the CBC's journalistic programming, and the new emphasis the CBC was now prepared to put on journalism, proved irresistible. Besides, the fascination of seeing at close hand the new and refreshing style of Prime Minister Pierre Elliott Trudeau added extra enticement. Finally I decided to accept the CBC offer, and in January, 1969, I hung up my trenchcoat and moved back home to Toronto, the city I had left twenty years before when I set off for the Halifax office of British United Press as an eager young journalist with a lot to learn. In 1978, after accomplishing many of the objectives I had set for myself, I would become anchor of *The National*. But that's another story.

Toronto, June 1, 1984 ...

Washington was once described by the great and sensitive CBS commentator Eric Severeid as "the greatest world centre of news since ancient Rome." I echo that sentiment, and as I reflect on my eighteen years in Washington, many thoughts and images come to mind. Standing high above all others are the images of John and Bob Kennedy, the most enriching public personalities I have ever met. I believe the history of the United States and, indeed, the history of the world in the last forty years of the twentieth century would have been profoundly different had it not been for Lee Harvey Oswald and Sirhan Sirhan. Vietnam would never have become the killing ground of a generation. The intensity of East-West confrontation would have been less. The social and economic disparity between the North and South of the world would have been less.

Both Kennedys instilled in people a sense of what they could be, of how they could be stretched. Jack Kennedy was a good President with much promise. But Bob Kennedy could have been a great President. He was less cool, less elegant, less distanced than his brother. He was more passionate, more human, more daring. He was soft-hearted and hard-headed. When John Kennedy was assassinated, it was a national and international calamity. When Bob Kennedy was assassinated, I felt it was a bigger tragedy because his potential seemed to be so much greater.

And, of course, in the images that march through my mind is that avalanche of a man, Lyndon Johnson. He lied, he cheated, he threatened. He whined and he bullied. He would never take "no" for an answer. To him, failure was unthinkable and unendurable. Yet, in the end, he was a failure, turning the folly of Vietnam into a disaster.

In my years in Washington I was extraordinarily lucky to have a front-row seat as the Presidents went by and as a parade of other memorable characters trotted across the stage, from Casey Stengel and Allen Dulles to Alger Hiss and Joe McCarthy. Of all the non-Americans I covered in those years, Ché Guevara stands out for the power that emanated from his quiet, gentle personality; so does Nikita Khrushchev for his flamboyant style.

I found it far more frightening to experience the terrorizing hatreds of the American racial crisis than I did the combat horrors of the wars in Vietnam and Santo Domingo. I was far more scared in Selma and Newark than in Dak To and Khesanh. My senses, too, were everlastingly seared by the horrible poverty I saw during my visits to the slums of Rio and Recife, Caracas and Bogota.

All these scenes and hundreds more crowd into my memory. So, too, does a feeling of pride about the news business itself, about the CBC's commitment to journalistic professionalism, and about the men and women in it. I was especially fortunate to be a part of the pioneering group of television correspondents in the early days of TV journalism. The big expansion of TV news in Canada grew out of the work of the CBC correspondents corps and particularly the work of our *Newsmagazine* producers such as Don Cameron, Bill Cunningham, and Bill Harcourt, always succoured and stimulated by our Chief News Editors, Bill Hogg and Don Macdonald.

In the 1960s, television correspondents had much more editorial freedom then than do correspondents today. Almost entirely on our own, we determined what stories we would do on our beat and what the story line would be. The idea of checking a script with the national "desk" in Toronto simply never entered our heads. Today, there is very tight script and editorial control. As a result, we've gained in consistency and production values, and lost in flair and individuality. It's a truism today that you can't fight city hall; you can't beat the taxman; and you can't win an argument with the "desk."

In my day, the hours were long, the pay was at best adequate, and the damage to family relationships was painful and often irretrievable. But for all the petty jealousies, individual foibles, and occasionally bitter rivalries, there was one common denominator among us: an irrepressible joy in being a correspondent and real pleasure in the camaraderie of our profession. We loved what we were doing; we also thought we were damned good at our jobs. And I believe we were.

Many of my friends and colleagues from the sixties have gone on to other jobs, or better worlds. Don Minifie retired after his stroke in 1967 and died seven years later. Stan Burke became anchor of *The National* and later moved to the West Coast to publish several newspapers there. Don Cameron carried on his peripatetic pace as vice-president of CTV News. Bill Cunningham became head of news at Global Television, later executive producer of CTV's *W-5*, and later still returned to the journalistic front lines as a correspondent for *W-5*. Michael Maclear went on to become an award-winning television documentary producer.

The frantic work pace and hectic private lives inevitably took their toll. Peter Reilly died in 1976 and Norman DePoe in 1980, both from the self-inflicted wounds of their lifestyle. In both cases the post-funeral reminiscences lasted long into the night. DePoe had the foresight to set money aside for his friends to throw a party at the Toronto Press Club on the night of his funeral. It was just the kind of bacchanal he would have loved and I could somehow hear his raspy voice singing above all the din.

One story told that night was of a BBC correspondent, whom I had known in Washington and who had died not long before. After Washington, he had been posted to Paris and then to Nairobi, where his excessive drinking finally caught up with him. Like most correspondents, he'd had a running feud with the BBC accountants over expense accounts and office details and he had willed his ashes to his particular accountant nemesis at BBC headquarters in London. The remains were duly sent, and the accountant, not knowing what else to do, put the box in a filing cabinet. There it rested for a few months until several journalistic colleagues decided it was entirely inappropriate for their friend to spend eternity in a BBC filing cabinet. So they took his ashes on a prodigious memorial London pub crawl, shaking a few ashes out of the box at every bar they visited. It's a story that would have pleased DePoe. All he wanted as an epitaph, he once told me, was simply, "He was a good reporter."

As I look back I'm struck by how lucky I've been. I've witnessed great events and rubbed shoulders with men and women who made history. These experiences have given me insights that have proved critically important in my work as a journalistic executive and anchor of *The National*.

I don't take myself too seriously, but I do take journalism seriously. To my mind journalism is democracy's two-way message centre, the communicating link between the governors and the governed. Only through the media can leaders talk to the mass of the people and the people talk to the leaders. Without free and independent media, you don't have a democracy.

The patron saint of journalism named by the pope in 1878 is St. Francis De Sales and I think he would endorse the idea that our job in a free society is to inform, to enlighten, to enrich, and to enlarge public understanding of uncomfortable problems, sometimes providing facts that painfully or fatally wound a theory. That puts heavy responsibility on our journalistic shoulders to try to be fair, accurate, honest, balanced, and thorough, in short, to be socially responsible. We are, after all, agents for the public and our credibility is the heart and soul of our business in providing "history on the run."

Our job as factual reporters is to provide, as Walter Lippmann once said, "the streams of fact that feed the rivers of opinion." In doing this, the media have enormous power because they "determine the agenda for society," to quote Senator Keith Davey. Although I've worked for news agencies, newspapers, magazines, and radio, it is television that I find to be the greatest challenge because it has the greatest potential. It is the most powerful vehicle of communication the world has ever known. Like it or not, more people these days depend on TV for their information than on any other single source of news. Therefore, television journalism has the greatest responsibility to provide a fair reflection of reality.

On the whole, I think the media are much better today than they used to be. For the most part, the yellow journalism of the fedora and trenchcoat days is long gone and the media are showing far more concern than ever before about their responsibility to the public. Reporters, editors, and producers are better educated and, in television especially, the technology is being better used to provide background for news stories. There are occasional excesses, there are lapses into bubble-gum journalism in the pursuit of higher circulation and audiences, and I worry about the cancerous spread of the idea that TV journalism is show business. It's not; it's news business and has a serious role to play as the communicating glue that holds together a democratic society.

As one of the CBC correspondents in the 1960s and as a reporter for the print media in Canada, I hope I've made a contribution to the credibility of the news business. In those days we all had a lot of fun, and I wonder today about whether our younger counterparts are having as much fun as we did. I think not.

INDEX

337

341

Ustinov, Peter, 230
U-2 spy plane, 131, 133, 135, 138

Valencia, Guillermo Leon, 171-72, 187
Valenti, Jack, 282
Vallee, Rudy, 29
Vallières, Pierre, 220
Vancouver, 26-29, 30, 35
Vancouver Sun, 8, 29, 174, 224
Vaughan, General Harry, 48
Venezuela, 90-91, 169, 171, 173-76
Victoria, Queen, 123
Victoria Times, 30
Vidal, Gore, 329
Vietnam, 121, 149, 207, 218, 223,
   229-30, 244, 246, 249-50, 251-54,
   261-74, 306, 328
Vietnam International Control
   Commission, 250, 265
Vietnam War, 186, 243, 248, 251-83,
   285, 287, 289, 294, 300, 303, 326,
   328, 333, 334
Vipond, Jim, 18
Virgin Islands, 102
Voting Rights Act, *1965*, 207-208, 209,
   282

Wade, Henry, 198, 200-201
Walinsky, Adam, 285
Walker, General Edwin A., 150-51,
   152
Wallace, George Corley, 206-207,
   323-25, 329
Wallace, Mike, 318
Wallas, Graham, 207
Walsh, Father Edmund, 207
Walter Reed Army Hospital, 316
Warren, Earl, 49, 66, 68
Washington, D.C., 7, 11-12, 33,
   34-156 *passim*, 221, 277, 279, 301,
   316, 330, 331
Washington, George, 99, 189
Washington Hilton, 330
Washington Post, 77, 104, 113, 123,
   252, 255, 330
"Washington Through Canadian Eyes,"
   82
Washington Times Herald, 51, 89
Watergate, 50, 275, 311, 330-31

Watts, Dan, 246
Waugh, Evelyn, 141
Way It Is, The, 279
Wedgeport, Nova Scotia, 25
Wegoda, Ron, 182
Welch, Joseph, 58
Welch, Robert, 66
Westmoreland, General William, 266,
   267, 268, 270, 272
West Virginia, 99
W-5, 334
Wheaton, Anne, 63
Wheeler, General Earle, 272
Wheeling, West Virginia, 51
White House, 11-12, 34-35, 45, 59,
   60-64, 77, 119-20, 122-24, 153, 190,
   194, 197, 242, 248-49, 252, 259
White House Correspondents
   Association, 291, 330
White, Lincoln, 136
Will, George, 239
Wilson, Harold, 154, 221
Wilson, Woodrow, 61
Winchell, Walter, 203-204
Windsor, Ontario, 30
Windsor Star, 8, 73, 74, 89, 223
Wingate, Orde, 39
Wisconsin, 99, 206, 288, 289, 313
Woodward, Bob, 330
World Bank, 37, 261
World at Eight, 286
World Health Organization (WHO), 37
World War I, 25, 64, 131, 269
World War II, 13, 16, 37, 46, 51, 52,
   131, 136, 142, 164, 280, 324
Wyoming, 102-103

Xuan Thuy, 280

Yalta Conference, *1945*, 47-48, 51
Yeats, W.B., 284
Yogi and the Commissar, The, 275
Yorty, Sam, 304
Young, Stephen, 78-79

Zambia, 42
Ziegler, Ron, 310, 314
Zionism, 20
Zwicker, General Ralph, 57